Mediating Europe

This book is for Maurice Roche, whose sociological imagination, scholarly vision and enjoyment of debate contribute greatly to the academic community.

Mediating Europe

*New Media, Mass Communications
and the European Public Sphere*

Edited by
Jackie Harrison and Bridgette Wessels

Berghahn Books
New York • Oxford

Published in 2009 by
Berghahn Books
www.berghahnbooks.com

Library of Congress Cataloging-in-Publication Data
Mediating Europe : new media, mass communications and the European public
sphere / edited by Jackie Harrison and Bridgette Wessels.
    p. cm.
Includes bibliographical references and index.
ISBN 978 1 84545 602 3 (alk. paper)
1. Mass media European Union countries. 2. Mass media policy European Union
countries. 3. Communication policy European Union countries. 4. Mass media
Political aspects European Union countries. 5. Public interest European Union
countries. 6. Intercultural communication European Union countries. I. Harrison,
Jackie, 1961 II. Wessels, Bridgette.
    P92.E9M43 2009
    302.23094 dc22
                                                          2009012950

British Library Cataloguing in Publication Data
A catalogue record for this book is available from the British Library
Printed in the United States on acid-free paper.

ISBN: 978-1-84545-602-3 (hardback)

Contents

Preface

These chapters represent a key collection of views made at the international conference 'Changing European Public Spheres: New Cultural and Media Contexts in Western and Eastern EU – Prospects and Challenges', hosted by the European Social and Cultural Studies Centre (ESCUS), University of Sheffield on 23–24 September 2004.

Chapter 1

Introduction: Mediating Europe and the Public Sphere

Jackie Harrison

Any attempt to understand a process called mediating Europe[1] needs to consider the following two points, either particularly, or as they interrelate to each other. First, the range of economic, political, social and cultural agendas set by or for the media,[2] and second, the constantly changing technical reconfiguration, content and service capacities of the media, accompanied by ever-emerging forms of new media. The former is no more than the current European habitat of the media and their local regulation by the European Union (EU) and its member states; the latter their current stage of development and their evolutionary adaptability. It is both these areas that the subsequent chapters will look at in detail and from very different points of view.

What follows immediately below is an introductory and therefore high-level overview of what I believe to be the key background problems to mediating Europe. These can be summarized as problems associated with the possible and plausible engagement of modern media in all its forms with an active civil society in all its diversity. I offer no solutions or recommendations to militate against these problems, as that is the domain of the subsequent chapters, but see these problems as the real barriers to the development and sustainability of a European public sphere,[3] or spheres, from which a more democratic and participative Europe can, in part, be developed. After this overview, I provide a brief account of each of the chapters.

In simple and reified terms the phrase 'mediating Europe' refers to what the media sector 'does' and wishes 'to do' to and with Europe and to what Europe 'does' and wishes 'to do' to and with the media. This simple reification is both helpful and important since it highlights the 'doing' that either side, private or public, undertakes or wishes to undertake, and which is carried out under the title 'mediating Europe' – in short, the way the current European communication space is occupied. This includes everything from junk content to networked citizens' groups, remotely distributed public and social services (particularly education and health), and high culture on a public service broadcast provider. European communication space is multifaceted in capacity, content, impact and significance. It is neither exclusively territorially nor functionally defined. Straightforwardly, mediating Europe refers not only to the current range of commercially provided communications options available to consumers and associated plans for the future that the private media sector chooses for itself, but also to the way EU policymakers agree or disagree with the private sector and have their own public plans for the media sector and for EU citizens. All of which begs the question of 'what is actually being done' by, with and to the media across Europe.

Answers to this question vary but are easily discernible, and can be characterized as follows:

1. The media sector consists of a few multinational companies that are beyond the reach or control of public authority and which do just as they like – often, it is said, against various versions of the public interest.

2. Public authority over the media is too meddlesome and restrains the ability of the media sector to be competitive and commercially successful.

3. Public authority improves, through versions of public service obligations, the media sector by ensuring that social and cultural aims are met.

4. Lack of intervention and regulation means that media content and standards are at their lowest and, although popular, distract from, or substitute for, political and high cultural activity.

5. There are reasons to be cheerful: broadcast news journalism still performs the role of the fourth estate; audiences domesticate the media and tame its influence; public social services, such as education and health, can increasingly be carried by the electronic media to just about anywhere; the media in some forms do stimulate democratic politics and participative citizenship; the threats to public service broadcasting are exaggerated; popular media culture is richer than

it is often credited with being; and finally, there is a communitarian-(or civil-) inspired revolution exemplified by the spontaneous use of new communication outlets, which shows the way forward in terms of a new spatial politics and new cultural opportunities.

Any one of these answers, or a coherent combination of them, points to the numerous ways in which Europe may be perceived by academics, commentators and analysts to be mediated.

The papers that follow this introduction provide arguments that variously seek to explain European audio-visual and information society policy (collectively referred to in this introduction as 'European media policy'), advocate certain stances, display the need for further research in some areas, or try to influence European media policy. Given the range of perspectives and arguments that follow, I choose to begin with the hapless figure of the EU media policymaker herself – using her as a rhetorical figure to explore the variety of vested interests involved in European media policymaking. It is she more than anyone who has the task of dealing with the media in overcoming perceived communication barriers to agreed European economic, political, social and cultural outcomes. Outcomes that are arrived at by listening to certain arguments and their attendant advocates who constantly knock on her door and seek to persuade her of what she must do for a successfully mediated Europe.

The first group of people to knock on her door are the economic liberalizers who wish to free the media market from public obligation and who pit their wits against the economic interventionists who wish, via the imposition on the media of public service obligation requirements, to promote European-inspired political ideals, participation and cultural values. Freeing the commercial imperative, it is argued, drives the European economy toward prosperity, buttresses the benefits of the knowledge sector, encourages consumer freedoms, maximizes choice and enables the subsequent creation of a decent European society. By contrast freeing the political and cultural imperative, it is argued, drives democratic politics and participative citizenship by helping to nurture and develop an engaged and informed citizenry, and by promoting positive externalities, merit goods and the subsequent creation of a decent European society. Leaving aside debates over the meaning of 'a decent European society', both arguments base themselves on a belief and recognition about the potential influence of the media to generate European-wide change and benefits (Morley and Robbins 1995), a point I shall return to later.

Following the economic liberalizers and economic interventionists into the office of our policymaker are the technocrats. Here the argument is how to manage the trend of technological change. Change, which occurs at a tremendous pace across the world, is manifest in increasing media convergence[4] and capacity, and produces communication boundaries that are increasingly 'liquid' (Bauman 2000). Instead of liberalizers and interventionists, we have optimists and pessimists. The optimists argue that European media policy must embrace the emancipatory tendencies of the new technology and welcome the promise of convergence to create multiple European communicative spaces in which all sorts of politically, culturally and socially desirable things can happen. It is a new communications world of direct democracy, virtual parliaments and town halls, political accountability, new forms of governance, interactive museums, global libraries, Wikipedia, easy-to-use databases, extended public services, new strategies for social inclusion and equal opportunities, MySpace, YouTube and blogs, media literacy programmes and realizable universal access. The pessimists fear the development of new media and the changing nature of the broadcasting environment, and call for regulation against the vertically constructed companies that own the infrastructure, the access and control technology and most of the content in the new communications world. These pessimists argue that power in this so-called 'new' communications world is as before and remains unequally distributed between private companies and public organisations (see also Barnett 1997; Curran and Seaton 2003); that ideas of European citizenship in this world have been overwhelmed by the now paramount conception of the European consumer (see also Morley and Robins 1995; Ward 2004) and that claims on behalf of the political, social and cultural benefits of the information society are extravagant and unrealistic. It is an argument that now ranges over the critical areas of who can access or afford what kind of media services; how universal access to these services is to be achieved and regulated in a digital world; and how the new communication options will be used and by whom and with what realistic and viable regulatory features in place.[5]

Following the technocrats into the office are the politicians. Here the argument is between the maximalist[6] and the irredentist. The maximalist politician simply says that the EU has competencies that are more extensive than is realized (even if such 'extended' competencies are flexibly and surreptitiously arrived at, Harrison and Woods 2007), and that they can, if necessary or required, cover a range of political, social and cultural issues. The irredentist politician reminds our policymaker of the limits imposed on EU competencies. Member states, they insist, retain the power to determine their own regulatory regimes in the media sector as long as the regulatory rules are compatible with the free trade rules contained in the Treaty.[7]

It is from this melange of views that our EU policymaker has to decide on how to use her influence to arrange matters to facilitate the successful mediation of Europe. And here a further problem arises – what is meant by successfully mediating Europe? From whose point of view and through what means and with what set of achieved outcomes is anything which is to be called successful in this instance to be arrived at? In other words, how is success to be described and for whom is a mediated Europe successful? Clearly the issue of mediating Europe for European media policymakers should begin with an answer to the direct question: for whose benefit is Europe mediated and how is this to be achieved?

The answer to the latter question currently given by European media policymakers stems from the basis of a belief that the media can generate changes and produce benefits. The media, it is believed, can simultaneously provide economic prosperity and improve the quality of democratic and public life through facilitating participative citizenship and fostering cultural cohesion and a sense of a European identity. In short, the media are perceived as hugely important economic, political and cultural phenomena for potential economic, political and cultural good. From this point on (though not pursued here), the issues of change and benefits become inextricably linked with the arguments listed above, which can now be seen to be centred on the management of the details required to produce such changes and benefits as desired by the various opinion holders and interest groups who knocked on our policymaker's door. This only leads us to ask again, rather more insistently this time, what specifically do European media policymakers want from the media? Given their rhetorical responses two things become very clear. What is wanted by European media policymakers is increasing and specific commercial freedoms for the media sector to allow it to generate economic benefits and, at the same time, the construction through regulation (or influence) of the publicly authorized circumstances whereby EU citizens can make use of the media to become increasingly enchanted with Europe and involved in its projects. In other words, a media environment that consists of a commercially free media sector adjacent to a publicly mediated Europe (Harrison and Woods 2007). Together and combined these would form a unique European communication environment. While this might appear contradictory (not to mention ambitious), it does sum up current EU media policy, which unsurprisingly is replete with tensions.

It is believed by European media policymakers that the media have the capacity to improve European democratic and public life. Somehow the media are seen as being able to stimulate involvement in the EU generally and its projects particularly, which means that the media are viewed as part of the machinery that enables democratic politics and participative citizenship to occur (Harrison and Woods 2000; Harrison and Woods 2007). Here we arrive at two subsidiary questions that bring us closer to understanding a version of what a successfully mediated Europe is. They are, first: under what circumstances can the media achieve such political influence? Second: how can the specific circumstances of enhancing democratic politics and participative citizenship be facilitated by the media?

One way of examining the first question is by looking at Habermas's conception of communicative action. In essence, communicative action consists of people speaking to one another and reaching agreement or common understanding about what it is they should do. Leaving aside Habermas's arguments about communicative rationality, which support the process of communicative action and the discursive ethical aspects of communicative action,[8] I wish to focus on the political aspects of what Habermas means. Habermas intends that we should understand that at the heart of any political project should be the recognition of the role of communication (both interpersonal and mediated). It is through communication that people discuss beliefs, events and goals, and, if those people are rational, it is via such discussions that these things are judged through evidence to be true, accurate and valid, or not. What should emerge as a result of such discourse are agreement and/or common understanding. Indeed, for Habermas the entire purpose of interpersonal communication is to achieve agreement and understanding (Habermas 1984: 286–88).[9] But where do these interpersonal communicative actions take place?

For Habermas there are two domains to society which act upon us and which we act within; these are the 'lifeworld' and the 'system' (Habermas 1987). The former is the intersubjective domain of our common background, our convictions, the taken-for-granted world of the everyday, the setting for our horizons, the 'to hand' of our language and culture, and the place of interpersonal discussion and agreement and/ or understanding. The latter is the place of instrumental rationality, of means-ends calculations, of technical thinking, of marketplace formulae, and of bureaucracy and government organizations. Today the system is detached from the lifeworld (for Habermas (1987: 153) it was not always so).[10] Importantly, the process that helps drive and keep the two apart is what Habermas calls the 'delinguistified media of communication'. He writes:

> the uncoupling of system and lifeworld is depicted in such a way that the lifeworld, which is at first coextensive with a scarcely differentiated social system, gets cut down more and more to one subsystem among others. In the process, system mechanisms get further and further detached from the social structures through which social integration takes place. As we shall see modern societies attain a level of system differentiation at which increasingly autonomous organizations are connected with one another via delinguistified media of communication. (Habermas 1987: 154)

What Habermas means by this is that the modern mass media and modern communication in general do not facilitate communicative action (whose linguistic and discursive purpose is common understanding and agreement)[11] and do not engender discussions about politics (or ethics); indeed, they potentially debase the lifeworld by steering social intercourse away from 'norms and values' (Habermas 1987: 154). The modern circumstances under which the media achieve their political influence are, for Habermas at this point, entirely negative and exist through the way they help to 'uncouple' the lifeworld from the system. In other words, the modern mass media limit the potential for rational and emancipatory politics and distort and trivialize public opinion – a point which would seem to stop our European media policymaker dead in her tracks with regard to achieving, as we said above, the publicly authorized circumstances whereby EU citizens via the media can become enchanted with Europe and get involved in its projects. Fortunately this is only half the story.

Paradoxically the way forward is to be found by asking the second question, albeit at this stage hypothetically: how are the specific circumstances of enhancing democratic politics and participative citizenship to be facilitated by the media? If Habermas were correct, such facilitation would have to fly in the face of the modern European communication circumstances under which genuine emancipatory political discourse is now utterly marginalized. Actually the answer is provided by Habermas himself in two works: *The Structural Transformation of the Public Sphere* (1989) and *Between Facts and Norms* (1996).

Habermas argues in *The Structural Transformation of the Public Sphere* that, in eighteenth-century Britain, France and Germany, there arose a bourgeois political/ social space, which could be called a public sphere.[12] It consisted primarily of the need by the bourgeoisie for commercial information and news. This need found its place in journals, newspapers, associations, clubs, dining societies and other public places (most famously coffee houses). From this basis civil society extended itself to include non-governmental settings. For Habermas this represents something very positive: it was a literary-based public sphere infused with Enlightenment values about reason, truth and law, and it served to mediate an early form of public opinion – in this case the claims for reform on behalf of the bourgeoisie themselves (although the eighteenth-century bourgeois public sphere was, however, exclusive of contemporary radical politics and women (Eley 1992)). *Tout court*, it can be argued that this European bourgeois public sphere was a series of civil and spatial settings for communicative action, which first saw rational-critical political debate and informed public opinion by tilting at the system.

The subsequent history of the debasement of the eighteenth-century public sphere and the corresponding manipulation of public opinion is not relevant here; suffice it to say that from such beginnings the modern mediated world of media distortion, its alliance with the system and the pursuit of its own commercial interests assumed greater and greater significance. The system was becoming increasingly dominant and accompanying its dominance (and increasing separation from the lifeworld) was the acceptance of the 'delinguistified media' and 'delinguistified forms of communication' as normal. And yet Habermas is optimistic that, from this relatively brief historical appearance of a public sphere, we can in modern Europe point to both the possibility (and plausibility) of a similar kind of discursive democratic politics and participative citizenship being developed once again. Again the development is through the relationship between civil society and the system, and again it is worked out, though in more detail, in what appears in *Between Facts and Norms* as the relationship between civil society, public opinion and communicative power and the political/legal system.

Beginning from a recognition that any public sphere is at best a communications 'network' (the word is Habermas's) and that it is necessarily limited in its ability to solve problems (here political problems), it needs, to be effective, to be engaged with the political/legal system. And this it can now do, both in theory and in practice, via the modern make-up of civil society, 'which has been rediscovered today in wholly new constellations' (Habermas 1996: 366), and it is in these that potential modern European public sphere(s) are, according to Habermas, now to be found. The reason for this is that the core of contemporary civil society now consists 'of those more or less spontaneously emergent associations, organisations, and movements, that attuned to how societal problems resonate in the private life spheres distil and transmit such reaction in amplified form to the public sphere' (Habermas 1996: 367). Importantly, these associations, organizations and movements are outside the scope of the 'delinguistifying' influence of the media (i.e., they are not 'delinguistified'), are rights based, and are in contrast to what he calls the panoptic state (Habermas 1996: 369).[13] The key to the modern political public sphere is an 'energetic civil society' (Habermas 1996: 369).[14] And for Habermas this can only develop, and has developed in Europe, through a liberal political culture that respects the distinction between private and public, that permits (or at least does not stop) people from acquiring communicative power (as public opinion/influence and distinct from political power) and that recognizes the limits of both state authority and corporate ambition. It is from this that public spheres without 'holistic aspirations' (Habermas 1996: 372)[15] (because they are self-limited – that is, they are 'bundles of topically specified *public opinion*')[16] can become the fora of influence about various issues and subsequently become democratically engaged through challenging the political/legal system. Habermas believes that under these liberal political circumstances civil society can acquire influence, not per se but through the development and sustainability of a variety (Habermas 1996: 373–74)[17] of public spheres, to bring about changes in the deliberations and actions of the political and legal system (Habermas 1996: 373–74). These public spheres are both accessible to laypersons and as such potentially influential on the deliberations and workings of the political/ legal system, and paradoxically, one of the most significant ways such influence can be achieved is via the media.[18]

Habermas believes that modern empirical research on the effects of the media has 'done away with the image of passive consumers as "cultural dopes" who are manipulated by the programmes offered them' (Habermas 1996: 377). Indeed, he says, viewers use 'strategies of interpretation', talk to each other and can be 'provoked to criticize or reject what is offered'. Citing with approval, Gurevitch and Blumler's list of tasks that the media ought to fulfil, Habermas (1996: 378) summarizes his own recommendations accordingly:

> the mass media ought to understand themselves as the mandatary of an enlightened public whose willingness to learn and capacity for criticism they at once presuppose, demand, and reinforce; like the judiciary, they ought to preserve their independence from political and social pressures, they ought to be receptive to the public's concerns and proposals, take up these issues and contributions impartially, augment criticisms and confront the political process with articulate demands for legitimation. (Habermas 1996: 378)

Of course, this is a normative argument and not an empirical one; the latter argument still recognizes the way that the media are still part of the system. But here Habermas's argument is based on his belief about what is achievable and possible and therefore provides grounds for some optimism. The reason for this is that 'the sociology of mass communications depicts the public sphere as infiltrated by administrative and social power and dominated by the mass media', but this 'estimate pertains only to a public sphere at rest' because in 'periods of mobilization ... the balance of power between civil society and the political system then shifts' (Habermas 1996: 379).

It is only through periods of mobilization that elements of the media have the potential, or can be utilized in an engaged way with civil-social public spheres, to become what Habermas thinks they ought to be and presumably what European media policymakers wish them to be, namely, an enabler and facilitator of democratic activity and participative citizenship. If Habermas is correct about the need for the mobilization of public spheres and the utilization of the media for civil purposes, then this leads our European media policymaker (assuming she is one with the political order) into the paradoxical position of recommending and advocating a state of affairs that facilitates civil society in generating active public spheres that, through their own communicative power, wrest power from the political order of which she is a part.

The two questions posed above asked: under what circumstances do the media achieve its political influence? And how are these specific circumstances of enhancing democratic politics and participative citizenship facilitated by the media? The answer to the first question is twofold. Currently, the commercial media do very little to adjust or adapt themselves to the circumstances required to stimulate civil society. While European media policy struggles with this brute fact and seeks to render it otherwise through its support of public service media, it is also required to promote the commercial imperative. Nevertheless, hope is increasingly being placed in the new communication circumstances constantly being thrown up by technological changes, service capacities and convergence, which now influence the media in all their aspects. It is under the aegis of these new communication circumstances that the belief in the potential for the media to be either used by or to stimulate civil-social activity is now placed.

This leads directly to an answer to the second question. Simply stated, facilitating the specific circumstances whereby the media enhance democratic politics and participative citizenship through the widespread utilization of these new communication circumstances is proving difficult for EU policymakers. Certainly we can say the following: the circumstances, which need to be so ordered as to achieve greater democratic involvement, are entirely communicative and are based upon the private life spheres of European citizens from which the detection of 'problems' first takes place and that these circumstances must be arranged so as to facilitate the mobilization and sustainability of active civil public spheres.

However, this does not tell us how those more or less spontaneously emergent associations, organizations and movements that characterize modern European civil society undertake to use the media successfully. Some uses of the media are well understood. For example, the use of 'sponsors' or 'patrons', or if 'a particular public sphere has within it large interest groups who do not have to obtain their resources from other spheres' and who have some 'social power', then the use of one's own communicators (marketing specialists, pollsters, PR professionals, etc.) is an option (Habermas 1996: 374–77). If a particular sphere is without such resources, then friendly members of the broadcast media, press journalists, or well-disposed publicity agents might be used to gain access to media outlets (1996: 374–77). But, to use Habermas's language once more, the path from the civil-social periphery to the political centres requires (in non-Habermasian language) the empirical and normative reconfiguration of the media and its imaginative use. Such reconfiguration requires that European media policymakers be critical of both their own political centres and the current commercially dominated configuration of the media.

How likely such criticism will be forthcoming is not the issue here; what is at issue is rather the coherence and usefulness of the claim that European media policymakers want to arrange circumstances in such a way that the media is a vehicle for enhanced democratic activity, participative citizenship and an open and improved European public life. To succeed in any of this, there needs to be (as we said above) a detailed recognition of the barriers that exist to achieving mobilized public spheres derived from an active civil Europe, since it is only from the basis of overcoming these barriers that the conjunction between European civil society and contemporary European political and economic reality can be achieved. European media policy is required by its own rhetoric to address this through creating a reconfigured European media, balancing commercial and public concerns. How willing and able it is to do this successfully is open to question.

At the moment, though, it is fair to suggest that the processes of European mediation must first occur between EU institutions and the variety of audiences and publics (here EU citizens) in their own public and private settings. These potential audiences and publics make sense of messages and representations through their own social norms and cultural values, which provides, in the case of the EU citizen, for a more or less strong version of being a European, or belonging to the EU. Thus what would be distinctive about an active EU public sphere, or spheres, would be 'the emergence of European-wide forums of communicative competence, discourses, themes and cultural models and repertoires of evaluation within different national contexts' (Delanty and Rumford 2005: 103) and, one could add, sub-national contexts. The significance of which (for Delanty and Rumford 2005: 104) is the potential for

> inter-societal cross fertilization … on the social and cultural level in the institutionally unique circumstances of the EU … The European public sphere differs from conventional, public spheres whether national or transnational, in that it is polyvocal, articulated in different languages and through different cultural models and repertoires of justification, and occurs in very different institutional contexts.

In short, any European public sphere(s) would, in order to merit the name European, have to be cosmopolitan. Ulrich Beck (2006: 164–65) writes: 'Only … a politically pragmatic image of humanity and culture deserves the label "European". This becomes clear when we ask "Where do you stand on Turkey?" which has become the critical question of European politics. It divides opinion and ignites the conflict between the old national and a new cosmopolitan Europe.'

How true it is that this is *the* issue, which divides the advocates of old nation state-based Europe from the new cosmopolitan Europe is interesting (although not pursued here). But from a European media policy point of view, what Beck is pointing to is revealing and adds another layer of complexity to the task of using the modern European media for democratic or civil purposes.

For Beck, Europe is neither a geography of nations nor a 'Christian West' bound together by some federal superstructure. Rather, cosmopolitan 'Europeanness' is the ability 'to combine in a single existence what appears to a narrow-minded ethnic mentality to be mutually exclusive characteristics; one can, after all, be a Muslim and a democrat, a socialist and a small business person, love the Bavarian landscape and way of life and support anti-immigration policies' (Beck 2006: 164–65). Or, in other words, cosmopolitan Europe has about itself a radical openness in which 'European civil society arises only when Christians and Muslims, white and black-skinned democrats, and so forth, struggle over the political reality of Europe' (Beck 2006: 164–65).[19]

Of course this is aspirational. But the point is that if it is true that energetic European public sphere(s) utilizing their communicative power must, as suggested above, bear the hallmarks of European cosmopolitanism, then the task of arranging matters whereby the media can be used to enable or to facilitate this is made even more difficult for European media policymakers. Cosmopolitanism has only a small foothold in the modern media. And, if this were not enough, European media policy has again to recognize that within itself it is forced to adopt and occupy a paradoxical position that, when wishing to stimulate European civil society and its attendant mobilized public spheres, it must recommend curbing the power and influence of the political centre of Europe, thereby allowing its cosmopolitan diversity more space and influence.

If Habermas is correct that an active civil society with its mobilized and energetic issues-based public spheres is Europe's only real chance of increasing democratic activity; and if Beck is right that these public spheres must be cosmopolitan; and if this requires the empirical and normative reconfiguration of the media by European media policymakers (who in their turn facilitate the movement of power away from the political centre to the civil-social periphery); then we are entitled to ask: what realistic chance is there of a mediated Europe emerging that includes civil-social activity, rather than the one that currently operates, according to European-wide commercial freedoms and with European-wide spaces of exclusion?[20] It is this last question which provides the rationale for this collection of essays, and it is the problems and barriers to mediating Europe associated with the successful achievement of a reconfigured European media that permits, encourages and facilitates active civil engagement through European public sphere(s) which are variously and diversely considered in the chapters that follow.

The book falls into two naturally distinct but related halves. The first half, Chapters 2 to 7, is speculative, concerning the possible nature, depth and structure of, as well as the risks to, the European public sphere(s). The second half, Chapters 8 to 12, are a critical evaluation of the stresses and strains of EU media policy, from which any European public sphere must develop and sustain itself. Given that the papers are different, the editors have deliberately kept some overlap because certain themes (such as defining the public sphere; liberalizers versus interventionists; culture versus commerce; managing the trend of technological convergence; the scope of EU competencies and, of course, the role of the media sector in the perplexing task of how to communicate the idea of Europe) are at the heart of the issue of the process of establishing European public sphere(s) and a consistent EU media policy.

Nick Stevenson's paper has a Kantian hue. He is not as hopeful of the media as others and explicitly requires that any public sphere, European or otherwise, has an ethical character. For him, European inertia about what should and should not be tolerated is the challenge that must be met, certainly if Europe is ever to address itself confidently and reflexively. Thus, for example, the disintegration of Yugoslavia is both a real and symbolic form of disgrace. It is certainly not a technical matter of the then Yugoslavia's status, as in or out of Europe. The disgrace is undiluted by such legalities. For Stevenson, the critical ethical characteristics of a European public sphere, or spheres, is conflict resolution (Kant's 'perpetual peace'), and one can almost hear him add, 'within the limits of reason alone'. The value of a European public sphere is as a place where disputes are articulated and settled. Concomitantly Stevenson's Europe is cosmopolitan – equally a place where tolerance is taken for granted and hospitality is the norm. Without such aims Europe is a geopolitical realm susceptible to the excesses of neo-liberal values and national self-interest. If Europe is to achieve a civil character it needs more than is currently provided by the media. Here Stevenson touches en passant on education. For Stevenson, European education (in the public sphere(s)) should intercede against uncivilized behaviour. Active communication in any public sphere requires the development of critically independent citizens who have an ability to think from the position of 'the other'.

Damian Tambini is concerned with the European public sphere as an ideal. But for him it offers a means of monitoring and evaluating a very broad range of developments in media law and policy and as such it is a very powerful background ideal. To the fore are the tasks of the identification and delineation of rules, which are emerging through the way law and policy impact upon the distribution and management of European media assets variously understood as public, private and personal. He argues that we must understand the bifurcated but related issues of the quality of any public sphere determined through the quality of the discourse it occasions and the quality of the participation it encourages, something current EU policy seems ill equipped to deal with directly. But how, he wonders, can we redress that? What is needed, he argues, is for research to be undertaken on the specific issue of a European way of communication and that this should focus on a methodological understanding of what constitutes the European path in law and policy in the audio-visual and wider media and communication fields.

Renée van Os, Nicholas W. Jankowski and Fred Wester are concerned with the processes of Europeanization through various forms of communication. They identify three approaches to the study of the communication of Europe and European issues and then analyse these approaches – what they have to tell us and how they should be understood. Following this they focus in detail on the communication of Europe via the World Wide Web and, applying their three approaches, they review recent empirical studies of European visibility and note the increasing significance for European citizens of Brussels-based news and wider European issues. While they caution us that availability of this content may not provide sufficient evidence for the development of a robust online European public sphere, they do counsel further investigation. A first step would be, they suggest, to explore the possibility of establishing an explicitly political European public sphere on the internet, since, at the moment, mediation is still very much a case of Europe talking to its citizens and not the other way around.

Errki Karvonen, like Stevenson, recognizes the dangers of 'uncivilized' behaviour. In particular, he fears the trivialization of a mediated Europe, where conflict resolution is reduced to theatrical posturing, supported by the popular media's diminishment of politics through their emphasis on entertainment values. It is an important sociological point. The celebrity, the cause célèbre and the images attendant on both are unfortunately common media fare and are cause for concern because, Karvonen believes, they substitute for public discussion and progressive politics. Karvonen is an advocate of public or civic journalism and believes that whatever cause we might have for hope in Europe resides in this and beyond the phantasmagorias of entertainment journalism, its agenda-setting powers and the postmodern support for it. His look at recent Politico-celebrity events in Finland is salutary and regrettably all too familiar.

Christiano Bee and Valeria Bello provide an assessment of the various factors that stand for the plausibility of genuine European democracy and a European democratic way of life. They outline some of the interventions made by the European Commission to try to reduce the democratic deficit, to promote network governance, to stimulate public communication and to facilitate European public sphere(s). Like Habermas, they suggest that it is only via active participation that a European public sphere has any real political value. Intriguingly, they provide a schema of the 'intersection between territorial and functional levels' of an ideal European public sphere. The schema owes much to Manuel Castells, but is an affirmative statement of a model of networked governance and as such provides a possibility for genuine political and democratic action. From this and against which, they add, we still need to address the asymmetrical solutions provided by the EU about the nature of communications between different actors and different institutions.

Bridgette Wessels discusses the possible influences that the development of a 'European Information Society' may have on the generation of a European Public Sphere (EPS). She argues that the analysis of an EPS needs to address three historical processes – namely, the concept of a 'public sphere', the relationship between nation states and the EU, and changes to forms of communication. Currently, both the public sphere and Europe lack a clear and unambiguous definition, rationale and vision. She points out that a key dimension in the development of an EPS involves considering the influence of the global networked information age in the shaping of public spheres that are traditionally shaped by, and understood through, the nation state. The question she addresses is: what is the influence of a global networked information age in developing an EPS within a collection of national public spheres? Taking a theme of participation, she shows how historically the public sphere has been shaped by who participates, the character of that participation and the means of communication. The current context of Europe and the emergence of new information and communication technologies are considered in relation to developments in the information society that may facilitate a public sphere for Europe in the twenty-first century. However, although these emergent forms of communication have the technological possibility of enabling participation, the issue remains the way in which the citizens of the EU nation states perceive Europe. In general terms, the lack of a European public and the democratic deficit within the EU mitigates against the dialogue and critical reasoning required for an active public sphere in Europe.

Peter Humphrey's paper introduces the second half of the book and sets the scene with a detailed and fluent account of the EU's regulatory competence in the audio-visual field. He finds the EU wanting on issues of public service broadcasting, but influential in the major area of the creation of an internal market and a competitive audio-visual market. The latter development, and what he refers to as the promotion of 'pan-European champion companies', seems to underlie EU policy and regulatory activism, as opposed to, say, its promotion of more publicly spirited audio-visual forms; a trend he thinks that will only become greater, although he recognizes some re-regulatory force in the Television Without Frontiers Directive and in the adoption of a French-style policy of cultural protection. For Humphreys, the Commission is both opportunistic in seeking to extend its influence in audio-visual policy and entrepreneurial when managing changes in technology and market stimulation. Consequently, a combination of tensions arises in the policymaking process that raises serious questions for the establishment of a European public sphere.

Max Craglia and Alessandro Annoni argue that the EU is developing a range of initiatives designed to increase the flow of two-way information between the European institutions and the European citizen. They take as an exemplar of this kind of thinking the original Aarhus Convention, which they see as establishing the EU citizen's right to information, the right to participate in decision-making processes and the right to redress. However, Aarhus has also been subject to amendments and these they argue are not entirely desirable, since they point to the priority of commercial ways of thinking. After this they offer an assessment of the INSPIRE proposal, itself a form of public sphere. This involves establishing a European Infrastructure for Spatial Information (in the first instance environmental information). They clearly approve of INSPIRE and address both the barriers to its success and measures to overcome them. Their conclusion contains a mixed message – what they desire, greater European democracy, is constantly frustrated by both the complexity and number of vested interests that have to be dealt with every time an information initiative is raised, but they believe that some progress is being made.

Katharine Sarikakis turns our attention to the role of the European Parliament and its influence. She argues that the role of the European Parliament in shaping EU communications policy has been understudied. Essentially, she believes that the European Parliament shapes the discourse surrounding media policy, constantly vying between cultural expressions and commercial imperatives (usually promoted by different Directorates-General). Although the European Parliament has managed to create spaces for more creative thinking about culture in the EU, often coming into conflict with the Commission and member states, its effectiveness has been constrained. The European Parliament's humanistic view of media and culture has been limited because of its own limited vision of Europeanness and the lack of a clear idea of what it is that it seeks to promote and protect. It needs to find ways to overcome this and, for Sarikakis, needs to address the problems of cultural dominance that occur within the EU itself, rather than focusing on either the protection and promotion of an un-reflexive European culture or growing a European commercial media that is primarily driven by its ability to compete in world markets. The European Parliament's relationship to an agreed media policy that deals with the diverse issue of what constitutes Europeanness is vital if engagement within the EU between the institution and EU citizens is to be fostered and maintained.

Mark Wheeler sees the tension in European audio-visual policy as one between the liberalizers, who argue that audio-visual policy should be based upon free market calculations, and the interventionists ('dirigistes'), who maintain that the media should be used to express public aims and European culture. For Wheeler, this dichotomy currently remains fixed in place, and consensus over European audio-visual policy is a long way off. If Wheeler were doing trend analysis he would suggest that those who support public aims for the media must be ever more watchful of the increasing influence of the EU Competition Directorate. Its remit is neo-liberal in economics and commercial in application. The domain over which it rules is expanding, and the extent to which it will protect public services and promote a European public sphere is questionable.

Gulseren Adakli provides a fascinating case study on recent Turkish media liberalization. She argues that a very traditional Turkish press (she uses the term 'artisan like') was subject in the 1980s and 1990s to the consequences of neo-liberal economic policies. The result was privatization and a flurry of mergers and acquisitions between various holdings to produce a few media groups defined by their horizontal, vertical and cross integration across different sectors. Within these media groups resided the stories of the real meaning of reform, of corruption and of the clash between media liberalizers and those who are critical of such changes. Her study of the Turkish press and its subsequent transformation, via issues of global media influence, changing journalistic values, cross-media integration, political pressures and ultimately European accession, reveals a paradox. In essence, liberalization was accompanied by a political desire to 'manage' the scope of press freedom, which was an agenda the new 'free' Turkish press seemed happy to go along with. The newly structured Turkish press was at best pragmatic, at worst unprincipled. But the issues were clear: the defence of capital and the introduction of Anglo-American corporate structures and governance became de rigueur, as did the desire to join Europe for what Adakli thinks are purely economic reasons that favour the new generation of Turkish large-scale media corporations who are, of course, advocates of the accession. To what extent Turkey has lost something of its own cultural and symbolic powers to reflect upon itself, indeed to remember and report itself, or to sustain civil public spheres, is an open question and one that poignantly stands as a reminder of the consequences of the clash between wider public aims and narrow corporate requirements.

Notes

1. Throughout this chapter the term 'Europe' is synonymous with the term 'European Union' (EU).
2. I include within the term 'media', and the phrase 'media sector', broadcasting, telecommunications, information and entertainment organizations and companies that range across radio, TV, computers, telephones, wireless applications and their various platform and distribution systems.

3. I take as my definition of 'public sphere' that provided by Habermas (1996: 360): 'The public sphere is a social phenomenon just as elementary as action, actor, association, or collectivity, but it eludes the conventional sociological concepts of "social order". The public sphere cannot be conceived as an institution and certainly not an organisation. It is not even a framework of norms with differentiated competencies and roles, membership regulations and so on. Just as little does it represent a system; although it permits one to draw internal boundaries, outwardly it is characterised by open, permeable, and shifting horizons. The public sphere can best be described as a network for communicating information and points of view (i.e. opinions expressing affirmative or negative attitudes); the streams of communication are, in the process, filtered and synthesised in such a way that they coalesce into bundles of topically specified public opinion.' On the issue of whether there is one public sphere or many, Habermas (1996: 374) has this to say: 'Despite the manifold differences [of public spheres] all the partial publics constituted by ordinary language remain porous to one another. The one text of "the" public sphere … is divided by internal boundaries into arbitrarily small texts for which everything else is context; yet one can always build hermeneutical bridges from one text to the next.'

4. An understanding of convergence and its impact on the media sector has also engendered different attitudes to the need for regulation. Some see the current regulatory structures as inadequate, as all platforms (traditionally regulated in different ways) will be able to receive the same material, and as regulation has retained a national focus this is inappropriate in an international services market. Others see convergence as having little impact, as audio-visual policy should continue to be distinguished from information society policy and continue to promote social, cultural and ethical values, regardless of which particular technology is used for delivering services. In the latter scenario, broadcasting would continue to have extra levels of obligation placed upon it (see Commission of the European Communities 1997, 1999).

5. For a detailed analysis of the way in which the needs of viewers are protected by European broadcasting law and policy, see Harrison and Woods 2007.

6. Needless to say, I am not referring here to the 1906 breakaway group from the Russian Socialist Revolutionary Party.

7. Despite the expansion of Union competence into areas such as culture and citizenship, its central focus remains the creation of a common market. To achieve the common market the EC Treaty provided for the free movement of goods, services, people and capital (the four freedoms).

8. Communicative rationality is the location of rationality in the structure of discourse itself as opposed to its location in the self-reflective subject or the world. Also by saying that I leave aside Habermas's ethical concerns I mean to say that, for reasons of brevity, I do not intend to discuss discourse ethics in what is, after all, a very brief and high-level account of a very difficult thinker.

9. This argument is in part derived from Habermas's adaptation of speech act philosophy (particularly Austin and Searle), and the argument that all

illocutionary speech acts have the purpose of achieving mutual agreement and understanding.

10. Social evolution for Habermas is to be understood as an account of the 'process of differentiation: system and lifeworld are differentiated in the sense that the complexity of one and the rationality of the other grow. But it is not only qua system and qua lifeworld that they are differentiated; they get differentiated from one another at the same time.'

11. Hence the term 'delinguistified' when talking of communications dominated by instrumental rationality, means-ends calculations, technical thinking and marketplace formulae, and of modern bureaucracy and government organizations.

12. For a definition of 'public sphere', see note 3.

13. The rights Habermas cites are freedoms of assembly, association and speech. These are accompanied by freedoms of press, radio and television to safeguard the media infrastructure of public communication and the freedom of parties 'to "collaborate" in the political will formation of the people'.

14. Habermas writes: 'Basic constitutional guarantees alone, of course, cannot preserve the public sphere and civil society from deformations. The communication structures of the public sphere must be kept intact by an energetic civil society.'

15. In essence, public spheres are not revolutionary in the Marxist sense because they do not seek complete political power.

16. See definitions in note 3.

17. Habermas gives examples not only of a variety of public spheres – popular science and literary publics, religious and artistic publics, feminist and 'alternative publics' concerned with healthcare issues, social welfare, or environmental policy – but also of their different levels according to their 'density of communication, organisational complexity, and range – from episodic publics found in taverns, coffee houses, or on the streets, through occasional or "arranged" publics of particular presentation and events, such as theatre performances, rock concerts, party assemblies, or church congresses; up to the abstract public sphere of isolated readers, listeners, and viewers scattered across large geographic areas, or even around the globe, and brought together only through the mass media.'

18. Within these are included sponsored communication campaigns, the use of market studies, opinion surveys, publications and publicity campaigns (Habermas 1996: 373–79). This is not to suggest that he still does not believe that 'public processes of communication can take place with less distortion the more they are left to the internal dynamic of civil society that emerges from the lifeworld' (Habermas 1996: 375), rather that public spheres can more and more utilize forms of media that were (prior to the emergence of modern energetic civil societies and new media possibilities) previously and otherwise unavailable to them. This is a point made constantly and forcefully by advocates of the emancipatory political potential for new media.

19. Taking his cue from both Kant and Habermas, Beck's argument comes down to this – for a cosmopolitan Europe to emerge it must acquire a cosmopolitan ethic to match its cosmopolitan make-up. This, in turn, must be based across a

cooperative of states, which in its turn utilizes the politics of reconciliation (with the interesting suggestion that in one sense this politics is accompanied by a cosmopolitan European history which began with the Nuremberg trials and the invention of the crime 'crimes against humanity'); advocates the real recognition and acceptance of diversity; enables the emergence of new intellectual elites who overthrow their parochial 'national lie' and curtails national egoism or tendencies when dealing with political events.

20. I have adapted Agamben's (2005) phrase 'spaces of exception' here.

Bibliography

Agamben, G. 2005. *State of Exception*, trans. Kevin Attell. Chicago: University of Chicago Press.

Barnett, S. 1997. 'New Media, Old Problems: New Technology and the Political Process', *European Journal of Communication* 12(2): 193–218.

Bauman, Z. 2000. *Liquid Modernity*. Cambridge: Polity Press.

Beck, U. 2006. *The Cosmopolitan Vision*, trans. Ciaran Cronin. Cambridge: Polity Press.

Calhoun, C. (ed.). 1992. *Habermas and the Public Sphere*. Cambridge, MA: The MIT Press.

Commission of the European Communities 1997. *Green Paper on the Convergence of the Telecommunications, Media and Information Technology Sectors, and the Implications for Regulation. Towards an Information Society Approach*, COM(1997)623.

———. 1999. *Public Consultation on the Convergence Green Paper: Communication to the European Parliament, the Council, the Economic and Social Committee and the Committee of the Regions*, COM(1999)108.

Curran, J. and Seaton, J. 2003. *Power without Responsibility*, 6th edn. London: Routledge.

Delanty, G. and Rumford, C. 2005. *Rethinking Europe: Social Theory and the Implications of Europeanization*. London: Routledge.

Eley, G. 1992. 'Nations, Publics, and Political Cultures: Placing Habermas in the Nineteenth Century', in C. Calhoun (ed.), *Habermas and the Public Sphere*. Cambridge: The MIT Press, pp. 289–339.

Habermas, J. 1984. *Theory of Communicative Action, Volume 1: Reason and the Rationalisation of Society*, trans. T. McCarthy. London: Heinemann.

———. 1987. *Theory of Communicative Action, Volume 2: Lifeworld and System*, trans. T. McCarthy. Cambridge: Polity Press.

——— 1989. *The Structural Transformation of the Public Sphere: An Inquiry into a Category of Bóurgeois Society*, trans. Thomas Burger assisted by Frederick Lawrence, reprinted 2003. Cambridge: Polity Press.

———. 1996. *Between Facts and Norms: Contributions to a Discourse Theory of Law and Democracy*, trans. William Rehg. Cambridge, MA: The MIT Press.

Harrison, J. and Woods, L. 2000. 'European Citizenship: Can European Audiovisual Policy Make a Difference?', *Journal of Common Market Studies* 38(3): 471–94.

————. 2007. *European Broadcasting Law and Policy.* Cambridge: Cambridge University Press.

Morley, D. and Robins, K. (eds). 1995. *Spaces of Identity: Global Media, Electronic Landscapes and Cultural Boundaries.* London: Routledge.

Ward, D. 2004. *European Union Democratic Deficit and the Public Sphere.* Oxford: IOS Press.

PART I

New Media, Mass Media and the European Public Sphere

Chapter 2

European Cosmopolitanism or Neo-liberalism? Questions of Media and Education

Nick Stevenson

Introduction

The idea of European identity has a long and mutable history. Many have sought to resolve the ambiguities generated by this by producing a European myth of origins that ultimately stamps its citizens with a definite identity. These identities include Europe as the origin of civilization, racially supreme, or as the founding place of Christianity. As Julia Kristeva (1993) reminds us, the cult of origins produces a rejection of the Other and cancels the possibility of development through inclusion of the Other. The risk of this is that we remain shackled to the past, unable to transcend our own historical identities. Yet if the game of European origins is best forgotten there remain European choices. Here I want to contrast two different versions of European futures, although of course there are others.

The first is a neo-liberal Europe defined by free trade and a loose association of nation states. The idea of Europe offered here is not one of participatory citizenship, but of consumption, indifference and market competition. The second offers a more cosmopolitan understanding of Europe that is built upon human rights, democracy, political participation and solidarity amongst strangers. A growing number of perspectives in this respect have begun to warn about the possible Americanization of Europe as it becomes increasingly detached from its core values. Here the argument has been that notions of European civilization are threatened by disappointing levels of engagement in elections, the rise of the far Right and an increasingly consumerist orientation to politics. Under this rubric, as American politics becomes increasingly captured by a fundamentalist Christianity, post-democracy and a repressive state, so the European project becomes ever more important in the global defence of civilized values. The commitment of the European Union (EU) to grant such values an institutional basis potentially makes it a global force that is able to preserve such values in the context of the polarizing rhetoric of the war on civilization and American power politics. Jeremy Rifkin (2004) has argued that, whereas the American dream is withering on the vine of massive social inequality and the decline of the work ethic and consumerism, the European dream is 'the' transnational project of the global age. If Americans continue to dream of wealth and power, Europe's peoples are more concerned with social solidarity, quality of life, human rights and democratic norms and the development of sustainable societies. Yet in the context of such sweeping generalizations, Europe clearly runs the risk of being both idealized and essentialized. According to Etienne Balibar (2003: 18), the idea that Europe can act as a bulwark against the one remaining superpower substitutes 'an imaginary Europe for the real one'. While European societies are more internally differentiated than scholars like Rifkin seem to realize, Europe, it should be remembered, has a long history of being unable to solve its own problems without American help. The war in the former Yugoslavia, which recorded the worst war crimes on Europe's continent since the Second World War, was halted only after the intervention of American military force. This is, of course, not to argue that the idea of Europe may not have a positive role to play in global power politics, but that we should be wary of inevitable displacements that accompany such essentializing rhetoric.

Key to which version of Europe will dominate our collective futures are the practices and definitions of culture. Here I shall argue that the question for Europe is whether it is able to articulate a form of cosmopolitanism that is able to engage global citizens as well as locals. The battle of ideas is not so much between America and Europe but between neo-liberalism and the rise of exclusive nationalisms and European cosmopolitanism. The project of fostering cosmopolitan institutions and identities remains Europe's best hope of both responding to its own barbarous past and preserving the ideals of democratic citizenship in the global arena. In other words, the collective memories of Europeans continue to promote a collective scepticism in respect of the inevitable dangers involved in the use of violence and the culture of militarism (Todorov 2003). However, this leaves open a wealth of questions. How might cosmopolitan sensibilities become more firmly embedded in the soil of culture, given the continued challenge of neo-liberalism and nationalism? What kinds of media and education systems are required to enhance cosmopolitan definitions and understandings? How might Europe build active and educated public spheres in the face of the threats posed by neo-liberalism and overt nationalism? Does Europe's own past provide any guidance as to the principles upon which these more engaged public spaces might be built?

These questions seem a long way from the preoccupations of global governance that are the usual fare of cosmopolitan discussion. However, my view is that if democratic and cosmopolitan sensibilities do not to some extent grow out of civil society then they are unlikely to find the necessary resonance in the lives of many ordinary citizens. If civic engagement and political participation appear to be increasingly irrelevant in the age of multinational corporations then citizenship will have been reduced to market-based choices. Public spaces such as the media and education, therefore, need to help foster the conditions that make a democratically engaged citizenship possible.

European Cosmopolitanism and Cultural Citizenship

Historically, cosmopolitanism has two related meanings. First, a cosmopolitan is someone who embraces plurality and difference. In this respect, modern cities are often seen as providing the backdrop for the development of cosmopolitan sensibilities in that they house a number of distinctive cultures, ethnic groups and lifestyles. A cosmopolitan is a polyglot who is able to move comfortably within multiple and diverse communities, while resisting the temptation to search for a purer and less complex identity. In recent debates, this meaning of cosmopolitanism has been connected to questions of cultural citizenship (Stevenson 2003). The need to preserve difference against the normalizing and exclusionary discourses and practices of the market, nation state and social movements has been important in this regard.

Cosmopolitan selves and communities in this understanding will thrive when the right to be different is both respected and encouraged. Post-colonial and queer theory have criticized the ways in which dominant discourses have helped construct a number of binary oppositions that reinforce the presumed superiority of 'Western' or 'heterosexual' lifestyles (Seidman 1997). The aim here is to subvert the ways that ideas of citizenship have sought to mask and normalize cultural difference. Homosexuality, feminism and black politics are not 'minority' issues, but are dependent upon the deconstruction of dominant codes and discourses. The attempt to fix the identities of the European and the non-European, men and women, and white and back people is the effect of powerful ideological discourses. Such codes and ideologies seek to impose unitary identities and thereby impose a normalized social order. The argument here seeks to question both the simple binaries between self and other and also the supposed unity of 'oppressed' groups in order to reveal the ways in which identities are constructed through language and culture.

These features have also introduced a shift from identity politics to a politics of difference. Whereas objectivist and interest-based traditions within the social sciences sought to develop a politics based upon unitary identities, such notions have been increasingly called into question. Instead, identities are being represented as the site of contestation and struggle, and as multiple and fragmented rather than pre-given and natural (Calhoun 1994). Claims to 'identity' are always caught up in the construction of an inside and an outside. Here it is the cultural production of the abject and the marginal that enforces processes of cultural and symbolic exclusion. A cultural politics in this respect seeks to make space for the 'Other' in democratic discourse.

Second, a cosmopolitan is literally a citizen of the world. This refers to a set of perspectives that have sought to jettison viewpoints which are determined solely by the nation, or their geographical standing within the world. The political philosophy of Immanuel Kant (1970) argued that a cosmopolitan democracy should be developed to replace the law of nations with a genuinely morally binding international law. For Kant, the spread of commerce and principles of republicanism could help foster cosmopolitan sentiments. Kant's vision of a peaceful cosmopolitan order based upon the obligation of states to settle their differences through the court of law has gained a new legitimacy in the twentieth century with the development of the United Nations and the EU. More recently, a number of political philosophers have argued that Kant's earlier vision can be revised to provide a new critical politics for an increasingly global age. A cosmopolitan political response is required where national politics has lost much of its power but little of its influence. Globalization has undermined the operation of national democracies, as it is increasingly unable to control the flow of money, refugees and asylum seekers, viruses and media images. Many have argued that to begin to address these problems requires the construction of overlapping forms of political community connecting citizens into local, national, regional and global forms of government. The development of cosmopolitan perspectives is fostered by the growing acceptance that many of the problems that face the world's citizens are shared and cannot be resolved by individual states.

The cosmopolitan project, then, seeks to revive democracy in an age where it is increasingly under threat. However, despite some of the earlier hopes to build a worldwide inclusive democracy after September 11, this now seems somewhat over-optimistic. If cosmopolitan democracy is to find expression then it is currently the EU that offers the best hope for its development. Here the idea of a cosmopolitan Europe does not attempt to dispense with the nation state, but recognizes its rise and fall as one actor amongst many in the European polity. If, as Ulrich Beck (2003: 463) has commented, 'the nation state is a state of mind', then cosmopolitanism has to be more than a process of institution building. In this respect, many have become concerned that the image of the European cosmopolitan is one that has been fostered by an elite who are able to move with ease between different languages and capital cities (Calhoun 2003). Others have been concerned that the two meanings of cosmopolitanism are not compatible with one another. Despite the acceptance of universal human rights and the rule of law and democracy, many communities remain excluded from participatory forms of democracy. A genuinely cosmopolitan Europe would need to move between republican and cultural forms of citizenship. The idea that we need not make a choice between the development of engaged, publicly oriented citizens and cultural politics has been articulated by all too few voices within current debates and perspectives.

European Identities and Media Cultures

The debate in respect of the connection between the EU and the media has been over-determined by the needs of capital and ideas of the nation. Many have pointed to the fact that the policy responses of the EU have contained a number of contradictory features. In this respect, directives from the EU seem to have been caught between the desire to maintain a plurality of media provision and enhance the competitiveness of the European media sector. In determining the specific balance between public and commercial media sectors, considerable autonomy has been left in the hands of member states (Wheeler 2004). At the European level, such features are usually represented through a struggle between the Competition Directorate's concern to foster liberalized communication environments and the European Parliament's desire to defend the values of public service broadcasting. The defence of public service broadcasting as a European ideal is considered important to both the maintenance of an informed citizenship and the fostering of diversity, with explicit reference to the serving of minority groups and populations. In particular, there has been the concern, due to the growth of commercial broadcasting since the 1980s, that publics are disintegrating under the pressure of new competition and the increasing provision of channels and services. The mass audiences enjoyed by public service channels can no longer be assumed in deregulated and individualized media environments (Harrison and Woods 2001).

Despite these arguments, others have pointed to the ways in which the defence of public service broadcasting has been mobilized in the face of a fear of subordinate cultures and cultural minorities. For example, Morley and Robbins (1995) report that many of the debates in 1950s Britain concerning the introduction of commercial television exhibited a fear of Americanization and the concern that a mostly working-class audience would be corrupted by commercial values. Further, it is also reported that ethnic minorities across Europe have responded enthusiastically to the development and provision of satellite broadcasting due to the perceived 'whiteness' of the official national public sphere (Morley 2000). Indeed, we could extend this argument further and suggest that the desire to defend the tradition of public service broadcasting may indeed be related to a specifically 'white' fear of the development of a more decentred communications universe (Creeber 2004).

Whatever the insights of this particular debate, it mostly leaves unquestioned the assumption that the link between communications policy and identity is the fostering and maintenance of national identity. Philip Schlesinger (1997: 70) argues that, in respect of political communications, 'the grand narrative of the nation is far from dead today'. Despite European directives that have sought to develop a European audio-visual culture, these can easily be dismissed as a pipe dream. The paradox of Europe is that it is actually an American entertainment–based culture that most easily traverses national barriers. The collapse of the 'iron curtain' within Europe has inevitably expanded the market for an American-style corporate culture (Schiller 1996). Neo-liberal media culture depends upon the active promotion of policies of privatization, consumerism, the development of new technology and a largely passive audience. This overtly commercial environment then effectively 'shuts out' the audience, reducing them to consumers of polished news programmes and eye-catching forms of entertainment in an increasingly competitive media environment (Hallin 1994). Despite the dominance of market-driven media cultures, in cultural-mediated terms Europe is best seen as a patchwork of nation states. For Schlesinger (1991), it is the nation which remains the primary organizing and structuring device of mediated cultural identities. This is a view shared by many anthropologists who complain that, unless Europe is able to become both a community of legal norms as well as an emotional and cultural community of affective connection, then European citizenship is likely to remain an empty shell. The idea of Europe, in this reading, becomes a technocratic project or a non-place when compared to the 'eros' of national cultures (Shore 2004).

Despite these considerations, there has been growing concern amongst many that these and similar arguments actually reify the idea of the national public sphere. For example, despite the continued power of national languages, what actually matters is communication on questions of European concern and interest. Here a cosmopolitan Europe is less a matter of a shared identity but more of the ability of divergent media to inform and respond to citizens' initiatives on matters of common concern. Indeed, there is some evidence to suggest that a diversity of national-based media communicates similar forms of public discourse on issues related to the EU (Van de Steeg 2002; Trenz 2004). In this respect, discourses about Europe can be said to both exist 'inside' and 'outside' the nation state providing relatively unified fields of communication across the EU. This is not to argue that there could ever be a single unified European media space but that such unified fields of communication that do exist will be mediated by nation states. There is also evidence amongst political and business elites that a number of publications like the European edition of the *Financial Times* and *The Economist* are widely read across Europe (Schlesinger 1999). However, it is evident that entrance to such debates is highly restrictive even amongst the circles of Europe's most powerful citizens.

The state of the current debate is that matters of shared European concern are either being communicated amongst an elite or would require a revived model of public service broadcasting in order to develop informed and critical perspectives on European identity. However, such views fail to recognize that public service broadcasting is more easily understood as a 'Western' European model of organizing communication. Further, the development of computer cultures, mobile phones and multi-channel television means that European societies are complex information-based societies. Notably, these transformations have been accompanied by the decline of specifically public service broadcasting and the privatization and commercialization of the media. There is then, perhaps, a need to rethink the role of the media and the ways in which they connect to the normative horizons of Europe's citizens. If Europe is to be built upon civic forms of solidarity that transgress the borders of nation states, then it requires enhanced levels of citizenship participation. Jürgen Habermas argues that Europe's citizens need 'to learn to mutually recognise one another as members of a common political existence beyond national borders' (Habermas 2001: 99). A cosmopolitan European identity actually requires a form of civic solidarity where fellow Europeans take responsibility for one another. These processes are dependent not only on the formulation of a common European civil society, constitution and social policy, but also on a sense of solidarity being created through political institutions. The development of a European cosmopolitan identity is dependent upon civic forms of solidarity being developed beyond the nation. Only when Europe is able to develop a genuinely post-national democracy will it be able to provide an alternative to both economic globalization and shared histories of barbaric nationalism.

If such a civic culture is to develop amongst Europeans then it will require enhanced forms of participation in mediated discussions on the future of Europe. In other words, we need to think more carefully as to how the norms of cosmopolitan democracy might be transferred into more practical contexts (Dahlgren 2002, 2004). Here I remain deeply sceptical of the view that a progressive European cosmopolitan solidarity can be ensured simply through a defence of national public service broadcasting. We need to remind ourselves that, even though public service broadcasting has provided a relatively decommodified zone for political forms of communication, it was built upon both deep structural inequalities as well as cultural forms of disrespect and misrecognition (Murdock 2000). In other words, the symbolic resources necessary for the participation of citizens are unevenly distributed in European societies and are enhanced by the structural divisions of class and powerful cultural forms of domination such as race and gender. This means that the power to speak, be heard and made visible is unevenly distributed in mass-mediated societies (Stevenson 2003). Further, we should also add that the structure of the media is such that it continues to reinforce a structural divide between those who are able to participate in the construction of media messages (conglomerates, politicians, political parties, NGOs, media professionals) and the vast majority of ordinary people who mostly consume such media (Couldry 2000). Despite the rise of the internet and other more interactive technologies, most media remain overwhelmingly one-way and leave most people in the role of viewers rather than participants. Indeed, such features might partially explain the reason why many young people have begun to turn their backs on conventional political debates.

There has been a trend of younger people moving away from mainstream journalism to more entertainment-oriented formats. Indeed, some have suggested that the huge interactive audiences across Europe for programmes like *Big Brother* actually signify a democratic revolution waiting to happen (Van Zoonen 2004). The claim here is that the public sphere needs to increase its level of digital interactivity to engage the horizons of increasingly disengaged young citizens. In this respect, many of the young have become enthusiastic users of both new forms of technology and more hybrid genres of journalism (so-called 'infotainment') and are more likely to 'surf' different forms of media than remain loyal to specific journalistic outlets (Dahlgren 2000). These mediated transformations can be read through the rubric of individualization, which entails the disembedding of the ways of industrial society and the reinvention of new communal ties and biographies. As more areas of social life become disconnected from the hold of tradition, the more our biographies require choice and planning. Individuals are 'condemned' to be both authors of their own lives and to 'choose' their level of engagement or disengagement from the public sphere. The disintegration of the nuclear family and rigid class hierarchies means that citizens are released from the structures of industrial society into the uncertainties of a risky and less certain world (Beck 1992).

However, I think we need to be careful of the view that more interactive forms of media equals more engaged forms of public space. For example, the development of the internet could indeed be understood as allowing enhanced possibilities in respect of political participation. There is considerable evidence that the internet has played an important role in enhancing communication across the borders of nation states, helping foster the role played by more internationally located public spheres (Serra 2000). We might also suggest that the web has had a democratizing effect, as in cyberspace the boundaries between journalism and non-journalism are partially deconstructed. Many social movements and critical citizens are able to set up web pages and information sites on issues that were previously excluded or marginalized by the 'big' media (Dahlgren 2001, 2004). Yet, while these are important developments, they can be overstated.

The idea that interactive television and the internet have enhanced meaningful forms of audience participation can be questioned on at least two levels. There is evidence that, despite calls to interactivity in television charity events, most of the audience most of the time remain passive (Devereux 1996). What is revealed here is an overwhelming refusal to become involved in mediated calls to pick up the telephone or indeed go online to make a donation. Mostly, such 'events', like more official versions in the public sphere, institute overwhelmingly one-way flows of information, although this is admittedly more disguised. Secondly, I would argue that a robust and democratic public sphere actually requires an exchange of different views and perspectives; however, this is precisely what certain aspects of virtual culture seem to cancel. For example, Jesús Martín-Barbero (2002) has argued that, despite the supposed democratizing effect evident in the development of new television channels and genres, the overall effect does not so much enhance engaged citizens as encourage a form of displaced nomadism. The development of new media technologies amongst the young enables them to avoid the definitions of the dominant parent culture while developing more fragmented subjectivities that are continuously on the move. In this respect, we could argue that virtual space is actually a relatively pacified space. Cyberspace is space that is both moved through quickly with the opportunity to close the conversation no more than a mouse click away. There is then no obligation to listen and engage with the otherness of the Other (Robins and Webster 1999). Here the argument is that a European civic culture that both promotes solidarity amongst strangers and the recognition and negotiation of difference will not be fostered by technological and mediated developments alone. While it is possible that I have painted an overly bleak picture of the current state of Europe's mediated public spaces, I think we need to be cautious about claims that mediated interactivity will of itself be able to push Europe in a cosmopolitan direction without considerable pressure from civil society.

What becomes critical at this point is the idea of what Habermas (1989) called the public sphere. Public sphere, in my understanding, depends more on what people actually do and on the general quality of their engagements than upon technological transformation. If Habermas's (1989) writing offers us two different definitions of human freedom then one points towards instrumentality and the other towards the ability to engage actively with the 'Other'. While it is true that many have argued that Habermas's insistence on consensus potentially cancels more enhanced forms of dialogue, his work continues to emphasize an important distinction between technocratic and communicative rationality (Mouffe 2000). The argument here is that recent media developments and more long-standing problems with media cultures are enhancing a future driven by markets and consumerism rather than an engagement with more democratic horizons and sensibilities. Further, we would also need to question the extent to which the development of modern media technologies will disrupt or normalize hierarchies or question the taken-for-granted borders of the nation state. The question becomes: how do we create a culture of communication through the media of mass communication that actually promotes communicative confrontation with the 'Other' rather than simply reaffirming existing group prejudices (Young 1999)?

We also need to consider the view that the fact that images and mediated texts cross over borders does not so much create solidarity as a generalized indifference. Keith Tester (1995: 475) argues that television cannot actually create moral solidarity, but it can provide a cultural resource for those who have a predisposition towards 'moral leaps of the imagination'. The representation of murder, war and suffering on television has no necessary connection to the development of cosmopolitan solidarity. In this respect, Zygmunt Bauman (1993) offers the notion of 'telecity' to explain some of these aspects. Telecity, Bauman argues, is where objects and subjects appear only as forms of pleasure and amusement. The television screen allows us to go travelling without leaving home, but its integration into privatized leisure patterns means that our experience of alterity becomes blunted. The space opened up by telecity allows the subject to wander through a variety of media texts without any strings attached. A world that is awash with images helps to foster a blasé attitude amongst the audience, whereby they repeatedly fail to be shocked by the pictures of horror and distress that are the daily diet of the television news. Television images are too fast and fleeting to leave any lasting moral trace of their presence. (Tester 2001).

The fear of mediated indifference undoubtedly articulates a Europe where privileged consumers can progressively delink themselves from place in ways that cannot be said of more local citizens. It is the ability of privileged global citizens to withdraw into the pleasures and comforts of their privatized space that destabilizes attempts to promote a strong transnational civic culture. We might argue that European citizenship is currently caught between a 'space of flows' on the one hand and other identities more tied to physical notions of place on the other. This has lead to increasing concern about disconnected citizens and the 'dual' city (Castells 1997; Delanty 2000).

Yet media cultures are capable of contributing to the building of a genuinely engaged and communicative European civic culture. The development of a mediated culture that respects difference, interrupts national imaginations and helps create new forms of solidarity amongst locals and globals, will have to be politically struggled for and is not the outcome of technological change. Cosmopolitan European citizenship, then, requires newly emerged communicative landscapes that make space for the 'Other'. The freedom of communication within civil society requires a constitutional defence that safeguards minimum standards in respect of ownership, funding and freedom from political interference (Keane 1991). A communications universe that has become overly controlled by powerful communications conglomerates that place profit before civic exchange does not best serve a vibrant media culture. What becomes important here is the building of mediated public spheres that take seriously questions of 'voice', 'visibility' and 'respect'. Along with traditions of public service broadcasting, we need to make a distinction between market and public values in an age where identities fostered by the market dominate over more publicly oriented concerns. Here media culture becomes about consumerism and market choice rather than the development of communicative engagement. In particular, the young need access to communicative public spaces where they can develop their own voices and thereby learn to become cultural producers as well as cultural consumers (Giroux 1999). Citizenship should become an engaged practice seeking to foster conversation that opens the possibility of learning through dialogue. As the work of Raymond Williams (1985) continues to remind us, the development of a politics of 'voice' requires a redefinition of who has a right to speak and make themselves heard in contested public spheres. This would mean challenging the dominance of communicative relations by large conglomerates and national political parties to make space for the materially and culturally excluded. These features necessarily require not only new media and communicative initiatives but, as we shall see, educational features as well.

If this seems like a luxury that the consumers of rich industrial societies could easily live without then they would do well to attend to the writing of Croatian journalist Slavenka Drakulic (2004). She describes the disintegration of the belief shared by many of her generation that the barbarity of the Second World War had been permanently banished from Europe, the human tragedy of the breakup of Yugoslavia being dramatized by the deaths of 7,475 Muslim men at Srebrenica. Inevitably the control of the media was only part of the story but, crucially, nonetheless shaped the cultural soil that allowed for the growth of extreme forms of cultural nationalism.

First, Drakulic demonstrates how the initial indifference of the West was mirrored by the silence of public opinion in the face of ethnic cleansing. More often than not, this was an attempt to cover up the fact that many people directly materially benefited from ethnic cleansing. She calls this 'the TV set syndrome' where locals would help themselves to the domestic goods of displaced peoples. Secondly, a nationalist-controlled history and media did not so much offer citizens histories of disputed engagement, but nationally inspired stories, myths and legends. There was then considerable resistance on the part of local populations when they were told that their heroes were actually war criminals. Finally, nationalist leaders, given the relative absence of democratic norms and ideals, easily exploited the young who had grown up in a largely unpolitical culture. Extreme nationalist ideologies seemingly converted a generation of mainly young men into organized killers. Lacking any formal democratic political education or any contexts within which democratic norms might be practised made this easier to achieve than it would otherwise have been.

Consumerism and nationalism in this analysis provide the two sides of the same coin that cancels a contested politics of the public. In other words, if the development of a cosmopolitan ethos amongst citizens more generally offers a challenge to mediated public spheres, the same could also be said of education, which can also act as a sphere of public communication.

Europe, Education and Citizenship

The need to lay the foundation for democratic values in European civil society has meant a renewed interest in the sphere of education. If Europe is understood as a project and a place of meaning, then a shared commitment to the norms of democracy and participation become key to its educational strategies. The European Commission from 1997 onwards has begun to develop a project called Education for Democratic Citizenship (EDC) (Forrester 2003). The project has mainly been developed in the context of the post-Yugoslavia situation and has mainly worked through a number of local projects to promote intercultural forms of understanding and social inclusion in Belgium, Bulgaria, Croatia, Spain and other areas. These projects are mainly targeted at young people and seek to develop citizenship norms through a number of learning activities. However, despite the virtues of such projects other commentators have emphasized the extent to which European educational strategies are overwhelmingly market-driven. In this respect, the aim of developing an attachment to democratic norms and principles amongst young Europeans comes second to the need to prepare citizens for a productive role in the labour market (Nova 2001). European-level educational polices have thus sought to develop educational environments that are suitable for knowledge-based and information societies. In particular, in this context the idea of lifelong learning and the flexible citizen have become key (Lawn 2001). Here education is no longer principally defined as a public good but as an individualized concern aiming to enhance personal development. Education literally becomes a passport, emphasizing the flexibility and malleability of modern citizens.

While capabilities of European citizens cannot afford to be indifferent to the needs of the economy, there is surely an argument for the realization of other more communicative capacities in the light of the declining fate of democratic and public participation. In this respect, we might focus upon the requirements of a cosmopolitan education. Here we need to guard against the idea that education should become the site of totalitarian indoctrination of the new cosmopolitan citizen (Arendt 1977). Indeed, a European education that merely insisted upon the heteronomy and conformity of its subjects would fail to learn the lessons of Europe's history of nationalist violence. When Adorno (2003) pondered what form of education becomes appropriate in the shadow of Auschwitz he answered unequivocally that it should be one that fosters the principles of self-reflection and an unwillingness to conform to agencies of power and control. In the context of European totalitarianism, education should emphasize the huge cost that is required of each of us to be obedient to external collectivities like nationalism. More recently, the philosopher Martha Nussbaum (1996) has argued that the requirement of a cosmopolitan education is that we learn to think less from the point of view of the nation and more from the point of view of the world. Notably, such a practice combines the two meanings of the term 'cosmopolitan' in that we are required to mutually respect difference while becoming world citizens. For example, a cosmopolitan education would require that we learn to view our identities and shared practices from the point of view of the 'Other'. Cosmopolitan dialogue would seek to disrupt what more local publics take to be normal and natural thereby disrupting the comfort of local truths and the passion of patriotism. It is surely no understatement to agree with Nussbaum (1996: 15) when she argues that 'becoming a citizen of the world is often a lonely business'. A cosmopolitan education therefore requires that educators strive not simply to reaffirm the views of their students but for a 'tolerable discomfort' (Rosaldo 1994: 407). Here the dominant national imaginations of Europe's young citizens need to be disrupted in terms of both questions of difference and the requirement that we reason from a European and perhaps even a global perspective.

The desire to foster a cosmopolitan education needs to go much further than prospective changes in the curriculum. Here a cosmopolitan education – returning to Adorno's remarks – needs to be principally concerned with fostering the autonomy of the subject. A cosmopolitan education requires the fostering of a politics of voice. Hence, instead of adopting the view that the education system should either equip young people for the world of work and/or civilize them into the routines and norms of society, we should require it to foster communicative competence. Special emphasis then is placed upon the students becoming cultural producers. The idea of thinking from the position of the other should be an active and not merely passive venture. Such features place importance on the development of written, verbal, visual and other communication skills. This would help foster a citizenry who could not only make their voices heard but were already well versed in doing so by making videos, writing in school newspapers and the like. In this respect, the primary role of education becomes the encouragement of actively communicating subjects rather than preparation for the job market. The emphasis upon education should therefore place less stress upon passing exams and league tables that chart performance and more on the ability to think critically and communicate effectively (Touraine 2000).

Further, the capacity of education to equip students with the ability to reason with one another needs to be coupled with knowledge concerning the struggles for citizenship, past and present. The identity of being a citizen is as much the matter of attaining a positive identity as it is about the ability to reason or the opportunity and ability to participate. The idea of citizenship requires not only the ability to be able to act autonomously, 'but also to believe that such struggles *are worth taking up*' (Giroux 2004: 131). Here I would agree with Chantel Mouffe (1993) that we should reject the false choice between the idea of the citizen as either atomized individuals or a status appropriate to those upholding a communal identity. If citizens today face a multitude of political questions, they require access to the knowledge and critical forms of understanding that will enable them to take up potentially heterogeneous political positions.

There remain, of course, considerable barriers to such a project. The continuation of societies built upon neo-liberal economics and cultural domination will make these principles hard to realize in practice. Further, there is much evidence that young people's disengagement from political questions is less a result of apathy and more a response to disenfranchisement (Buckingham 2000). In this sense, new public spaces need to be created both within education and the media where young people can be both seen and heard. New forms of civic engagement in the age of privatization and the withering of public space can be promoted only by forms of education that introduce more new critical narratives into the classroom and also enable students to find their own voice. A new form of civic courage is required in an age where market principles and nationalist rhetorics are inscribed into the dominant culture (Giroux 2004). As Raymond Williams argued, a democratic participatory society requires 'not only the general "recovery" of specifically alienated human capacities, but is also, and much more decisively, the necessary institution of new and very complex communicative capacities and relationships' (Williams 1980: 62). The recovery of 'voice' only makes sense in a culture that expects more of its citizens than that of becoming employees and consumers.

For Democratic Cosmopolitan Publics

This article has argued that the defence and development of democratic public spaces and identities can be linked to the struggle for a cosmopolitan Europe. In this context the development of engaged public citizens through contemporary media and education systems becomes crucial. The idea of a 'citizens' Europe' refers usually to the institutional protection of human rights and democratic rights. Others have argued that a democratic and social Europe requires the maintenance of a substantial public realm against the rule of the market. Here the growth of social inequality, the downsizing of public provision and enhanced forms of individual competition progressively abandon the functions of the media and education to the market (Bourdieu 2001). Further, the rise of aggressive nationalist politics across Europe means that there is an urgent need both to defend the social state and to develop new forms of cosmopolitan solidarity within the European context. However, my view has been that the response to these pressures should not be purely defensive. The active construction of a cosmopolitan Europe requires the development of new competencies and engagements, particularly amongst Europe's newest citizens. The relative decline of democratic sensibilities and the rise of a form of cool cynicism amongst the young require not so much moralism but new mediated and educative initiatives at the European level. European identity then becomes not so much a matter of civilizations, national identities or consumerism, but is defined through a project to build active and engaged public spheres within and across a number of cultural borders and boundaries.

Bibliography

Adorno, T. 2003. 'Education after Auschwitz', in R. Tiedmann (ed.), *Can One Live after Auschwitz?* Stanford: Stanford University Press.
Arendt, H. 1977. *Between Past and Future.* London: Penguin.
Balibar, E. 2003. 'Europe: Vanishing Mediator', *Constellations* 10(3): 312–38.
Bauman, Z. 1993. *Postmodern Ethics.* London: Blackwell.
Beck, U. 1992. *Risk Society.* London: Sage.
———. 2003. 'Toward a New Critical Theory with a Cosmopolitan Intent', *Constellations* 10(4): 453–68.

Bourdieu, P. 2001. *Acts of Resistance: Against the New Myths of Our Time*. London: Verso.

Buckingham, D. 2000. *The Making of Citizens: Young People, News and Politics*. London: Routledge.

Calhoun, C. 1994. 'Social Theory and the Politics of Identity', in C. Calhoun (ed.), *Social Theory and the Politics of Identity*. Oxford: Blackwell.

————. 2003. 'The Class Consciousness of Frequent Travellers: Towards a Critique of Actually Existing Cosmopolitanism', in D. Arhibugi (ed.), *Debating Cosmopolis*. London: Verso.

Castells, M. 1997. *The Power of Identity*. Oxford: Blackwell.

Couldry, N. 2000. *The Place of Media Power: Pilgrims and Witnesses of the Media Age*. London: Routledge.

Creeber, G. 2004. 'Hideously White: British Television, Globalization and National Identity', *Television and New Media* 5(1): 27–39.

Dahlgren, P. 2000. 'Media, Citizenship and Civic Culture', in J. Curran and M. Gurevitch (eds), *Mass Media and Society*. London: Arnold.

————. 2001. 'The Transformation of Democracy', in B. Axford and R. Huggins (eds), *New Media and Politics*. London: Sage.

————. 2002. 'In Search of the Talkative Public', *IAMCR Conference, Barcelona, 2002*.

————. 2004. 'Reconfiguring Civic Culture in the New Media Milieu', in J. Corner and D. Pels (eds), *Media and the Restyling of Politics*. London: Sage.

Delanty, G. 2000. 'The Resurgence of the City in Europe?', in E.F. Isin (ed.), *Democracy, Citizenship and the Global City*. London: Routledge.

Devereux, E. 1996. 'Good Causes, God's Poor and Telethon Television', *Media, Culture and Society* 18: 47–68.

Drakulic, S. 2004. *They Would Never Hurt a Fly*. London: Abacus.

Forrester, K. 2003. 'Leaving the Academic Towers: The Council of Europe and the Education for Democratic Citizenship Project', *International Journal of Lifelong Education* 22(3): 221–34.

Giroux, H. 1999. *The Mouse that Roared: Disney and the End of Innocence*. Oxford: Rowman and Littlefield.

————. 2004. *The Terror of Neoliberalism*. London: Paradigm.

Habermas, J. 1989. *The Structural Transformation of the Public Sphere*. Cambridge: Polity Press.

Hallin, D. (1994) We Keep America on Top of the World, London, Routledge.

————. 2001. *The Postnational Constellation*. Cambridge: Polity Press.

Harrison, J. and Woods, L.M. 2001. 'Defining European Public Service Broadcasting', *European Journal of Communication* 16(4): 477–504.

Kant, I. 1970 'Perpetual Peace. A Philosophical Sketch', in H. Reiss (ed.), *Kant: Political Writings*. Cambridge: Cambridge University Press.

Keane, J. 1991. *Media and Democracy*. Cambridge: Polity Press.

Kristeva, J. 1993. *Nations without Nationalism*. New York: Columbia University Press.

Lawn, M. 2003. 'The "Usefulness" of Learning: The Struggle over Governance, Meaning and the European Education Space', *Discourse: Studies in the Cultural Politics of Education* 24(3): 325–36.

Martín-Barbero, J. 2002. 'Identities: Traditions and New Communities', *Media, Culture and Society* 24(5): 621–41.

Morley, D. 2000. *Home Territories: Media, Mobility and Identity.* London: Routledge.

Morley, D. and Robins, K. 1995. *Spaces of Identity: Global Media, Electronic Landscapes and Cultural Boundaries.* London: Routledge.

Mouffe, C. 1993. *The Return of the Political.* London: Verso.

Murdock, G. 2000. 'Reconstructing the Ruined Tower', in J. Curran and M. Gurevitch (eds), *Mass Media and Society.* London: Arnold.

Novoa, A. 2001. 'The Restructuring of the European Educational Space: Changing Relations amongst States, Citizens and Educational Communities', in G. Lewis, J. Fink, and J. Clarke (eds), *Rethinking European Welfare.* London: Open University Press.

Nussbaum, M.C. 1996. 'Patriotism and Cosmopolitanism', in J. Cohen (ed.), *For Love of Country.* Boston, MA: Beacon Press.

Rifkin, J. 2004. *The European Dream.* Cambridge: Polity Press.

Robins, K. and Webster, F. 1999. *Times of the Technoculture.* London: Routledge.

Rosaldo, R. 1994. 'Cultural Citizenship and Educational Democracy', *Cultural Anthropology* 9(3): 402–11.

Schlesinger, P. (1991) Media, State, and Nation, London, Sage.

Schiller, H. 1996. *Information Inequality: The Deepening of Social Crisis in America.* London: Routledge.

Schlesinger, P. 1997. 'Wishful Thinking: Cultural Politics, Media and Collective Identities in Europe', in A. Sreberny-Mohammadi (ed.), *Media in a Global Context: A Reader.* London: Arnold.

―――. 1999. 'Changing Spaces of Political Communication: The Case of the European Union', *Political Communication* 16: 263–79.

Seidman, S. 1997. *Difference Troubles: Queering Social Theory and Sexual Politics.* Cambridge: Cambridge University Press.

Serra, S. 2000. 'The Killing of Brazilian Street Children and the Rise of the International Public Sphere', in J. Curran (ed.), *Media Organisations.* London: Edward Arnold.

Shore, C. 2004. 'Whither European Citizenship? Eros and Civilisation Revisited', *European Journal of Social Theory* 7(1): 27–44.

Stevenson, N. 2003. *Cultural Citizenship: Cosmopolitan Questions.* Maidenhead: Open University Press.

Tester, K. 1995. 'Moral Solidarity and the Technological Reproduction of Images', *Media, Culture and Society* 17: 469–82.

―――. 2001. *Compassion, Morality and the Media.* Buckingham: Open University Press.

Todorov, T. 2003. *Hope and Memory.* London: Atlantic Books.

Touraine, A. 2000. *We Can Live Together?* Cambridge: Polity Press.

Trenz, H.J. 2004. 'Media Coverage on European Governance: Exploring the European Public Sphere in National Quality Newspapers', *European Journal of Communication* 19(3): 291–319.

Van de Steeg, M. 2002. 'Rethinking the Conditions for a Public Sphere in the European Union', *European Journal of Social Theory* 5(4): 499–519.

Van Zoonen, L. 2004. 'Imagining the Fan Democracy', *European Journal of Communication* 19: 39–52.

Wheeler, M. 2004. 'Supranational Regulation: Television and the European Union', *European Journal of Communication* 19(3): 349–69.

Williams, R. 1980. *Problems in Materialism and Culture*. London: Verso.

———. 1985. *Towards 2000*. London: Pelican.

Young, I.M. 1999. 'Difference as a Resource for Democratic Communication?', in J. Bohman and W. Rehg (eds), Deliberative Democracy: Essays on Reason and Politics. Cambridge, MA: MIT Press.

Chapter 3

Transformation of the Public Sphere: Law, Policy and the Boundaries of Publicness

Damian Tambini

Introduction

Do new technologies usher in a new age of equal, active citizenship or will they lead to new inequalities and forms of unaccountable power? Clearly, technologies alone are not decisive. How they are used depends on how they are managed, regulated and institutionalized in a changing socio-political context.

This chapter[1] examines how media and communications law and policy are being reformed in Europe during this process of technological and market change in the media sector, and how this impacts on the 'publicness' of communication in Europe. I treat the public sphere as an ideal: the idea that there should be a site of rational-critical debate and social learning in which articulation of a 'general interest' is possible, beyond sectoral and private interest. Behind this notion of the public sphere is a normative commitment to participatory citizenship. Reclaiming the normative critique will enable me to address anew some of the familiar debates about the civic potential of new technologies. I focus on the issue of how law and policy articulate the impact of new technologies on the development of the public sphere in relation to discrete areas such as intellectual property law, public broadcasting and digital rights management technologies. I argue that discussion of the public sphere must engage with the law and policy debates that are reshaping our communications environment.

The concern for the public sphere is a concern for, as Calhoun put it, 'the quality of discourse and the quality of participation' (Calhoun 1992: 2). Writing on the public sphere is centrally concerned with the potential of communicative processes to emancipate and to promote social integration. I use the term 'public sphere' in a somewhat loose and dynamic way, taking Habermas's work as a springboard rather than a constant reference point. In Habermas's account, the rise in the family sphere of a particular form of subjectivity, together with other conditions such as the gradual elimination of censorship formed the backdrop to the rise of a public sphere. The emergence of a reading public occurred in relatively open-access participatory fora such as coffee houses, within in the context of a more clearly defined national territorial power.

Habermas was writing an historical account, at a time, during the late 1950s, that preceded the rise of mass television in Europe, and his focus was on a much earlier period. Subsequent authors (Garnham 1992; Calhoun 1992; Dahlgren 1995) have explored the role of broadcasting and other mass media in the subsequent development of the public sphere. These and other authors have argued that a contemporary, developing account of publicness[2] must take into account new technologies such as broadcasting and the question of technology and it's implication for the public sphere remains fundamental to the field.

Habermas's concern was with finding a way between liberals such as John Stuart Mill, who saw free public debate as part of a search for Truth, and Marx who dismissed it as mere false consciousness. My concern in this paper is an empirical question: what are the implications of the 'European Information Society' – which I define as the bundle of contemporary policies and laws around which *European* countries are converging – for public communication, and for the publicness of communication in Europe? Publicness is defined as the degree of accessibility, visibility and openness of processes of communication.

We are aware of the pitfalls of a technologically determinist approach to the media and the public sphere. Clearly technologies are important, but articulated through processes of management, regulation and political economy. My thesis is that law and policy are a crucial and neglected part of this process and at the same time can be seen as a crucial indicator of publicness. Increasingly, law and policy institutionalize and regulate communications processes, creating new boundaries of publicness in communications.

Law is continuously involved in drawing distinctions between public
and private domains. Henry Sumner Maine (Maine 1861) argued that
modernization of societies generally involves a move from status to contract
in resolution of disputes and allocation of resources. Communications is
marked by a similar trend: with the embedding of electronic communications
technologies in everyday life, the formal regime of law and regulation is ever
more important in allocating information resources and resolving disputes.
Even though property and privacy are routinely ignored on the internet,
the policy debates and balances being struck, and decisions over whether
to enforce in cases of infringement, are moments where the new boundaries
of the public sphere are being drawn. The constitutional, legal, regulatory
and self-regulatory framework for communication, surprisingly neglected
in studies of the public sphere, should therefore be subject to more analysis.
Systematic analysis of changing standards in law and policy can offer a
means to mark out the 'new boundaries of publicness'.

According to Kees Brants, 'critical "publicity" as Habermas called it,
depended on access to open dialogue, participation of and no barriers for
a reasoning public of citizens, and the formation of public opinion as the
end product of private discourse over public issues by educated, informed,
and rational people' (Brants 2005: 144). Barriers to publicity and access to
dialogue can be physical, economic or social-institutional (e.g. taboos and
norms). However, to an increasing extent they are legal.

This chapter proposes that the size, shape, richness, accessibility and
content of the public sphere are structured by the legal and regulatory
framework that surrounds decisions to publish, and by the competing public
and private claims over particular forms of information. In the context of
the increasing ubiquity of electronic communication and digitalization
and internationalization of media, this communication is subject to rules,
contracts, codes, licences and agreements that mark out the degree to which
any text is public and published, and for which public it is available. I will
focus on the following main aspects of regulation of publicness:
1. Public service in broadcasting.
2. Communication for public value: economic theory of public
   information goods.
3. Public taboos: regulation of profanity.
4. Deciding to publish: freedom of speech, and the risk of liability.
5. Private property and the public domain: copyright in the information
   society.
6. Self-regulation as private regulation.

The aim of this tour of the horizon is not to provide an exhaustive survey. Rather it is to outline a future research direction that may go some way to address the central conundrum of contemporary media. In some ways, contemporary developments in communications seem to undermine our treasured institutions of publicness: public service broadcasting is under threat; commercialization and casualization appear to undermine many of the key ethics and values of journalism; private consumption decisions rather than public accountability determine the content of our public sphere. On the other hand – abundance: new technologies, particularly the internet, offer cultural and communicative riches to the public that would have been beyond the wildest dreams of the fathers of cultural critique in the Frankfurt School. Clearly, this exaggerated opposition must be unpacked to offer a nuanced, detailed and operationalized account. I argue that the study of law and policy can provide such a framework. Each of the areas of law and regulation I identified draws a distinction between what should be considered public (public access, public ownership, public interest) and what should be considered private. These distinctions form the central institutional references for the emergence and development of the European public sphere. The more pressing question for the European public sphere is then not a topographical one regarding the geographical scope of 'publics' and their relation to the nation state; it is the broader question for public spheres worldwide: whether public communication can continue to provide a site for social integration and democratic citizenship, given the radical shifts currently taking place in our communications institutions.

Behind any decision to publish – to make public via print, broadcasting or some new platform such as the internet – is a complex calculation and balancing act. On one hand are rights to speech freedom and motivations to publish, and on the other hand are the restrictions considered necessary according to law in a democratic society: restrictions in the name of intellectual property, and also socially enforced taboos, laws relating to privacy, confidence, protection of reputation and so forth. Decisions to publish occur when benefits of publication outweigh risks of liability derived from such laws. These balances, in a liberal age, are increasingly the subject of formal rules, and less the subject of informal norms or sanctions.

Where competition is increasingly enforced in publishing, broadcasting and elsewhere, the role of intermediaries changes: it becomes more difficult not to respond to public demand, more difficult to couple cultural and economic bottleneck power in communications processes. Even where editors are not directly consulting their lawyers, formal rules are incorporated in the rules of thumb, consent procedures, and risk assessments of journalists, film-makers even artists. It is the combination of those rules of thumb and formal rules that determines the quality and quantity of information in the public domain, and the terms upon which it is accessed, and thus marks out the boundaries of publicness today. Technological and market changes necessitate revision of these rules, various aspects of which are outlined in the next sections.

Public Service in Broadcasting: A Vulnerable Public Sphere?

With changes to communications technologies and markets come new struggles over the boundaries of publicness. According to Nicholas Garnham,

> those institutions within which we construct, distribute, and consume symbolic forms, are themselves undergoing a profound change. This change is characterised by a reinforcement of the market and the progressive destruction, at least in Western Europe, of public service as the preferred mode for the allocation of cultural resources ... The result of this trend will be to shift the balance in the cultural sector between the market and public service decisively in favour of the market and to shift the dominant definition of public information from that of a public good to that of a privately appropriable commodity. (Garnham 1992: 362–63)

In all European countries, broadcasting has been publicly regulated to serve the public interest, mainly through licence fees or direct subsidies and/or through setting aside the 'airwaves' (electromagnetic spectrum) for broadcasting under a licensing regime.[3] Access to the scarce resource of spectrum has been granted on a non-market basis, and broadcasters have been obliged to provide transmissions that serve public purposes as defined by legislation, codes and licences, rather than private purposes of advertisers or consumers. Garnham's predictions have proved correct. The point made in this article is that to gain further point and purchase, such a critique needs to be empirically instantiated with reference to the unfolding process of policy, regulation and law. The onward march of commercialization is surely a simplification: every aspect of the process is contested in policy and law, and research should trace this. It is by no means the case that public service broadcasting is in a decline from a golden age. But some aspects, for example the provision of openly accessible public service television funded by advertising, may be under threat.

The uniquely European inheritance of a mixed economy in electronic communications is reflected directly in the European Convention on Human Rights, which specifically mentions broadcast licensing as permissible in the context of rights to free expression,[4] and indirectly in the Amsterdam Protocol to the Treaty of Amsterdam, which establishes support for public service broadcasting.[5] The European approach to public broadcasting assumes that the public sphere needs to be protected from two directions: on one hand it needs to be protected from the privatizing impact of unconstrained capitalism, and on the other hand it needs to be protected from the state.

Broadcast licensing and public broadcasting have therefore been the cornerstones of the European approach to electronic communications. Many have argued that the continuation of this European approach is crucial to the continuation of the fragile public spheres of Europe that have emerged in the face of state pressure and under increasing pressure from pressures of globalization and commercialism. In this view, broadcasting provides some of the conditions for the development of an autonomous sphere of rational-critical debate to which citizens have equal rights of access.

Taking the example of the German public service broadcasters (PSBs), according to Bernd Holznagel (2000) the functional remit of the German PSBs covers eight main dimensions:

1. *Information remit*: PSBs have a duty to convey objective information as a basis for free opinion forming. Coverage, therefore, has to be comprehensive, truthful and factual.

2. *Guiding role*: as a source of independent and unbiased information, PSBs provide reliable, credible reference points and, consequently, guidance for free opinion forming.

3. *Role of forum*: PSBs have to ensure that all relevant opinions on a particular subject receive a hearing. They have to offer a forum for public discussion in which the relevant social groups can participate.

4. *Integration role*: PSBs should aim for mutual understanding and, thus, foster social cohesion.

5. *Benchmark*: PSBs have the obligation to provide guiding, high-quality and innovative programming. In this way it sets standards.

6. *Cultural mission*: PSBs' programming has to reflect Germany's cultural diversity and the events taking place in all the *Länder*.

7. *Mission to produce*: appropriate fulfilment of the respective obligations cannot be guaranteed by the mere acquisition of foreign productions. Because of that, PSBs have a mission to produce independently and creatively.
8. *Innovative role*: PSBs are encouraged to take an innovative lead in testing and using new technology and new services in the broadcasting sector.

In recent years the public-service, public-interest settlement for broadcasting in Europe has come under increasing pressure. The key challenge is how the regulatory and economic framework will facilitate the evolution of European PSBs during a period of rapid digital innovation. The gradual introduction of commercial broadcasting – first in the larger European markets in the 1960s and later in Scandinavia and finally Austria and the new EU member-states in the 1990s – provided commercial competition to the state-funded broadcasters, and the rise of digital technologies has subsequently seen a rapid rise in the number of television channels. The U.K., like other markets such as Spain that depended on analogue terrestrial broadcasting rather than cable, has experienced a rapid and marked increase in the numbers of television channels available to consumers. In the U.K., most homes have gained a fourth and fifth channel since the early 1980s, and in the decade following 1995, 60 per cent of homes went digital and therefore have at least 30 and up to 200 TV channels available. The European Commission has recommended that all countries execute a digital switchover plan by around 2012. The public demand for more choice emerged as soon as there was a supply of satellite cable and DTT services to supply it, and not to have one was never, realistically, an option.

The rise of increased channel choice has far-reaching implications for the European tradition of public service in broadcasting (PSB), which are only now becoming clear. As Figure 3.1 shows, when consumers have access to more channels, their viewing of public service genres declines rapidly. This trend is not peculiar to Germany, but is reflected in audience data for other European countries and represents a major shift away from PSB. This undermines licence fee–funded channels' audience because they are obliged to carry such genres, and also the commercial providers of such public service genres, who face a decline in advertising sales. In the U.K., the new communications regulator, Ofcom, conducted an impressive programme of research into public service broadcasting, publishing three major reports in 2004–5 and a further review during 2008–9. The overall findings are

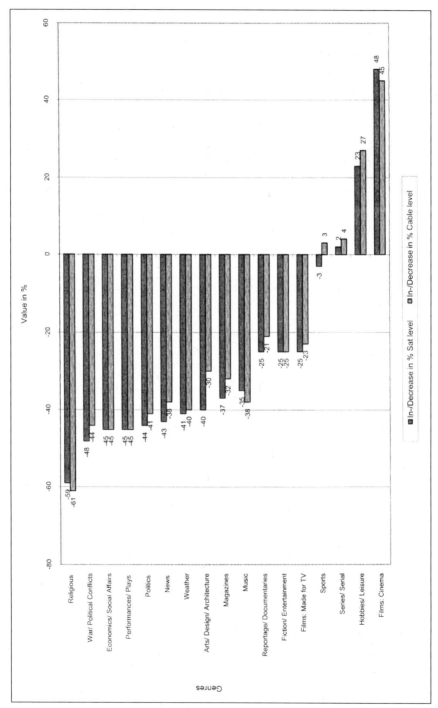

Figure 3.1: Drop in Share through Cable/Satellite: Germany.

bad news for PSBs as traditionally understood. The thrust of the Ofcom research is that public service broadcasting faces fundamental challenges in the long term. Notably, the commercial spectrum for service compact is fundamentally undermined. Regulators no longer control entry to audio-visual markets, and in a world of broadband and on-demand services, broadcasters are no longer able to deliver captive audiences to content considered to serve the public interest. In this view, the leading public service broadcasting market in Europe, the U.K., will be fundamentally altered by the shift to digital. The BBC and potentially a reformed Channel Four will continue to operate public interest broadcasting in the U.K., but others will become more purely commercial (Ofcom 2004; 2008)

In other European countries such as France and Germany the obligations on advertising funded public service broadcasters were always lower and are remaining constant. On the other hand, publicly funded broadcasters face long-term challenges. Licence-fee legitimacy declines along with the audience, and in any case collection of fees for television receivers is difficult when reception shifts to other devices. The Spanish government commissioned a report by Enrique Bustamentes, which offered a robust defence of traditional public service broadcasting in 2005, and in France the CSA opposes 'graduated regulation', preferring to continue to impose public service requirements on all digital terrestrial (TNT) broadcasters in France. How long these defences of traditional public service broadcasting can last in an era of audience choice and power remains to be seen.

The mission of the BBC has in its first eighty years been broad and somewhat loosely regulated. Under its previous Royal Charter, the BBC was permitted to provide new, non-broadcasting services of information, education and entertainment, subject to the approval of the Secretary of State. But as the BBC entered many non-broadcasting markets in new services there have been calls from government-appointed commissions to more clearly define the remit of the BBC, in order to provide certainty to encourage private investment in communications markets.[6] In a process echoed in public broadcasting policy in continental Europe, Japan and elsewhere, U.K. broadcasting policy is undergoing significant reform. The broader mission outlined in previous BBC charters – to 'inform, educate and entertain' in broadcasting and in other services – has been revised under a new charter to run to 2016, in part because European State Aid regulations require a clearer remit for PSBs across Europe. This charter will determine the broad goals of the BBC in the period of the transition to 100-per-cent digital television and of the rise of online delivery of a much wider array of audio-visual services, so these general purposes of the BBC will have a huge impact on the balance between public and private communications markets in the U.K.

The BBC public purposes are: sustaining citizenship and civil society; promoting education and learning; stimulating creativity and cultural excellence; representing the U.K., its nations, regions and communities; bringing the U.K. to the world and the world to the U.K.; and building digital Britain. These purposes were outlined in a Green Paper in 2005 and a White Paper issued in March 2006 and approved broadly by a parliamentary committee and by the independent regulator. The public purposes of the commercially funded public broadcasters as defined in the Communications Act are broadly similar.

Current changes in broadcasting threaten to undermine the public sphere function of broadcasting, but the implications of this are less clear. In some European contexts, not least Russia and the former Soviet Union more generally, the relaxation of state control is a key to developing the public media. Many former Soviet countries have failed to develop public service media and, given the political influence of large media companies, it may be difficult or impossible to rectify this (see OSI 2005).

The fate of public service broadcasting in this context depends on the interaction between audience behaviour and the policy process. But the political sustainability of PSB is under question given audience decline and the increase in value of publicly owned resources such as the airwaves which have been gifted to PSBs in the past. If laws and policies providing PSB have been a key aspect of the institutional framework of 'publicness' in Europe, these institutions are increasingly under question.

Communications for Public Value: The Economic Theory of Public Information Goods and Externalities

Underlying the public service broadcasting model is a theory of the peculiar characteristics of broadcasting markets. This theory has historically formed part of the justification for providing broadcasting that is universally available and publicly funded. In economic terms, broadcasting is often seen as a public good because of its non-excludable, non-rival nature. Before the advent of encryption technologies and the end-user hardware to support it, it was more difficult and expensive to charge for subscription services. It was cheaper to provide broadcasting that could be received by anyone, funded by taxation/ license fees or by scattergun mass advertising. The Ofcom reports cited earlier accepted that these public good characteristics were strongly present in the analogue world, but argued that with the rise of digital they are in decline (Ofcom 2004, 2008). But broadcasting is still a non-rival good. Unlike, for example, apples, consumption of a publicly available broadcast by one viewer does not take away from a rival viewer, so there remain some public good characteristics of broadcasting.

More recently, defenders of public broadcasting have attempted to develop this economic rationale for public broadcasting, by arguing that broadcasting provides positive externalities. This is at the theoretical heart of the BBC's 'Public Value' approach (BBC 2004). The point here is that the overall utility of media content to society as a whole, and even to those who do not consume the material, will not be taken into account in decisions to consume the material, and therefore the market would fail to provide the optimum level for social welfare. Educational material, for example, may have positive spin-off effects and violent material may have negative impacts. Where the market fails to provide optimal welfare, regulation for public service broadcasting is justified.

Gavyn Davies, the former chairman of the BBC, has outlined a summary of the economic characteristics of broadcasting markets which lead to failure of market distribution to deliver socially optimal outcomes. Basically, he argues that broadcasting is, in economic terms, a public good, that it creates externalities, and that there are strong economies of scale in production and information asymmetries (Davies 2005: 140–47).

Controversy reigns among economists regarding the impact of technological and market changes on the economic characteristics of broadcasting outlined in Table 3.1, and the extent to which they can also be applied to other communications technologies. Clearly, familiar research challenges – such as the 'impact' or 'effect' of media, both positive and negative – could be framed in a way useful for this debate, and rendered within the dominant language of welfare economics. The central problem is that externalities are difficult – perhaps impossible to measure accurately – and policymakers tend to use broad and hopeful estimates. This elegant table in itself could provide a framework for a programme of empirical research, bringing together a long tradition of research on effects with a sense of 'externalities' in the language of regulatory economics.

Table 3.1: The Economics of Public Service Broadcasting.

Type of television service	Public good		Externalities create 'Public Value'?	Economics of scale in production?	Information asymetrics?
	Non-rival?	Non-excludable?			
Pornographic/ violent content	Yes	No - encrypted	Strongly negative	Yes	No
Imported mass entertainment	Yes	Often encrypted	Mildly positive	Yes	Unlikely
Mainstream popular entertainment	Yes	Yes	Positive	Strongly positive	Possible
Informative/ educative content	Yes	Yes	Strongly positive	Strongly positive	Strong

Source: **Davies 2005**

In terms of the transformation of the public sphere, to summarize, public service media are undergoing a major shift. It is well known that mass services are giving away to niche services, and as we have seen the regulatory consensus now acknowledges that the fundamental economic characteristics of PSB have changed so that public service is now considered a less efficient policy solution. Unless the fundamental terms of the debate can be changed, it may be only a matter of time before PSB is gradually phased out, particularly in those European Countries where it is already less popular. The broader European support for PSBs in the context of competition law (see Larouche 1998), and the constitutional underpinning of this in the Council of Europe countries remain strong, but the institutions of public service communications are far from guaranteed in the current context, given the undermining of the economic arguments for regulation.

Public Taboos: Regulation of Profanities

The 'negative externalities' associated with sexual and violent images and sounds have traditionally been regulated by taboos and social norms, and also by law. In the era of public accountability and regulation of the electronic media, these norms have been applied more formally through licensing schemes and codes which reflected the ideal that public media should maintain higher standards – because of their particularly invasive, pervasive, influential nature (Forgan and Tambini 2001).

The process of digital convergence raises new definitional questions relating to whether a particular delivery method is to be considered public or private and correspondingly whether publicly held norms should be implemented through accountability mechanisms. At what point should peer-to-peer, handheld, encrypted and narrowcast material be subject to the standards of the most public media, and which of the public media should be treated as sacred space, entirely free of material considered profane? Given the global nature of new media such as those based on internet protocols, which national or regional standard should apply? Crucially, will the new regulation of taboos close down or open up public communication?

Clearly, the main broadcast channels remain subject to specific rules about taste, violence and decency. These are contained in the national laws and broadcasting licences, and in the Television Without Frontiers/Audiovisual Services Directive. The dispute between European governments in 2005–6 about which services should be subject to the directive, and whether internet television should be included, was emblematic of the debate about standards for 'public' media.

It is a long-established truism that standards relating to taste, decency and offence in media content vary throughout Europe. The same film might have widely varying certifications in different European countries (Tambini et al. 2008). Each European member state has a different self-regulatory scheme for classifying films and videos. In the context of the emergence of a single market, however, these schemes are converging over time, and some newer media (e.g. electronic games, but not mobile internet) are establishing European-wide standards for definitions of what content is suitable for which age group.

Like the VCR; the internet and, increasingly, mobile communications have had a major impact on the business models for delivery of pornographic and violent content, and other content considered harmful for children. As such they have opened up a new sphere of public/private media which are private in the sense of private consumption and social taboos in many countries, but which increasingly challenge private/public distinctions.

Obscenity law in Europe has not been radically altered in the light of new technologies, though the decade of the mass internet has seen a continuation of the general trend to liberalization that characterized the previous half-century. Calls for restriction of 'harmful' content meet with resistance on freedom of expression grounds, and constitutional protection of freedom of expression constitutes a permanent challenge to any form of restriction. In liberal countries, 'accepted' public standards of what constitutes taste and decency have been replaced with an evidence-based attempt to identify harm and offence (Millwood Hargrave and Livingstone 2006). In broadcasting, the crucial matter here is the 'invasiveness' of the medium. New technology impacts on the regulatory framework in several distinct ways. First, by increasing excludability through V-chips and pin numbers, which make it theoretically possible for parents to regulate children's viewing (Price 1999) thereby lowering the rationale for public intervention. Secondly, by reducing the mass impact of single transmissions. Negative externalities will be smaller with a smaller audience and choice of alternative viewing greater. Overall, the picture is of ever-greater consumer control of media, though the question of to what extent users do in fact exercise the control at their disposals – such as internet filter software – is unclear.

In general, therefore, the framework for regulating taboos in the new context places a greater onus on individual consumers to regulate their own behaviour, and on service providers to restrain themselves. There is some evidence that new media codes reflect a 'Europeanization' of taboos – as common codes are applied in videogames and mobile content services across Europe. But this is occurring only within 'voluntary' self regulation schemes.. In general calls for statutory regulation of internet content have gone unheeded in Europe. Depending on one's viewpoint it could be argued that this lack of statutory regulation has been responsible for a growth in the distribution and publicness of objectionable content, or for a richer and freer public sphere. There are, however, specific issues such as that of the Danish cartoons[7] and other specific taboo breaches that continue to 'chill' public expression and therefore diminish the public sphere.

Deciding to Publish: Freedom of Expression and Its Counterparts

Formal regulation of taste and taboo are only one of many limitations on freedom of expression. Those who oppose regulation raise the possibility of a 'chilling effect' that regulatory measures may have on publications. This refers to the risk assessments that determine what material is placed in the public domain. What gets into the public sphere, and the conditions, economic and otherwise, under which people may be able to access it, depends on decisions to publish. How publishers balance the risks of liabilities on one hand and potential benefits such as profit or public service on the other depends on the careful assessment of law and regulation and the balance between their freedoms to publish and any countervailing rights. In the following section I deal more specifically with the issue of the monetization of content and the incentives to publish. Here I outline some of the parameters that might impact upon the risk of liabilities of providing for the public sphere using new technologies. Whilst the United States and Europe in particular have strong traditions of free speech (and increasingly of freedom of information), which protect those who provide information to and for the public, these must be balanced with rights that potentially conflict.

The tradition, particularly in the United States, of constitutional protection for freedom of expression is in many ways linked to the notion of the public sphere. What U.S. jurisprudence describes as 'the marketplace for ideas' is in fact similar in many ways to the public sphere concept. J.S. Mill was the first to isolate the basic philosophical underpinning of the right, in terms of the three arguments – from truth, from self-determination and from democracy (Barendt 1985). In decisions within the U.S. court system and later in Europe, these arguments constitute the three master categories of argument in support of free speech.

In the context of discussion of the European approach to public communications, it is worth noting a difference between American and European approaches to free expression. The First Amendment to the U.S. Constitution reads: 'Congress shall make no law respecting an establishment of religion, or prohibiting the free exercise thereof; or abridging the freedom of speech or of the press; or the right of the people peaceably to assemble...' The emergent European tradition of jurisprudence emerging around the European Convention on Human Rights (ECHR), by contrast, focuses not only on state actions (or 'Congress') but potentially also on the private regulation of communications. ECHR Article 10 can be applied not only vertically (against states) but horizontally (against others and private bodies).

Freedom of expression protection in Europe is spreading and, arguably, strengthening. Freedom of expression is not an absolute, however. It must be balanced with other countervailing rights, such as the rights to reputation (protection from defamation), to privacy, and legal standards on hate speech. One vector of the matrix of publicness in law and policy is the right to private life. If law marks out large swathes of material that the public is interested in as protected by legal rights to private and family life, and as a result publishers do not risk publication, the public sphere will be diminished as a result. In a similar way the right to reputation, formalized in a variety of traditions of national defamation laws, marks out the terms under which material that can affect a person's reputation can be published.

New digital technologies of many kinds have led to a revisiting of the long-term debate over the boundary between privacy and the public interest. Use of CCTV footage, the ubiquity of recording devices, interception of mobile telephony and use of database records have tested the supply side, and the nature of publication on internet, niche publishing and global media have led to new debates on the distribution side. Our concern in this essay is the public access rather than the rights of the individual to be left alone: has the response to new technology resulted in a transformation – even an impoverishment – of the public sphere of communication and, if so, of what kind?

European countries operate with varying legal standards regarding what constitutes an invasion into privacy. The ECHR enshrines a right to private life in Article 8, and the European Court of Human Rights is (to a limited extent) gradually developing a common European standard. Legal enforcement of boundaries between public and private in Europe varies. A cabinet minister in the U.K. can expect little protection of private and family matters, whereas matters of sexuality and family are treated with more circumspection in most European countries: a French Prime Minister might be able, for example, to maintain a mistress and a daughter in the knowledge of his immediate colleagues, without this being published in public media.

A great deal has been written, particularly in the U.K., on the impact of the European Convention on Human Rights, and the question whether it will result in a common European standard on a right to privacy. This is vehemently opposed by many journalists in the U.K., where the press has a lot to lose. But less has been written about the technological drivers of this process in supply and distribution, which are redefining approaches to privacy and its breach.

This shifting balance between fundamental rights may seem academic, but it is clearly extremely practical when we consider the impact it has on decisions to publish. The entry of any material into the public domain occurs only if benefits outweigh risks. The extent to which in-house media lawyers rationally weigh risk associated with publication on the internet is, of course, open to discussion. Potential litigation arising from invasion of privacy is only one potential liability that will be taken into account. Defamation is another risk, as is incitement of racial or religious hatred.

Levels of criminal or civil liability for content generally depend on whether, how, and to what extent material can be considered to have entered the public domain. These vary depending on the issue at stake. For example, levels of compensation (and thus levels of potential liability risk) for defamation will depend on the extent of damage to reputation, which depends in turn on assumptions about the extent of publication. Key online defamation cases such as the *Demon Internet* v. *Laurence Godfrey* case in 2000 and the Guttnick case[1] raised new questions about what constitutes publication. In an asynchronous medium which is easily searchable by name, how can damage to reputation be established? Just how public is the material published? What about linking to other sites? Does this constitute publication of them?

---

1   *Dow Jones & Company Inc v Gutnick* [2002] High Court of Australia 56 10 December 2002.

Linking liability is only one of the new questions for media law which will shape accessibility and publicness, particularly for archive material. If legal liability was calculated accurately, it may be that very little would be published. As Joshua Rozenberg reports, 'under the Limitation Act 1980, as amended, a libel action cannot normally be started more than a year after the offending article was published … However, each individual act of publication gives rise to a fresh cause of action.' If each download of a news story from a website constitutes a new publication, therefore, it is likely that newspapers will be vulnerable to libel suits for as long as they maintain an archive (Rozenberg 2004: 204). So whilst the dream of an infinitely rich treasure trove of searchable archive material on the internet is seductive, and the direct costs of providing material may be low, the legal risks that accompany providing this material may be prohibitive. Uncertainty about liability acts as a brake on archive provision; a case could be (and probably is) made for removing archive material to reduce risk. Law and policy is engaged in a continuing redefinition of what constitutes publication. This in turn informs the liability risk assessments made by publishers. Subtle shifts in the balance of these decisions may result in a 'chilling' of speech or an impoverishment of the public sphere. In particular, it may be possible to control liability risk for example by restricting audience. A small number of higher paying subscribers might be less risky than an open publication model and law and policy may therefore result in a bias against public media.

Clearly, research must take more account of exactly how these assessments of risk are made. Newsrooms and in-house lawyers would be key objects of such studies. But risks are only part of the picture. Where the financial rewards are great enough (for example, the impact of celebrity photos on sales of magazines), it may be rational to accept a degree of risk. Where potential audiences are low, on the other hand, media companies may be less likely to accept the risk. Much will depend on the development of new business models.

Copyright and the Public Domain

Copyright protects the integrity of a work and the right of the author to be credited. It also, creates and maintains some of the motivations of creators to produce by providing income streams.[8] But the development of intellectual property rights is in constant tension with the right of the public to access culture freely. Many argue that intellectual property rights coupled with technologies of digital rights management are fundamentally threatening the public domain, or at least that the balance between freedom and innovation on one hand and protection on the other hand has been lost in favour of protection (Lessig 2001).

Current critiques of copyright focus on two broad areas: first, the development and extension of the law of copyright and its enforcement in the new context and, second, the use of software code, labelled Digital Rights Management (DRM), to 'lock down' intellectual property to a greater extent than was the case in law. Both of these result in an impoverishment of the public domain according to campaigners and theorists in this field (Lessig 1999).

Previous mass media, whilst in some cases involving price barriers for subscription or receiver equipment, often tended to be public goods in economic terms: as we noted, it is difficult to exclude potential users from broadcasting, for example, even when it is provided by a commercial channel. But where it is possible to create exclusivity there are strong economic incentives to do so. A previously relatively simple value chain of content delivery in the past, with production done in-house or by independents for a few powerful distributors to a mass audience, is breaking down. Where distribution by time window is not a means to create distinct publics over time, subscription offers a means for synchronous distinction. More complex DRM and encryption basically increase the ability of content providers to exclude potential users, target content and thereby increase returns. Whereas the previous distribution window hierarchy for film ran from theatre to video to television with a tiny on-demand slice of the market, the basic logic of new platforms is one which enables content to behave as a medium for ever more complex processes of Bordieuian distinction (Bourdieu 2002).

DRM offers still more smart means to exploit the maximum value from content, and will result in more pressures to move away from a 'public good' model of distribution to a 'private good' model. Even the BBC is experimenting with models of delivery and storage of content that incorporate DRM technologies to enable users to use content a limited number of times and not to store or share it. DRM standards and interoperability will clearly determine boundaries to access in the new environment and will constitute the new boundaries of publicness. 'Exploitable' content, or what we used to call premium content, will be sold. There will remain a much more accessible, rich and multimedia 'public domain', but the extent of public access – and therefore perhaps the extent of 'information citizen equality' – depends on key decisions relating to standards, interoperability and competition policy.

What is relatively clear is that smart DRM and innovation in control and exploitation of intellectual property tend to lead to a process of exclusivization: of slicing and dicing content and more tightly controlling distribution. This has very far-reaching implications for the operation of a public sphere. We may even go so far as to say that we are witnessing a technologically driven break-up of the public sphere, abetted by law, as a public sphere based on public information goods and non-excludability of consumption is replaced by multiple fragmented 'spheres' and a process of information exclusion whereby only a lucky few will access the best information services. This process is almost wholly unresearched, and at a policy level little thought has been given to its long-term civic consequences.

Self-regulation as Private Regulation

Regulation, as Lawrence Lessig has outlined, can be provided by law, by software code and by the market. It can also be provided through voluntary self-restraint, and these various forms of regulation often compete and interact. For example, it is very common for private players in the media, as in other sectors, to offer to develop a code of conduct or voluntary self-restraint as a means to face down public or political demands for statutory regulation. Private self regulation is displacing public regulation with implications for the public accountability of rule making and enforcement.

Where U.K. journalists were seen to have pushed the boundaries of decency too far in the early and mid 1990s, committees of MPs called for statutory regulation, but the press in the U.K. headed them off by setting up and then tightening a self-regulatory regime under the Press Council (Soley and O'Malley 1999; see also HMSO 1991, 1993). When mobile operators in the U.K. and Japan first developed 3G and i-mode services that would deliver video, they worried that the new services might expose children to harmful content (and about the impact this would have on their market). The mobile operators responded by developing a rule book which they then committed themselves to observing. And in the internet space, European ISPs, with strong encouragement from the European Commission, have been working on detailed codes of conduct which make clear their obligations and intentions with respect to their consumers. In this section, I raise the question of whether many of the functions of public regulation are increasingly shifting to private actors and what the consequences might be for the public sphere.

Private self-regulation is not new. It is as old as the Hippocratic Oath. But there are several reasons that the trend in recent years has been to a much greater reliance on self-regulation rather than regulation by law or by public authorities established under statute in the media sector. Self-regulation has gained ground because it answers many pressing questions for the existing regulatory framework. It appears to be flexible and able to respond to challenges of a rapidly changing media sector. It enlists the close cooperation of the regulated in designing rules, policing observation of them, and any sanctions that may be applied. There has been a huge amount of public and political support for self-regulation[9] and many supporters of self-regulation argue in addition that self-regulation is more freedom of expression friendly.

But the apparent advantages of self-regulation are also its alleged drawbacks. Flexibility is seen as weakness and closeness to industry is seen as capture. And the freedom of expression argument is a complex issue. Whilst it may in certain circumstances be preferable for non-state bodies to exercise censorship functions (as they are at least independent of Government), it must be noted that private bodies are not subject to the same level of accountability or review as public authorities. Whilst there are instances in which self-regulation can operate as a powerful mechanism of enlightened self-interest, there are others in which it is nothing of the sort.[10] Further – and critically – the embrace of private regulation has been a pragmatic one, with little concern for the broader impact on the public sphere: whilst self-regulatory codes may be entrusted with developing and applying codes of conduct to deal with specific harms, they are arguably less successful when entrusted with protecting the public interest generally. (Tambini, Leonardi and Marsden, 2008).

Conclusion: A 'Common European Information Space'?

In the twentieth century a unique European path for media policy was developed which combined strong but qualified protection for free speech and a strong commitment to public provision and accountability of broadcasting. The combination of a mixed broadcasting system, press freedom in print media, and a general commitment to free speech did provide some positive benefits in terms of access and inclusion in rational critical debate about the challenges facing society. In the light of the review of law and policy presented above, it seems clear that the institutional framework is now entering a phase of fundamental change in which traditional legal and regulatory balances are bring recast.

Is 'publicness' growing or shrinking in Europe? Is the principle of universal equal access to public information resources and communication spaces being developed or undermined? This short chapter has provided only an overview of a particular way of engaging with this familiar set of issues. The short answer, provided by this chapter is that whilst the new communicative abundance provides everyone with more communications resources, law and policy are not being developed in ways that protect key resources of _public_ communication. Intellectual property law and DRM is increasingly used to lock down cultural content and maximize revenue, and there are associated processes of fragmentation of audiences and services. Liability risk assessments and legal uncertainty may tend to undermine some of the more radical approaches to public provision and publishing, and the future model of public service broadcasting is under strain. I have charted some ways in which new rules are being formalized through media law and policy and old rules are being called into question.

Some forms of media consumption occur increasingly outside the scope of the formal, publicly accountable regulatory authorities which – arguably – sought to protect European public spheres as sites for rational-critical debate. Electronic distribution of audio-visual content, for instance, increasingly takes place outside the scope of the detailed regulation that surrounds broadcasting. And law and policy is being developed to respond to the new configuration of balances between publicity and harm which may further undermine the universal public availability of media texts. In light of this, decisions to publish are taken and new businesses developed which may further undermine the universal public availability of media texts.

Where does all this leave the 'quality of discourse and the quality of participation?' Whilst no final answers are possible, it is possible to identify some of the mechanisms involved in the current transformation of the public sphere and some of the foci of research that should be carried out: research on the behaviour of increasingly empowered audiences in a situation of increased choice; the definition of taste and taboos in global media; the risk assessments and benefit calculations that are made before any decision to enrich the public sphere through publication is carried through. We may be able to build a theory of the process of fragmentation of public spheres which could be used to measure empirical change. These are not the only questions, but they can deliver some key indicators of the health of the public sphere and the direction of its development.

It is worth also remarking on current policy, such as the European Commission's calls for a 'common information space'[11] in Europe as a key target for its i2010 communications policy. The European policy framework, which draws competencies from competition and single-market laws and powers, seems ill-equipped to deal with the more profound challenges to a European tradition of communications: the idea of a public sphere of rational-critical debate to which all citizens have access has been absent from policy and public debate on developing the 'European Way' in communications.

This policy context raises some fundamental questions for those with an interest in the European approach to the development of the public sphere. The vexed question of whether anything approaching a pan-European public sphere might exist is only a part of this. If we assume that people will seek information about and participation in the debates that impact their lives, a sphere of participation in EU affairs should gradually build. But the infrastructure that supports public sphere participation more generally is complex, fragile and contingent upon broader issues of regulation, law and policy. Whether we are concerned with participation at the local, national or European level, conditions for that participation – e.g. that all citizens have access to the key fora and texts – are being undermined. The outcome of the processes outlined in this paper is far from clear. I have outlined some of the key contours of the relevant changes, and argued that discussion of the fate of the public sphere should examine law and policy.

The irony for Europe is that the European Commission Directorate-General with powers in this field has scant competencies to pursue a distinctive 'European Path' in the protection of the public sphere. DG Infso's powers are derived from competition and infrastructure objectives, whilst cultural, civic and educational powers tend to be jealously guarded at the member state level.

Public sphere theory should not only engage with law and policy in order to understand how 'publicness' is being transformed, it should attempt to forge a new European framework for the protection of citizen access to rational critical debate. Where once the right to impart ideas as defined in the ECHR was at the centre of the debate, now the right to receive ideas is gaining in importance in a situation of communicative abundance

Notes

1. An early version of this paper was presented at the conference *Changing European Public Spheres, ECSUS, University of Sheffield, 22 September 2004*. I am grateful to the organizers for the invitation and to the participants for discussion and comments. I am grateful also to Carles Llorens and Seeta Gangadharan for their comments on an earlier draft.

2. It has been frequently pointed out that Habermas's original term 'Öffentlichkeit' has been rather clumsily translated using the spatial metaphor of the public *sphere*, whilst the more appropriate translation would have been 'publicness' or 'publicité' in the older French sense. I use the terms interchangeably and the somewhat awkward 'publicness' where appropriate.

3. For a full survey, see Price and Raboy 2003; OSI 2005.

4. Convention for the Protection of Human Rights and Fundamental Freedoms as amended by Protocol No. 11 (ECHR), Article 10 Freedom of Expression: 'Everyone has the right to freedom of expression. This right shall include freedom to hold opinions and to receive and impart information and ideas without interference by public authority and regardless of frontiers. This article shall not prevent States from requiring the licensing of broadcasting, television or cinema enterprises.'

5. The relevant section of the protocol to the Treaty of Amsterdam reads: 'The provisions of the Treaty establishing the European Community shall be without prejudice to the competence of Member States to provide for the funding of public service broadcasting insofar as such funding is granted to broadcasting organisations for the fulfilment of the public service remit as conferred, defined and organised by each Member State, and insofar as such funding does not affect trading conditions and competition in the Community to an extent which would be contrary to the common interest, while the realisation of the remit of that public service shall be taken into account.' 10. 11. 97 E N *Official Journal of the European Communities* C 340/109.

6. The BBC has been subject to a series of 'new services' reviews since 2000, covering new television and radio channels and online, including the Gardam, Barwise and Graf reviews.

7. Twelve editorial cartoons, most of which depicted the prophet Muhammad, were published in the Danish newspaper *Jyllands-Posten* on 20 September 2005, leading to widespread protest.

8. A useful basic introduction to property rights can be found at: http://www. intellectual-property.gov.uk/faq/. For a more in-depth analysis, see Thierer and Crews 2001, esp. 'Introduction' and Chapters 1 and 15.

9. For examples at the European level, see: *Green Paper on the Protection of Minors and Human Dignity in Audiovisual and Information Services*, COM(96)483, 16.10.97; *Communication on Illegal and Harmful Content on the Internet*, COM(97)487, 16.10.97; *Council Recommendation 98/560/EC on the Development of the Competitiveness of the European Audiovisual and Information Services Industry by Promoting National Frameworks Aimed at Achieving a Comparable and Effective Level of Protection of Minors and Human Dignity*, OJ L 270, 7.10.1998.

10. Research has been carried out on how ISPs, in contrast to other groups, set rules (codes of conduct) and police themselves and their users accordingly. Unhappy with the lack of information provided by ISPs themselves, and with a suspicion that the ISPs were routinely censoring their servers, researchers at PCMLP decided to test the regime. They established that a spook website, in this case ostensibly a fan site for J.S. Mill, was removed by some ISPs without sufficient review when

spurious complaints were made about it. See 'How "Liberty" Disappeared from Cyberspace': http://pcmlp.socleg.ox.ac.uk/text/liberty.pdf.

11. Brussels, 1.6.2005 COM(2005)229 *Final Communication from the Commission to the Council, the European Parliament, the European Economic and Social Committee and the Committee of the Regions 'i2010 – A European Information Society for Growth and Employment'* (SEC(2005)717).

Bibliography

Armstrong, N. 2008. 'Blog and be Damned?' *New Law Journal* 158: 387–89.

BBC. 2004. *Building Public Value.* London: BBC.

Bourdieu, P. 2002. *Distinction : A Social Critique of the Judgement of Taste.* Cambridge, MA: Harvard University Press.

Brants, K. 2005. 'Guest Editor's Introduction: The Internet and the Public Sphere', *Political Communication* 22(2): 143–46.

Calhoun, C. (ed). 1992. Habermas and The Public Sphere. MIT Press.

Cammaerts, B. and Audenhove, L. van. 2005. 'Online, Political Debate, Unbounded Citizenship and the Problematic Nature of a Transnational Public Sphere', *Political Communication* 22(2). Retrieved from http://www.metapress.com/app/home/contribution.

Chalmers, D. 2003. 'The Reconstitution of European Public Spheres', *European Law Journal* 9: 127–89.

Chang, A. 2004. 'How Low Is the Lowest Common Denominator? Online News Media in England and Fears of New Global Standard for Internet Defamation after *Gutnick'*, MSt thesis. Magdalen College, University of Oxford.

Dahlgren 1995.

Dahlgren, P. 2005. 'The Internet, Public Spheres, and Political Communication: Dispersion and Deliberation', *Political Communication* 22(2): 147–62.

Davies, G. 2005. 'The BBC and Public Value', in D. Helm, *Can the Market Deliver?* Eastleigh: John Libbey.

Eriksen, E. 2004. 'Conceptualizing European Public Spheres General, Segmented and Strong Publics', ARENA Working Paper 3/04. Oslo: Centre for European Studies, University of Oslo.

Forgan, L. and Tambini, D. 2001. 'Content', in D. Tambini et al., *Communications: Revolution and Reform.* London: IPPR.

Fraser, N. 1992. 'Rethinking the Public Sphere: A Contribution to the Critique of Actually Existing Democracy', in C. Calhoun (ed.), *Habermas and the Public Sphere.* Boston, MA: The MIT Press, pp. 109–42.

Garnham, N. 1992 'The Media and the Public Sphere', in C. Calhoun (ed.), 1992. *Habermas and the Public Sphere.* Boston, MA: The MIT Press, pp. 37–53.

Habermas, J. 1994. 'Three Models of Democracy', *Constellations* 1(1): 1–10.

HMSO. 1991, 1993. *The Report of the Calcutt Review on the Press.* London: HMSO.

Holznagel, B. 2003. 'The Mission of Public Service Broadcasters', in M.E. Price and M. Raboy (eds), *Public Service Broadcasting: A Reader*. Alphen an den Rijn: Kluwer Law International.

Kunelius, R. and Sparks, C. 2001. 'Problems with a European Public Sphere: An Introduction', *Javnost– The Public* 8(1).pp 5–20.

Larouche, P. 1998. 'EC Competition Law and the Convergence of the Telecommunications and Broadcasting Sectors', *Telecommunications Policy* 22(3).

Lessig, L. 1999. *Code and Other Laws of Cyberspace*. New York: Basic Books.

———. 2001. *The Future of Ideas: The Fate of the Commons in a Connected World*. New York: Random House.

Maine, H.S. 1986. (first published 1861). *Ancient Law: Its Connection with the Early History of Society, and Its Relation to Modern Ideas*. Dorset Press.

Meyer, J.H. 2004. 'Is there a European Public Sphere? Recent Analyses on the Democratic Deficit, Legitimation and Control in Europe', *Berliner Journal für Soziologie* 14(1): 135–43.

Millwood Hargrave, A. and Livingstone, S. 2006. *Harm and Offence in Media Content: A Review of the Evidence*. Bristol: Intellect.

Ofcom, 2004; 2005. *Review of Public Service Television Broadcasting*. Phase 1, 2, 3. Reports.

Ofcom 2008. *Second Review of Public Service Television Broadcasting*.

OSI (Open Society Institute) 2005. Television Across Europe – Regulation, Policy and Independence.

Owen, L. 2001. *Selling Rights*. London: Routledge.

Price, M. 1996. *Television, the Public Sphere and National Identity*. Oxford: Oxford University Press.

Price, M.E. and Raboy, M. (eds). 2003. *Public Service Broadcasting: A Reader*. Alphen an den Rijn: Kluwer Law International.

Rozenberg Joshua 2004. Privacy and the Press Oxford University Press.

Soley, C. and O'Malley, T. 1999. *Regulating the Press*. London: Pluto Press.

Seifert, F. 2003. 'The Critical European Discourse on Genetic Engineering and the Deficit of a European Public Sphere', *Berliner Journal for Soziologie* 13(4).

Simon, J. 2005. 'New Business Models for Audiovisual Content', report by the British Screen Advisory Council (BSAC), *UK Presidency Creative Economy Conference, 5–7 October*.

Tambini, D. 2001. 'The Civic Networking Movement: The Internet as a New Democratic Public Sphere', in C. Crouch et al. (eds), *Citizenship, Markets and the State*. Oxford: Oxford University Press, pp. 238–60.

———. 2006. 'On-demand in Demand: Public Service Broadcasters, New Services and Copyright', in C.S. Nissen (ed.), *Making a Difference: Public Service Broadcasting in the European Media Landscape*. Eastleigh: John Libbey.

Tambini, D., Leonardi, D. and Marsden, C. 2008. Codifying Cyberspace. Communications Self-Regulation in the age of Internet convergence. Routledge, London and New York.

Theirer, A. and Crews, C.W. (eds). 2002. *Copy Fights: The Future of Intellectual Property in the Information Age*. Washington, D.C.: Cato Institute.

Chapter 4

Exploring the Online European Public Sphere: The Web and Europeanization of Political Communication in the European Union

Renée van Os, Nicholas W. Jankowski and Fred Wester

Introduction

This chapter commences with a sketch of the manner in which the notion of the Europeanization of political communication and the related concept of a 'European public sphere' have been formulated and investigated during the past decade. We elaborate on our interpretation of what constitutes a European public sphere by placing emphasis on political actors, including citizens, communicating about Europe. We review a number of studies related to this interpretation, mainly performed within a mass-mediated environment.

The first part of the chapter considers the potential of the Web to contribute to or enhance a European public sphere. Particularly in the case of European issues, it is important for political actors to maintain websites as means of communication with supporters and the electorate at large, inasmuch as these issues are generally less intensely covered by the mass media than national political issues. In this chapter, we argue that such online communication about Europe by political parties deserves scholarly attention. It is through their websites that political actors – participants in the public sphere – can offer a particular perspective on European news, issues and events, suggesting whether and why issues concerning Europe are socially and politically relevant. Such utilization of the Web can be considered an indicator of Europeanization of political communication on the Web and, consequently, of an online European public sphere.

In the second part of the chapter, several research projects are presented that focus on the Europeanization of political communication on the internet, specifically the World Wide Web, within three areas of research: visibility of communication, interpretative schemes in which European issues are addressed, and the online structure of communication about Europe as determined through hyperlink analysis. The research designs and outcomes of these studies are examined. Finally, the chapter concludes with recommendations for a more overarching empirical investigation of the European public sphere.

Conceptualizing the European Public Sphere

Against the background of the democratic deficit of the European Union (EU), scholars recognize that the process of European integration must be accompanied by Europeanization of political communication in order to overcome the lack of legitimacy and popular involvement in the EU by European citizens (Koopmans and Pfetsch 2003). The concept of public sphere, initially elaborated by Habermas in *The Structural Transformations of the Public Sphere* (1962/1989), has more recently begun to play a central role in discussions about European integration.[1] Various models regarding Europeanization of political communication across the EU, and the possible development of a European public sphere, have been presented in the last decade by a variety of scholars, and several of these are outlined in this section. In general, scholars seem to agree that the mass media serve as the main venue for public representation of a public sphere functioning at the European level. The actual development of a European public sphere, however, is lagging behind economic and political integration at the European level as argued by, for example, Gerhards (2000).

Yet scholars disagree about how to deal, both theoretically and empirically, with the notion of public sphere at the European level. Early scholars, dealing with the possibility of a public sphere functioning at the European level, such as Gerhards (1993), Grimm (1995), Graham (1992), Kielmansegg (1996) and Schlesinger (1996, 1999), retain the original Habermasian notion of the public sphere. This notion, generally speaking, involves 'the space within which the affairs of the state could be subjected to public scrutiny' (Kunelius and Sparks 2001: 11). These scholars are willing to consider the possibility of a European public sphere at the supranational level only on the condition that Brussels becomes more of a political centre in which decisions are taken independently of national governments. They, to different degrees, place emphasis on the lack of political actors, such as political parties and interest groups, operating at the European level. They also refer to the lack of European-level mass media, to the diversity of languages across Europe, and to the absence of a collective European identity. Schlesinger, for example, considers the lack of a single European public problematic: 'without the broad mass of European media consumers organised transnationally as common audiences or readerships, there is no basis for talking about a single European public for political communications' (Schlesinger 1999: 276–77). These scholars prefer to speak of 'Europeanization of national public spheres' instead of the development of a 'European public sphere' when referring to Europeanzation of political communication across the EU.

Other scholars have criticized this view as being excessively strict and based on an idealized notion of an essentially homogeneous national public sphere to be replicated at the European level (Eder, Kantner and Trenz 2000; Koopmans et al., 2004; Risse 2002, 2003; Van de Steeg 2002, 2004). In this regard, early scholars such as Schlesinger, Gerhards and Grimm 'base their conceptualisation on unsubstantiated assumptions concerning the character of the public sphere and its relation to key concepts such as language, the media system and the state's frontiers' (Van de Steeg et al. 2003: 2). Instead of considering a pre-existing community that almost automatically translates into a public sphere, Risse and Van de Steeg propose considering public sphere as a discursive community that emerges around debating a specific issue (Risse 2002, 2003; Risse and Van de Steeg 2003; Van de Steeg et al. 2003). As Risse argues:

> A European public sphere does not fall from heaven, and does not pre-exist outside social and political discourse. Rather, it is being constructed through social and discursive practices creating a common horizon of reference and, at the same time, a transnational community of communication over issues that concern 'us as Europeans' rather than British, French, Germans or Dutch. (Risse 2003: 2)

Although it is not our intention here to take a position in this debate about the (non-) existence of a European public sphere – this seems to be essentially a matter of definition – we do agree with Risse and colleagues on the centrality of communicative interaction about common European issues or events, either directly (face-to-face) or indirectly through media or internet-based representations. Therefore, scholarly research should focus foremost on the extent to which, and the nature of which political actors (including citizens) are communicating about Europe.

Communicating about Europe: Review of Empirical Studies

Few empirical studies measure aspects of the Europeanization of political communication. One study by Eder and Kantner does take on this challenge and the authors suggest a valuable point of departure (Eder and Kantner 2000). They place emphasis on the 'parallelization', or transnationalization, of public debates across Europe. For them, the key indicator of a shared public debate and, at the same time, of a European public sphere, is whether similar European issues are being simultaneously addressed in different national media.[2] Gerhards, extending the proposal made by Eder and Kantner, advocates a more normatively demanding stance towards what constitutes Europeanization of political communication (Gerhards 2000). He argues that it is not only important that actors communicate about a European issue or event; they should also 'evaluate it from a perspective that extends beyond one's country and interest'. This position, formulated succinctly, emphasizes that Europeanization involves communication from a European perspective (Gerhards 1993, 2000: 293). Related to these differences in interpretation, Risse and Van de Steeg, in a review of recent empirical studies, distinguish two approaches in measuring Europeanization of political communication: measuring first, visibility of communication about Europe and second, cross-national appearance of similar interpretive schemes in which Europe is addressed in the mass media (Risse and Van de Steeg 2003); Trenz distinguishes a third approach, namely via connectivity of communication across Europe (Trenz 2004). These three approaches, which we call 'visibility of communication', 'interpretive schemes' and 'connectivity of communication', are discussed in turn in the next three sub-sections.

Visibility of Communication
The first approach essentially counts how often Europe, European institutions and European affairs are mentioned in the mass media

(Gerhards 1993, 2000; Groothues 2004; Hodess 1997; Kevin 2001; Trenz 2004). Four studies are discussed here that measure visibility of communication about Europe. First, Gerhards (2000) investigates news coverage about European issues within three German newspapers in the period 1951–1995, and compares the extent of European issues coverage with coverage of national and international issues. Overall, during the entire period, 60 per cent of the news coverage dealt with national issues; 40 per cent dealt with international issues (a news item can deal with both international and national issues); only 7 per cent of the news coverage during the entire period dealt with European issues, with no large variation; slightly higher percentages (about 10 per cent) could be noted for the period 1951–1955, right after the foundation of the Union, and for the most recent period in the study, 1991–1995 (Gerhards 2000: 294–95).

Second, Groothues compares the number of (primetime) news items dealing with EU affairs to:

1. news items dealing with other European countries
2. domestic news items, and
3. non-European items

during two 'routine' weeks in 2003, for three television stations: one in France (France 2), one in Germany (ARD) and one in the U.K. (BBC1). For all three stations, only a small percentage of news items dealt with strict EU affairs: 2–4 per cent. On average, 25 per cent of the news items dealt with events/issues in other European countries (variation between the stations: 20 per cent for France 2, 31 per cent for ARD); a majority of the news items, however, dealt with purely domestic issues (an average of 68 per cent, with differences between the three stations ranging from 57 per cent for ARD and 75 per cent for France 2) (Groothues 2004: 9).

Third, Kevin investigates the extent to which national media outlets in eight EU member states[3] (both print and television) covered the 1999 European Parliament election during the last week of the campaign. She finds considerable variation between the various EU member states regarding the number of articles dealing with the election: 263 for France, compared to 99 for the U.K. and 47 for the Netherlands (Kevin 2001: 27–28).

A final example is a study conducted by Trenz (2004), who investigates eleven newspapers in six EU member states[4] in the period September to December 2000. Trenz differentiates between:

1. *European articles* – articles that discuss European topics as the dominant issue.

2. *Europeanized articles* – articles that discuss national topics as the dominant issue with reference to one or several European sub-issues.

3. *Articles with a European referential frame* – articles that discuss non-European issues but make different rhetorical references to Europe (Trenz 2004: 293–94).

The outcomes of the study show that European political communication (all three of the above categories) constitutes 35 per cent of the newspaper articles. Differences were noted between the newspapers, however, ranging from 55 per cent for the German *Frankfurter Allgemeine Zeitung*, to 24 per cent for the French *Libération* (Trenz 2004: 297–98).

Overall, when recapitulating the studies presented in this section, one can say that considerable variation exists between the EU member states investigated regarding the level of Europeanization of political communication, conceptualized as visibility of European affairs in the mass media. Also, for individual member states, the results of the studies vary: Kevin observes European issues to be relatively salient in the French news media, in contrast to Groothues and Trenz, who discover low salience of European issues in the French print news media.

However, in a general sense, one can conclude that the issue salience (visibility) of European affairs in the mass media has increased during the last ten years (see also Risse and Van de Steeg 2003; Trenz 2004 makes a similar argument). But, compared to coverage of national political issues, 'European' issues are still less addressed by the mass media. Future research can investigate whether the trend of an increasing visibility of European issues in the mass media persists.

Interpretative Schemes

A second, more qualitative approach concentrates on the interpretative schemes in which media address European issues, referred to by others as 'framing' (De Vreese 2003; Eder and Kantner 2000; Eder, Kantner and Trenz 2000; Gavin 2000; Risse and Van de Steeg 2003; Semetko, De Vreese and Peter 2000; Trenz 2000, 2004; Van de Steeg 2002, 2004). These studies observe that European issues are being discussed and reported in various media across Europe at the same time, at similar levels of attention in the issue cycle of media reporting, and in a similar fashion. Risse and Van de Steeg view the framing of particular European issues in similar ways across national media as being 'an important precondition for the emergence of a viable European public sphere' (Risse and Van de Steeg

2003: 4). Similarly, Trenz speaks of 'the specific meanings, expectations and world views that are channelled through and conveyed by debates' (Trenz 2004: 308). He criticizes studies that only measure the visibility of European affairs in the news media, considering this a 'minimalist indicator for the emergence of a European public sphere'. He argues that scholars should not only observe what is communicated, but also how and why it is communicated. Gavin makes a similar argument, stating that 'we need not to think just about the level of prominence of European news; the way it portrays Europe's political institutions and processes is also important' (Gavin 2000: 369). A first empirical investigation within the second approach, measuring interpretative schemes in which media address European issues, is executed by Gavin (2000). In particular, Gavin investigates economic entitlements offered to British citizens, and the portrayal of material benefits or losses for Britain, in European economic news coverage on British television. Gavin found that British coverage put a greater emphasis on the negative economic implications of engagement with Europe, rather than economic benefits (Gavin 2000: 364–66).

Second, Semetko, De Vreese and Peter investigate the extent to which European issues, events and persons in national news in Britain and Germany are framed as 'European' or 'domestic'. They conclude that a 'European' frame is increasingly present in national news, versus a national frame. European integration and the EU are not only present in news coverage of genuinely European issues, but are also increasingly an integral part of national political and economic coverage (Semetko, De Vreese and Peter 2000: 129).

Third, Van de Steeg (2002) presents an explorative study on the debate on EU enlargement in national weeklies in four EU member states. She observes two interpretative schemes being discussed in all four weeklies, namely: 1. 'widening and deepening' (similar rhetorical moves and arguments are put forward in the four weeklies in comparable quantity), and 2. costs and benefits of enlargement for the EU. An interpretative scheme that did not appear similarly across the four weeklies was the categorization of EU enlargement as something 'foreign' or something 'domestic'; only the Dutch *Elsevier* categorized EU enlargement as taking place across national frontiers (Van de Steeg 2002: 514–15). To a certain extent, Van de Steeg considers this cross-national occurrence of similar interpretative schemes an indicator of public opinion formation taking place at the European level and, similarly, of development of a European public sphere (Van de Steeg 2002: 517).

Fourth, Risse and Van de Steeg consider the debate that emerged across Europe in 2000 regarding the rise of a right-wing populist party in Austria, Jörg Haider's FPÖ. They investigate the extent to which newspapers from various countries used similar interpretative schemes when addressing the so-called Haider issue (Risse and Van de Steeg 2003; Van de Steeg et al. 2003). Risse and Van de Steeg discover that six similar interpretative schemes emerged frequently across all fifteen newspapers in five EU member states included in the study.[5] Four interpretative schemes related directly to Jörg Haider, for example 'Haider as a Nazi or xenophobe'. Two of them were directly related to Europe: 'Europe as a moral community' and 'European legal standards' (Risse and Van de Steeg 2003: 6–7).

Finally, Eder, Kantner and Trenz (2000) investigate to what degree the three interpretative schemes – interests, identity and values – are shared across European countries within different national news media (see also Trenz 2004).[6] Eder, Kantner and Trenz argue that these interpretative schemes tell us whether and why an issue is relevant, and therefore that their cross-national appearance should be considered 'the qualitative criteria for the existence of a European public sphere' (Trenz 2004: 308–9). In an analysis of news coverage of European governance and policymaking during 2000, 85 per cent of the articles in the sample contained an 'interests' frame, 38 per cent were coded in normative terms ('values' frame), and 27 per cent contained an 'identity' frame. Typical issues, which were linked to interest negotiations among Europeans, are institutional reform, competition policy and the debate on the euro. Few articles referred to purely normative or identity-based framings; 45 per cent of the articles made use of multiple framings, raising issues in the context of interests and/or values and/or identities. The enlargement of the EU to include countries located in Eastern Europe, for example, was predominantly framed in instrumental terms (interests), but was regularly linked to normative questions and questions of collective identity. The relationship between the EU and Turkey was mainly framed in identity-related terms (Trenz 2004: 309–10).

A diverse picture emerges from these studies investigating the cross-national appearance of similar interpretative schemes in which European issues are addressed. First, scholars have investigated whether European issues/events have been framed as 'European' ('foreign' in the terminology of Van de Steeg), or as national or 'domestic'. In a general sense, an increase in usage of a 'European' frame by various mass media across the EU has been observed (for example, by Semetko, De Vreese and Peter 2000). Second, scholars have identified specific interpretative schemes in which the mass media address European issues: 1. a material benefits-and-losses frame (as put forward by Gavin 2000 and Van de Steeg 2002), which is also covered by the 'interests' frame identified by Eder and colleagues[7] (their 'interests' frame also includes legal issues, identified by Risse and Van de Steeg 2003); 2. the frame 'Europe as moral community' of Risse and Van de Steeg (2003) roughly corresponds to the 'values' frame identified by Eder and colleagues; and 3. the 'identity' frame identified by Eder, Kantner and Trenz (2000). In conclusion, the three frames identified by Eder, Kantner and Trenz (see also Trenz 2004) seem to be the all-inclusive, overarching general frames that, in our opinion, deserve more scholarly attention in the future. We believe that the scarcely examined academic field investigating the interpretative schemes in which European issues are addressed, should benefit from structured research following the typology as proposed by Eder and colleagues.

Connectivity of Communication

Trenz (2004) mentions a third approach that measures Europeanization of political communication: via the connectivity of communication within a given, but changeable, communicative context. This corresponds to what others have referred to as the 'structure of communication' (e.g. Koopmans and Erbe 2004). In this regard, Koopmans and Pfetsch argue that 'the spatial reach and boundaries of public communication can be determined by investigating patterns of communicative flows and assessing the relative density of public communication with and between different political spaces' (Koopmans and Pfetsch 2003: 13).[8] First, they define three levels of communication: the national public sphere; other national public spaces – which comprise the EU (candidate) member states; and the transnational, European political space – in which the European institutions and common policies are situated. The degree to which public spheres can be deemed national, transnational or European depends, according to Koopmans and colleagues, on the density of communicative linkages within and between these spaces (Koopmans and Pfetsch 2003: 11–12). Accordingly, they speak of 'horizontal Europeanization' if, for example, the German media report on what happens in other national public spaces, and of 'vertical Europeanization' when communicative linkages are made between the national and the European public space (Koopmans and Erbe 2004: 103–4).

Second, in order to assess the role of the media as compared to other actors, Koopmans and Pfetsch recommend moving 'beyond the usual article-level types of content analysis to consider individual public claims by different collective actors' as a means to measure communicative linkages (Koopmans and Pfetsch 2003: 13–14). Thus, their units of analysis are individual acts of political communication, which they term 'public claims'.[9] One of the main conclusions of the EUROPUB project was that for all countries included in the study (except the non-EU country Switzerland), the number of claims on European integration was higher in 2002 than in 1990. Especially regarding the issue fields of 'monetary politics' and 'agriculture', the number of claims with a European scope (claims made by European-level actors – vertical Europe anization) increased from 40 per cent and 36 per cent respectively in 1990 to 78 per cent and 61 per cent in 2002. Within other issue fields only a modest increase in vertical Europeanization could be observed; no clear vertical tendencies could be found within fields in which the EU has very little power and influence (e.g. education and pension issues). For horizontal Europeanization, they observed a slight decrease – from 18 per cent across all countries in 1990 to 17 per cent in 2002 (Koopmans et al. 2004).

One of the conclusions of the EUROPUB project corresponds with the outcomes of research related to the first approach measuring Europeanization of political communication presented at the beginning of this section: increased visibility of European issues in the mass media. However, Koopmans and colleagues provide additional information on the nature of this increased Europeanization of political communication. European-level actors, particularly, are increasingly raising their voices in the (national) public sphere, within selected issue fields.

Public Sphere and the Internet

The internet and, more specifically, the World Wide Web (WWW) are often said to have the potential to provide a public forum where everyone is able to obtain and maintain a virtual presence (e.g. Mitra and Cohen 1999: 180). For the politically concerned – interest groups, NGOs, political parties and candidates, governments and lay citizens – the internet potentially serves as a space where information can be shared, issues discussed and where those interested can engage in political action. These elements are often considered important components of the political process and, accordingly, the public sphere. Expectations have, however, lowered considerably since the rise and popularization of the internet in the 1990s. Early 'cyber optimists' like Rheingold (1993), who claimed that the internet could fuel the process of democratization through opportunities for deliberation and direct decision-making, have been succeeded by 'cyber pessimists' like Margolis and Resnick (2000), who warned that the internet could even widen the gap between the engaged and the apathetic. Scholars like Norris (2000, 2001), Foot and Schneider (2002), Schneider and Foot (2002) and Ward, Gibson and Lusoli (2003) take a more 'middle ground' position, suggesting that a balance should, and can, be found between these two extremes. First, Foot and Schneider stress the importance of independent political websites developed by national and state advocacy groups, civic organizations, and mainstream and alternative press. In their research, they concentrate upon the online structure of politically oriented websites and the political action such online structure facilitates: information gathering and persuasion, political education, political talk, voter mobilization and candidate promotion (Foot and Schneider 2002). Second, Norris mentions the existence of websites prepared by minor and fringe parties, and considers these an asset for democracy, enabling citizens to learn more about the range of electoral choices than was previously possible (Norris 2003). In this context, she speaks of the emergence of a 'virtual political system' (Norris 2001: 95).

During recent years, more and more websites, produced by a variety of political actors, have become available to citizens of European countries for political communication about European issues. In the case of European (political) issues and events, it is particularly important for political actors to maintain websites as a means of communication with supporters and the electorate at large, since these issues are generally less intensely covered by the mass media than are national political issues (Hix 2005: 193; Thomassen and Schmitt 1997). In this chapter, we argue that, similar to the mass media research presented in the previous section, one can measure Europeanization of political communication and the possible development of a European public sphere by looking at the extent to which and the nature of political actors (including citizens) communicate about Europe on their websites. The proposed conceptual frameworks within a mass-mediated environment, as elaborated in the former section, can be used in the investigation of online communication on websites produced by political actors. Moreover, such online content contains indications about the Europe political actors have in mind, in contrast to the opinions or attitudes towards Europe the mass media attributes to actors when reporting on them. It is through their websites that political actors – participants in the public sphere – can offer a particular perspective on European news, issues and events, suggesting whether and why issues concerning Europe are socially and politically relevant. Similar to Trenz and colleagues, we consider an increased visibility of political communication about Europe, as the cross-national appearance of similar 'interpretative schemes' in which European issues are discussed, are indicators of the existence of an online European public sphere.

Empirical Research: European Public Sphere and the Web

This section elaborates on empirical research conducted within the online environment of the Web, and is similarly structured around the previously mentioned three approaches which are analytical elements for measuring Europeanization of political communication: visibility of communication, interpretative schemes and connectivity of communication.

Visibility of Communication

Zimmermann and Koopmans (2003) investigate the degree of Europeanization of political communication on the internet within six different policy categories, plus one 'European integration' category, as unfolded via search engines within six EU member states and Switzerland in two periods in 2002. In order to determine the degree of Europeanization of this online political communication, Zimmermann and Koopmans look at various dimensions of transnationalism at the level of each website:

1. Language used.
2. External linking to actors from other EU countries or from the EU level.
3. Reference to actors and the information provided on the site from other EU countries or from the EU level.
4. Reference to sources from other EU countries or from the EU level.
5. Actors that become visible as 'claimants' on the site and their (European/national) scope.
6. The perceived (European/national) scope of the issues they address.

For the entire sample,[10] 23 per cent of the cases included a European dimension, either because one of the actor types involved was organized at the European level or because the issue was seen in a European frame of reference. Zimmermann and Koopmans refer to this situation as 'vertical Europeanization' (Zimmermann and Koopmans 2003: 41–42). They distinguish a second form of Europeanization: 'horizontal Europeanization', meaning the establishment of horizontal communicative linkages between EU member states. A considerably lower amount of horizontal Europeanization (10 per cent) was found, as compared to vertical Europeanization (Zimmermann and Koopmans 2003: 42). As concerns vertical Europeanization, variation was observed between the countries included in the study, especially between the EU countries and the one non-EU country, Switzerland, in which only 12 per cent of the claims had a European dimension. This percentage contrasts to the relatively higher figures for Italy (32 per cent) and Spain (31 per cent). For the other countries included in the study, the percentages fluctuated around the overall mean. As concerns horizontal Europeanization, these two countries score relatively low: 5 per cent for Italy and 8 per cent for Spain in comparison to 16 per cent for the U.K. and 12 per cent for Denmark (Zimmermann and Koopmans 2003: 42). As with the other dimension, the horizontal Europeanization measured for the other countries fluctuated around the overall mean – see Table 4.1.

Table 4.1: Horizontal and Vertical Europeanization of Online Political Communication.

Country	Vertical Europeanization (%)	Horizontal Europeanization (%)
Germany	23	12
Spain	31	8
France	18	11
Italy	32	5
Netherlands	24	9
U.K.	20	16
Switzerland	12	12
Total	23	10

Source: Zimmermann and Koopmans (2003: 42)

In contrast to Zimmermann and Koopmans, who investigate online political communication with regard to general policy issues at a randomly chosen point in time and determine the degree of Europeanization by looking at the presence of a European dimension within that online communication, Van Os, Jankowski and Vergeer (2007) study the specific online communication about Europe provided by a selection of political actors on their websites during the 2004 European Parliament (EP) election campaign.

This study focuses on nine EU countries, including three new member states. For each country, in the two months before the 2004 EP election, coders searched for sites they expected to be involved in the 2004 EP election campaign by consulting search engines, politically oriented portals and other depositories of potential website addresses. Stratified samples of 100 sites were drawn from the collection of identified sites per country within five actor-type categories: candidates, political parties, governmental sites, NGOs and labour unions, and other actors. For each site, four features were coded as contributors to Europeanization of political communication, and subsequently a European public sphere, two of them being: 'EP election content on front page', 'European content on front page'. In this study, 68 per cent of the websites included in the study actually had EP election-related content on the front pages at the time of the election, a percentage the researchers considered relatively low, in particular because of the search strategy followed. The researchers interpret this limited referencing of the election as an indication that political actors considered the election not particularly important (Van Os, Jankowski and Vergeer 2007). NGOs and labour unions in particular provided relatively little EP election-related content: only 38 per cent.

However, when examining the second feature, 'European content on front page', which included not only EP election-related content, but also more general content on European issues, NGOs and labour unions scored higher: 46 per cent. For all actor types together, the total score for this second feature was 73 per cent (compared to 67 per cent of EP election-related content). Apparently some actors considered Europe sufficiently important to note on their websites, but not the 2004 EP election. A possible explanation for this difference may be the negative reputation of the EP regarding legitimacy and power in relation to the other EU governmental bodies. Variations existed between the countries included in the study. Ireland, for example, scored low on both EP election-related content (31 per cent) and European content on front page (47 per cent). The U.K. scored high on both features – 92 per cent and 88 per cent respectively. In France, much variation between the two features was observed: 52 per cent for EP election-related content, compared to 77 per cent for European content on the front page – see Table 4.2.

Table 4.2: EP Election/European Content on Front Page Websites.

Country	EP content (%)	European content (%)
Czech Republic	74	89
Finland	77	83
France	52	77
Hungary	58	70
Ireland	31	47
Italy	64	58
Netherlands	65	63
Slovenia	97	96
U.K.	92	88
Total	**68**	**73**

Source: Van Os, Jankowski and Vergeer (2007)

Both studies presented in this section compare, in a quantitative manner, various countries with each other as concerns the degree of Europeanization of political communication present on websites produced by a variety of actors in these countries. However, the two studies vary considerably in the operationalization of this notion, as well as in search strategy used to select websites, and, as a result, they cannot be compared. In a general sense, there are no countries that turn out to be extreme exceptions in both studies, either in a positive or a negative manner. Only the U.K. seems to reside in the upper region in both studies as concerns the degree of Europeanization of political online communication.

Interpretative Schemes

An exploratory investigation by Van Os (2005) is structured around the three interpretative schemes – interests, identity and values – identified by Eder, Kantner and Trenz (2000, 2002). Van Os investigates these three interpretative schemes within political communication about Europe present on websites maintained by the eleven largest French political parties in the context of the 2004 EP election. Van Os adds one component to the typology of Eder and colleagues: whether interests and identities mentioned in the online communication of parties have a national or European orientation. First, Van Os observes that most political parties emphasized to some degree European interests in their online communication, usually in combination with an indication of benefits of European integration for the French electorate. Second, only about half of the political parties mentioned a European identity in their communication about the 2004 EP election; others firmly expressed a French, national identity. Third, universal values, such as democratic principles and governmental transparency, were mentioned by almost all parties in relation to the EU: political parties consider sharing these values as necessary for a well-functioning EU. Van Os argues that these expressions, related to the three interpretative schemes (interests, identity and values), as formulated by French political parties on their websites, 'can be considered indicators of a feeling of "belonging to Europe", and qualitative measurements of Europeanization of political communication, and possibly the development of a European public sphere' (Van Os 2005: 214).

In a subsequent paper, Van Os, Wester and Jankowski (2007) compare the online communication of French, British and Dutch political parties, again investigating the interpretative schemes – interests, identity and values – in which Europe is addressed on political party websites in the context of the 2004 EP election. Again, this paper differentiates between European and national interests, and a European and national identity frame. Another additional indicator was included, namely 'tenor of reporting', which measures the general attitude towards Europe a party shows in its online communication: as advantageous/positive, or merely disadvantageous/negative. Variation was observed between the three countries as concerns the appearance of the interpretative schemes within political parties' online communication – see Table 4.3.

British parties more often mentioned national interests and a national identity frame in their online communication compared to Dutch and French parties, which more often mentioned European interests and a European identity frame (percentages are noted in Table 4.3). British parties also showed the most negative attitude towards Europe. However, most parties did not mention values very often. Van Os, Wester and Jankowski also compare the appearance of the three interpretative schemes cross-nationally along parties' positions in the political spectrum. They discover cross-national similarities in parties' online communication, especially among the liberal (democratic) parties, the 'green' parties, and the sovereign/extreme right-wing parties; more diversity was observed among the social democratic parties and centre-right parties. First, the liberal parties united in the European group Alliance of Liberal Democrats in Europe (ALDE, with national delegations: VVD (Netherlands), UDF (France), Liberal Democrats (UK), D'66 (Netherlands) mentioned European interests relatively often and, in some cases, a European identity frame. These parties generally approve the focus on EU economic development, which was manifest in a positive tenor of reporting. In contrast, the sovereign/extreme right-wing parties (Front National (France), the British National Party (U.K.), Nieuw Rechts (Netherlands), French sovereign parties (MPF, RPF and CPNT) mentioned national interests relatively more and often a national identity frame. These parties, in a general sense, are opposed to European integration, which was manifest in a negative tenor of reporting. Finally, the 'green' parties Green Party (U.K.), Les Verts (France), GroenLinks (Netherlands) mentioned values relatively often in their online communication. These parties almost only stressed European interests, and a European identity frame. In a general sense, more similarities in interpretative schemes were observed cross-nationally among parties

Table 4.3: Aggregated Means Frames per Country.

Country		Interests (%)	Identity (%)	Values (%)	Tenor*
U.K.	European	23	10	18	2.15
	National	31	25		
	Regional	16	15		
Netherlands	European	42	18	24	1.93
	National	17	13		
	Regional	1	0		
France	European	51	24	26	2.08
	National	25	17		
	Regional	1	0		
Total (N=1701)	European	41	18	23	2.04
	National	23	18		
	Regional	-	-		

*Note: * N tenor = 1294; Tenor scale: 1 = positive   2 = neutral   3 = negative*
Source: Van Os, Wester and Jankowski (2007)

with similar political orientation than among parties within one country. Van Os, Wester and Jankowski considers these cross-national similarities in interpretative schemes an indicator for the Europeanization of political communication and for the development of a European public sphere (Van Os, Wester and Jankowski 2007).

Connectivity of Communication

Zimmermann, Koopmans and Schlecht (2004: 26) investigate the EUROPUB conceptualization of (horizontal versus vertical) Europeanization, as previously described, in an online environment, by looking at hyperlink structures among websites of a pre-selected group of social actors already active in the 'offline' world, relating to issues regarding agriculture, immigration and European integration in six EU member states and Switzerland. The aim of the study is 'to explore the degree to which newly-emerged communicative and informative spaces on the internet may contribute to a Europeanisation of European public spheres' (Zimmermann, Koopmans, and Schlecht 2004: 3). A Web crawler was employed that automatically collected the information (hyperlinks) from the selected URLs. Each (outgoing) hyperlink was then examined and coded for country of actor, actor type, party/issue affiliation and organizational scope (for example, local, national, EU). The results suggest, first of all, that 50 per cent of all hyperlinks were directed to national actors, followed by actors from other countries (19 per cent). European actors received 14 per cent of the total number of hyperlinks (N = 17,951). Furthermore, 68 per cent of the hyperlinks provided by national actors directed visitors towards actors of the own country; 11 per cent of these hyperlinks directed visitors towards EU actors. Slightly more often, hyperlinks to national actors from other countries (12 per cent) were provided. More than half (54 per cent) of the EU-level actors provided hyperlinks to other EU-level actors. According to Zimmermann, Koopmans and Schlecht, these figures suggest a low degree of horizontal Europeanization through hyperlinks. Forms of vertical Europeanization through hyperlinks from national actors to European actors were more developed, but strongly concentrated on state actors (Zimmermann, Koopmans and Schlecht 2004: 26). The authors also report on the density of the hyperlinked groups of actors. No significant hyperlink relations appeared to exist between the countries in the sample. Significant vertical relationships were, however, observed between the national and EU level, the latter being mainly EU institutions.

A preliminary report about the debate around the European constitution in France in 2005, as played out on the internet, is prepared by Ghitalla and Fouetillou (2005). The objective of the study is to obtain an overview of the political debate on the Web and to comprehend how the online debate on the European constitution was organized in terms of relations between the sites. Between 30 May and 1 June 2005, a Web crawler searched for website addresses by following hyperlinks present on other websites. The search started from a dozen sites addressing the European constitution identified by the researchers. Some 12,000 sites were collected, of which more than 6,000 were in English and therefore excluded from the study. Ultimately, 5,000 sites were accessed and, of those sites dealing with the European constitution, 295 were selected for further study. These sites were classified as 'YES-sites', 'NO-sites', 'sites that do not take position', 'sites produced by institutions', and 'sites produced by media corporations'. Actors taking a position against the European Constitution produced two-thirds of the sites (the 'NO-sites'). This is, Ghitalla and Fouetillou note, in contrast to the debate that emerged on the three largest television channels: in that medium, 70 per cent of the speakers claimed to be in favour of the European Constitution. Ghitalla and Fouetillou (2005) suggest that: 'the Web has served as a public outlet for those who feel rejected by the mainstream mass media of television'.[11] They conclude that two almost distinct 'competitive communities' emerged on the Web around the YES and NO camps. The NO camp turned out to be less open than the YES camp: 79 per cent of the links provided on NO-sites were 'intra-community', in comparison to 64 per cent for the YES camp.

These two studies, although, again, different in the operationalization of Europeanization of political communication, present interesting results. In both studies, Europeanization is measured by looking at hyperlink structures on the Web. A central analytical element in the first study by Zimmermann and colleagues is the level on which actors who produced the sites operated: European, national or another EU member state. The degree of Europeanization is determined by the degree of connectivity between these levels. Koopmans and colleagues found a higher degree of Europeanization between the levels (vertical) than within the levels. In contrast, a central analytical element in the study by Ghitalla and Fouetillou is the attitude (opinion) towards Europe (the European Constitution) a French actor displayed on its website. By far the most hyperlinks were identified between websites displaying a similar position towards the European Constitution. When speaking about Europeanization of political communication, Ghitalla and Fouetillou's study shows us that attitudes towards Europe, becoming manifest through hyperlink analysis, can be a binding factor between actors 'belonging' to a particular community. Relationships, measured by the degree of hyperlinks, between the actors within one group were much higher than between actors belonging to different groups.

Conclusion: Suggestions for Future Research

In this chapter, various conceptualizations of, and empirical research about, European political communication, and a related European public sphere are discussed. In our interpretation, we place emphasis on political actors, including citizens, communicating about Europe. Despite the growing body of research focusing on the Europeanization of mass-mediated communication, almost no research has been conducted to examine online communication/internet-based representations of European issues.

In the second part of this chapter we reviewed the few studies available on the Europeanization of political communication on the World Wide Web. Only two studies focused on the visibility of European issues on the Web. Both the study by Zimmermann and Koopmans (2003) and by Van Os, Jankowski and Vergeer (2007) draw comparisons between different EU member states regarding the degree of Europeanization. Although these studies differ in operationalization of the notion of Europeanization, in both studies the U.K. scored in the upper region. Through these two studies on the visibility of communication about Europe on the Web, we have initiated exploration of Europeanization of political communication and, subsequently, development of an online European public sphere. It is through measuring visibility of political communication about Europe on diverse political actors' websites that we can say something meaningful about the extent to which a European public sphere is developing on the Web. The studies presented in this chapter, and especially the study performed by Van Os, Jankowski and Vergeer, suggest that variation exists not only between the different countries included in the study, but also between different types of actors concerning the extent to which they communicate about Europe on their websites. Therefore, this – tentative

– online European public sphere seems incomplete in a sense that both institutionalized and non-institutionalized actors are participating in it.

Second, although network analysis as an approach to analyse the Web is becoming popular, only two studies were found that investigated Europeanization of communicative interaction measured through hyperlink analysis. The focus and conclusions vary substantially: one study reports a partially 'European' network of national- and European-level actors (Zimmermann, Koopmans and Schlecht 2004); the other study notes two distinct competitive communities of mainly national actors emerging around one particular European issue (Ghitalla and Fouetillou 2005). Both studies reveal the emergence of (hyperlinked) networks of political actors on the Web, either evolving at the national level about a particular European issue, or at the pan-European level about general policy issues. This suggests some form of Europeanization of political communication and that a European public sphere is developing on the Web.

Finally, two exploratory investigations conducted by Van Os and colleagues are discussed with regard to the interpretative schemes in which political actors – in these particular studies political parties – address European issues on their websites (Van Os 2005; Van Os, Wester and Jankowski 2007). Although more research is needed, these studies provide a model for further investigation. It is through measuring the cross-national appearance of interpretative schemes in which European issues are addressed by political actors on their websites (or by the mass media) that we can obtain a more profound understanding of the way these participants in the public sphere view and feel about Europe; by discovering similarities in this online political communication about Europe, we can draw the contours of a developing European public sphere. In the studies conducted by Van Os, differences were observed in interpretative schemes and the 'portrayal' of Europe between the three countries included in the study. British parties in particular scored low on the presence of European interests and European identity in their online communication; these parties mainly mentioned national interests and a national identity frame. In contrast, some cross-national similarities in interpretative schemes in which Europe is addressed were observed among parties with a similar political orientation in France, the U.K. and the Netherlands, which is considered an indicator for Europeanization of political communication and possibly for development of a European public sphere.

The six studies presented in this chapter that examine online communication/internet-based representations of European issues are too few by far. Much more research is needed in order to assess the potential of the Web to incorporate or enhance a European public sphere. As previously mentioned, the internet is increasingly becoming an object of study in empirical investigations of the public sphere, especially because of the possibility for political actors to maintain websites as a means of direct, unfiltered communication with supporters and with the electorate at large. We have argued that, in the case of European issues and affairs, this possibility is particularly important. Not only can political actors themselves determine the extent of communication about Europe, but they can also determine the manner in which European issues are addressed, rather than being dependent on the mass media. For academic researchers, this opens up a new field of investigation. Online documents as research material are, in a sense, comparable to mass media material. Conceptual frameworks proposed in a mass-mediated environment can therefore be used in the investigation of online communication. Research is needed within all three areas discussed in this chapter: visibility of communication about Europe on the Web, the cross-national appearance of interpretative schemes in which European issues are addressed on political actors' websites, and the online structure of communication about Europe.

It seems particularly interesting to draw comparisons between the extent to which and the nature of Europeanization of political communication is becoming manifest simultaneously on the Web and in the mass media, for example during a future European event. These communicative interactions, in our opinion, all contribute to, or enhance, a single European public sphere. Through such an integrated research design studying simultaneously online and offline political communication about Europe, it becomes possible to determine whether such a single European public sphere is developing; at this moment, online and offline communicative interactions are investigated too far apart from each other. Cross-national research is of the utmost importance, as is the inclusion of more diverse EU member states – especially 'new' Eastern European member states – so that a more complete picture of 'Europe', or at least of the EU, can be obtained.

Notes

1. This discussion is – at least partially – nourished by normative demands. Scholars argue about the need for the EU to have a public sphere, and the need for political actors to address or discuss European issues and events.
2. Eder and Kantner are inspired by Habermas, who considers a public sphere 'a political public sphere which enables citizens to take positions at the same time on the same topics of the same relevance' (Habermas 1996: 190). See also Eder, Kantner and Trenz (2000) and Koopmans et al. (2004).
3. Countries included in this study are: France, Germany, Ireland, Italy, the Netherlands, Spain, Sweden and the United Kingdom.
4. Countries included in this study are: Austria, France, Germany, Italy, Spain and the United Kingdom.
5. Countries included in this study are: Austria, Belgium, Germany, France and Italy.
6. Countries included in this study are: Austria, France, Germany, Italy, Spain and the United Kingdom.
7. For a more extensive elaboration on the three frames identified by Eder, Kantner and Trenz (2000), see Van Os (2005).
8. Koopmans is coordinator of the EUROPUB project; see http://europub.wz-berlin.de for more information.
9. The EUROPUB project analyses the communication through which political actors make public demands on selected issues. A claim is defined as 'an instance of strategic action in the public sphere' (Koopmans and Erbe 2004: 98).
10. Six policy categories are included here; the category 'European integration' is excluded.
11. This text has been translated from French by the first author.

Bibliography

De Vreese, C.H. 2003. *Framing Europe: Television News and European Integration.* Amsterdam: Aksant.

Eder, K. and Kantner, C. 2000. 'Transnationale Resonanzstrukturen in Europa: Eine Kritik der Rede vom Öffentlichtkeitsdefizit', in M. Bach (ed.), *Die Europäisierung nationaler Gesellschaften*, special issue of *Kölner Zeitschrift für Soziologie und Sozialpsychologie* 40: 277–305.

Eder, K., Kantner, C. and Trenz, H.-J. 2000. *Transnationale Öffentlichkeiten und die Strukturierung politischer Kommunikation in Europa. Antrag auf Forderung eines Forschungsvorhabens im Rahmen des DFG-Schwerpunkts Regieren in Europa.*

Foot, K.A. and Schneider, S.M. 2002. 'Online Action in Campaign 2000: An Exploratory Analysis of the U.S. Political Web Sphere', *Journal of Broadcasting and Electronic Media* 46(2): 222–44.

Gavin, N.T. 2000. 'Imagining Europe: Political Identity and British Television Coverage of the European Economy', *British Journal of Politics and International Relations* 2(3): 352–73.

Gerhards, J. 1993. 'Westeuropäische Integration und die Schwierigkeiten der Entstehung einer Europäischen Öffentlichkeit', *Zeitschrift für Soziologie* 22(2): 96–110.

———. 2000. 'Europäisierung von Ökonomie und Politik und die Trägheit der Entstehung einer Europäischen Öffentlichkeit', in M. Bach (ed.), *Die Europäisierung Nationaler Gesellschaften. Sonderheft der Kölner Zeitschrift fur Soziologie und Sozialpsychologie* 40: 277–305.

Ghitalla, F., and Fouetillou, G. 2005. *Le Web et le débat sur la constitution européenne en France*. Retrieved from http://www.utc.fr/rtgi/index.php?rubrique=1andsousru brique=0andstudy=constitution.

Graham, N. 1992. 'Habermas and the Public Sphere', in C. Calhoun (ed.), *The Media and the Public Sphere*. Cambridge, MA: MIT Press.

Grimm, D. 1995. 'Does Europe Need a Constitution?', *European Law Journal* 1(3): 282–302.

Groothues, F. 2004. *Television News and the European Public Sphere: A Preliminary Investigation*. Leeds: Centre for European Political Communications.

Habermas, J. 1989. *The Structural Transformation of the Public Sphere*. Cambridge: Polity Press.

———. 1996. 'Braucht Europa eine Verfassung? Bemerkungen zu Dieter Grimm', in J. Habermas (ed.), *Die Einbeziehung des Anderen: Studien zur politischen Theorie*. Frankfurt am Main: Suhrkamp, pp. 185–91.

Hix, S. 2005. *The Political System of the European Union*, 2nd edn. Houndmills: Palgrave Macmillan.

Hodess, R.B. 1997. 'The Role of the Mass Media in European Integration: A Framework of Analysis for Political Science', *Res Publica* 39: 215–27.

Kevin, D. 2001. 'Coverage of the European Parliament Elections of 1999: National Spheres and European Debates', *Javnost – The Public* 8(1): 21–38.

Kielmansegg, P.G. 1996. 'Integration und Demokratie', in M. Jachtenfuchs and B. Kohler-Koch (eds), *Europäische Integration*. Opladen: Leske und Budrich, pp. 47–71.

Koopmans, R. and Erbe, J. 2004. 'Towards a European Public Sphere? Vertical and Horizontal Dimensions of Europeanized Political Communication', *Innovation* 17(2): 97–118.

Koopmans, R. and Pfetsch, B. 2003. *Towards a Europeanised Public Sphere? Comparing Political Actors and the Media in Germany*, ARENA Working Paper 23/03. Retrieved from http://www.arena.uio.no/publications/wp03_23.pdf.

Koopmans, R., Statham, P., Kriesi, H., Della Porta, D., De Beus, J., Guiraudon, V. et al. 2004. *The Transformation of Political Mobilisation and Communication in European Public Spheres – Preliminary Draft of End Report*, Europub.com project. Retrieved from http://europub.wz-berlin.de.

Kunelius, R. and Sparks, C. 2001. 'Problems with a European Public Sphere', *Javnost – The Public* 8(1): 5–20.

Margolis, M. and Resnick, D. 2000. *Politics as Usual: The Cyberspace Revolution*. London: Sage.

Mitra, A. and Cohen, E. 1999. 'Analyzing the Web: Directions and Challenges', in S. Jones (ed.), *Doing Internet Research: Critical Issues and Methods for Examining the Net*. Thousand Oaks, CA: Sage, pp. 179–202.

Norris, P. 2000. *A Virtuous Circle: Political Communication in Post-industrial Societies.* Cambridge: Cambridge University Press.

———. 2001. *Digital Divide: Civic Engagement, Information Poverty, and the Internet Worldwide.* Cambridge: Cambridge University Press.

———. 2003. 'Preaching to the Converted: Pluralism, Participation and Party Websites', *Party Politics* 9(1): 21–45.

Rheingold, H. 1993. *The Virtual Community: Homesteading on the Electronic Frontier.* Reading, MA: Addison-Wesley.

Risse, T. 2002. 'How Do We Know a European Public Sphere When We See One? Theoretical Clarifications and Empirical Indicators', *IDNET Workshop 'Europeanisation and the Public Sphere', European University Institute, Florence, 20–21 February.*

———. 2003. 'An Emerging European Public Sphere? Theoretical Clarifications and Empirical Indicators', *Annual Meeting of the European Union Studies Association (EUSA), Nashville, TN, March 27–30.*

Risse, T. and Van de Steeg, M. 2003. 'An Emerging European Public Sphere? Empirical Evidence and Theoretical Clarifications', *International Conference: Europeanisation of Public Spheres, Political Mobilisation, Public Communication and the European Union, Science Center Berlin, June 2–22.*

Schlesinger, P. 1996. 'The Babel of Europe? An Essay on Networks and Communicative Spaces', in D. Castiglione and C. Longman (eds), *The Public Discourse of Law and Political in Multilingual Societies.* Oxford: Hart Publishing.

———. P. 1999. 'Changing Spaces of Political Communication: The Case of the European Union', *Political Communication* 16: 263–79.

Schneider, S.M. and Foot, K.A. 2002. 'Online Structure for Political Action: Exploring Presidential Campaign Websites from the 2000 American election', *Javnost – The Public* 9(2): 43–60.

Semetko, H.A., DeVreese, C.H. and Peter, J. 2000. 'Europeanised Politics, Europeanised Media? European Integration and Political Communication', *West European Politics* 23(4): 121–42.

Thomassen, J. and Schmitt, H. 1997. 'Policy Representation', *European Journal of Political Research* 32: 165–84.

Trenz, H.-J. 2000. 'Korruption und politischer Skandal in der EU: Auf dem Weg zu einer Europäischen politischen Öffentlichkeit', in M. Bach (ed.), *Die Europäisierung nationaler Gesellschaften*, special issue of *Kölner Zeitschrift für Soziologie und Sozialpsychologie* 40: 277–305.

———. 2004. 'Media Coverage on European Governance: Exploring the European Public Sphere in National Quality Newspapers', *European Journal of Communication* 19(3): 291–319.

Van de Steeg, M. 2002. 'Rethinking the Conditions for a Public Sphere in the European Union', *European Journal of Social Theory* 5(4): 499–519.

———. 2004. *The Public Sphere in the European Union: A Media Analysis of Public Discourse on EU Enlargement and on the Haider Case.* Florence: European University Institute, Department of Political and Social Sciences.

Van de Steeg, M., Rauer, V., Rivet, S. and Risse, T. 2003. 'The EU as a Political Community: A Media Analysis of the "Haider Debate" in the European Union',

Annual Meeting of the European Union Studies Association (EUSA), Nashville TN, 27–30 March.

Van Os, R. 2005. 'Framing Europe Online: French Political Parties and the European Election of 2004', *Information Polity: An International Journal of Government and Democracy in the Information Age* 10(3–4): 205–18.

Van Os, R., Wester, F. and Jankowski, N.W. 2007. 'Presentations of Europe on Political Party Websites during the 2004 EP Election Campaign'. *Javnost - The Public,* 14(2): 63–82.

Van Os, R., Jankowski, N.W. and Vergeer, M. 2007. 'Political Communication about Europe on the Internet during the 2004 European Parliament Election Campaign in nine EU member states '. *European Societies* 9(5): 755–75.

Ward, S., Gibson, R.K. and Lusoli, W. 2003. 'Participation and Mobilisation Online: Hype, Hope and Reality', *Parliamentary Affairs* 56(3): 652–68.

Zimmermann, A. and Koopmans, R. 2003. *Political Communication on the Internet. Report WP 4 Part 1: Representative Sample of Websites,* Europub.com project. Retrieved from http://europub.wz-berlin.de.

Zimmermann, A., Koopmans, R. and Schlecht, T. 2004. *Political Communication on the Internet. Report WP 4 Part 2: Link Structure among Political Actors in Europe,* Europub.com project. Retrieved from http://europub.wz-berlin.de.

Chapter 5

Entertainmentization of the European Public Sphere and Politics

Erkki Karvonen

Introduction

Media intrusion into private lives of politicians is an internationally observed phenomenon. The British journal *Parliamentary affairs* dedicated its issue 1/2004 on this topic and editors James Stanyer and Dominic Wring wrote:

Matters once deemed personal are now widely reported and commented upon in 'quality' as well as 'populist' media formats. This has led to the boundaries that once defined the public and private being significantly redrawn. ... The transformation of the media environment inevitably changes the political nature of communication. Personality has, for instance, become a more central aspect of modern election campaigning. ... Here and elsewhere there is a growing perception that senior politicians have become the key players in kind of national (and, at times, a global) soap opera. (Stanyer and Wring 2004: 1–2)

This is what I mean by the 'entertainmentization' of the public sphere and politics. Politics is represented as a sort of entertainment or popular culture. Lilleker (2006: 69) explains that the term 'dumbing down' essentially means 'making the presentation of politics similar to that of popular culture'. Great Britain is perhaps a leading country in this. David Beacon (2004: 10) writes how media hyper-competitiveness combined with lightly regulated press, weak legal right to individual privacy, the rise of political marketing and spin make Britain one of the leading countries for media intrusion into politicians' private lives. France, Germany and Spain, for instance, are not so advanced in this transformation. Those countries have stricter regulatory framework and more deferential journalistic culture, but media practices are changing in these countries, too.

My analysis of the 'entertainmentization' of the public sphere and politics is based upon recent political happenings and their associated media uproar in Finland. The following attempts to illustrate contemporary practices in the journalistic reporting of politics and reveal the uneasy relations between politicians and journalists in modern Finland.

In April 2005 the Finnish Prime Minister, Matti Vanhanen, and his wife unexpectedly divorced. This made front-page news in all the Finnish media, including the quality newspapers. Wild speculations about the reasons for the divorce burgeoned in internet discussion groups, and soon the tabloid press also got hold of these rumours. One magazine suggested that Mr Vanhanen and the then Minister of Culture, Ms Tanja Karpela, had had a 'secret' nocturnal assignation in a hotel room six years earlier during a party conference and that this covert love story was the real cause of the ensuing divorce. Only one anonymous informant had witnessed the alleged meeting, and this provoked a debate among journalists as to whether it is professionally correct to rely on one informant, especially one with possibly malicious intentions.

However, the tabloids went into a frenzy about the 'revelation' and made an enormous issue of it. In fact, the press had its own reasons for doing so. Ms Karpela happens to have been Miss Finland 1991, and as a celebrity she had been an object of constant media interest. Moreover, some years ago Ms Karpela – then an MP – was romantically involved with another party leader and minister, Mr Sauli Niinistö. The romance was monitored on the front pages like a soap opera: 'A Surprise Romance!' – 'They are the King and Queen of Finland!' – 'Ms Karpela not Pregnant!' – 'The Affair is Over!' – 'Together Again!' – 'Peaceable Break-up!' The plot thickened as Mr Niinistö and Mr Vanhanen both became candidates of their respective parties for the presidency of Finland in 2006.

Tanja Karpela became a member of parliament in 1999 and in 2003 she was appointed a minister. At first, she had very favourable media exposure, but later the media became more critical of her. During Prime Minister Vanhanen's divorce scandal Ms Karpela felt the full fury of the media powers. She came down with an illness and her press adviser accused the press of causing the minister's health troubles. A war broke out between the minister and the media. One tabloid paper viciously attacked her, insisting that she had exploited the media and that she was completely incompetent in her office. The story was a merciless 'political character assassination'.

Ms Karpela retaliated, pointing out twenty-seven errors in the tabloid's story: she published the list of incorrect statements on her personal website. A week later one quality magazine struck back on behalf of journalism, analysing in its main story how the minister had 'spin-doctored' the media to project a positive image of her. However, there were also newspapers that defended the minister and criticized other papers for being too aggressive and judgmental. Many women viewed the case as an unjustified attack against a woman who had actually done nothing wrong and had not neglected her duties.

But this was not the end of this entertaining political show. Soon after this case the Deputy Parliamentary Speaker, Ilkka Kanerva, was upbraided for sending inappropriate SMS messages to certain young women celebrities. It seems that at least one woman was hired by a leading gossip magazine to entrap Mr Kanerva into these contacts. The issue was a favourite topic in the headlines for a week.

Only a couple of weeks later Prime Minister Vanhanen was under fire again. This time a celebrity magazine published a serial in three successive issues on an alleged extramarital affair between the Prime Minister and an anonymous woman. Again the story was based on information sourced from a single person, someone who did not want her name to be published. But what was her motivation for making her 'revelation'? Was she paid a large amount of money? This theme dominated the Finnish media agenda throughout the summer; it was a topic of discussion both in the media and among the general public. But there was more to come.

In spring 2006 Prime Minister Vanhanen was once more in the headlines of a tabloid paper. This time Mr Vanhanen's SMS message to a certain woman was made public. Indeed, the paper implied that the minister was involved with several women. It subsequently emerged that the message was the unattached Prime Minister's shy and harmless invitation to meet over a cup of coffee. Vanhanen protested to the paper, saying that it had no right to publish such a private communication, and went on to mention in his blog that he would be taking up the case with his lawyer. This proved an unwise move, as it provoked even the broadsheets and the public service television channels to make the affair their leading news item. The media interpreted Vanhanen's incautious statement as a threat and framed the affair as a question of freedom of speech. However, the majority of Finnish citizens quickly grew tired of this hullabaloo about one trivial SMS message. 'Let the Prime Minister have some minimum privacy to live a normal life,' people pronounced.

What happened then? Mr Vanhanen and the other politicians mentioned did not resign, because the uproar concerned only their private lives and there had been no misconduct in office. Mr Vanhanen refused to make public or explain his private life, insisting that this was nobody else's business. According to a Gallup poll, the great majority of the Finnish population supported Vanhanen's right to keep the details of his offstage life private. Nevertheless, Mr Vanhanen was running for the presidency of Finland and the story had a negative impact on his campaign. Devoutly religious people from rural northern areas, especially, hesitated about voting for him. This turned out to benefit another candidate, Mr Sauli Niinistö, who lost only narrowly to the incumbent candidate, President Tarja Halonen.

However, this was not the end of the story. Mr Vanhanen's ex-girlfriend, an ordinary single parent mother, published in February 2007 a kiss-and-tell type book depicting her and the PM in a romantic, intimate setting. Matti Vanhanen sued her for violation of privacy. This resulted in a court case (February 2007) which, at the time of writing, is going to the Court of Appeal. Equally and immediately after Mr Vanhanen's trial, Mr Ilkka Kanerva, now Minister of Foreign Affairs, was in deep trouble with a new series of flirtatious SMS messages sent to a young 'exotic dancer'. Needless to say, this case also caused a great deal of media interest resulting in the sacking of Mr Kanerva from his ministerial post in April 2008.

With regard to the femme fatale, Tanja Karpela? She was married to the film director and professor of film production Olli Saarela. Of course, much has already been written about 'Tanja's new love' and a couple of unfortunate revelations about her husband's life have also been published. In March 2006 the press reported that the legend of the lovely Tanja and Prime Minister Vanhanen had travelled all the way from Scandinavia to Turkey. Over a year after the brouhaha in Finland, and seven years after the alleged hotel-room assignation, the press in Turkey finally got round to reporting that there was 'a scandal and a love story going on at the top level in Finnish politics'. This detail nicely depicts the 'bardic' character of this kind of political reporting.

These examples represent tabloid journalism, which is perhaps the most conspicuous and the most influential part of contemporary journalism. The tabloid press seems to handle politicians like celebrities:

The brutal reality of the modern age is that all famous people are treated like celebrities by the mass media, whether they be a serial killer or Maureen of *Driving School* [a reality TV programme]. The newspapers and television programmes responsible for their publicity do not draw any meaningful distinction between how they are publicised. (Giles 2000: 5)

Graeme Turner (2004: 8) agrees with Giles, saying that:

Politicians, television stars, pop stars, and the latest evictee from the *Big Brother* house, all seem to be integrated into the same 'publicity regimes and fame making apparatus'... The modern celebrity then, is a product of media representation: understanding it demands close attention to the representational repertoires and patterns employed in this discursive regime.

According to Turner, the discursive regime of celebrity is defined by a number of elements. It crosses the boundary between public and the private worlds, preferring the personal, the private or 'veridical' self, as a privileged object of revelation. The entertainment industry, including the popular press, makes its living from celebrities. A good celebrity story covers the revelations of intimate lives and morally questionable actions of the protagonists. In these anecdotes, complicated issues and events are simplified and turned into personal stories in a process of personalization. From a critical perspective, these stories are full of trivia, details devoid of real social significance. (see Mckee 2005: 32–65).

In many cases, Aristotle's definition of comedy as 'the action of men worse than ourselves' is characteristic of tabloid tales; while serious drama, tragedy, is defined as 'the action of men superior to us' (Aristotle, *Poetics*, parts 2 and 5). Perhaps a significant part of our enjoyment of political scandals is the malicious pleasure felt when someone 'up there' is brought down and ridiculed. Politicians, like other celebrities, are used as raw material for the fabrication of entertaining public drama. This could be the preliminary understanding of the entertainmentization of the political public sphere. Scholars have debated entertainmentization: is it a danger for democracy or does it benefit politics by fostering citizens' participation? I will discuss this later.

Politics in the Hall of Mirrors

On the basis of the examples above one may think that Finnish political life is a soap opera rich in love affairs and adultery. If we think that the media only mirror a neutrally objective reality, then we have to conclude that the Finnish Parliament must be a veritable 'love boat'. It seems that politicians do nothing else than flirt or intrigue with each other in order to be the king of the castle. A former beauty queen elected in the general election and later appointed a minister – the fact seems to confirm that we have entered into the era of image politics in which the 'telegenic' attributes of a political candidate are what counts.

On the other hand, everyday political work is far from any kind of intimate bonding. Very few politicians get the attention of the media, and only a very small proportion of the activities of these prominent persons are sensational. Prime Minister Vanhanen, for instance, with his deliberative, calm, rational and unexciting style of communicating, is the embodiment of matter-of-fact politics. All the Finnish politicians mentioned have good reputations for their work, both in legislation and in governance. It seems as if the most visible media coverage of politics is biased. To make use of our optical metaphor, the popular media are like 'funny mirrors', giving grotesque distortions that accentuate some aspects of reality while all but concealing others.

The entertainmentization of the political public sphere may be seen as a reflection of a bizarre political reality. Politicians often provide plenty of material for the entertainment industry with some politicians acting more like films stars; as John Street (2003, 2004) has argued. This is not to excuse the media and we must keep in mind that they remain part of the problem. Understood in a social constructivist manner, the media do not only mirror politics but also create social reality. The media are players that influence society by producing representations of it in a highly selective process. In our mediatized society we rarely meet politicians or are able to participate in a plenary session of Parliament, but can only follow the representations of such people and events as created by journalists. In terms of the agenda-setting approach, media have the power to influence the salience of topics on the public agenda: 'Through their day-by-day selection and display of the news, editors and news directors focus our attention and influence our perceptions of what are the most important issues of the day' (McCombs 2004: 1). Attention is a very valuable asset in contemporary society. Davenport and Beck (2001) state that we are living in an 'attention economy', in which attention is intrinsically scarce and therefore a most valuable economic resource.

The media determine the issues that are worth our discussion, but do not necessarily dictate our opinions of them; this is a premise of the original agenda-setting theory as set out by Maxwell McCombs and Donald Shaw (1972). However, media representations also strongly suggest how to define situations and make sense of events. Agenda-setting theory is often supplemented by frame analysis: 'To frame is to select some aspects of a perceived reality and make them more salient in a communicating text, in such a way as to promote a particular problem definition, causal interpretation, moral evaluation, and/or treatment recommendation' (Entman 1993: 52). McCombs (2004: 86–97) has recently explained framing as 'second-level agenda-setting', whereas first-level agenda-setting influences what is important in the world. The media have power to structure which parts of reality become noticed and how we should understand these aspects. The tabloid press can propagate on every street corner the idea that the most important national issue of the day is an SMS message sent by the Prime Minister. In every pub and café what we should really be doing – the press suggests – is debating whether the PM has been misbehaving or not, and asking why on earth he just didn't send flowers.

Entertainmentization of Political Reporting

Many scholars have been concerned about the entertainmentization of public sphere and politics. One of the best-known writers about the changing nature of the public sphere is Neil Postman. He believes that the public sphere is degenerating and democracy is in danger: 'When a population becomes distracted by trivia, when cultural life is redefined as a perpetual round of entertainments, when serious public conversation becomes a form of baby talk, when, in short, a people become an audience and their public business a vaudeville act, then a nation finds itself at risk; culture death is a clear possibility' (Postman 1985: 5–6). The German political scientist Thomas Meyer (2002) is equally concerned:

> We must never lose sight of the fact that communication cannot fulfil its political function of democratic legitimation unless it maintains a nucleus of rationality, discussion, and reliable information; unless it is subject to argumentative accountability and capable of generating consensus. This holds true even in the media age, however much communication may have come to resemble entertainment in its quest for a wider audience. If this rational core should ever disappear from communication, it would no longer be political in the sense of promoting democratic legitimation and control … Democracy reduced to sheer entertainment ceases to be democracy. (Meyer 2002: 81)

Bob Franklin (1997) states that journalism's editorial priorities have changed:

> Entertainment has superseded the provision of information; human interest has supplanted the public interest; measured judgment has succumbed to sensationalism; the trivial has triumphed over the weighty; the intimate relationships of celebrities from soap operas, the world of sport or the royal family are judged more 'newsworthy' than the reporting of significant issues and events of international consequence. Traditional news values have been undermined by new values; 'infotainment' is rampant. (Franklin 1997: 4)

Since the late 1980s, the pressures on news media to win viewers and readers in an increasingly competitive market have generated revised editorial ambitions (Stanyer and Wring 2004:1). Franklin (1997) continues: 'News media have increasingly become a part of the entertainment industry instead of providing a forum for informed debate on key issues of public concern. Journalists are more concerned with reporting stories which interest the public than stories that are in the public interest.' Franklin characterizes this phenomenon by Malcolm Muggeridge's neologism 'Newszak' (a play on the term applied, usually pejoratively, to easy-listening background music – 'muzak').

Parliamentary reporting has also changed: 'Items discussing personal scandal or allegations of misconduct by MPs now enjoy a greater prominence in parliamentary coverage than significant areas of government policy such as health, education and law and order.' Another novel feature of parliamentary reporting is a growing trend for journalists to be highly critical in their appraisals of political events (Franklin 1997: 236, 238). We can add to this that coverage of politics is also highly personalized: 'The purveyors of political entertainment love to focus on the "personal" side of politics, especially the all-too-human weaknesses of political actors. Indeed, success stories in policy-making are always portrayed as lucky hits, while corruption is declared to be the nature of the system' (Meyer 2002: 81). On the other hand, politics itself has become more personalized. Often it seems that when all parties pitch their campaigns around appeals to the middle classes it follows that their respective messages become quite similar. Consequently personality becomes an increasingly more central aspect of modern election campaign coverage, particularly when television reinforces this with the concomitant idea that the leader of a party is the same as the 'party' itself (cf. Stanyer and Wring 2004: 2). The logic of the mass media is closely interwoven with its economic structure. The products of commercial media are first and foremost commodities, and sales figures are the essential justification of journalistic activities. The media producers have to consider if this or that subject can capture the audience's attention to maximum extent. What aspects should be highlighted in order to boost the sales figures? The media system as a whole has become more commercial and competitive. There is a process of 'tabloidization' of the news media, which means that broadsheets and other 'quality media' tend to adopt the sensational style of tabloid papers (Esser 1999; Sparks and Tulloch 2000; Turner 1999). This can mean that even tabloids have to go more downmarket and, in severe competition, are compelled to be more sensational than ever. The process of tabloidization is usually considered the sacrifice of information for entertainment and accuracy for sensation. This also means 'entertainmentization' of political reporting, or that politics becomes 'politainment', a form of popular culture (Dörner 2001).

Meyer depicts (2002: 56) how we live in a 'media democracy' and how the media has indeed colonized politics. According to Jürgen Habermas, one societal domain can colonize another and make it function according its own rules. Contemporary politics is heavily dependent on the media, which provide politicians with almost the only effective way to communicate with citizens or voters. Almost everything we know about politics is mediated by media institutions, which, however, represent political processes in a selective way and following their own logic.

In order to maximize their visibility, politicians have adapted themselves to fit in with the specific interests of the media, and in this way politics begins to follow a media logic rather than its own internal logic. If the media are interested mostly in the personal or entertaining aspects of a politician, then he or she must provide this kind of material. This process is called 'mediatization' or 'mediazation' of politics. More generally, the term 'mediatization' refers to the penetration of mass media and of their functional and operational logic into all social systems (cf. Altheide and Snow 1979).

Kent Asp and Peter Esaiasson (1996) explain that mediatization of politics in Sweden has developed in three stages:
1. In the 1960s mass media became the dominant communication channel between politicians and citizens
2. In the 1970s the media turned into independent actors who exercise great influence on governing body and the people.

3. In the 1980s political players began to adapt themselves to demands of the media. This adaptation to the needs of the media is regarded as 'spin' among journalists.

Public Sphere as Rational Debate

One of the traditional functions attributed to the mass media is to inform citizens about the public affairs of their societies (McNair 2003; Negrine 1996). However, the shift towards entertainment-based content leaves less and less room for the informative function and rational discussion. Public discourse is generally acknowledged as being an essential constituent of democratic society, whether its arena is the marketplace, the *agora* of Athens, or newspapers, radio and television, or the internet.

In his classic work (Habermas 1991, 2004), Jürgen Habermas reconstructed an ideal of a bourgeois public sphere, which was a certain kind of social space between the state and the family. In the salons and coffee houses of the eighteenth century, bourgeois citizens (adult, white, economically free men) were able to meet each other as equals and everybody had a right to speak. In these forums, citizens debated and argued about public issues in a rational and critical manner; the best argument would win in this domination-free communication. Three major features of this Enlightenment idea of rational-critical public reasoning can be identified: universal access, rational debate and a disregard of rank.

Habermas's appraisal of the contemporary public sphere is gloomy: it does not meet the high standards of the bourgeois public sphere. A debating and reasoning public has been transformed into a merely consuming audience. There has been a process of 'refeudalization' of the public sphere, which means that publicness is based on staging and the appearances of idolized 'courtiers' (now: celebrities) and not on debate that disregards rank. Now experts and civil servants make decisions on behalf of citizens. Public opinion is not formed by a reasoning public but is a result of skilful persuasion and public-relations work (Habermas 1991: 181–235).

Habermas's work has been fruitful for the discussion on the role of media in contemporary society (Curran 1991). Peter Dahlgren (1995), for instance, studies the relationship between television journalism and the public sphere. Nicholas Garnham (2004) focuses on broadcasting and argues that the public service model may be seen as the embodiment of the principles of the public sphere. John Keane (2004) proposes that we should distinguish three different sizes of public spheres: micro, meso and macro scale. Zizi Papacharissi (2004) claims that the internet now promises to revive the public sphere. Yet she points out several aspects that could curtail the democratic potential of the internet: not everyone has an internet connection; access does not guarantee participation; discussion groups are fragmented and do not provide any discussion on common issues; in many cases the internet does not foster rational discourse, but rather gives rise to emotional 'flaming' and irresponsible mischief, or 'trolling' (see also Karvonen 2004).

Habermas's theory has been found to contain a number of blind spots. He was silent on 'plebeian' – that is, popular – public spheres of informal exchange of information, gossip and rumours; he did not identify the patriarchal character of the bourgeois public sphere (Fraser 1992); and his work was restricted by the discourses of Enlightenment and Western modernity (Dahlgren and Sparks 1991: 6). Moreover, we can justly ask if there ever historically existed a bourgeois public sphere with rational-critical political discourse (Schudson 1992).

Why Shouldn't Politics Be Entertaining?

Among scholars there are also divergent approaches to the entertainmentization of the political public sphere. Tabloidization is itself a debated issue. Some scholars are critical of the modernist, elitist attitudes that glorify the educated 'high culture' discourse of broadsheet papers and despise the 'low culture' discourse of the tabloids, and which suggest that middle- or upper-class culture is superior to working-class culture (Turner 1999).

In cultural studies, it is commonplace to deconstruct this kind of hierarchical distinction between low and high cultures. Moreover, in culturally oriented media studies, the emphasis has been on the active receiver, who makes his/her own culture out of the cultural ingredients available. Accordingly, the dominant question has been 'what do people do to the media?', while the contrary question 'what do the media do to people?' has been ignored (see Katz 1959). Perhaps we should conclude that the notion of an active audience does not imply that mass communication has no influence at all. On the contrary, the media have power to frame, signify and define politics as a particular kind of activity, although we may discuss whether this effect on people's minds is conducive to democracy or not.

John Corner and Dick Pels (2003: 3–4) introduce two different approaches to changing media-politics relationship. In the 'enabling perspective' the media are conceived necessary agents of the practice of modern, popular democracy. 'Free press' enable circulation of knowledge, presentation of diverse views and critical scrutiny of those in power, and this all will act as a guarantor of political health and active citizenship. In its earliest versions, this is behind the Enlightenment or Liberal view of media-political relations. As the question of 'influence' of the media is raised at all, it is raised in a way that emphasises the potential for good.

The scholars contrast such a position with what they call the 'disabling perspective'.

In this far more familiar view, the media are seen as variously undermining the practice of democracy, or, at least, of having a strong propensity to do so. They perform their subversive function through such routes as the substitution of entertainment for knowledge, the closing off of true diversity, the pursuit of an agenda determined primarily by market factors and their susceptibility to control by government and corporate agencies. … It is the disabling view that has provided the focus for the majority of studies in political communication. The key question has been: in what ways and to what extent do the media impact negatively upon political practice? … Address to the negative rather than to the positive has provided the primary point of reference (Corner and Pels 2003: 4)

Liesbeth van Zoonen (2005) agrees with the observation that the political public sphere has become more entertaining, but she challenges the common criticism of this process. From a postmodernist feminist position, she suggests we should abandon the modernist Habermasian notion of the public sphere as rational discussion and open our minds to learn how citizens are informed, engaged and mobilized by popular culture. The behaviour of fans in relation to their favourite programmes is not fundamentally different from what is required of active citizens in a healthy democracy (Van Zoonen 2005: 16). It really seems that younger people conditioned to influence the course of a reality TV programme can also become engaged with some sort of political activism.

Instead of discarding the popular as irrelevant or dangerous to the democratic process, Van Zoonen discerns the positive opportunities of popular culture. If citizens' detachment, apathy and passiveness are the main problem of Western democracies, why not learn from popular culture where this kind of indifference is unknown? She proposes deconstruction of the distinctions between private v public, emotional v rational and personal v political. Van Zoonen studies the pejorative use of a 'soap opera' metaphor in commenting politics: she argues that 'proper' politics is defined through masculine metaphors (like battle), and that 'corrupt' politics is understood in feminine terms. Jeffrey Jones (2005) also takes the view that entertaining television programmes on politics creates positive effects for democracy.

Beyond the Postmodern Attitude?

A postmodern attitude among scholars of the political public sphere seems to be quite trendy at the moment. For instance, Alan McKee (2005) and the contributors to Corner and Pels (2003) have adopted a postmodern approach that is critical of the modernist, Habermasian vision of a public sphere.

Corner and Pels support the 'enabling' or optimistic view to media and politics. Or should we say that they are critical to the older critical paradigm of political communication research? A critique of the critique could be a negation of the negation, which equals affirmation. This stance can lead to an affirmative and completely uncritical approach to the entertainment industries. Ironically, this is not a brand new position but rather a centuries old traditional strand of classical Anglo-saxon liberalism.

Tuija Pulkkinen (2000) has analysed the underlying premises of liberalism and argues that the basic metaphor of liberal ontology is free movement of an individual: freedom is understood fundamentally as unrestricted movement of the 'body'. This notion originates from Galileo Galilei and was adopted in liberalist discourse by Thomas Hobbes. Any interference or blocking of free movement is viewed negatively as damaging of the original freedom belonging to everyone. This is why power, those in power and the state are understood as inherently bad and dubious. Political debate in terms of liberal ontology inevitably revolves around the issues of resisting power, liberating from power – getting rid of power. The media's role as a watchdog of power may be directly derived from liberalist premises. On the contrary, the historical alternative to liberalism, the tradition of German idealism views the role of the state positively. Liberalist Anglo-saxon discourses and communitarian continental discourses are competing today in the European public sphere. Liberalism seems to be in the lead in this competition.

Moreover, the strongly oppositional nature of this discourse makes it look suspicious: it seems to be even a binary opposition or antithesis of earlier leftist ('disabling') discourse. Earlier information content was emphasised, now it is style (or form) that matters. Modernism used to value Enlightenment and reason, now it is Romantic tradition with emphasis on emotion that is appreciated. Science, ethics and responsibility were central in former discourse; on the contrary art, aesthetics and freedoms are now the important aspects of life. Earlier state regulation and Marxism were worth supporting, now market liberalism and even Fascism seem to be fashionable. One can challenge the idea that such an opposition or antithesis only can be good science and former position completely useless. Rather, I prefer to understand this contribution as an introduction of new approaches and new metaphors to be used in the study of political communication.

Kevin Glynn (2000: 16) also represents the postmodern view: 'The public sphere concept thus entails problematic normative assumptions about the "irrationality" of many cultural practices and configurations external to the modern West or marginalised and dominated within it.' For Glynn (2000: 17–18), characteristics of postmodernity include:

> Increasing prioritisation of images over the real, a general instability and uncertainty regarding key modernist organisational categories (including, for example, distinctions between public and private, reality and representation), a generalised pluralisation, relativisation, and fragmentation of discourses and knowledge games; an increase in cultural products marked by stylistic eclecticism and bricolage, and growth of incredulity toward grand narratives, including those that underwrite modern claims for the universality and 'objectivity' of scientific rationalism.

According to Glynn (2000: 18), commodification of culture lies at the heart of many working definitions of postmodernity, the consequence of which is a profound destabilization of differences between 'news' and 'entertainment'. Legitimate journalism has historically been produced according to the tastes and knowledge practices of the most privileged. Tabloid journalism, on the contrary, has learned to operate according to popular tastes (i.e., it is populist). Science, among other things, is one of those 'matters of taste' (and 'there's no use arguing about taste'). The tabloid press and television are free from the rigid requirements of scientific knowledge. Thus, encounters with UFOs and humanoids are the accepted content of supermarket tabloids.

Discourses of modernity surely deserve criticism. But postmodern thinking is also problematic, which is why I am looking for some kind of post-postmodern approach. Modern thinking was based on a Cartesian-style 'Subject (consciousness) v Object (reality)' ontological dichotomy. Realism based on this distinction leads to universalism and absolutism: there is only one true description of the world. Postmodern thinking is usually rooted in a poststructuralist premise, which in turn is a certain (neo-)Kantian modulation of Cartesian dichotomy (see Grossberg 1992: 43, 47–52). In this distinction, the linguistically constituted Subject is ontologically detached from the rest of the world and is epistemologically capable of structuring the world arbitrarily. This kind of constructivism easily leads to 'anything goes' relativism: every description of the world is basically as good as another. After all, it is a matter of taste which kind of representation you prefer. The preference for different representations is resolved in power struggles between social groups. Something called 'truth' is therefore only an expression of the dominance of some coalition. Now, the mission of the social scientist is to find the alternative representations pushed to the periphery and celebrate them.

The starting point of postmodern thinking is in literature and the arts, and from this point it is extended to cover all other textualities: all of reality is textuality. Art is not evaluated on grounds of its factuality; the only criteria are its aesthetic originality and its deviation from the canon, the norms of expression. Hence, this makes sense of why 'political style' (i.e., aesthetics) is seen as the most important aspect of politics in current postmodern commentary. Norms, morals and ethics are only rules to be transgressed. When 'quality journalism' is a norm, then it is inherently something bad for a postmodernist, while maligned and disregarded tabloid journalism must be something valuable. Since 'social responsibility' is a question of ethics and rules, it does not belong to the vocabulary of postmodern discourse. Social concerns about the influence of media representations are usually ridiculed by the pejorative expression 'moral panic'. In its 'anything goes' liberalism, postmodern thinking seems to support the neo-liberalist values of unregulated trade and markets.

Ethics seem to be absent from postmodern theory, while it is strongly present in Habermasian discourse ethics. However, ethics should be acknowledged in the theory of public sphere, and human life cannot be reduced to aesthetics. Is the so-called 'circumcision' of girls only a question of taste or an interesting cultural choice? Is the pollution of the environment only a matter of taste? Does it matter if somebody insists that the Holocaust never happened and that the whole story is only a version of the winning party? Is it only an aesthetic choice to eat junk food? If your child has diabetes, is it only a matter of taste if you choose to use homeopathic baths or contact a medical doctor?

Perhaps it is not just a question of taste if marginalized people use only tabloid products and thus remain marginalized? Perhaps it does matter if, instead of relevant political information, people's minds are filled with a sort of junk information. If we care about what we eat, why don't we care about the 'nutrition' we give to our minds? And if we care about environmental issues, why don't we care about issues of our symbolic (media) environment? Who dares to say that environmental concerns are just 'moral panic'?

What kind of discourse would come after postmodern thinking? The problematic character of both modernist and postmodernist discourse derives from their underlying, excessively abstract premises concerning the nature of the Subject. They both insist that the Subject is somehow detached and separate from rest of the world, from reality. I believe that more concrete and mundane ontological and epistemological premises may help in transcending the weaknesses of these two discourses.

Such 'third way' insights may be derived from pragmatic materialism, from contextualist approaches, from the 'ontology of encounter' developed in the existential phenomenology of Martin Heidegger and Maurice Merleau-Ponty, from Donna Haraway's ideas of the situated, embodied subject, and from Evander Bradley McGilvary's idea of perspective realism (see Cherwitz and Hikins 1986), based on relational ontology. These are in line with Lawrence Grossberg's view: 'I believe it is necessary to bring "the real" back onto the agenda of cultural studies ...' (Grossberg 1992: 48). Reality could be understood as effects appearing in encountering the world practically and corporeally. The reality itself is relational but real; our knowledge of the world is perspective, because it is derived from relational effects. Most of the postmodernist ideas are still valid, but postmodernist 'anything goes' relativism is replaced by relational ontologies. The possibility of ethics and responsibility is retrieved (see Karvonen 1997; 1999a and b).

A sort of 'third way' solution for journalism could be 'public journalism' or 'civic journalism'. According to this approach, the ambition of journalism is to foster democratic life; to be a sort of midwife that helps people give birth to deliberate discussion and problem solving.

If journalism is a promoter of democracy, then it cannot be inherently hostile towards politicians as representatives of citizens. Jay Rosen is one of the earliest advocates of the public journalism movement. He defines it as follows:

> Public journalism is an approach to the daily business of the craft that calls on journalists to: (1) address people as citizens, potential participants in public affairs, rather than victims or spectators; (2) help the political community act upon, rather than just learn about, its problems; (3) improve the climate of public discussion, rather than simply watch it deteriorate; and (4) help make public life go well, so that it earns its claim on our attention. If journalists can find a way to do these things, they may in time restore public confidence in the press, re-connect with an audience that has been drifting away, rekindle the idealism that brought many of them into the craft and contribute, in a more substantial fashion, to the health of American democracy, which is the reason we afford journalists their many privileges and protections. (Rosen 1999: 22)

'Intimization' of the Public Sphere

The entertainmentization and personalization of politics mean, practically, the 'intimization' of the political public sphere. In order to depict gender positions of Western modernity, Bryan S. Turner (1984: 38) has made a useful sketch of the social and spatial separation between the public sphere and the private, intimate (secret) sphere:

PRIVATE	PUBLIC
Gemeinschaft	*Gesellschaft*
Desire	Reason
Female	Male
Informal	Formal
Affectivity	Neutrality
Particularity	Universality
Diffusion	Specificity
Hedonism	Asceticism
Consumption	Production

According to Turner, bourgeois city houses were divided into public departments, such as the salon, and private spaces such as bedrooms, kitchen, living rooms, and servants' rooms. The public part was a front stage for social life and the private part was a backstage or an offstage, which was 'none of your business'. Similarly, coffee houses were front-stage places dedicated to public reasoning. In this original bourgeois arrangement, politics was a part of the public domain: it represents masculinity, reason, universalism. In this social construction, women do not belong in politics at all. Women are represented as an antithesis of politics, belonging to the private, 'soap opera' domain.

From the feminist perspective, this bourgeois arrangement of Western modernity is unsatisfactory because women and their issues are excluded from politics and the public sphere. Many issues close to women are branded as trivial in patriarchal culture. Women were kept in the private sphere, where they were often treated badly. For instance, marital rape, wife beating and child abuse were problems that nobody could interfere in because these occurrences belonged to a ruling man's internal realm. By making public issues of these malpractices, women could share their experiences and recognize that these were not just individual problems but problems in society in generally. By publishing abuses they can be stopped (McKee 2005: 47).

But how about the case in which a woman politician's alleged love affairs were made the most important issue of the national public sphere? In this case it is hard to see any emancipatory aspects. The publicity made her political work almost impossible. Applying here Mary Douglas's view, we could say that in the modern setting a woman in politics was and still is somehow an anomaly or 'dirt'. Douglas argues that 'dirt' is something that is out of its proper place:

> We are left with a very old definition of dirt as matter out of place. This is a very suggestive approach. It implies two conditions: a set of ordered relations and a contravention of that order. Dirt, then, is never a unique, isolated event. Where there is dirt there is a system. Dirt is the by-product of a systematic ordering and classification of matter, in so far as ordering involves rejecting inappropriate elements. (Douglas 1988: 35)

From this point of view what is dirty is relative. It is not sand per se that is dirty, but sand in the wrong place or out of place:

> It is a relative idea. Shoes are not dirty in themselves, but it is dirty to place them on the dining table; food is not dirty in itself, but it is dirty to leave cooking utensils in the bedroom, or food bespattered on clothing; similarly, bathroom equipment in the drawing room, ... out-door things in-doors; upstairs things downstairs ... (Douglas 1988: 35–36)

To revert to the case of the Finnish Minister of Culture, Tanja Karpela, we can now perhaps explain something about the extraordinarily hostile (masculine) reaction she has suffered since she became a minister. Being a former beauty queen, Ms Karpela is not only a woman, but also a kind of superfeminine creature from the intimate sphere. As such, her place is preferably in the bedroom rather than at the heart of the public sphere. According to the traditional order, she is considered to be a totally improper person to be placed in the ministerial cabinet; there she is annoying 'dirt' to be cleaned up.

Yet Ms Karpela has a university degree, and other politicians as well as 'cultural people' evaluate her political achievements to be better than average. She is a single parent of two young children. Other female ministers in the Finnish government have coped better with the media than Ms Karpela. A woman politician always meets conflicting demands: on the one hand she has to adopt attributes of the masculine public sphere, while on the other she cannot compromise her womanhood (Van Zoonen 2005: 73).

Karen Ross (2002: 17) also remarks that there are normative assumptions about the 'place' of women in society. Due to this, 'women have to spend a lot of campaign time presenting themselves as 'serious politicians'... For men, this is not an issue which they need to confront' (Ross 2002: 17). Women 'need to convince a traditional polity that they are competent as politicians *despite* their gender, not *because* of it' (Ross 2002: 43). In Ross's interview, many women MPs reported that they have been reduced to their basic sexuality and rumoured by male colleagues to be having affairs in order to achieve success (Ross 2002: 50).

Another interesting observation can be made from the private v public binary oppositions listed above. A traditional broadsheet or quality paper typically represents the public area, whereas tabloid papers represent the private area (common gossip to discuss, emotions, sex, personal experiences). Now, the right column attributes that used to characterize the public sphere are, in contemporary media publicness, being replaced more and more by the left column attributes of the private, intimate sphere. It seems that the public sphere has become more intimate.

A further point concerns Tönnies's classic sociological distinction *Gemeinschaft* v *Gesellschaft*. Crudely, *Gemeinschaft* refers to village-like community, where each member knows the others' business all too well, due to informal face-to-face communication or gossiping. The moral pressure for uniformity is high in such a small community. By contrast, *Gesellschaft* represents urban city life, in which inhabitants are not familiar with others' affairs. Everybody can engage in whatever they want; the moral pressure is low. Most contemporary urban people actually live in *Gesellschaft*. Now, it seems that celebrity (gossip) magazines are creating for us a kind of virtual village populated by celebrities. We do not know each other's business, but we certainly know and chat about the private lives of celebrities. And with help of the tabloids, we can disapprove of the moral weaknesses of celebrities and politicians. With notable rewards, magazines encourage us to be 'denouncers', watchers, informants of what celebrities do in restaurants, and so on. Mobile phones with cameras are very useful for this celebrity-spotting. Interestingly, the monitoring of celebrities has a parallel phenomenon in contemporary society, namely reality TV programmes like *Big Brother*, which are based on observation.

The Celebritization of Politics

The reporting of politics seems to become more entertaining regardless of how we evaluate it. This process of entertainmentization could also be understood as the 'celebritization' of politics (Turner 2004). Politicians are treated in the media like celebrities.

According to Turner, the discursive regime of celebrity is defined by a number of elements. It crosses the boundary between the public and private worlds, preferring the personal, the private or 'veridical' self, as a privileged object of revelation. However, Turner remarks that there is a certain difference between a public figure and a celebrity:

> We can map a precise moment a public figure becomes a celebrity. It occurs at the point at which media interest in their activities is transferred from reporting their public role (such as their specific achievement in politics or sport) to investigating the details of their private lives. Paradoxically, it is most often the high profile achieved by their public activities that provides the alibi for this process of 'celebritisation'. (Turner 2004: 8)

Turner (2004: 9) defines celebrity as follows: 'Celebrity, then, is a genre of representation and a discursive effect; it is a commodity traded by the promotions, publicity, and media industries that produce these representations and their effects; and it is a cultural formation that has a social function we can better understand.' Turner concurs with Marshall, who states that celebrities have become one of the key places where cultural meanings are negotiated and organized (Marshall 1997: 72–73). According to Turner, the salience of celebrities reflects an ontological shift in contemporary culture (Turner 2004: 5–6).

Daniel Boorstin had already noticed in the early 1960s the rise of celebrity culture as a symptom of cultural change (Boorstin 1962).

Boorstin did not use term the 'postmodern culture' but later scholars have traced back the beginning of this era to the end of the 1950s or the early 1960s (Jameson 1991). Boorstin (1962: 57) defined 'celebrity' tautologically in his *The Image*: 'The celebrity is a person who is known for his well-knownness'. Boorstin made a distinction between 'celebrity' and 'hero', explaining that the first is merely a known 'face', but the latter has really done a heroic deed.

Battlefield of Publicity

Politicians, among other public figures, are potential raw material for the media industry. In a 'mediated society' media publicity is the only effective way to reach citizens (and voters), and that is why politicians are desperately seeking media exposure. Politicians prefer serious media, but they do not despise entertaining television programmes because they provide them with an easy way to present themselves as belonging to the ordinary people (i.e., not belonging to the alienated members of the elite). Just like celebrities, politicians have to be paradoxically 'ordinary' and 'special' at the same time (cf. Van Zoonen 2005: 83).

Entertaining publicity also enables contact with the people who are not interested in politics or social issues. In the case of artists, revelation of private life events is the cost that the artist has to pay if he/she would like to get publicity for his/her newest release. Politicians can also live in symbiosis with the media – although this relationship can rapidly change from mutualism to predation or parasitism. Political journalism is one of the most critical (or even cynical) breeds of journalism, since journalists are accentuating their integrity or detachment.

Seen from the journalistic side, politicians always seek free publicity in order to market themselves, and because of this journalists have to protect their integrity as much as possible. Politicians are eager for sympathetic publicity, but when the time comes to report negative aspects of their actions they protest vociferously. In many cases, politicians try to accuse journalists of biased reporting. Political parties have hired public-relations professionals to hide the regrettable aspects of their activities and to manipulate media coverage in order to make the public favourable towards the dubious plans of the ruling elite (as with the Iraq war). This activity is often called 'media management', 'news management', 'information management' or (pejoratively) 'image building', 'spin' and 'propaganda' (e.g. Franklin 1994; Jones 1996; McNair 2003). Journalists, on the contrary, try to find out and tell the truth. Journalism is the watchdog of those in power, and freedom of expression is a guarantee of democracy against autocracy and dictatorship.

However, seen from the political side, journalism or media do not appear so 'truthful', 'unbiased', 'full' or 'fair' – to use John Merrill's (1997) encapsulation of the ethical principles of journalism. Nor does journalism tell the essential, relevant societal facts necessary for the well-informed citizen to make wise decisions. Instead, it seems that the greater part of journalistic activity seeks out the negative or entertaining aspects of politics in order to maximize circulation. Good news is no news. Journalism is often focused on the irrelevant details of the private lives of politicians. Journalism seems to react in an allergic way. It is known that allergies develop when our immune defence system does not have proper microbes to fight against. When there is a lack of real enemies, the immune system makes harmless particles into its enemy. In a similar fashion, real maladies are not available every day for journalism to attack; thus quite harmless things are trumpeted as great news.

Journalism also indoctrinates citizens to view politics from the outsider's position, encouraging them to observe it as a horse race or as a battle of political gladiators. Freedom of expression is, of course, an important standard in Western liberal democracy, but protection of privacy is also a guiding principle in the liberal tradition; in many cases, both principles are expressed in the constitutions of European countries. Granted, it is important to monitor the powerful, which is why the media, acting as the Fourth Estate, have somehow to be looked after.

Moreover, politics was not the house that began the 'rearmament' race of information management. Rather, politics was forced to hire PR professionals to counter the tendency of some elements of the media to represent politicians as negative character types or to engage in 'political character assassinations' (Turner 2004: 132). To sum up: from the politician's view, it is journalism that is not acting in a responsible way.

These uneasy relations between politics and news media are analysed in Karen Ross's (2002) empirical study based on interviews with women politicians in the U.K., Australia and South Africa. According to Ross:

> Women politicians themselves are very clear that the way in which politics is reported has changed over time, and certainly not for the better in their almost unanimous view. In general, women from all three case studies were very negative about how the news media choose to portray politics, the political process, and politicians more generally, with a broad consensus among women from all political colours that the media has become depressingly tabloid, …

that political speeches and policy positions are constantly filtered through a journalistic lens which seems intent on 'dumbing down' to the lowest common denominator soundbite. (Ross 2002: 69)

Women parliamentarians suggested that the media are only interested in sensation instead of reporting what was said in Parliament. The media have now 'much greater interest in the sex lives of politicians' (Ross 2002: 70). Investigative journalism seems to be almost completely preoccupied with the disclosure of scandal (see Arja Alho 2004; Alho is a Finnish woman parliamentarian and former minister, forced to resign due to a political scandal).

The women politicians in Ross's study reported that almost the only way for backbenchers to get any publicity is to take a line which is against their own party:

> The media are always looking for an angle, a story and therefore the way in which they report is to sensationalise everything that comes up … They want spicy stories. So whatever you say, it's not enough to make good points. You must be prepared to say inflammatory things, to rant and rave, before you'll get column inches. (Hilary Armstrong, Labour MP, U.K., quoted in Ross 2002: 72)

Another U.K. parliamentarian said that the danger with the media is twofold: the first is sheer triviality and the second is hype:

> Media's idea of a good discussion is one Labour person there saying that the Tories are rubbish, one Tory person there saying that Labour is rubbish but not actually a discussion of the issue. But hype is even worse than triviality. I find my own comments are very frequently hyped into something which is utterly unrecognisable. (Ann Widdecombe, Conservative MP, U.K., quoted in Ross 2002: 70)

In the Finnish case described above, the press vehemently attacked Minister Tanja Karpela, insisting that she had spin-doctored and exploited the media. Consequently, we are bound to wonder: which is exploiting the other – journalism or politics? Ms Karpela certainly had a seller's market position in relation to the media, while rank-and-file MPs are in a buyer's market position. MPs have to work hard to get any publicity in the media and they have to take all they can get. The setting changes when a politician becomes a minister or party leader: this means that he or she will be able to pick and choose whom to give interviews to. The same is true in the case of celebrity politicians. When Ms Karpela became a minister, she became an extremely desirable object for the media for those two reasons. It is claimed that about two hundred journalists were queuing to get an interview with her after her inauguration. Of course, the minister give preference to some representatives of the media above others and in this way she was powerful. But in accusing her, the media blamed her for being all too attractive an object that could not be resisted.

Media management or 'spin' is a controversial issue. As scholars, we should not take sides too readily between journalism and politics (cf Beacon 2004: 22). Both of these parties view themselves as the genuine representatives of the people, and see no faults in their own activity, but blame the other side. It is better to adopt a more sociological view and try to give voice to both the competing powers in the arena of the public sphere. Moreover, we should not forget to ask how citizens themselves signify the issue of political public sphere – and its evident entertainmentization.

Conclusion

The media constitute an essential part of the European public sphere. Of course, internet newsgroups and blogs, as well as real life face-to-face discussions, are important, but still the commercial media dominate the public sphere or public spheres. The most visible part of the media is the tabloid press with its entertainment values. One problem is that these media nowadays have so much agenda-setting power that they can dominate the whole public sphere. Entertainment is undeniably needed, but perhaps it should not become the main substance of public sphere. Instead of eating the main course first and then dessert, we now have dessert and sweeties all the time. Are we, then, living in a tabloid democracy?

The media can focus our attention on, and influence our perceptions of, what are the most important issues of the day. Due to the media's commercial interests, however, the most important topics tend to be revelations about the private lives of celebrities. Politicians, too, are now treated as celebrities. Is entertainmentization corrupting serious public discussion and democracy or, on the contrary, does it support democracy? This is what we have discussed here. The focus has been on the journalistic reporting of politics and the troubled relations between politicians and journalists.

Viewed theoretically from the Habermasian, modernist perspective, the processes of entertainmentization, tabloidization, trivialization, celebritization, personalization and so on. processes are devastating rational-critical discussions of common significant issues. However, from the feminist viewpoint, this arrangement of private sphere v public sphere of Western modernity is unsatisfactory, because women and their issues are excluded from politics and the public sphere. Many issues close to women were branded as trivial in patriarchal culture and women were kept in the private sphere, where they were often treated very badly. Making these 'trivial' issues public has led to an emancipatory process. Another question considered above was: does any published private detail bring about this positive effect?

The modernist conception of public sphere is also challenged from the postmodern view. If citizens' detachment, apathy and passiveness are the main problem of Western democracies, why not learn from popular culture, where such a lack of interest is unknown? Legitimate journalism has historically been produced according to the tastes and knowledge practices of the most privileged. By contrast, tabloid journalism has learned to operate according to popular, and populist, tastes. In this way, tabloidization and entertainmentization can be regarded as a positive development.

However, one could criticize postmodern discourse, which has its starting point in literature and the arts, and from where it has extended to cover all other textualities. Art is not evaluated on grounds of its factuality, but the only criteria are its aesthetic originality and its deviation from the canon, the norms of expression. As a norm, 'quality journalism' is inherently something bad for postmodernism, while oppressed and disregarded tabloid journalism must be something valuable. Aesthetic premises lead to 'anything goes' relativism and the absence of ethics, and 'social responsibility' of the press.

Therefore 'third way' approaches were proposed. From the premises of contextualism or perspective realism, most of the postmodernist ideas remain valid, but postmodernist relativism is replaced by relational ontologies. The possibility of ethics and responsibility is retrieved. The media can be understood as an environmental issue. There are indeed signs that activism critical of the media is developing among citizens.

Political reporting can be seen from different angles. We have seen that journalists and politicians have radically differing opinions of the state of current political reporting. Both sides viewed themselves as genuine representatives of the people and blame the competing partner. Politicians evaluated the press very critically, but we seldom hear about this critique because, after all, journalists are the gatekeepers of publicity. Perhaps it is helpful to let both of the competing powers have a say and try to support dialogue.

As a 'third way' solution for journalism, 'public journalism' was introduced. According to this approach, the ambition of journalism is to foster democratic life, and therefore it cannot be inherently hostile towards politicians as representatives of the people.

Bibliography

Alho, A. 2004. 'Silent Democracy, Noisy Media', Ph.D. dissertation. University of Helsinki, Department of Sociology. Retrieved from http://ethesis.helsinki.fi/julkaisut/val/sosio/vk/alho/silentde.pdf.

Altheide, D.L. and Snow, R.P. 1979. *Media Logic*. London and Beverly Hills, CA: Sage.

Asp, K. and Esaiasson, P. 1996. 'The Modernization of Swedish Campaigns: Individualization, Professionalization and Mediazation', in D.L. Swanson and P. Macini (eds), *Politics, Media and Modern Democracy*. Westport, Conn: Praeger.

Beacon, D. 2004. 'Politicians, Privacy and Media Intrusion in Britain', *Parliamentary Affairs* 57 (1): 9–23.

Boorstin, D.J. 1962. *The Image. Or What Happened to the American Dream*. New York: Atheneum.

Cherwitz, R.A. and Hikins, J.W. 1986. *Communication and Knowledge: An Investigation in Rhetorical Epistemology*. Columbia: University of South Carolina Press.

Corner, J. and Pels, D. (eds). 2003. *Media and the Restyling of Politics: Consumerism, Celebrity and Cynicism*. London, Thousand Oaks, CA and New Dehli: Sage.

Curran, J. 1991. 'Rethinking the Media as a Public Sphere', in P. Dahlgren and C. Sparks (eds), *Communication and Citizenship: Journalism and the Public Sphere in the New Media Age*. London and New York: Routledge.

Dahlgren, P. 1995. *Television and the Public Sphere: Citizenship, Democracy and the Media*. London: Sage.

Dahlgren, P. and Sparks, C. (eds). 1991. *Communication and Citizenship: Journalism and the Public Sphere in the New Media Age*. London and New York: Routledge.

Davenport, T.H. and Beck, J.C. 2001. *The Attention Economy: Understanding the New Currency of Business*. Boston, MA: Harvard Business School.

Dörner, A. 2001. *Politainment: Politik in der medialen Erlebnisgesellschaft*. Frankfurt am Main: Suhrkamp.

Douglas, M. 1988. *Purity and Danger: An Analysis of the Concepts of Pollution and Taboo*. London: ARK.

Entman, R.M. 1993. 'Framing: Toward Clarification of a Fractured Paradigm', *Journal of Communication* 43(4): 51–58.

Esser, F. 1999. 'Tabloidisation of News: A Comparative Analysis of Anglo-American and German Press Journalism', *European Journal of Communication* 14: 3.

Franklin, B. 1994. *Packaging Politics: Political Communications in Britain's Media Democracy*. London: Edward Arnold.

———. 1997. *Newszak and Newsmedia*. London: Arnold.

Fraser, N. 1992. 'Rethinking the Public Sphere: A Contribution to the Critique of Actually Existing Democracy', in C. Calhoun (ed.), *Habermas and the Public Sphere*. Cambridge, MA and London: The MIT Press.

Garnham, N. 2004. 'The Media and the Public Sphere', in F. Webster (ed.), *The Information Society Reader*. London and New York: Routledge; originally published in N. Garnham, *Capitalism and Communication*. London: Sage, 1990.

Giles, D. 2000. *Illusions of Immortality: A Psychology of Fame and Celebrity*. London: Macmillan.

Glasser, T. (ed.). 1999. *The Idea of Public Journalism*. New York: Guilford Press.

Glynn, K. 2000. *Tabloid Culture: Trash Taste, Popular Power, and the Transformation of American Television*. Durham, NC: Duke University Press.

Grossberg, L. 1992. *We Gotta Get Out of this Place: Popular Conservatism and Postmodern Culture*. New York and London: Routledge.

Habermas, J. 1991. *The Structural Transformation of the Public Sphere*. Cambridge, MA: The MIT Press. Originally published in 1962 as *Strukturwandel der Öffentlichkeit*.

———. 2004. 'The Public Sphere', in F. Webster (ed.), *The Information Society Reader*. London and New York: Routledge. Originally published in *New German Critique* 3 (Fall), 1974.

Jameson, F. 1991. *Postmodernism; or, The Cultural Logic of Late Capitalism*. Durham, NC: Duke University Press.

Jones, J.P. 2005. *Entertaining Politics: New Political Television and Civic Culture*. Lanham, MD: Rowman & Littlefield.

Jones, N. 1996. *Soundbites and Spin Doctors: How Politicians Manipulate the Media – and Vice Versa*. London: Indigo.

Karvonen, E. 1997. *Imagologia. Imagon teorioiden esittelyä, analyysiä, kritiikkiä* [Imagology. Presentation of Public Image Theories: An Analysis and Critique], Acta Universitatis Tamperensis 544. Tampere, Finland: University of Tampere. Main ideas available in English: http://www.uta.fi/~tierka/centrid.htm.

———. 1999a. *Elämää mielikuvayhteiskunnassa. Imago ja maine menestystekijöinä myöhäismodernissa maailmassa* [Living in the Image Society. Public Image and Reputation as Key Factors to Success]. Helsinki: Gaudeamus. Main ideas available in English: http://www.uta.fi/~tierka/centrid.htm.

———. 1999b. 'Perspektiivinen realismi – parempi perusta kansalaisjournalismille?' [Perspective Realism: A Stronger Foundation for Public Journalism?]. *Tiedotustutkimus* [The Finnish Journal for Mass Communication Research] 27(2): 44–59. Abstract available in English: http://www.uta.fi/~tierka/perspect.htm.

————. 2004. 'Introduction' to Part 7: 'Democracy', in F.Webster (ed.), with the assistance of R. Blom, E. Karvonen, H. Melin, K. Nordenstreng and E. Puoskari, *The Information Society Reader*. London and New York: Routledge.

Katz, E. 1959. 'Mass Communications Research and the Study of Popular Culture', *Studies in Public Communication* 2: 1–6.

Keane, J. 2004. 'Structural Transformation of the Public Sphere', in F. Webster (ed.), *The Information Society Reader*. London and New York: Routledge. Originally published in *Communication Review* 1(1), 1995.

Lilleker, D.G. 2006. *Key Concepts in Political Communication*. London etc.: Sage.

Marshall, P.D. 1997. *Celebrity and Power: Fame in Contemporary Culture*. Minneapolis: University of Minnesota Press.

McCombs, M. 2004. *Setting the Agenda: The Mass Media and Public Opinion*. Cambridge: Polity Press.

McCombs M.E. and Shaw, D.L. 1972. 'The Agenda-setting Function of Mass Media', *Public Opinion Quarterly* 36: 176–87.

McKee, A. 2005. *The Public Sphere: An Introduction*. Cambridge: Cambridge University Press.

McNair, B. 2003. *An Introduction to Political Communication*. London: Routledge.

Merrill, J. 1997. *Journalism Ethics: Philosophical Foundations for News Media*. New York: St. Martin's Press.

Meyer, T. with Hinchman, L. 2002. *Media Democracy: How the Media Colonize Politics*. Cambridge: Polity.

Negrine, R. 1996. *The Communication of Politics*. London and Thousand Oaks, CA: Sage.

Papacharissi, Z. 2004. 'The Virtual Sphere: The Internet as a Public Sphere', in F. Webster (ed.), *The Information Society Reader*. London and New York: Routledge.

Postman, N. 1985. *Amusing Ourselves to Death: Public Discourse in the Age of Show Business*. London: Methuen.

Pulkkinen, T. 2000. *The Postmodern and Political Agency*. Jyväskylä: SoPhi, University of Jyväskylä.

Rosen, J. 1999. 'The Action of the Idea: Public Journalism in Built Form', in *The Idea of Public Journalism*. New York: Guilford Press, pp. 21–48.

Ross, K. 2002. *Women, Politics, Media: Uneasy Relations in Comparative Perspective*. Cresskill, NJ: Hampton Press.

Schudson, M. 1992. 'Was There Ever a Public Sphere? If So, When? Reflections on the American Case', in C. Calhoun (ed.), *Habermas and the Public Sphere*. Cambridge, MA and London: The MIT Press.

Sparks, C. and Tulloch, J. (eds). 2000. *Tabloid Tales*. Boulder, CO: Rowman and Littlefield.

Stanyer, J. and Wring, D. 2004. 'Public Images, Private Lives: An Introduction', *Parliamentary Affairs* 57(1).

Street, J. 2003. 'The Celebrity Politician: Political Style and Popular Culture', in J. Corner and D.Pels (eds), *Media and the Restyling of Politics. Consumerism, Celebrity and Cynicism*. London, Thousand Oaks, New Delhi: Sage Publications.

Street, J. 2004. 'Celebrity Politicians: Popular Culture and Political Representation', *The British Journal of Politics and International Relations* 6: 435–52.

Turner, B.S. 1984. *The Body and Society: Explorations in Social Theory.* Oxford and New York: Basil Blackwell.

Turner, G. 1999. 'Tabloidisation, Journalism and Possibility of Critique', *International Journal of Cultural Studies* 2: 1.

———. 2004. *Understanding Celebrity.* London: Sage.

Van Zoonen, L. 2005. *Entertaining the Citizen: When Politics and Popular Culture Converge.* Boulder, CO: Rowman and Littlefield.

Chapter 6

A European Model of the Public Sphere: Towards a Networked Governance Model

Cristiano Bee and Valeria Bello

Introduction

In the last decade, the development of the globalizing phenomenon has threatened the political life of the modern nation state, which has become incapable of managing inside its boundaries all those problems arising in an ever more interdependent world. Indeed, particularly in the economic sector, the mechanisms through which modern societies have exercised political control over economic constraints have been inhibited by the centres of private economic power that dominate the global market.

In this context, the European Union (EU) has been considered a new kind of institutional entity organizing the socio-political space, which could be able to face the problems arising from both external and internal events through the interdependence and the cooperation among its member states. Following the developments that have concerned the EU and its order in these years, sociological theories have tried to clarify both the possibilities and necessities of this new political dimension represented by the EU. In this, different sociological theories have focused their attention on the issue of the public sphere these have followed Habermas's efforts to level out the principle of shared interests from a universalistic point of view and the modern form of pluralism, in order to find a solution to the main concerns linked to the phenomena of the postmodern era.

However, the solutions proposed are as widely diverse as the basic perspectives on the context in which the EU operates are disparate. Most authors, starting from different approaches to the question, indeed consider the EU system, as it currently functions, as a risk to the democratic life of the European member states for different reasons. Scharpf, for example, begins from the viewpoint that the political capacity of the European member states to shape the destiny of their own communities has been impaired by both the economic interdependence of the globalized world and the context created by the European integration process (Scharpf 1994). This threatens the consistency of their democratic processes because the process of policymaking should be the result of the real manifestation of the people's will. It is obvious, however, that the policies adopted cannot satisfy and represent the will of all the members of the European community. Nonetheless, thanks to the collective identity inside a country, the concerns of individuals about their own personal interests are overcome by the solidarity between the members of the community (Scharpf 1998).

In response to the problems menacing the democratic life of communities, Habermas developed the concept of 'deliberative democracy', which is conceived to represent a bridge between the input and output-oriented legitimizing arguments (Habermas 1996). The idea is that specific input-oriented procedures would provide for qualitatively adequate output-oriented results. According to the Habermas school of thought, this goal could be achieved by adjusting the stream of communications and discourses that derive from the different options and formations of will. The consequent decisions reached – even if possibly fallible and imperfect – have a presumption of reasonableness and consistency. This solution to the difficulties faced by the democratic life of communities in the era of interdependence and globalization is one that aims at the construction of a public sphere that should exist not only at a national level but also at a European one.

A European public sphere thus seems to be needed to solve the question posed to democracy by the consensual system of the EU. In any case, Scharpf, who is one of the main critics of the EU system on this point, considers that deliberative democracy could certainly be theoretically a solution but it requires very sophisticated public debates on both an ethical and an intellectual level, in order to avoid a descent into populist attitudes by governments. Nevertheless, this would mean that public debates should be dedicated and engaged only for small elites of philosopher-kings (Scharpf 1998). What Scharpf argues is that, in reality, politically-oriented debates are filtered and manipulated by the media.

The Habermasian reply to Scharpf's arguments is that it is not correct to talk about a democratic deficit in the EU, as European governance rests on a different kind of legitimacy, both of a direct and indirect type. Moreover, the same discourse on the democratic deficit of the EU is part of this emerging public sphere in the European Union.

The debate on the European public sphere has thus recently achieved a new prominence in the sector of studies concerning the European integration process. It is worth saying that it is part of a wider debate regarding the relationship between the EU and its citizens, which has become crucial since the middle of the 1970s and 1980s, when documents such as the *Tindemans Report on the Future of the Union* and the *Adonnino Report on the Citizens' Europe* were published. Moreover, the institution of a European citizenship, the first measures on Social Europe and the constitution of policies in areas such as education, culture, information and communication could be considered crucial for forging this relationship between the EU and its citizens (Goddard, Llobera and Shore 1994). Furthermore, as Cris Shore (2000: 26) underlines, the EU has developed a system of agents of consciousness with the clear aim of reinventing a European identity.

In this context, the concept of the public sphere is important as 'a precondition for the realisation of popular sovereignty because, in principle, it entitles everybody to speak without limitations, whether on themes, participation, questions, time or resources' (Eriksen 2004: 1). The question of the public sphere is important, as Calhoun argues, because it enables participation in collective choice; it allows for the production, reproduction or transformation of a 'social imaginary' and it is a medium of social integration, a form of social solidarity, as well as an arena for debating with others (Calhoun 2003: 1).

Leaving behind theories which tend to derive the basis of the EU from a common identity and a common space, in this article we will try to focus our attention on the salience of networks in Europe, with particular attention to the principles of network governance made by the European Commission.

After having briefly discussed the importance of the concept of the public sphere and given some insights gained from the very broad literature, we offer an overview of the most recent contributions which have considered the development of the European public sphere, showing how this concept is directly related to such questions as European identity, the formulation of a European *demos* and issues of belonging and citizenship within the European space. An overview of these issues allows us to go a step further and to conceive of such a space as a networked space, insofar as it seems not possible to develop a structure similar to that of the nation state. This is developed alongside an analysis of the multilevel structure of the EU, looking at those authors who have recently considered it as an entity formed by different networks, constituting the European publics, which at different levels and with different possibilities of influence cooperate with the European institutions. This leads us to argue that there is a convergence between the literature advocating the idea of Europe as networked space and what the Commission has been doing over the last few years in the area of information and communication policy. In order to create a communicative space, a networked structure of the public sphere has been developed, composed by different actors such as civil-society organizations, relays, media infrastructures, and so on, which interact with different institutions not only at the EU but also national, regional and local levels.

Public Sphere and Spheres of Publics

The principal assumptions on the concept of the public sphere have been made by Habermas (1989, 1996), who considers the concept as an arena within which a set of ideas, opinions and public concerns are discussed and developed through a deliberative process, which should gradually produce consent over time.

The concept of the public sphere would thus be inclusive, as everyone should be able to participate and interact together in a debate. This is underlined also by Eriksen and Fossum (2002: 403), who describe the public sphere as a 'precondition for realising popular sovereignty'. Following this, it can be affirmed that one of the main features of this social construct is that it would allow everybody, without any limitations, to express questions of public concern insofar as it is assured by the basilar principles of democracy. This possibility is given by the guarantee of legal rights such as the freedom of expression and association. It is a common space of free discussion where some problems of public concern are uncovered and debated but also concretely realized; thus, political institutions have to take into consideration the results of such processes of deliberation.

Calhoun underlined another important aspect, taking into account the function that the public sphere assumes when it is considered as 'a setting for communication and participation in collective action that can shape identities and interests, not only reflect them' (Calhoun 2003: 252). As the contributions of some important scholars belonging to the constructivist theory show (e.g. Anderson 1996; Deutsch 1994; Gellner 1997), shaping identities within a political arena is fundamental in order to develop a sense of belonging to a community.

The role of social communication (Deutsch 1994) and the role of education (Gellner 1997) are fundamental for forging national entity – for allowing all the people who belong to a certain geographical area to imagine themselves as a nation (Anderson 1996). From these considerations, the main source of alienation derives from being excluded from a particular political system and its structure, composed by means of communication, and its cultural, social and educational system, as Calhoun (2003) argues. This has also been remarked upon by Nancy Fraser who argues that the concept of the public sphere allows us 'to study the social construction of social problems and social identities… The idea of the public sphere enables us to study the ways in which culture is embedded in social structure and affected by social relations of domination' (Fraser 1995: 287). In her model, Fraser stresses the necessity of stimulating participation through the elimination of social inequalities, allowing the development of multiple publics – even opponents – and creating the space for the inclusion of different interests and issues.

These statements are fundamental to bear in mind when we consider the transformations of the concept and the model of public sphere in a transnational context.

The European Public Sphere

A central question investigated by different authors (Calhoun 2003; Eriksen 2004; Schlesinger and Kevin 2000; Schlesinger 2003; Trenz and Eder 2004; Van de Steeg 2002; Bee *et al.* 2008) is about the relevance and possibility of the existence of a public sphere that transcends the structure of nation states and assumes a new transnational or post-national character. A crucial point, for example, has been made by Philip Schlesinger and Deirdre Kevin (2000: 209) when they try to answer the following question: 'is a sphere of publics that is distinct from those of the member states actually emerging at a European level?' In other words, can we speak about a European communicative space, and, if so, how is it structured?

Hence, the debate on the consequences for the democratic life of the different communities inside the EU is strictly linked to the question of identity. Some who are convinced that there is a problem concerning the legitimacy of EU decision-making based this thesis on the absence in the context of the EU of the solidarity that would allow decisions to be reinforced by output-oriented legitimacy (Scharpf 1999; Bellamy and Castiglione 2000b).

The major problem for the foundation of the European *demos* is considered to be the existence of autonomous sources of power, which challenge the development of a strong European citizenship and identity. Indeed, people still identify more with nationally or regionally controlled bodies. Thus, what they propose is 'the development of the mechanism of identification, participation and representation offered by political constitutionalism' (Bellamy and Castiglione 2000a: 11). Constitutionalism is considered to be able to allow the functioning of a political system even if the interested groups do not share other values apart from a belief in the same system as a public good (Bellamy and Castiglione 1996).

It is important to stress that the question of a European public has been a question of academic debate for a long time, with some arguing that what is missing within the European space is a bond between peoples and institutions. The main exponent of the so-called 'no *demos* thesis' is Dieter Grimm, who affirms: 'What exactly obstructs democracy is accordingly not the lack of cohesion of Union citizens as a people, but their weakly developed collective identity and low capacity for trans-national discourse. This certainly means that the European democracy deficit is structurally determined' (Grimm 1995: 297). The lack of possibility of a European public emerging, together with a weak sense of collective identification between Europeans, produces the European democratic deficit.

On the other hand, the counter thesis, developed by Habermas (1999), considers the development of a European *demos* as the result of a process of European constitutionalism, through a configuration of strong citizenship (cf. La Torre 1998), a sense of civic solidarity (cf. Rusconi 1999) between European citizens and a form of political identification with the European structure. To some extent, we could say that Habermas's idea is related to Durkheim's conclusions, which argued that 'among European people there is a tendency to form, by spontaneous movement a European society which has, at present, some idea of itself and the beginning of organisation' (Durkheim 1960: 405). The Constitution process is just the major realization of community organization and the main expression of shared civic values among people, this latter being the way through which a *demos* – the membership of a political community – expresses its collective conscience, the representation of itself. This allows us to say that a form of community in Europe could exist, at least in a dimension of citizenship, which involves both the formal question of a status conferred by the state – as mentioned in the liberal-pluralist discourse – and the substantive aspect of participation indicated by the neo-republican tradition.

However, if the concept of participation is considered to be linked to the decision-making process along the lines of the framework set out in the *Social Contract* of Rousseau, it presently also takes the form of a discursive democracy in the so-called public sphere (Habermas 1996; but cf. Arendt 1988). Thus, on the one hand, thanks to the likely realization of a European Constitution, the question 'Is there a European Society?' (Delanty 1998) – which in Delanty's view is most definitively negative – could be transformed in a real fact, as Habermas suggested (Habermas 1999). On the other hand, the existence of a European public sphere could offer the feature of substantive citizenship and thus avoid the lack of the participatory dimension claimed by Delanty (Delanty 1998: 2.2).

Deliberative democracy indeed involves the public in an active participation in the decision-making process through the influence that discourses emerging from the deliberative process could have on the political centre (Habermas 1996: 442). In our opinion, the EU institutions seem to have come around to the same conclusion, as the results of empirical research into 'The Cultural Citizenship and the Creation of European Identity' (Delgado-Moreira 1997) have suggested. Delgado-Moreira, considering the content of the EU official documents, found that the idea of citizenship proposed was a mixture of certain universal values and the search for an active participation in the democratic process through the deliberative procedure. Thus, 'European identity is closer [than American cultural citizenship] to the liberal concept of citizenship: comprised of political and civil rights in the public sphere' (Delgado-Moreira 1997: 7). Nevertheless, this analysis reveals the assumption that the European institutions wish to create a super-state, because the European identity portrayed in the official texts considered by the author 'intends to overcome the pressure both from underneath (unemployment, minorities, etc.) and outside (growing immigration), and aims to be effective in terms of propaganda, militarism, primary education, rewriting of histories and affirmation of identity' (Delgado-Moreira 1997: 8).

This argument seems to be hazardous, since it is often stated in the same research that there is no will to threaten the national identities of the different member states, as 'there are two typical contexts for the use of the word identity... First, there exists the need for identity at the level of the Union. Such identity has to be perceived as clear and distinct both inside and outside. Second, there is the need to respect existing national identities of the Member States' (Delgado-Moreira 1997: 4). Moreover, Delgado-Moreira himself admits that, as far as the European identity project is concerned, the EU institutions have made 'a choice between culture and citizenship', where culture is left to the national level, demanding collective sources of identity at the state level.

These arguments seem to indicate a lack of coherence with the conclusions of the research. The creation of a super-state does not square with the persistence of national systems and the will of the member states, which is undeniably sensitive to the matter of their sovereignties. If this is the case, we think there is a particular model that has been overlooked, and which could explain the abundant references to European identity in the official documents. What appears to be the context capable of putting together the rhetoric of European identity and the need for the defence of national ones expressed in the content of the analysed texts is the notion of the multilevel public sphere and the concept of network governance.

Public Sphere and Networks in Europe

In introducing the system of networked governance which is under development in the European Union, a necessary reference has to be made to Castells' work on the network society and in particular to his theory of the network state (Castells 1996). This is based on the assumption that by consequence of the processes of globalization and the consequent crisis of the traditional national states' structure there has been a search for new forms of governance: 'the increasing inability of nation states to confront and manage the processes of globalisation of the issues that are objects of their governance lead to ad hoc forms of global governance and, ultimately, to a new form of state' (Castells 2008: 87). In particular Castells indicates three mechanisms through which nation states can adapt to these supranational processes: through associations of states and the development of networks; through the development of associations of international institutions and supranational organizations, and through the development of processes of decentralization. The combination of these three elements is fundamental in order to understand the new processes going on both at the local and supranational levels. Under these circumstances also the concept of the public sphere and the new arena is characterized by being transformed by the different communicative relations existing between institutional actors – such as the UN, the WTO, and the EU – and non institutional, such as NGOs, private companies, media .

The concept of network elaborated by Castells can be fully applied to the case of European integration. Indeed the author says that 'around the process of formation of the European Union, new forms of governance, and new institutions of government, are being created, at the European, national, regional, and local levels, inducing a new form of state that I propose to call *the network state*' (1998: 339); therefore he claims that Europe is governed by a *network state* which is composed of shared sovereignties and different levels of negotiated *decision making* (see also Castells 2002: 16). Peculiarity of this form of state is not only the different levels involved, but the diverse kinds of actors included in this process. The European Union, with its system of governance, which is networked around different levels and different actors, then seems to respond to these exigencies.

As will be underlined later in this article, the complexity of the EU is shown by the different processes of governance characterizing this supranational form of governance and by the spectrum of actors who are in communicative relationships with each other.

The role of networking has in fact gained a new relevance in the EU context as Kohler-Koch and Eising explained in their book 'The transformation of governance in the European union' (1999), as the European Commission involved sub-national actors such as agencies, NGO groups and so on. Although the Commission has a prominent role in shaping and stimulating the development of networks in Europe, Kohler-Koch (Kohler-Koch 1999: 19) asserts that there are different actors interested in redefining the political space, such as regions represented by the 'Committee of the Regions' and functional collectives such as interest associations. Moreover, in assuming the EU to be a network system, it becomes possible to manage this differentiation, which means that the EU is based on 'the recognition of a plurality of interests and it is linked to a reductionist concept of legitimacy which is equated with efficient performance' (Kohler-Koch 1999: 25). In the view, the concept of network governance implies the existence of organized social sub-systems and the political system assumes characteristics of being an activator, which means that being 'vertically and horizontally segmented' – there are different actors and organisations which become active in the political process (Eising and Kohler-Koch 1999: 5).

In considering the EU as a multilevel system, it should be stressed that the participation of its citizens in the European integration process, although necessary, does not imply a European *demos* in the traditional sense (Soysal 2002: 265). The European space is thus constituted by a multiplicity of levels and subjects and defined by the interaction of different social and political actors activated by the EU's institutions. The transnational level, as with the national and the sub-national, constitutes and needs to be considered in equal terms when managing this space. The European public space is a network which is structured on a different basis when compared to the traditional model of the nation state. The concept of network governance is thus central when applied to the case of a public space, which should be considered multilevel.

In considering the concept of multilevel governance, Schlesinger (Schlesinger and Kevin 2000; Schlesinger 2003) does agree on these points (cf. Bernard 2002; Hooghe 2001) and assumes that the most realistic way of applying the concept of the public sphere to the EU is to take into account the definition of the multiple publics that effectively exist and deliberate: 'The political communication processes, which take place in terms of policy consultation, lobbying, public affairs, and interest representation, reflect the "multi-level governance" of the European Polity. Consequently the processes are at times national, supranational and sub-national, and often combine all three levels' (Schlesinger and Kevin 2000: 217–18). Moreover, Schlesinger explains how this concept of a sphere of publics acts inside the European communicative space. He gathers that this space is more and more constituted by networks in which different actors interact and exchange information (cf. Koopmans and Pfetsch 2003; Trenz and Eder 2004) and that the institutionalization of the EU has allowed the development of strong and weak publics, often oriented towards national publics, which have traditionally been influenced by national interests (Schlesinger 2003: 1). The EU could thus be considered as a body entitled to generate a wide and deep social communication able to connect different spheres of publics (Schlesinger 2003: 4).

Eriksen has contributed to this scenario with an innovative work (2004) in which he distinguishes between the general, segmented and strong publics that characterize the European public sphere. Here, it is posited that there are some traits of a 'general public' – communicative spaces of civil society in which all can participate on a free and equal basis. The main examples include magazines and televisions spread out on a continental basis, social movements that facilitate transnational European debate, and traits of discussions about European issues (Eriksen 2004: 16).

The second level of the model elaborated by Eriksen consists of 'transnational segmented publics', which evolve around 'policy networks composed of a selection of actors with a common interest in certain issues, problems and solutions' (Eriksen 2004: 16). These create transnational public spheres emanating from the policy networks of the Union. Common debates stimulated by public communication campaigns of the EU are examples of events creating transnational but segmented public spheres. Some examples of such campaigns are those implemented for launching the euro, but also all the initiatives taken by the Commission under the so-called 'Plan D'. The result is a public sphere that Eriksen defines as 'fragmented, differentiated and in flux' (Eriksen 2004: 18).

Instead, 'strong publics', which, according to Eriksen, could be considered the institutional hardware of the EU, are 'legally institutionalised and regulated discourses specialised upon collective will-formation at the polity centre' (Eriksen 2004: 16). Strong publics are constituted by 'A) open deliberative spaces B) in which deliberation takes place prior to decision-making and C) decision makers are held to account' (Eriksen 2004: 19). Eriksen discusses the Convention which elaborated the Charter of Fundamental Rights as an example testifying for open debate, insofar as civil society and other organizations have been included.

However, it is important to underline that Eriksen criticizes the method of the Convention by stating that 'the link between institutionalised debates and the general public is largely missing' (Eriksen 2004: 23). Even if, as the author's theoretical contribution has shown, there are various degrees of public spaces in Europe, what does not exist is the 'ability to filter themes and topics, the problems and solutions aired in the civil society and verbalised in the general public into the decision making via transnational networks and strong publics' (Eriksen 2004: 23).

Again, some central issues emerge from this discussion. First, despite the fact that public spaces and different publics exist within the EU, these do not communicate with each other. Second, common opinion and will developed through common themes, shared interpretative frames and inclusive fora are missing. Third, the segmentation and differentiation of the European public sphere seems to be more a limitation to this model than a support. Last, the lack of communication between different spheres of publics is to be considered to be another form of democratic deficit.

In framing their theory into contributions which relate the democratic deficit of the EU to the lack of a substantial communicative space in Europe, Trenz and Eder present a theory of democratic functionalism based on the idea that there are self-constituting dynamics of the European public sphere which connect the development of some transnational spaces of political communication with the process of communication of the EU institutional system (Trenz and Eder 2004). The self-constituting dynamics of a European public sphere are supported by two mechanisms: the increase of communication within the European institutions and an increased awareness of the public towards European themes. In particular, Trenz and Eder take into account all the mechanisms that generate discussions. These include 'not only those who take an active part in the debate but also presupposes that communication resonates among others who constitute a public for this communication' (Trenz and Eder 2004: 9). In the self-constitution of a public sphere, it is thus important to consider the intersection of these two elements, which are the resonance of public actors and the external public resonance addressing these actors and institutions.

In considering various contributions (Calhoun 2003; Eriksen 2004; Koopmans and Erbe 2003; Schlesinger 2003), we can identify two main dimensions of the European public sphere which emerge from a network governance approach.

The first dimension, which we can define as the horizontal dimension, considers the debate stimulated from an institutional point of view at the different European levels (EU, nation state, regions etc.), whereas the second dimension, defined as the vertical dimension, regards all those agencies, relays, organizations, media and so on that furnish the basis for an effective debate about EU issues. The connection between these two dimensions is fundamental in order to overcome some of the limits that have characterized the European space until now. In the following section we will try to look at what the European Commission has recently done to stimulate the constitution of a horizontal dimension of such a space.

The Concept of Network Governance in European Official Documents

In this section we provide an overview of the main official documents produced by the Commission in the area of information and communication policy in recent years, in order to ascertain the main features characterizing a networked European public space. These documents have emerged from a political context formed by the period of crisis endured by the EU at the end of the 1990s – for example, the resignation of the Commission in 1999 due to scandals and the imminent adoption of the euro, which preceded a controversial debate about its meaning for the construction of Europe. The so-called 'democratic deficit' and the never-resolved dilemma of the distance between citizens and institutions had become more and more evident, as different studies conducted at the end of the 1990s demonstrated. Moreover, the debates that followed the adoption of the Treaty of Nice in 2000 and the Convention for the Charter of Fundamental Rights were quite critical moments, at which it was clear that divisions between the different views that each of the member states were taking into the European integration process could bring a halt to the process itself. In addition, negotiations about enlargement brought home the necessity of thinking about new directions that the EU could take.

The concept of network governance has thus become an important feature of the new developments the EU is currently facing, and has characterized the 'look for a new strategy' objective of the European Commission, at least since the White Paper on European governance was elaborated in 2001. Similarly, the idea that communication should become a central tool for enhancing citizens' participation has been clearly stated and reaffirmed in the *White Paper on European Communication Policy* published on 1 February 2006.

A number of documents regarding the EU's communication and information policy have been produced by the Commission in the last five years. In these documents (as identified in this section), the concepts 'decentralization' and 'involvement' have been of particular concern. This demonstrates, as Kohler-Koch underlines, that the Commission is 'active as an actor – although not the only one – interested in redefining the boundaries of the European political space' (Kohler-Koch 1999: 19). This position is clearly stated within the 2001 White Paper on European governance, where information and communication are considered two central tools for creating an effective bond with European citizens, who, according to the Commission, would become concretely active in the process of policymaking: 'Providing more information and more effective communication are a precondition for generating a sense of belonging to Europe. The aim should be to create a transnational "space" where citizens from different countries can discuss what they perceive as being the important challenges for the Union' (Commission of the European Communities [CEC] 2001a: 12).

The adoption of a network governance approach clearly results from the process that led to the composition of the White Paper in 2001. Twelve working groups in six different areas were formed in order to prepare the document. The emphasis on the necessity of enhancing a network structure has been addressed in different working groups and has thus influenced the structure of the working paper.

The link between this approach and the necessity of stimulating a better involvement of European citizens was highlighted by Working Group 1a, which said in its report that:

> The working group's objective was to provide helpful suggestions on how to transform the citizens of the European Union into actors in the European political process... Among the questions we asked ourselves there were how to make communications a strategic tool of governance for the Commission and how to inject relevant European aspects into political debates still dominated by national discourses, concerns and actors. (Working Group 2001a: 5)

The two concerns seem to be relevant in reforming the European integration process. First of all, the issue is not only of 'getting Europe close to the citizens', but doing something more important: making them active and aware of the EU political process.

This is noted in the White Paper on Governance, which stated that one of the future objectives of the EU should be enacting and enforcing citizens' involvement (CEC 2001a: 15). Indeed, from the quotation taken above it follows that communication should be considered as a tool of governance in order to stimulate discussion about Europe within national systems in which other concerns prevail. The concept of decentralization is considered fundamental in defining the European public space and in order to engage a dialogue with the citizens, which has been identified several times as one of the founding principles of the Information and Communication Policy of the EU.

Thus, in this scenario, the concept and the meaning of network governance becomes an essential tool for realizing these objectives. Networks, from the Commission's point of view, are important as a tool for improving governance and solving crucial problems inherent in modern public policies by providing the flexibility required to deal with the wide diversity and sometimes 'very fundamental differences existing between administrative cultures and structures in Europe' (Working Group 2001b: ii). The questions of openness and transparency, and those of representation and inclusiveness, are thus considered vital and fundamental in order to develop an effective and well-structured networked Europe (Working Group 2001b: 2).

It is worth moving towards the definition of the new structure of the communication and information policy since the adoption of these principles. In fact, some crucial documents have been published in the last years in which the principles of networked governance have been adopted with the emergence of the principle of decentralization as a well-defined feature.

It is not surprising that the decision to define a new communicative framework was taken in 2001, when a 'new framework for cooperation on activities concerning the information and communication policy of the European Union' was welcomed with the aim of establishing 'a new inter-institutional relationship based on a new type of co-operation where common subjects and interests are concerned. These will involve joint implementation of information policies, management arrangements that are easy to handle, decentralised and involve as little bureaucracy as possible' (CEC 2001b: 3). This document did not give any real insights that could make it possible to move beyond mere declarations of intents, but it surely diffused the idea that an improvement in the Communication Policy was necessary in order to realize the Commission's classical statement which says that the aim of the EU is to 'bring Europe closer to its citizens' (CEC 2001b: 4).

A real cornerstone by which the approach was clearly defined has to be considered the well-known DOC 350 published in 2002. In this document, the principles of governance were finally adopted:

In order to exist, the European public space needs temporal, spatial and ideological points of reference. It also needs active public involvement. This will mean developing all forms of representation (opinion leaders, interest groups, parliamentarians, etc.) at European level and building on all forms of cooperation, whether from journalists, the major media or national institutions. (CEC 2002: 8)

An entire section was dedicated to defining what decentralization would mean. In fact, the need for better cooperation between the European institution, the member states and also the regional and local governments was recognized.

At the same time, in considering that 'the Union's information and communication strategy cannot stand alone' (CEC 2002: 24), it proposed to elaborate a Memorandum of Understanding in order to recognize 'at national level the role of the networks and relays in transmitting a regular flow of information, thereby ensuring ongoing public debate in Europe' and to provide for the systematic networking of information correspondents in each member state, and the Commission, the Council and the European Parliament, to 'give Member States the freedom to form more specific partnerships' (CEC 2002: 24).

The realization of a 'Europe as close to the people as possible' would be made possible through the opening up of a second dimension of European information policy – that is, the horizontal one. The third section of the document was thus dedicated to the role and functions that the institutional and non-institutional networks and relays might assume:

Their experience, flexibility and immediate proximity to the representatives of civil society and the general public make them invaluable and a favoured instrument for implementing the European Union's information and communication strategy. On the ground, they embody the synergy of resources available to the European Union, the Member States and civil society, translating into practice the principle of the decentralisation of information. (CEC 2002: 25)

The need to improve information and communication policy has drastically increased since the referendum for approving the Constitutional Treaty failed in France and the Netherlands in 2005. A new context of crisis, consisting of the evident distance between citizens and the EU's institutions, has in some ways stopped the evolution of the integration process. Following this, a period of reflection aimed at spreading the debate on Europe has been opened under the direction of Commissioner Margaret Wallström. The aim of the new 'Plan D for

Democracy, Dialogue and Debate' is that of setting out 'a long term plan to reinvigorate European democracy and help the emergence of a European Public Sphere, where citizens are given information and the tools to actively participate in the decision making process and gain ownership of the European project' (CEC 2005b: 3). Together with Plan D, an 'Action Plan to Improve Communicating Europe by the Commission' has been established, showing the growing importance given to this area of policy. The main principles of these documents are those of listening and communicating with citizens, and adopting a new strategy based on transparency. These goals are clearly stated in different documents: those of giving the 'EU a single face' and of putting 'its own house in order' (CEC 2005a: 2). The strategy is that of 'Going Local', referring to an expression used by the Commission: 'Good communication requires excellent understanding of local audiences. The Commission's communication activities must be resourced and organised in such a way as to address matching demographic and national and local concerns, and to convey information through the channels citizens prefer in the language they can understand' (CEC 2005a: 4).

The new *White Paper on a European Communication Policy* published on 1 February 2006 clearly summarizes all the concerns raised in the previous five years and remarked upon in this section. The scope is that of creating a 'citizens centred communication' involving a wide range of partners, both institutional and non-institutional, in order to overcome the image of a EU which remains too bureaucratic and remote: 'national public authorities, civil society, and the European Union institutions need to work together to develop Europe's place in the public sphere' (CEC 2006: 5).

From this view, the levels under consideration are determined both by territorial criteria (European, national, regional and local) but also by functional criteria according to specific expertise (public authorities, economic community, social partners and other civil society organizations) (cf. CES 2002). The public space is thus formed by different nodes constituted by the interaction between these two dimensions. A schema has been elaborated in order to show the complexity resulting from the intersection between territorial and functional levels (Figure 6.1).

Each of the functional levels could be considered as a distinctive sphere in which debate is created, which to a various extent influences and binds European activity in the decision-making process. The publics that are created could be considered as the segmented publics indicated

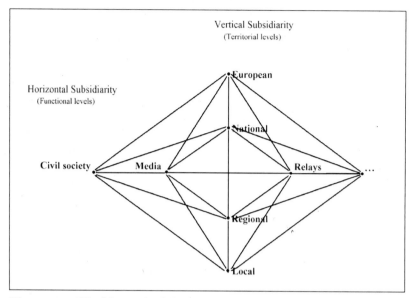

Figure 6.1: The Networked Governance Model.

by Eriksen (2004), which stimulate a sort of link between strong publics and general publics. Public administration offices, economic and social partners, civil society groups and mass media should act as mediators between strong groups composed of officials, intellectuals and so on, and general publics composed of citizens. Realizing that this communicative flow would result in a better involvement of the latter in the activities of the former, it would make the self-constituting dynamics of the European public sphere as represented by Trenz and Eder (2004) possible.

Conclusions

The form of a network state that characterizes the EU, according to the contribution by Castells, is constituted by nodes of different sizes which are linked by asymmetrical relationships, making its structure as different from a centred political system, as it is from a nation state one. In fact, as Castells avers: 'regardless of these asymmetries, the various nodes of the European network state are interdependent on each other, so that a node, even the most powerful, can ignore the others, even the smallest, in the decision making process. If some political nodes do so, the whole system is called into question' (Castells 1998: 352).

The EU, in adopting a network governance approach, becomes an entity that appears very similar to the form of a network state as described by Castells. The debate on the public sphere has been strictly influenced, as we attempted to show, by these features. Indeed, in following the theoretical contributions we have taken into consideration, the result is that the European space is characterized by different actors (movements, NGOs, media, etc.) and different kinds of institutions interacting with each other, constituting different arenas in which discussions about European issues take place.

As has been shown, the European Commission has clearly stated that, in order to bring Europe close to its citizens, some crucial principles such as those of decentralization and subsidiarity should be adopted for making network governance feasible. The approach taken by the Commission is that of activating and engaging all the local authorities, environments and actors. This is part of the strategy of proximity of the EU, represented in the principle of decentralization, whose aim is to ensure that decisions are taken as closely as possible to the level of the citizens by regularly checking whether action taken at Community level could equally well be taken at national, regional or local level. In practice, the principle means that, except in areas for which it has exclusive competence, the EU shall only act when this is more effective than action at national level. Deriving from this, the quality of European communication should be based on such a concern. The messages should be given and should be structured following this representation of proximity, fragmenting the communicative initiatives in relation to the different kinds of publics that exist in Europe.

In principle, the idea of the European public space which emerges from the Commission's point of view follows the theoretical background within which the European public sphere has been considered and discussed in the literature. One point that has been missing until now is the effective activation of all those actors standing at the horizontal and functional levels who need to find concrete ways to communicate with the vertical and territorial levels constituted by European institutions, governments and local entities. Future evolution, under the reform initiated with the publication of the new White Paper concerning this area of policy, will have to take into consideration the development of a bidirectional flow of communication between actors and institutions, in order to reduce drastically the fragmentation existing between different spheres of publics in Europe.

Bibliography

Anderson, B. 1996. *Comunità immaginate: Origini e diffusione dei nazionalismi.* Rome: Manifesto Libri.

Arendt, H. 1988. *Vita Activa.* Milan: Bompiani.

Bee C., Scartezzini R. and Scott A. (eds.) 2008. 'The Development of a European Public Sphere: A stalled project?', *European Political Science Special Issue,* 7/3.

Bellamy, R. and Castiglione, D. 1996. *Constitutionalism in Transformation: European and Theoretical Perspectives.* Oxford: Blackwell.

_____. 2000a. 'The Normative Turn in European Union Studies: Legitimacy, Identity and Democracy', RUSEL Working Paper 38. Exeter: University of Exeter, Department of Politics, Retrieved from http://www.ex.ac.uk/shipss/politics/research/rusel/rusel38.pdf.

_____. 2000b. 'The Uses of Democracy: Reflections on the European Democratic Deficit', in J.E. Eriksen and E.O. Fossum (eds), *Democracy in the EU: Integration through Deliberation.* London: Routledge: 65–84.

Bernard, N. 2002. *Multilevel Governance in the EU.* The Hague: Kluwer Law International.

Calhoun, C. 2003. 'The Democratic Integration of Europe: Interests, Identity, and the Public Sphere', in M. Berezin and M. Schain (eds), *Europe without Borders: Re-mapping Territory, Citizenship and Identity in a Transnational Age.* Baltimore, MD: Johns Hopkins University Press: 243–75.

Castells, M. 1996. *The Rise of the Network Society. The Information Age: Economy, Society and Culture.* Oxford: Blackwell.

Castells, M. 1998. *End of Millennium.* Oxford: Blackwell.

_____. 2002. 'La costruzione dell'identità europea', *Fodeus* 3: 545–60.

_____. 2008. 'The New Public Spere: Global Civil Society, Communication Networks, and Global Governance', *The Annals of the American Academy of Political and Social Science* 616: 78–92.

CES. 2001. *Opinion on European Governance – A White Paper.* Brussels, 20 March 2002.

Commission of the European Communities. 2001a. *European Governance: A White Paper,* COM(2001)428 final. Brussels: CEC.

_____. 2001b. *New Framework for Co-operation on Activities concerning the Information and Communication Policy of the European Union,* COM(2001)354 final. Brussels: CEC.

_____. 2002. *An Information and Communication Strategy for the European Union,* COM(2002)350 final/2. Brussels: CEC.

_____. 2004. *Implementing the Information and Communication Strategy for the European Union,* COM(2004)196 final. Brussels: CEC.

_____. 2005a. *Action Plan to Improve Communicating Europe by the Commission,* 20.07.2005. Brussels: CEC.

_____. 2005b. *Plan-D for Democracy, Dialogue and Debate,* COM(2005)494 final, Brussels: CEC.

_____. 2006. *White Paper on a European Communication Policy,* COM(2006)35 final. Brussels: CEC.

Delanty, G. 1998. 'Social Theory and European Transformation: Is There a European Society?' *Sociological Research Online* 3(1). Retrieved from http://www.socresonline.org.uk.

Delgado-Moreira, J.M. 1997. 'Cultural Citizenship and the Creation of European Identity', *Electronic Journal of Sociology* 2. Retrieved from http://www.sociology.org/content/vol002.003/delgado.html.

Deutsch, K. 1994. 'Nationalism and Social Communication', in J. Hutchinson and A.D. Smith (eds), *Nationalism*. Oxford and New York: Oxford University Press: 26–29.

Downing, J. and Husband C. 2002. 'Intercultural Communication, Multiculturalism, and Social Inequality', *IAMCR Conference Special Sessions on Intercultural Communication, Barcelona, 21–26 July*. Retrieved from http://www.portalcomunicacion.com/forumv/forum1/pdf/f1_eng.pdf.

Durkheim, E. 1960. *The Division of Labour in Society.* Glencoe, IL: Free Press.

Eising R. and B. Kohler-Koch 1999. 'Introduction: Network governance in the European Union', in B. Kohler-Koch and R. Eising (eds), *The transformation of governance in the European union.* London; New York, N.Y.: Routledge: 8–13.

Eriksen, E.O. 2004. 'Conceptualising European Public Spheres. General, Segmented and Strong Publics', ARENA Working Paper 3/04. Centre for European Studies, University of Oslo.

Eriksen, E.O and Fossum, J.E. 2002. 'Democracy through Strong Publics in the European Union?' *Journal of Common Market Studies* 40: 401–24.

Fraser, N. 1995. 'Politics, Culture and the Public Sphere: Toward a Postmodern Conception', in L. Nicholson and S. Seidman (eds), *Social Postmodernism: Beyond Identity Politics.* Cambridge: Cambridge University Press: 287–312.

Gellner, E. 1997. *Nazioni e nazionalismo.* Rome: Editori Riuniti.

Goddard, V.A., Llobera, J.R. and Shore, C. (eds). 1994. *The Anthropology of Europe: Identities and Boundaries in Conflict.* Oxford: Berg.

Grimm, D. 1995. 'Does Europe Need a Constitution?', *European Law Journal* 1(3): 282–302.

Habermas, J. 1989. *The Structural Transformation of the Public Sphere.* Cambridge: MIT Press.

————. 1996. *Between Facts and Norms.* Cambridge, MA: MIT Press.

————. 1999. *La costellazione postnazionale.* Milan: Feltrinelli.

Hooghe, L. and Marks, G. 2001. *Multilevel Governance and European Integration.* Lanham, MD: Rowman & Littlefield.

Husband, C. 1996. 'The Right to be Understood: Conceiving the Multi-ethnic Public Sphere', *Innovation* 9(2): 205–16.

————. 2000. 'Media and the Public Sphere in Multi-ethnic Societies', in S. Cottle (ed.), *Ethnic Minorities and the Media.* Buckingham: Open University Press.

Kohler-Koch B. 1999. 'The evolution and transformation of European governance', in B. Kohler-Koch and R. Eising (eds), *The transformation of governance in the European Union.* London; New York, N.Y.: Routledge: 14–35.

Kohler-Koch B. and Eising R. 1999. *The transformation of governance in the European union.* London; New York, N.Y.: Routledge.

Koopmans, R. and Pfetsch, B. 2003. 'Towards an Europeanised Public sphere? Comparing Political Actors and the Media in Germany', ARENA Working Paper 23/03. Centre for European Studies, University of Oslo.

Koopmans, R. and Erbe, J. 2003. 'Towards a European Public Sphere? Vertical and Horizontal Dimensions of Europeanised Political Communication', Discussion Paper SP IV 2003–403 WZB.

Kymlicka, W. 1995. *Multicultural Citizenship*. New York and Oxford: Oxford University Press.

La Torre, M. 1998. *European Citizenship: An Institutional Challenge*. Netherlands: Kluwer Law.

Rusconi G.E. (1999). *Possiamo fare a meno di una religione civile?* Roma; Bari: Laterza, 1999.

Scharpf, F.W. 1994. 'Community and Autonomy Multilevel Policy-making in the European Union', in *Journal of European Public Policy*, 1(2): 219–42.

————. 1998. 'Interdependence and Democratic Legitimation', RSC, European University Institute, Fiesole.

————. 1999. *Governare l'Europa: legittimità democratica ed efficacia delle politiche dell'Unione Europea*. Bologna: Il Mulino.

Schlesinger, P. 2003. 'The Babel of Europe? An Essay on Networks and Communicative Spaces', ARENA Working Paper 22/03. Centre for European Studies, University of Oslo.

Schlesinger, P. and Kevin, D. 2000, 'Can the EU Become a Sphere of Publics?', in E.O. Eriksen and J.E. Fossum (eds), *Democracy in the EU: Integration through Deliberation*. London: Routledge: 206–29.

Shore, C. 2000. *Building Europe: The Cultural Politics of European Integration*. London: Routledge.

Soysal, Y.N. 2002. 'Locating Europe', *European Societies* 4(3): 265–84.

Trenz, H.J. and Eder, K. 2004. 'The Democratising Dynamics of a European Public Sphere', *European Journal of Social Theory* 7(1): 5–25.

Van de Steeg, M. 2002. 'Rethinking the Conditions for a Public Sphere in the European Union', *European Journal of Social Theory* 5(4): 499–519.

Working Group. 2001a. *Broadening and Enriching the Public Debate on European Matters* (Group 1a, June 2001), White Paper on European Governance Work area no. 1 (Broadening and enriching the public debate on European matters).

Working Group. 2001b. *Networking People for a Good Governance in Europe* (Group 4b, May 2001), White Paper on Governance Work Area no. 4 (Coherence and cooperation in a networked Europe).

Young, I.M. 1996. *Le politiche della differenza*. Milan: Feltrinelli.

Chapter 7

Exploring the Role of European Information Society Developments in the Europeanization of Public Spheres

Bridgette Wessels

Introduction[1]

In this paper I discuss the idea of a European public sphere (EPS) in relation to three historical processes, namely: the concept of a 'public sphere'; the relationship between nation states and the European Union (EU); and changes to forms of communication. A public sphere is shaped through forms of public participation, the role of the state within socio-economic conditions, and the means of communication. At this historical moment, both the public sphere and Europe lack a clear and unambiguous definition, rationale and vision. A key dimension in the development of an EPS involves considering the influence of the global networked information age in the shaping of public spheres that are traditionally shaped by, and understood through, the nation state. The question to address is: what is the influence of a global networked information age in developing an EPS within a collection of national public spheres?

Given the above context, a significant aspect of rethinking a public sphere for Europe is the development of a 'European Information Society', which is characterized by new forms of communication via digital technologies that are socially organized through networks. These developments, however, need to be understood within the broader dynamics of participation, both socially and in democratic processes, and the rise of neo-liberalism, which are part of the emergence of the networking logic of the current socio-political environment. In this chapter, I trace the historical contexts of the public sphere, which illustrate the national character of public spheres as well as the adaptation of communicative media within socio-political realities that have fostered particular forms of participation in public life. I then question the ways in which developments within the EU information society may or may not influence the shaping of a public sphere for Europe in the twenty-first century, and then draw the discussion to issues concerning participation in Europe more generally.

The broad context of the debates underpinning the development of an EPS is one of an emergent post-national globalizing world. Within this context, some nation states and empires have broken up, generating sub-national conflict, whilst some existing nation states are configuring and reconfiguring in supranational organizations within world regions (Rex 1999, cited in Smith and Wright 1999). Western Europe and, increasingly, Eastern Europe is seeking to develop an economic, political, social and cultural unit from numerous nation states that are geographically situated in the sub-continent of the peninsula of the Eurasian landmass (ibid.). Key reasons for building such a unit include ensuring peace and cohesion across the states of Europe, combining to become a strong economic and political player in the global economy, and offering another perspective in international relations and (especially from a continental European view) as a counter to American hegemony.[2]

The development of an integrated and enlarging Europe is contested: it is hard to identify a strongly held sense of European identity and pan-European discourse, and there is a lack of a well-supported European political process and European media (ibid.). These characteristics, alongside the absence of an enduring European public, generate a difficult context in which to develop an EPS. Instead Europe, and any EPS, institutionally speaking, is seen as segmented (Eriksen 2004). This segmentation is seen not only in the exclusiveness of national publics but also in the different strands within the EU policy sector. Although this segmented sensibility of Europe is pervasive, there are instances that bring a sense of European commonality publicly to the fore. These are mainly episodic occurrences generated through cultural events or major political issues that make transient cross-European mass interests manifest, such as opinion regarding the 2003 Iraq war (Roche 2005).

Another form of EPS activity is characterized as potentially 'conflictual' in that it is generated through structural change in the EU, which includes cross-European transformation in areas such as the EU's Single Market project (Roche 2005). These types of developments have the potential to generate conflict through the adaptive responses of member states, especially in the context of enlargement and the inclusion of transitional nation states in the EU.

This context involves the interlayering and interrelationships between social, political and economic change, as well as changes to the means of communication in the innovation and development of digital technologies and the World Wide Web (WWW) and the ongoing commercialization of the traditional mass media. A central strand that weaves though changes to these domains is the fulfilment of meaningful participation by a diversity of individuals and publics in democratic processes, whether at national or supranational levels. If one understands participation in its fullest sense (Steinert and Pilgram 2003), then participation encompasses the way in which public institutions are accountable and responsive to the public and private concerns of a diverse and multicultural populace, which moves participation beyond public opinion. It includes the ways in which individuals and groups can participate in public debate and democratic processes. Participation is not just at the level of individuals and groups voicing their own concerns but is also one in which understanding between different social and cultural perspectives can be fostered, which can develop a collective sense of 'public good' at the European level.

The characteristics of participation need to be understood within specific socio-economic and political frameworks. Currently, the framework is heavily biased towards neo-liberalism. This framework posits the market as the arbiter of resources, as the most efficient mechanism for the distribution of resources, and as helping to ensure individual freedom. This has implications for key institutions vested with the responsibility of building Europe within democratic liberalism, chiefly the European Parliament, the European Commission and European Council, as policy has to engage with the ideology of the market and address social cohesion, inclusion and social justice. In terms of participation, there is the rise of 'different partial arenas of cultural and social sub-politics – media publicity, judiciary, privacy, citizens' initiative groups and the new social movements ... [that] add up to forms of new culture' (Beck 1992: 198). This trend becomes ever more complex in the context of the diverse populace of the EU, and any straightforward adaptation of either a universalistic argument or relativist argument regarding a public sphere for Europe struggles to address the issue of participation in Europe in the context of a networked global economy (Borradori 2003). A key issue within these dynamics is the provision of information and communication for both governors and citizens of Europe that can facilitate informing a citizenry and developing and sustaining dialogue regarding European concerns, to ensure participation in Europe. Together these conditions – the economic, social and political and the means of communication – point to debates regarding the public sphere, and its role and character not just in Europe, but also at national and global levels as they relate to Europe in the twenty-first century.

History of the Public Sphere

The notion of the public sphere is a contested one but it points to a more or less autonomous and open arena for public debate in civil society and one that involves the use of various forms of media including pamphlets, the mass media and the internet. The public sphere is largely a national construct, gaining credence through national socio-economic and political contexts and, symbolically, through cultural forms identified within a national sensibility and in the national organization of media and communication. The history of the public sphere illustrates the way in which information and communication is used to develop public sensibilities within particular historical social orders, which influences the character of participation in a public realm. The sphere for public dialogue has, therefore, changed from early capitalism, through organized and disorganized capitalism to the current (as yet emergent) networked global capitalism. The current change requires a re-examination of communication and participation at nation state level, but also in the context of developing a European Information Society, which forms the communicative infrastructure for an EPS in a global economy.

In general terms, the emergence of a space between the private and domestic lives of individuals and families and the state occurred at the demise of feudalism. Mercantilism saw the separation of the state from economic activity, the Church and, in varying ways, from the monarchy. The emergence of the bourgeoisie in European nation states saw the development of a reading public that generated practices of debate. The literary public sphere protected the practice of debate, and it was through engagement with cultural forms such as the novel as well as letters, pamphlets and the press that the bourgeoisie reflected both on itself and on the role of the state in the formation of a good society (Goode 2005). The bourgeois public sphere saw itself to be comprised of private people coming together to counter public power, and was underpinned by universal principles: 'The bourgeois public's critical public debate took place in principle without regard to all pre-existing social and political rank and in accord with universal rules' (Habermas 1989: 54).

However, the bourgeois public sphere moved beyond printed material and exclusive groups of pedagogues and philosophers to the political public spheres of coffee houses and salons of the early eighteenth century. The aim of this political public sphere was to protect and secure the integrity of the private sphere (Habermas 1989: 52–55). To ensure this relationship between 'the private and the political the bourgeoisie took on the mantle of the universal class by asserting the meritocratic ideals of the free market' (Goode 2005: 9), which sought to neutralize power so that a civil society could emerge and function. The ideals of the political public sphere granted rights of participation regardless of status and privilege achieved through civil society and on a constitutional framework of freedom of contract and laissez-faire trade policies (Habermas 1989: 73–89). Alongside these developments was the formation of public opinion, which developed in different ways in England, France and Germany, but nonetheless the national press was the key medium of this critical reasoning in national political public spheres and became established as the Fourth Estate of the realm.

The idea of 'publicity' underpinned the public sphere and pointed to the public use of reason, free of manipulation and coercion. As Goode points out: 'a key virtue was to think for one's self publicly, that is, as a member of humanity and not as a private individual' (Goode 2005: 13, citing Habermas 1989: 104–6). A key dimension of this publicity was that participants in the public sphere were autonomous, which Kant argued was ensured by the participants being property owners. Furthermore, the role of public deliberation, for Kant, was not to generate consensus or compromise; rather that pure reasoning – not just dialogue – would reveal the 'truth' of things (Goode 2005). Habermas follows Kant in developing a universalistic framework, although, as Goode (ibid.) points out, Habermas 'substitutes the monologic conceit of "pure reasoning" for the rule of dialogue and open-ended argumentation; and he favours Kant's model of a reasoning public over Rousseau's "common sense", though he is only interested in a republicanism that can accommodate liberalism's concern for the rights of individuals' (ibid.: 13).

As the conditions for sustaining a bourgeois public sphere were eroded, the abstract and universal reasoning of Kant was criticized by Marx and Hegel. Hegel argued that both privilege and conflict in civil society meant that public opinion could not sustain the universalism and permanence needed for a Kantian system, and that politics could not be subsumed into an abstract 'universal morality' (in Habermas 1989: 109). The state had to intervene in civil society and could, in fact, stand above public opinion to unify society. Hegel sought to embody the zeitgeist of the populace and give it meaning through a public sphere that aimed to educate, motivate and assemble and thus activate public opinion (Habermas 1989: 121).

Marx also raised the point that society was ridden with contradictions and argued that the bourgeois public sphere was not a 'radical revolution or universal emancipation ... it is the partial, merely political revolution ...' (Marx 1843: 4, in Livingstone and Benton 1992: 253–54). Marx argued that one particular class, the middle class, was seeking to undertake the emancipation of society, but from its own perspective. Of course, in the spirit of Marx's analysis and politics, he argued that the workers would see through an illusory freedom to sell their labour in the 'free market' to throw off their actual conditions of alienation and exploitation to find truly universal emancipation.

Habermas (1989: 128–29) saw in Marx's call for a socialist public sphere an inversion of the public–private relationship: one that was not based on property-owning private individuals along with the state as forming a public sphere, but rather that free individuals would secure a truly autonomous public sphere of personal freedom, leisure and freedom of movement. However, Marx was working at a time that did not foresee changes to the public sphere, and as the nineteenth century unfolded, the political public sphere became concerned with conflict management rather than dissolution of power (Goode 2005). The focus became one of securing compromise between interest groups and factions. Habermas commented that 'with liberalism ... the bourgeois self-interpretation of the public sphere abandoned the form of a philosophy of history in favour of common-sense meliorism – it became realistic' (Habermas 1989: 131).

Key trends of this 'realistic turn' emerged over the nineteenth and twentieth centuries, interacting with changing perceptions of the role of the state as well as understandings of the private sphere, and have logically worked their way through to twenty-first-century thought and debate, as well as historical realities within Europe (Goode 2005). Centrally, the narrow notion of a property-owning, middle-class and male domain forming the basis of a public sphere started to become eroded through the interrelation of two trends: the public sphere began expanding through the growth of the press and the spread of literacy on the one hand, and through working-class consciousness and political activity, the rise of trade unions, women's movements, and the anti-slavery and race movements on the other hand. Conflict, therefore, occurred not just between classes but also in relation to race and gender politics. Furthermore, interacting with these developments, the growing power of public opinion in the form of populism threatened individual liberties. Mills and de Tocqueville argued that these conditions undermined the public sphere, first through the tyrannical aspects of public opinion and second with the extension of state power through the increasing bureaucratization and centralization of organized capitalism (Goode 2005).

The transition to organized capitalism led to the state taking a more interventionist role. Habermas characterizes this as a process of refeudalization, in which the distinction between public and private could no longer be applied, and in which organized capitalism required the interlocking of state and society (Habermas 1989: 142). During this period the perceived coherence of civil society was challenged, as imperfections of the market system were regularly highlighted in the endemic crises inherent in the contradictions of capitalism. These crises resulted in organized private interest groups vying for state power, with some demanding protectionism and others liberalization, which politicized civil society further (Goode 2005). Working-class pressure and other factors such as Keynesian redistribution, the 'publification' of contractual law, collective wage bargaining and the provision of state welfare were further factors shaping the public sphere and defining the role of the state under organized capitalism (Goode 2005). These trends resulted in changed understandings of the public and private spheres, with public interest seen as facilitating compromise between private interests, and the private realm became 'hollowed out', increasingly focusing on leisure, consumption and lifestyle – what Habermas was later to call 'privatism' (Habermas 1976).

It was within these dynamics that the twentieth-century mass media and cultural industries developed and played a particular role in national public spheres of the era. Habermas (1989) recognized the democratizing and progressive opportunities within the commodification of culture in the mass media and cultural industries. However, as they developed, Habermas argued that the mass media and cultural industries were drawn towards the lowest common denominator in which publics became less debating publics and more consuming publics. Habermas (1989) argued that the expansion of the public sphere in these conditions creates a logic in which cultural products are simplified to make them more saleable, so that individuals as members of mass or niche markets do not have to raise their understanding and reflection to engage in cultural activity and cultural products (Goode 2005). In this context, the expansion of the public sphere was through the commercialism of mass culture, which was, and is, characterized by formulaic packages of human-interest stories, advice columns, 'real life stories', the rise of celebrities, reality TV shows and so on. These trends in the commercialization of the media and the commodification of culture leads to private life being publicized and public life being privatized, and culture as a site of critical debate and self-improvement becoming emptied of meaning (Habermas 1989).

Habermas's analysis of socio-cultural change raises issues in the development of a public sphere in which notions of a just and good society can be discussed. There are, however, further dimensions to consider in changes to society in late modernity, which open up a debate around identity, participation and exclusion, as well as the development of new media and information communication technologies (ICTs) that are pertinent and require the setting of new agendas and policies. This opening of debate highlights Habermas's own admission that his analysis is overly unilinear and simplistic – as seen, for example, in his argument of the move from a culture-debating to a culture-consuming public (Habermas in Calhoun 1992: 438).

Calhoun (1992) identifies weaknesses in Habermas's analysis of the public sphere, primarily pointing to a methodological imbalance in his analysis of a classical (bourgeois) public sphere on the one hand, with the public sphere of organized capitalism on the other hand. Critique is levelled at his emphasis on rational bourgeois communication at the expense of the various modes of public discourse in the public sphere (Eley in Calhoun 1992: 307) and in emphasizing the exclusive character of the public sphere and so de-emphasising working-class discourse in the critical publicity (Baker in Calhoun 1992: 191–92). Crossley and Roberts (2004) further assert that Habermas's narrow view of the public sphere, especially that of the bourgeoisie, leads him to underplay the strategizing of powerful agencies in seeking political influence (2004: 11). Theoretical critiques from late-modern, postmodern and relational and institutional schools in different ways all question his use of the 'universal' and 'truth' in considering the public sphere as a site for reasoned debate.

Some of the critiques can be illustrated by concrete examples, such as the rise of women in the workplace and the reorganization of the family following early feminist activity, which might necessitate public debate regarding gender issues. As Fraser (1992) suggests, the role of women in the public sphere, as a focus on the emotional as well as rational aspects of society, needs addressing. This was not at the forefront in the bourgeois public sphere and was not fully addressed in Habermas's analysis. Furthermore, society is increasingly complex and multicultural, which means that any active and fully functioning public sphere needs to be able to accommodate many different social groups, identities, ethnicities and interests, something which the bourgeois public sphere did not, in real terms, facilitate (Siltanen and Stanworth 1984). Another factor is the fluidity and deterritorialization of globalization, which has altered the meaning of public spheres through, for example, the emergence of global events, the development of global economic organizations such as the World Bank, the rise of global political publics such as the UN, UNESCO and Amnesty International – all of which in broad terms raises questions about who are the 'general public' in a globalized world (Sheller and Urry 2003).

As indicated at the beginning of this discussion, participation means understanding the roles and relationships between the state, individuals and groups, and the means of communication. Habermas (1989) tries to envisage the ways in which critical publicity can be developed in late capitalism in a 'reconstructive turn'. He argues for a new role for the state, requiring an alteration in its scope to increase critical publicity and scrutiny, which extends to agencies that interact with the state such as special interest groups, corporations, professional associations, parties and so on. These groups all contribute to and are part of the formation of public interest and must be open to scrutiny, forming a reflexive publicity (Habermas 1989). Any reconstructed public sphere, therefore, needs to be developed by applying critical publicity to existing institutions such as political parties, unions, the media, extra-parliamentary decision-making spheres and so on. In the case of a public sphere for Europe, this entails addressing the means of communication in the mediation of the social, economic and political conditions in relation to what it means to be both a member-state citizen and a citizen of Europe in a networked global economy. Communication, moreover, that is embedded within socio-economic and political contexts and understood and shaped culturally, in the everyday sense and in popular and high-cultural forms. The re-imagining of communication and publicness requires addressing the co-presence of the consumption of commoditized culture and engagement in culture in the negotiation of social life, as both are intrinsic in contemporary cultural change.

The Context of EU Information Society Policy in the Shaping of a Public Sphere

The current emergence of an information society provides the context for the development of a twenty-first century public sphere, which may include some sort of EPS. The development of such a public sphere is not straightforward in conceptual, technological or institutional terms, or in terms of public participation. Rather, as the bourgeois public sphere emerged out of several contributing factors, the development of an e-enabled EPS is also situated in a variety of factors, some of which are seen in the way in which the EU aims to foster a European Information Society. Policymakers have not directly focused on a European public sphere, but intended to build a European Information Society that would address the building of a technological infrastructure and technological capacity through R&D and fostering the relevant skill sets, as well as recognizing the dangers of exclusion from an information society.

There is debate regarding the character of an information society on the one hand, and debate as to whether there is any significant transformation to a radically different society on the other hand (Webster 2003). However, the use and development of ICT is situated within broader socio-economic and cultural change, materializing with the rise of a networked society, within the dynamics of globalization (Castells 2001). Furthermore, social actors in an information age do experience the mediated and informational character of contemporary society via new ways of organizing work and education as well as leisure time and everyday life (Dutton 1999; Haddon 2004). In economic as well as social terms, key features underpinning an information age are: networked informational appliances and the networks that support them, which facilitate new forms of exchange in and between organizations and throughout society (Mansell and Steinmuller 2000: 453). Examples given by Mansell and Steinmuller (2000) include the emphasis on social networks in the production of knowledge, networks of users in innovation processes, and networks of suppliers in competitive industrial sectors.

Political consequences emerging from these dynamics include a crisis in liberal democracy in which citizens are finding that their respective nation states are ineffective and that transnational institutions hold power but make little provision for democratic citizenship (Barney 2004). Interacting with these changes is a democratic malaise in which citizens distrust and feel alienated from democratic processes. Within this situation, commentators such as Webster (2001) and Castells (1997) see the rise of 'informational politics' in which electronic media comprise the privileged space of politics. Whether or not 'informational politics' is necessarily a new politics, this trend highlights the role of networked technologies in political processes and, by association, in the public sphere.

In theory, ICT has the potential to enhance liberal democracy, since information and communication underpin democratic processes. Technically speaking, ICT offers new opportunities for citizens to engage in dialogue and to participate in a public sphere because of its decentralized architecture and interactive applications. It thus moves beyond the limitations of the centralized and one-way broadcast media of the mass press, radio and television. Barney (2004) summarizes the possible contribution that ICT might make to democratic politics, including:

1. More convenient, generalized access to significant volumes of politically relevant information.
2. A medium for publication for all.
3. A tool for organizing and mobilizing action.
4. A means of enhanced, routine vertical communication between citizens and officials.
5. A medium of enhanced horizontal communication amongst citizens, which includes expanded opportunities for public dialogue and deliberation.
6. A mechanism to enable more direct forms of popular participation in democratic decision-making, such as online voting and deliberative opinion polling (ibid. p.134).

These factors combine to provide 'an infrastructure for the erection and maintenance of a more inclusive and politicised public sphere than that mediated by existing, commercial mass media' (Barney 2004: 134). It is, however, the way in which these technologies are socially shaped and used that will influence the way they can contribute to the public sphere. As Mansell and Steinmuller (2000) argue, the ways in which technologies are developed and used is complex, and is negotiated through various social and economic factors that influence their cultural significance and meaningfulness to society.

The importance of networks leads Mansell and Steinmuller to argue that there is a growing recognition of the 'crucial role of interdependency in modern societies and economies' (Mansell and Steinmuller 2000: 453). In relation to Europe, they point out that 'concerns about the extent and nature of interdependencies not only have a long history, but they also have considerable contemporary significance' (Mansell and Steinmuller 2000: 453). In this context, as Mansell and Steinmuller (2000: 453) conclude, it is not surprising that Europe has a special interest in a networked environment involving ICT. Europe was a key player in the drive to push forward an information society, and there is a specific European vision of an 'information society', which 'implies a goal of achieving ubiquitous and accessible information resources as a foundation for economic growth and development. It also describes the increasing extent to which information is becoming a central feature of social and cultural life' (Mansell and Steinmuller 2000: 453).

Developments in the European Information Society are envisaged as contributing to European economic growth, increasing employment, fostering social and economic cohesion across the Union, as well as transforming governance systems. Although there are potentially negative consequences, such as the development of digital divides, policymakers feel that this could be mitigated through policy (Mansell and Steinmuller 2000). The early vision of development of an information society was that of a single evolutionary pathway in which broadly accessible ICT infrastructures would create opportunities for beneficial and progressive change. However, as Mansell and Steinmuller (2000: 1) argue, 'there are many possible European Information Societies depending on the rate and implementation of technological developments, how these technologies interact with users, and the actions of those in other parts of the world.'

Thus, there is no set evolutionary path for a European Information Society, and much less for the development of an EPS from these developments. Rather, it is the developments in information society that provide and generate opportunities for users and developers to shape a public sphere for Europe in the twenty-first century. Although information society policy does not specifically focus on the development of an EPS, information society development is generating a communications infrastructure that may facilitate a public sphere. These emergent forms of communication may generate new forms of participation embedded in the socio-economic and political change of an emerging information society in a global economy.

The trajectory of EU information society policy starts with the economic emphasis of gaining EU competitiveness in global markets. Mansell and Steinmuller (2000) point out that worldwide change in ICT and service markets are related to developments in the EU,[3] such as the international momentum towards a market-led development of the telecoms industry through liberalization and privatization, leading to the opening of the European telecom industry to the market. These trends interact with the rising importance of networks, as ICT-enabled organizational forms, reflecting the new organization of capitalism and the interdependencies both within and between modern societies and economies in a global economy, variously talked about as the new economy, the knowledge economy or society, and the information society or information age. In Europe, interdependencies, for example in trade and politics, have a long history and remain significant in that the EU stresses the role of 'trans-European' networks as a means of extending linkages across borders of member states. Mansell and Steinmuller (2000) argue that the European Information Society is a transnational construction[4] and is illustrative of the broadly consensual character of European policy-making

> that aggregates national diversity into a loose structure where boundaries between national and supra-national initiatives are fluid ... Although each member state has articulated its own perspective on, and approach to, information society developments, the value of a common perspective on the broad outlines of defining a European Information Society is recognised. (Mansell and Steinmuller 2000: 453–54)

Early developments of an information society were detailed in the 1993 EU White Paper *Growth, Competitiveness, Employment: The Challenges and Ways Forward in the 21st Century*. Early developments of an information society were detailed in the 1993 EU White Paper 'Growth, Competitiveness, Employment: the Challenges and Ways Forward in the 21st Century'. This White Paper set an agenda for using ICT as a tool to foster economic growth and improve levels of employment. However, The 1994 Report of the Members of the High Level Group on the Information Society: 'Europe and the Global Information Society: Recommendations to the European Council' set a broader strategy for the development and use of ICT. The report stated that the widespread use of ICT had the potential to 'build a more equal and balanced society', 'reinforce social cohesion' and provide a' wider choice of services and entertainment' (1994: 6).

Frameworks of European funded Research and Development supported this vision. Projects in the 4th Framework, for instance focused on Telematics applications in a range of social contexts (Wessels 2007). For example the 'Advanced TransEuropean Telematics for Community Help' project (ATTACH, 1995–1998) developed multi-media information kiosks for community help. The 'Delivery and Access to Local Information and Services' project (DALI, 1995–1998) fostered multi-media services[5] for the elderly. The 'Telematics Applications and Strategies Combating Social and Economic Exclusion project (PERIPHERA project, 1995–1998) produced multi-media applications for training and educational purposes. The 'Citizens Access Networks and Services' project (CANS, 1995–1998) addressed the needs migrant groups through multi-media assisted language and skills training. Research in the 5th Framework broadened out to address the dynamics of the social take-up and use of ICT. For instance, EMTEL, the European Media Technology and Everyday Life network (2000–2003) focused on the way ICT was used by different groups across Europe. Their research shows how ICT is appropriated and adapted differently in varying contexts of use, for example Greek communities in London use Internet cafes to communicate with their Diaspora network, the lack of joined-up accessible ICT training is proving to be a barrier to employment for those living in Liege, and rural Irish families use the Internet for personal communication and not civic engagement (Silverstone ed 2005: 1–13). The foci of the 4th and 5th Framework have produced a base of ICT applications and studies of use that is informing current strategy and development.

The current strategic goal for 2010 is that the EU should 'become the most competitive and dynamic knowledge-based economy in the world, capable of sustainable economic growth with more and better jobs and greater social cohesion' (Lisbon European Council, March 2000), a hugely ambitious but laudable aim. Policies such as 'eEurope', and 'i2010: European Information Society 2010' continue to shape developments through the alliances that are formed and reformed as Europe adapts the logic of a networked society through various economic and social initiatives. The development of these networks is understood via the notion of a European Information Society, in which low-cost information and ICT are in general use, and as a knowledge-based economy that stresses investment in human and social capital and knowledge and creativity.

The current Information Society and Media portfolio extends and takes forward the understanding of EU economic competitiveness more fully into an information society and knowledge-based economy by focusing on the underlying communications infrastructures and, beyond, to the content and services they deliver. It encompasses telecommunication networks, broadband internet access and satellite communications, new communications technologies such as '3G' mobile communications and internet telephony, and digital material as diverse as cinema releases and eHealth services, as well as channel strategies and portal services. One can see the way in which an information society and media perspective is beginning to bring a more convergent view to communication within a European Information Society framework, albeit still within a perspective that sees ICT as a key enabler in facilitating a variety of cultural and political initiatives.

There are developments in the area of culture, eGovernment, and eInclusion that are generating ways in which the citizens within the EU can participate in forms of cultural and political activity.[6] These policy agendas and initiatives are laying the foundations for new forms of communication in a networked economy and society. They are situated in the pervasive ethos of market liberalism, which is integral to the new economy and is influential in shaping the organization of networked societies, seen primarily in the retrenchment of the state in the organization of national societies. This reorientation to market liberalism and the rise of transnational economic activity, seen in a string of bilateral and multilateral economic covenants such as the treaties of the EU, as well as the new ICT, is generating a context in which culture, politics and social life are being renegotiated. Given that national public spheres emerged out of a set of economic, political, and social and cultural conditions, it is necessary to explore the ways in which policy is considering culture, politics and social life in the information society, which may provide the basis for a public sphere for the twenty-first century.

In the area of culture, there are a range of activities. The 'Culture in the Digital Era' programme, for example, sees itself as a catalyst for creativity and for stimulating innovation in the arts, with the underpinning role of culture being one of ensuring sustainable cultural development throughout society, both in the creative industries and in the intrinsic meaningfulness of social life. The creative industries are gaining a new significance in advanced capitalist societies as they adapt to the knowledge economy in which cultural products, images and processes are the new commodities of exchange across global networks. In relation to culture more generally, as Raymond Williams (1958) argued, culture, both ordinary and as it is manifested in many cultural forms, gives meaning to – or indeed is – the meaning of social life. The explicit 'turn to culture' occurred in the late industrial period and in the rise of consumer society. Although, as discussed earlier, this can lead to passive consumption of a commodified culture, there is also engagement in cultural activity that can enhance dialogue and understanding of lifeworlds. Engaging in cultural activity gains a new significance in the global economy, understanding difference in a multicultural society and, if supported by humanistic principles, countering intolerance on the one hand (Silverstone 2006) and, given the transnational nature of capitalism, managing cultural markets on the other hand. This, in the fullest sense, requires cultural intelligence. It is also within the appropriate cultural frameworks that freedom of expression, pluralism, protection of minors and consumers are secured in a competitive and dynamic knowledge-based economy. Culture, in this context, is seen as being crucial to maintain quality of life and social cohesion, especially in the context of the mobility of people and the dynamics of intercultural dialogue[7] in a knowledge-based economy.

In this context, EU policymakers have devised strategies for the creation of a digitally literate Europe within the ethos and framework of entrepreneurialism and market liberalism in a knowledge economy. The eEurope 2005 Action Plan, for example, proposed that all European museums, libraries and archives should be connected to broadband networks by the end of 2005, which would entail partnerships between private-sector network providers and part state-funded and visitor revenue supporting public organizations. In this spirit, the Lund Principles aim to establish an agenda for actions to be carried out by member states and/or the Commission to help coordinate the mechanism for digitisation programmes across Europe.[8] To overcome barriers such as differences of language, culture and administrative practice, and to enable the cross-border use of digital content, the eContent initiative, again a market-oriented programme, aims to support the production, use and distribution of European digital content and to promote linguistic and cultural diversity via global networks.

Another aspect of change in the arena of political processes, and a central initiative across Europe, both at national level and across the Union, is 'eGovernment'. EGovernment means the use of ICT in public administrations which, when combined with organizational change and new skills, seeks to improve public services and democratic processes and to strengthen support for public policies. The Commission, in line with Castells (1996), who argues that that the internet can be used by citizens to watch their governments, believes that eGovernment is a way for public administrations to become:

1. More open and transparent, and to reinforce democratic participation.
2. More service-oriented, providing personalized and inclusive services to each citizen.
3. More productive, delivering maximum value for taxpayers' money.

EGovernment is an eEurope 2005 policy priority[9] and touches on many areas of government and administration. Some of these areas have a European focus as well as each nation's own eGovernment national applications and content. The EU's eGovernment activities are diverse and reflect the vision they have of eGovernment itself.[10] Significantly, they operate directly at the EU level through initiatives such as:

1. Your Voice in Europe – the European Commission's 'single access point' to a wide variety of consultations, discussions and other tools that enable citizens to play an active role in the European policy-making process.
2. The European Parliament's Citizens' Portal – a mailbox for questions, requests for information, proposals and suggestions addressed to the European Parliament by members of the public.
3. The European Ombudsman – which deals with complaints about maladministration by the institutions and bodies of the European Community.

Each of these initiatives promotes a European perspective and participation on a European level, and combine, at a minimum, to initiate dialogue and foster democratic accountability across the Union.

The third dimension underpinning any public sphere is the social one, which needs to be inclusive to enable participation (Steinert and Pilgram 2003; Wessels and Meidema 2003). The eInclusion programme focuses on participation for all in the knowledge-based economy. The Lisbon Strategy (2000) set the ambitious goal of ensuring that every citizen should have the appropriate skills needed to live and work in an information society. The strategic challenge for eInclusion is twofold: to exploit the potential of ICT to overcome traditional forms of exclusion, while ensuring that all citizens benefit from the information society. The Commission puts emphasis on ICT to turn the risk of a digital divide into 'digital cohesion' and to generate 'digital opportunities' across the Union. The agenda is to bring some perceived benefits of an information society to all segments of the population, including those disadvantaged through limited resources, education, age, gender, ethnicity, disability, and from living in less-favoured areas.

To support these objectives, the 'Open Method of Coordination' encourages member states to set out steps in National Action Plans to improve access to ICTs and to the opportunities ICTs can provide. New member states have outlined their key challenges in the area of eInclusion in their Joint Inclusion Memorandum. The eEurope 2005 Action Plan focuses on ensuring the equal participation of all citizens in the mainstream development of modern online public services. The new regulatory framework for electronic communications networks and services contains a series of rules and principles to ensure that the liberalization of the electronic communications market does not occur at the expense of end-users. It assumes that competition and market forces are the most effective means of satisfying user needs but, at the same time, it provides national regulatory authorities (NRAs) with the relevant powers to act to protect users when necessary.

The dynamics of these initiatives are articulated in the objective of the Single European Information Space, which aims to offer affordable and secure high-bandwidth communications, rich and diverse content, and digital services. This initiative aims to review the electronic communications regulatory framework (2006), which includes defining an efficient spectrum management strategy (2005). It further seeks to create a consistent internal market framework for information society and media services by modernizing the legal framework for audio-visual services, starting with a Commission proposal in 2005 for revising the Television Without Frontiers Directive, analysing and making any necessary adaptations to the Community acquis affecting information society and media services (2007). Part of the agenda is to promote fast and efficient implementation of the acquis governing the information society and media services. There is continued support for the creation and circulation of European content, defining and implementing a strategy for a secure European Information Society (2006), and identifying and promoting targeted actions on interoperability, particularly digital rights management (2006/2007). These tasks are the necessary prerequisites for building an information and communications infrastructure for a European Information Society, which is also the means for the development of a public sphere for Europe.

However, notions of a European Information Society are based on a loose network of member states and there is a strong focus on the technological development needed to underpin such a society. Although there is some evidence that information society and media agendas are beginning to converge, little direct attention is paid to the development of an EPS; rather, attention has focused on the ways in which the new digital technologies for information and communication can be integrated into social and economic networks. The initiatives in culture, eGovernment and eInclusion aim to enable participation. Each of these initiatives addresses dimensions that underpin the fostering of a European sensibility that may in time generate a European public willing and able to participate in an EPS. Thus, for example, the culture agenda has the potential to foster understanding across Europe and move towards genuine dialogue across member states – a prerequisite for a public sphere of a democratic world region such as Europe. The focus on eInclusion is aiming to ensure that everyone can participate in a society that is increasingly organized around digital networks – again a prerequisite for democratic society and for activating a public sphere. Finally, the initiatives in the area of eGovernment are specifically aimed at providing information, communicative spaces and democratic procedures at the European level.

These initiatives show that there is a European vision in the development of the infrastructure and framework for a European Information Society that is resourced through European collaboration. But these activities do not comprise a cohesive single path towards developing a European Information Society, let alone an EPS. Instead, the nature of the innovation cycle is one of incremental change, at technological, institutional and social levels. Mansell and Steinmuller (2000) argue that this incremental and cumulative process has the potential to develop an inclusive European Information Society. Nonetheless, the key question is whether the networking capacity and more open communication can facilitate different forms of participation in public discussion and democratic processes in late modernity. This question requires an analysis of the socio-economic and political context that may, in cultural terms, foster new forms of engagement in public life in Europe.

Participation in Europe

However, it is too early to see if the networked spaces of EU information society initiatives will foster publics, whether with a sense of national identity or a European identity, to engage with European issues and in European democratic processes. Thus as yet, for example, the European Information Society does not function as a public sphere for a European polity, but if supported by changing institutional practices and greater identification with Europe by citizens of member states, it may well be a step towards building and, in the longer term, sustaining an EPS. Both of these complex processes need addressing if Europe is to have its own public sphere. This involves examining the democratic deficit, public identification with Europe, being European, and ways of building an EPS.

A European Information Society may be a necessary prerequisite for an EPS, but on its own it is not sufficient for an EPS. In general terms, the EU suffers from a lack of democracy (Scharpf 1996; Weidenfeld 1990) and, as Grundmann (1999) asserts, a requirement for European democracy is a European public, which currently is hard to identify. The lack of democracy and a European public is interlinked with the lack of any common European identity, resulting a very weak sense of an EPS. In relation to the democratic deficit, the history of European integration is primarily characterized by a technocratic approach of an elite in an era when public approval was not seen as important (Grundmann 1999: 128). The process of European integration was marked by a 'permissive support' or 'diffuse support' (Easton 1965; Key 1961; Lindberg and Scheingold 1970). Diffuse support means that there is a 'reservoir of goodwill' and a commitment to institutions which is not contingent upon short-term policy outputs and outcomes (Smith and Wright 1999). However, in the 1990s and 2000s this permissive support has been undermined, as national referenda have often rejected EU objectives.

In relation to the ways in which publics identify with Europe, Europe is generally unpopular. Leonard (1998) identifies three interconnected reasons for this. First, EU institutions are detached from people's everyday life. Second, the priorities of EU policymakers are not those of most voters. Third, the benefits of the EU are spread unevenly within member states, with most of the direct benefits going to minority groups, declining industries and underdeveloped regions. Furthermore, in their attempts to foster integration, the Commission's role is undermined by a lack of public legitimacy (Featherstone 1994: 163). Publics are largely unable to identify political leaders in the Commission, and many are not unduly concerned with the balance of power within European institutions – between the Commission, the Council and the Parliament. Additionally, the Parliament does not have the powers of a national government, it does not control European politicians or the budget, and it does not have legislative functions (Grundmann 1999: 131).

These issues pose problems for the development of a transnational European democracy. In addressing the ways in which more democratic control and greater legitimacy may be achieved, one could consider a division between the legislative and executive or perhaps direct election of members to the Commission via the mass electorate. One could also envisage the European Parliament having more power – electing and dismissing members of the Commission (Grundmann 1999), for instance. However, as Grundmann (1999) points out, a prerequisite for accountability and transparency is the politicization of the decision-making process, which is constrained by the pervasive ethos of consensus. He further argues that simply providing more information will not address the democratic deficit because information that is uninteresting to the public will not remedy the lack of transparency, and might generate information overload, that could deter engagement in European issues (in Smith and Wright 1999).

Lodge adds another dimension to the issue of information by stating that: 'filling an alleged information deficit will not necessarily restore confidence among people who mistrust political processes, for whatever reason' (Lodge 1994: 361). Although ICT can provide wider access to information, it needs to be designed to meet the needs of citizens. Thus, for example, 'Lexcalibur' is a virtual European public square that aims to empower actors by providing information on the decision-making processes of the Community (Grundmann 1999). Although it seeks to provide citizens with access to information, the information is presented in a technical way and not in ways that make the information intelligible and interesting for the citizen. Therefore, as Weiler (1997) argues, 'the most immediate direct beneficiaries of Euro-governance on the Internet would in fact be the media, interested pressure groups, non-governmental organisations, and the like' (Weiler 1997: 515).

The quest for participation in Europe requires a European public, which raises the question of 'who are the Europeans?' Given the Western notion of *demos* as signifying (national) territory, common institutions and a political community that binds people together, it is hard to identify Europe, let alone Europeans. Whereas national identities are vivid, accessible, established, popular and widely believed (Grundmann 1999: 133),[11] European identity is none of these. As Grundmann suggests, 'Europe is deficient as idea and as process' (1999: 133), and, as Smith says, 'it lacks a pre-modern past – a 'prehistory' that can provide it with emotional sustenance and historical depth' (Smith 1995: 327). Given this context, the notion of Europe as being a 'project' rather than a deeply held belief reflects the sensibility and imagination of efforts to integrate Europe. For some, the idea of the European project is expressive of ideas about postmodern society. As Pocock argues:

> 'Europe' could become 'the ideology of a post-historical culture, in which varying affluent and varying alienated masses ... float from one environment to another with no awareness of moving from one past, and one commitment to it, to another ... The affluent populations wander as tourists – which is to say consumers of images – from one former historical culture to another, delightfully free from the need to commit themselves to any, and free to criticise while determining for themselves the extent of their responsibility. (Pocock, 1997: 303–4, 312)

Although this position serves to illustrate some of the ways in which integration may be envisaged, it nonetheless offers a superficial account of the social and political dynamics of building a world region. Some commentators identify with a more progressive approach and envisage a 'New European', who has to be 'as sophisticated as the merchants and courtiers of the Renaissance or the multinational and multilingual inhabitants of Central and Eastern Europe before Hitler and Stalin ... He has to know foreign languages beyond the superficial and unreliable *koine*' (Picht 1993: 87). In practical terms, this is a lot to expect from the average citizen, who has to balance work and home in their everyday lives, and may reinforce the existing elitism within Europe. One aspect of developing a progressive European sensibility can be found in the humanistic ideal of intercultural training, especially if the aim is not a rejection of identity but addressing other identities in an open way (Grundmann 1999: 134). However, identity is not always a straightforward concept, as many people have multiple identities and can move between them according to need and circumstance, and intercultural training on its own is not sufficient to generate a democratic Europe (Smith and Wright 1999).

It would be naive not to acknowledge that alongside the concern to build a European identity, or at least some feeling of European commonality, there is the reassertion of national identities. Weiler (1997) raises a key point in relation to the link between identity and national citizenship and European citizenship. He points out that there is a flaw in the assumption that speaks of European citizenship in the same tones as national citizenship. He suggests a version of multiple *demoi* in which individuals see themselves belonging to two *demoi*, and that member-state nationality and European citizenship are understood as being interdependent. Logically, as Weiler (1997) points out, one cannot be a European citizen without being a member-state national. Weiler sees a civilizing aspect in his suggestion, in that:

> The acceptance by its members that, in a range of areas of public life, one will accept the legitimacy and authority of decisions adopted by fellow European citizens in the realisation that in these areas preference is given to choices made by the outreaching, non-organic, *demos*, rather than by an in reaching one. (Weiler 1997: 510)

However, to arrive at this point requires changing people's perceptions and attitudes greatly, and requires vehicles for this cultural change. The development of a public sphere relevant to twenty-first-century Europe may help to facilitate change to the idea and process of citizens' integration and engagement in Europe. Grundmann (1999) argues that a homogeneous EPS is a precondition for a European polity, where 'homogenous' means a 'public sphere in which the same issues are debated at the same time with a view to the same political processes' (1999: 143). The rationale for a homogenous public is that the public has the agenda-setting function in a democracy and it is voters who can change their political representatives as well as selecting politically relevant issues (Grundmann 1999: 136). As Grundmann (1999) further argues, there are national public spheres but no common European political agenda, and therefore politicians do not need to respond, or be accountable, to a 'European constituency'. He argues for strengthening a public sphere in Europe that is based on the distinction of, on the one hand, the Europeanization of national public spheres, and, on the other hand, on the emergence of a transnational European public. The first step, Grundmann (1999) argues, is a synchronization; the second is a homogenization of national public spheres. The homogenization of public spheres is more ambitious, and Grundmann (1999) argues that this will follow on from national public spheres becoming synchronized in relation to debate on key political issues. Grundmann (1999) sees this distinction as a way to build a public sphere for Europe.

However, he does see problems in achieving even modest amounts of synchronization and homogenization of national public spheres, and although there are increased technological possibilities, there is no common media system. Obstacles to this include the heterogeneity of culture and language (de Swaan 1991; Groze-PecLum 1990). Other difficulties include the fact that news correspondents tend to be nationally aligned and are primarily interested in European topics that relate to their domestic policy agenda (Gerhards 1993), while member states tend to pursue a national line in European policy debates. Both these processes strengthen national discourses about Europe rather than fostering a European perspective on policy debates. Furthermore, most member states 'look to Brussels' and, apart from the European elite, do not consider the other member states, which means that there is less crossing over of interests at a grounded national interest level to form a European perspective (Smith and Wright 1999).

An ironic factor in the re-emergence of nationalist movements is the growing importance of the means of communication and the provision of information, which often leads to the emergence of smaller and denser networks of homogenous ethno-linguistic groups (Grundmann 1999: 133). This dimension, alongside the difficulties of imagining a European community for the twenty-first-century global economy, poses real challenges for developing an EPS. There is some evidence of transnational European interests, such as the single currency (euro) and the BSE crisis in the early 1990s. These types of pan-European concerns may well contribute to the synchronization of a transnational public sphere at a European level. There are also some signs of the Europeanization of media coverage and public sphere activity in the area of international and security policy (Risse 2003; Kantner 2004; Martin 2004). It is, however, unclear as to how this policy sector links with broader European institutional processes that can, in the longer term, generate a broader interest in European policy by citizens.

This discussion of the historical development of the public sphere, information society and participation in Europe shows how the public sphere is embedded in historical conditions and shaped through economic, political, social and cultural factors. The materialization of a public sphere occurs through a negotiation of the role of the state, forms of participation in and identification with national or supranational geopolitical configurations, and the media and forms of communication within society. These factors shaping the public sphere in the twenty-first century are situated within broader globalizing trends in which commercialized culture interacts with a multiplicity of cultures of everyday life across and within multicultural experience. Currently there is only a weak sense of European sensibility across member states and a general lack of interest in Europe, a lack of awareness of European institutions, and a perceived sense of a lack of democratic accountability by member-state citizens. The domestic agenda of many national media providers reinforces a national rather than European perspective to current affairs (c.f. Smith and Wright 1999).

The networked technologies have the potential to provide an infrastructure for new forms of participation across the EU. Information society policy does aim to be economically and socially inclusive and to foster intercultural dialogue and political engagement. If publics can access these technologies and form networked debating publics, then they may develop intercultural dialogue in which to negotiate place, identity and multiple *demoi* that, in time, could generate a European sensibility. The working through of networked societies as they develop alliances across interest groups in Europe may generate new spaces in which interests, both public and private, can start to inform and shape a public sphere for the twenty-first century in Europe. However, to exploit these information and communication technologies fully requires institutional change regarding the governance of Europe and an increased identification with Europe by the citizens of member states.

Conclusion

By tracing the way in which policy has developed, one can start to ascertain which opportunities are emerging that might foster an EPS within a European Information Society, and one that is relevant and appropriate in a global economy of networked societies. The interaction of policy and commercial activity in the new economy is part of the reshaping of society and of nation states but, as yet, there is a lack of understanding of the ways in which various groups and individuals engage in civil society and political processes in the development of supranational developments such as the fostering of a more integrated Europe. The ways in which

ICT is emerging in this new environment may generate new possibilities for citizens to engage at a European level in world affairs, which would reflect back into European, national and regional concerns. The incremental and complex realisation of an information society in Europe currently generates an ambiguous situation in which to predict whether an information society based on networking is conducive to fostering an EPS. Given that information policy has not focused directly on EPS, policymakers and commentators could explore the emerging networked environment for opportunities to develop new forms of public spheres, including an EPS.

The changes over historical time show both continuity and change: continuity in the negotiation of market, state, and individual liberty to participate in the public good; and change in relation to who participates and how individuals and groups can participate. The current quest to develop Europe as a world region within the global economy as well as providing a distinct cultural and political alternative to American hegemony and the homogenising of culture requires a radical rethinking of what a public sphere might be within a supranational entity such as Europe. This problem is the context in which the media as a form of communication in the public sphere has to facilitate spaces for public reasoning – both critical and normative – whilst at the same time the media as an institution is being shaped by contemporary social, political and economic trends. The current socio-economic climate of neoliberalism generates new forms of exclusion, which may reduce social justice to one of ameliorating the effects of the market with little concern for securing a 'good society' beyond individualistic and market freedom(s). The historical concerns of our European forbears are, therefore, being fully re-enacted beyond the nation state to the configuration of states in Europe. A key part of this is the shaping of a European information society, which may have a part to play in the mediation of Europe, and hence in the development, shaping and sustainability of a public sphere for Europe.

Thus, regarding the question of the influence of networked information society developments, the issue is one of a potential reshaping of media and communication, of governance systems, and of moving beyond universalistic and relativistic discourses regarding a public sphere. The potential lies in working towards a situation in which networking allows for, and facilitates, the emergence of twenty-first century publics that can engage meaningfully in intercultural discourses publicly and with a global understanding. However, as Hegel wrote: 'The Owl of Minerva spreads its wings only with the falling of dusk' (Hegel 195: 13), meaning that historical change can only be understood after a particular period of change has run its course. The opportunities and threats for Europe in a networked global economy underpinned by ICT are uncertain, but it does present an opportunity for Europe to reflect upon its history and culture and consider the ways in which it, as a world region, may foster participation and critical debate by its peoples in a global world.

Notes

1.   This Chapter has been adapted and worked up from: Wessels, B. (in press): 'The Public Sphere and the European Information Society'[1] in Bee and Bozzini *European Public Sphere: Spaces and Communication* (ed). Ashgate: Aldershot.

2.   The role of Europe in world events is, however, much debated, and the public debate between Habermas and Derrida illustrates the complexity of Europe's position and role. See Borradori (2003).

3.   Mansell and Steinmuller argue, for example, that the international momentum towards the market-led development of the telecommunications industry through liberalization and privatization resulted by January 1998 in the official opening of the European telecommunication market to competition. By then, the main directives promoting this change were being transposed, implemented and enforced by the member states. In the audio-visual sector, in the same year, there were major initiatives to launch digital broadcasting. There were moves to encourage a wide range of 'information push' technologies and services as well as the promotion and diffusion of electronic commerce applications (Mansell and Steinmuller 2000: 2).

4.   This covers the various transnational alliances that are formed out of supranational and national networks which are increasingly based on specific projects.

5.   Thus, multimedia is defined as a technology whose general characteristics are: digital, convergent, involving computers and communication technologies, involving a combination of video, sound and text, possibly involving video conferencing, scanning, interactive tracking and smart card technologies, touch screens etc., and requiring content to be interpolated from it: i.e., it has no intrinsic content or context of its own. The term 'telematics' developed out of a need to describe the specific context of the integration of ICT to deliver new kinds of services electronically, and is defined in this book as: involving the use of multimedia technologies to deliver various services. The factors that contribute to the contextual definitions are:the ability of various organizations to provide access to information and services for the public via information and communication technologies, the promise of which is an enhanced service for the public (Wessels 2007: 3)

6. The other main areas of activity are: 'Work and Employment', which covers employment, SMEs, eBusiness, economy sectors and eWork; 'Education and Training', which covers 'enhancing education and training' and 'skills', and 'Quality of Life', which covers the environment and health. Other areas of activity include 'IS Industry', which covers 'communications' and 'content and services'. Other areas of activity include 'Regions/World', which covers EU regions and the world. And there is 'Information Society Research'.

7. This means moving beyond a superficial understanding of other cultures and each other to foster a genuine understanding of each other in developing progressive relationships.

8. In the audio-visual sector, digital technology is a tool in the reshaping of broadcasting, programming production, delivery and payment systems, and at the same time adds to the intensity of commercial, regulatory and cultural debates worldwide.

9. See 'eEurope 2005, eGovernment' for an overview of the eGovernment targets in the eEurope 2005 Action Plan, including a summary of the Commission's *Communication on the Role of eGovernment for Europe's Future* and the 2005 *eGovernment Benchmarking Report*.

10. Examples include:
    1. The IDABC eGovernment Observatory: created by the Interoperable Delivery of European eGovernment Services to Public Administrations, Businesses and Citizens programme. This provides reference information on eGovernment issues and developments across Europe.
    2. EGovernment research: there is a plethora of open research issues on eGovernment. Research in this area is driven by policy, learns from best practice, and should provide input to future policy.
    3. The eGovernment action line of the eTEN programme.

11. Another factor is that many ethnic sentiments persist and may become visible, as seen in the periodic revivals of national identities.

Bibliography

Baker, K. 1992. 'Defining the Public Sphere in Eighteenth-century France: Variations on a Theme by Habermas', in C. Calhoun (ed.), *Habermas and the Public Sphere*. Cambridge, MA: The MIT Press. pp. 181–211.

Barney, D. 2004. *The Network Society*. Cambridge: Polity Press.

Beck, U. 1992. *Risk Society: Towards a New Modernity*, trans. M. Ritter. London: Sage.

Borradori, G. 2003. *Philosophy in the Time of Terror: Dialogues with Jürgen Habermas and Jacques Derrida*. Chicago: University of Chicago Press.

Calhoun, C. (ed.). 1992. *Habermas and the Public Sphere*. Cambridge, MA: The MIT Press.

Castells, M. 1997. *The Power of Identity*. Oxford: Blackwell.

———. 2001. *The Internet Galaxy: Reflections on the Internet, Business and Society*. Oxford: Oxford University Press.

Crossley, N. and Roberts, J.M. (eds). 2004. *After Habermas: New Perspectives on the Public Sphere*, Sociological Review Monographs. Oxford: Blackwell.

Dutton, W. (ed.). 1999. *Society on the Line: Information Politics in the Digital Age*. Oxford: Oxford University Press.

Easton. D. 1965. *A Systems Analysis of Political Life*. New York: Wiley.

Eley, G. 1992: 'Nations, Publics and Political Cultures: Placing Habermas in the Nineteenth Century', in C. Calhoun (ed.), *Habermas and the Public Sphere*. Cambridge, MA: The MIT Press. pp. 289–339.

Eriksen, E. 2004. 'Conceptualizing European Public Spheres: General, Segmented and Strong Publics', ARENA Working Paper 3/04. Centre for European Studies, University of Oslo.

Featherstone, K. 1994. 'Jean Monnet and the "Democratic Deficit" in the European Union', *Journal of Common Market Studies* 34: 149–70.

Fraser, N. 1992. 'Rethinking the Public Sphere: A Contribution to the Critique of Actually Existing Democracy', in C. Calhoun (ed.), *Habermas and the Public Sphere*. Cambridge, MA: The MIT Press.

Gerhards, J. 1993. 'Westeuropäische Integration und die Schwierigkeiten der Entstehung einer europäischen Öffentlichkeit', *Zeitschrift für Soziologie* 22: 86–110.

Goode, L. 2005. *Jürgen Habermas: Democracy and the Public Sphere*. London: Pluto.

Groze-PecLum, M.-L. 1990. 'Gibt es den europäischen Zuschauer?' *Zeitschrift für Kulturaustausch* 40: 185–94.

Grundmann, R. 1999. 'The European Public Sphere and the Deficit of Democracy', in D. Smith and S. Wright (eds), *Whose Europe? The Turn towards Democracy*. Oxford: Blackwell, pp. 125–46.

Habermas, J. 1976. *Legitimation Crisis*. London: Heinemann.

———. 1989. *The Structural Transformation of the Public Sphere: An Inquiry into a Category of Bourgeois Society*, trans. T. Burger. Cambridge: Polity Press.

Haddon, L. 2004. *Information and Communication Technologies and Everyday Life*. Oxford: Berg.

Hegel, G.W.F. 1952. *Philosophy of Right*. Oxford: Oxford University Press.

Kantner, C. 2004. Waiting for an European 'Progressive Era': The European Public and Its Problems. Florence: European University Institute.

Key, V.O., Jr. 1961. *Public Opinion and American Democracy*. New York: Knopf.

Leonard, M. 1998. *Rediscovering Europe*. London: Demos.

Lindberg, L. and Scheingold, S.A. 1970. *Europe's Would Be Policy Pattern of Change*. Englewood Cliffs, NJ: Prentice Hall.

Lodge, J. 1994. 'Transparency and Democratic Legitimacy', *Journal of Common Market Studies* 32: 343–68.

Mansell, R. and Steinmuller, W.E. 2000. *Mobilizing the Information Society: Strategies for Growth and Opportunity*. Oxford: Oxford University Press.

Martin, M. 2004. 'The European Public Sphere after 9/11: Discursive Constructions of the War on Terrorism in Britain and Germany', *EPS Conference, ESCUS, University of Sheffield, September*.

Marx, K. 1992. 'A Contribution to the Critique of Hegel's Philosophy of the Right: Introduction', in *Early Writings*, ed. R. Livingstone and G. Benton. Harmondsworth: Penguin Books. Originally published 1843–44.

Papacharissi, Z. 2002. 'The Virtual Public Sphere: The Internet as a Public Sphere', *New Media and Society* 4(1): 9–27.

Picht, P. 1993. 'Disturbed Identities: Social and Cultural Mutations in Contemporary Europe', in S. Garcia (ed.), *European Identity and the Search for Legitimacy*. London: Pinter, pp. 81–94.

Pocock, J.G.A. 1997. 'What Do We Mean by Europe?' *The Wilson Quarterly* 21(1): 12–35.

Rex, J. 1999. 'Prologue', in D. Smith and S. Wright (eds), *Whose Europe? The Turn towards Democracy*. Oxford: Blackwell, pp. vii–ix.

Risse, T. 2003: 'An Emerging European Public Sphere? Theoretical Clarifications and Empirical Indicators', *IDNET F5 Project (EUI) and the Centre for Transatlantic* Paper presented to the Annual Meeting of the European Union Studies Association (EUSA), Nashville TN, March 27–30. Berlin: Free University.

Roche, M. 2005. 'Developing the Public Sphere in Europe – Background Notes', Notes for a revised bid for an IP under F6: 7.1.1. (23/3/2005).

Scharpf, F.W. 1996. 'Democracy in Transnational Politics', *Internationale Politik* 51(12): 11–20.

Sheller, M. and Urry, J. 2003. 'Mobile Transformations of "Public" and "Private" Life', *Theory, Culture and Society* 20(3): 107–25.

Siltanen, J. and Stanworth, M. 1984. 'The Politics of Private Woman and Public Man', *Theory and Society* 13 (1): 91–118.

Silverstone, R. ed. 2005. *Media, Technology and Everyday Life in Europe: From Information to Communiation*. Aldershot: Ashgate.

Silverstone, R. 2006. *Media and Morality: On the Rise of the Mediapolis*. Cambridge: Polity Press.

Smith, A.D. 1995. 'National Identity and the Idea of European Unity', in P. Gower and P. Anderson (eds), *The Question of Europe*. London: Verso, pp. 318–42.

Smith, D. and Wright, S. (eds) (1999), *Whose Europe? The Turn towards Democracy*, Oxford: Blackwell.

Steinert, H. and Pilgram, A. 2003. *Welfare Policy from Below: Struggles against Social Exclusion in Europe*. Aldershot: Ashgate.

Swaan, A. de. 1991. 'Notes on the Emerging Global Language System – Regional, National and Supranational', *Media, Culture and Society* 13(3): 309–23.

Webster, F. 2001. 'A New Politics?' in F. Webster (ed.), *Culture and Politics in the Information Age: A New Politics?* London: Routledge.

———. (ed.). 2003. *The Information Society Reader*. London: Routledge.

Weiderfeld, W. (ed.). 1990. *Wie Europa verfasst sein soll*. Gutersloh: Bertelsmann Stiftung.

Weiler, J.H.H. 1997. 'To Be a European Citizen – Eros and Civilisation', *Journal of European Public Policy* 4(4): 495–519.

Wessels, B. 2007. *Inside the Digital Revolution: Policing and Changing Communication with the Public*. Aldershot: Ashagate.

Wessels, B. and Miedema, S. 2003. 'Towards Understanding Situations of Exclusion', in H. Steinert and A. Pilgram (eds), *Welfare Policy from Below: Struggles against Social Exclusion in Europe*. Aldershot: Ashgate, pp. 61–76.

Williams, R. 1958. *Culture*. Harmondsworth: Penguin.

PART II

EU Audio-visual and Information
Society Policies: Developments
and Challenges for the Mediation
of Europe

Chapter 8

EU Audio-visual Policy, Cultural Diversity and the Future of Public Service Broadcasting

Peter Humphreys

Introduction

Since the 1980s in the audio-visual sector new forms and arenas of regulation have developed, as policymakers have sought to adapt to new market and technological realities, principally: globalization, trans-frontier broadcasting by satellite, and the digital convergence of broadcasting, telecoms and the internet. One key element of regulatory change is the European Union's (EU) accumulation of regulatory influence in the audio-visual field, in part to re-establish problem-solving capacity that is escaping the national level as the result of the new technologies (satellite broadcasting, etc.). At first sight, the regulation of cross-border broadcasting appears to be an excellent example of the EU's development as a 'regulatory' political system (Majone 1996; Harcourt 2005: 7).

This chapter examines this process of the EU's accretion of influence, asking whether its role in the audio-visual field has been 'deregulatory' or 're-regulatory'. Precisely, it explores the hypotheses: first, that the EU has the capacity either to amplify or to moderate deregulatory competition ('racing to the bottom') among its member states; but, second, that it has an inherent deregulatory bias. The chapter highlights the distinction between the EU's powers of negative integration, notably the market-making powers that EU institutions wield from the economic goals enshrined in the Union's treaty base, and on the other hand, the EU's potential for positive integration, notably the harmonization of market-correcting rules. The chapter suggests that, in the politically sensitive audio-visual field, EU 'negative integration' appears to be far easier to achieve than positive integration. The chapter focuses on policies to promote public service goals in broadcasting, notably national (and social) cultural diversity and media pluralism[1].

The Analytical Framework

Globalization is often seen as naturally encouraging a (de)regulatory competition (see, e.g., McKenzie and Lee 1991) between 'competition states' (Cerny 1997), which are eager to retain and attract investment within their regulatory jurisdictions. Some public lawyers and political scientists have argued that, from the perspective of the public interest, this can lead to a 'race to the bottom'. Policymakers engage in regulatory competition where economic actors can choose locations on the basis of their relative regulatory attractiveness, referred to as 'regulatory arbitrage' in the political economy literature; regulatory competition may lead policymakers and regulators to lower regulatory standards in order to maintain investment or attract it from abroad and to promote national champions, the so-called 'Delaware effect' (after the U.S. state that attracted firms by offering lax incorporation standards). However, not all political scientists are convinced. David Vogel (1995), for example, suggests that there is nothing inevitably 'deregulatory' about regulatory competition, which under certain circumstances may actually drive regulatory standards upwards, the 'California effect'.

In this connection, the EU is particularly interesting because of its potential to provide problem-solving capacity in areas where the national capacity of its member states is being eroded under the impact of forces such as technological change and globalization (Scharpf 1997, 1999). As Vivien Schmidt (1999: 172) has argued, the EU has the potential either to reinforce the pressures of globalization or to moderate them. Several studies suggest that the EU has not contributed significantly to downward regulatory competition – the 'Delaware effect' (Woolcock 1994; Sun and Pelkmans 1995; Goodhart 1998). David Vogel's (1995) study of consumer protection and environmental regulation even found that the EU contributed to a 'race to(ward) the top' – the 'California effect'. However, in some sectors, such as road haulage, the EU's concern with economic competition means that it has tended to accentuate the process of deregulation, while in other sectors the EU's regulatory capacity has been kept minimal by member states jealously guarding national sovereignty . This is clearly the case with regard to social policy, industrial relations, and business and capital taxes. In relation to cultural policy in the media, the picture so far is mixed and to an extent open, in that policy developments at both the EU and global level are ongoing.

A diversity of EU media policies exert an impact – direct or indirect – on cultural diversity and the fulfilment of public service goals in broadcasting. Thus, EU policies regarding the regulation of the European audio-visual market determine the increasingly commercial international context within which national cultural policies for broadcasting and public service broadcasters operate. The EU's stance in world trade talks bears on the European countries' ability to protect and promote cultural production and, ultimately, concerns the long-term future of state aid (i.e., licence-fee) supported public service broadcasting. The EU's policies regarding the 'convergence' of broadcasting, IT and telecoms, under the impact of digital technologies, provide another important constraint on public service goals in broadcasting and media pluralism. Here, EU policies regarding access for public service broadcasters to digital networks will prove to be very important. EU competition policy, some say, places a question mark over the future funding basis of public service channels.

EU policies vary according to the balance of influence between member states, between member states and the supranational institutions, notably the Court and the Commission, and between the internal branches even of the Commission. The member states have diverse views, reflected in the generally complex negotiations surrounding draft directives. Thus, the goals of culturally protectionist France have often been at odds with those of the more 'open' U.K. or Germany. Collectively, though, member states have sought to retain primary responsibility for media policy, with the EU relegated to a supportive role. The Commission, on the other hand, acting as a 'purposeful opportunist' (Cram 1997) and as a 'policy entrepreneur' (Radaelli 2000) has sought both to expand its competences and to coordinate a European response to the new international market and technological challenges. However, the Commission's priorities vary according to particular Directorates-General (DGs). Collins (1994: 18–19) has famously described a broad conflict between 'liberals' (e.g. DG Competition) and '*dirigistes*' (e.g. DG Culture). Policies emerge from a complex process of negotiation, with member states and EU institutions seeking to respond to – and promoting and allying themselves with – important economic and other political interests, these operating increasingly at transnational, as well as national, level.

Complex though the EU policy process is, one general hypothesis promises to provide some clarity. Fritz Scharpf (1997, 1999) has argued that EU 'negative integration' is easier to achieve because the Commission and the European Court of Justice can rule unilaterally on market-making and competition-related matters, whereas the harmonization of market-correcting rules – 'positive integration' – is rendered more difficult to achieve because of the need for agreement in the Council of Ministers and Parliament. Negative integration has generally been deregulatory, in the sense of removing rules that obstruct the free movement of goods and services and impede competition in the single market. Positive integration implies EU regulatory harmonization, in other words a re-regulation, generally to provide common 'market correcting' measures. With this in mind, Figure 8.1 shows that the complexity of EU audio-visual policies can be clarified by plotting the EU's audio-visual policies diagrammatically in terms of the degree to which regulatory capacity has shifted to the EU level, or not (for a comparison with telecoms, see Humphreys 2006: 114).

Figure 8.1: National and European Capacity for Regulation

European capacity high

• Single audiovisual market (negative integration) • Convergence: regulating 'electronic communications' carriage (negative integration) • Competition policy with a 'Community dimension'(negative integration)	• GATT/WTO negotiations (shared competence between EC and member states)

National capacity Low	**National capacity high**
• Anti-concentration rules and cross-media ownership (failed EU positive integration) • Broadcasting content regulation/ international commercial broadcasters)	• National audiovisual production support schemes • Broadcasting content regulation/ public service broadcasting • Conditional-access regulation

European capacity low

Source: Adapted from a table ('National and European Problem-solving') in Scharpf 1997.

Negative Integration: Television Without Frontiers.

EU negative integration in the audio-visual field was achieved formally by the enactment of the 1989 Television Without Frontiers (TWF) Directive (Council of the European Communities 1989), creating the legal framework for a single European audio-visual market. There were a number of pressures behind the formulation of TWF during the 1980s apart from the obvious one of the EU's 1992 Single Market Initiative. A key factor was technological. The spread of cable and (the arrival of) large-scale satellite broadcasting undermined the 'scarcity of frequencies' rationale for public service broadcasting monopolies. Across Europe, governments re-regulated broadcasting to allow private commercial companies to enter the sector. At the same time, trans-frontier satellite broadcasting – notably, by means of the Luxembourg-based SES-Astra satellite series – offered commercial broadcasters an opportunity to circumvent restrictive national regulation. The weakened regulatory capacity of its member states provided a rationale for the EU to become the locus of at least some regulatory policymaking in the audio-visual field (Humphreys 1996: 169–70). Satellite broadcasting also appeared to promise the creation of a pan-European audio-visual market, attracting the interest of important transnational and supranational actors (Krebber 2002). Internationally, ambitious commercial companies wanted to exploit the economies of scale and scope promised by a 'single European market' (or, more accurately, its three principal linguistic markets: English, French and German). The Brussels-based European advertising lobby saw Europeanization as a way of achieving liberalization of advertising regulations in the member states. Liberalization was favoured by 'media-exporting' member states with strong media industries, notably the U.K., Germany[2] and Luxembourg (given the latter's role in satellite broadcasting and the strong international orientation of its domestic broadcaster, CLT). For their part, Commission officials drafted the TWF Directive in the belief that EU market liberalization was required in order to create the kind of economies of scale and scope for European companies that might boost the international competitiveness of the European audio-visual industry vis-à-vis that of the United States. Moreover, during the 1990s, the Commission came to deem the audio-visual sector, now 'digitally converging' with telecoms and the internet, to be of high strategic importance for Europe's competitiveness in the emerging 'global Information Society' (Humphreys 1996: 293–94).

The authority of the European Court of Justice (ECJ) was indirectly of key importance in paving the way for the Commission to liberalize the sector. The process of producing the TWF Directive had actually been preceded by two key ECJ rulings[3] – in 1974 and 1980 – on specific competition issues. Crucially, these rulings had defined broadcasting as a tradeable service subject to the European Community treaties and specified the illegality of any discrimination against broadcasting services from other member states. In its 1984 Green Paper on 'Television Without Frontiers' the Commission referred to these ECJ rulings to justify its involvement in the sector on economic grounds, since culture was not yet recognized as an area of EU activity (which was an innovation of the 1992 Maastricht Treaty) and, at the time, the development of an EU audio-visual policy was still contested (Krebber 2002: 86–87). Through drafting the TWF Green Paper and subsequent directive, the Commission played the role of a very active 'policy entrepreneur', exploiting to the full its power to set the agenda and formulate policy. Moreover, at a key stage during the negotiations, the Commission employed the threat of infringement suits regarding free movement of services, non-tariff barriers and competition issues against hesitant member states in order to exert pressure on them to accept its proposals for TWF (Krebber 2002: 115–16). Nonetheless, given the need for the intergovernmental negotiation of a minimum of harmonized rules for an internal audio-visual market, the negotiations in the Council of Ministers were laborious. Not until 1989 – five years after release of the Green Paper – was the market-liberalizing EU TWF Directive (Council of the European Communities 1989) finally enacted.

TWF opened up the European TV market by mandating the free reception and establishment of broadcasting services from other member states subject to the observation of fairly liberal minimum content and advertising regulations that were harmonized at the EU level by the directive. TWF established 'mutual recognition' as the core internal market principle for the audio-visual sector, with the country of origin – not the country of reception – exercising regulatory jurisdiction. Since the 1989 enactment of TWF, the ECJ has played a direct role, ruling on a number of occasions against 'protectionist' member states for failing to comply with the liberalising requirements of the directive. According to Harcourt (2005: 22), in numerous rulings the ECJ 'has paid attention to TWF's provisions on market liberalization (e.g. cross-border broadcasting), whilst ignoring those relating to public interest goals (e.g. restriction of advertising time, content quotas) and sometimes overriding them (e.g. protection of minors). This has eroded the national capacity to regulate media markets and created a situation of regulatory arbitrage in Europe.'

The main thrust of the 1989 TWF Directive was plainly deregulatory, the removal of national legal and regulatory barriers from a single European audio-visual market. Harcourt (2002, 2005) has suggested that TWF, and the ECJ's related interventions, actually provided a stimulus for an element of (de)regulatory competition within Europe, as certain member states sought to exploit the opportunities presented by the new EU legal context of a single European market to attract media investment, by providing a suitably relaxed regulatory environment for satellite broadcasters. Luxembourg, with a very light regulatory regime for broadcasting, was conspicuously successful in building up its satellite broadcasting industry (notably the SES-Astra satellites) and attracting international media business. So was the U.K., which introduced a very light regulatory regime for satellite broadcasters during the Thatcher era. This view is supported by Levy's (1999: 34–35) suggestion that companies could obtain an ITC (Independent Television Commission) licence 'more or less on demand', making the country an attractive location for 'TV stations keen to beam their signals into neighbouring EU territories while escaping the tighter regulatory regime that was often applied to them in those states'. Harcourt (2005: 28) observes that 'the UK's lax regulatory regime for satellite broadcasters had created a situation of regulatory arbitrage in Europe. A significant number of broadcasting companies had relocated to the UK, away from their original locations'. Similarly, Ward (2002: 62) suggests that the U.K. government thus promoted the London market for TV production.

Cultural Protectionism: Quotas and Subsidies

However, it is important to understand that the 1989 TWF Directive was a political compromise between economic liberal and culturally protectionist-minded member states. Although the directive was mostly deregulatory, it contained two protectionist measures to reduce the cultural and economic impact of U.S. audio-visual imports. Article 4 stated that a majority of broadcasting time (not counting news, sports, games, advertising and teletext) should be reserved for 'made-in-Europe' programmes. Article 5 specified that broadcasters should reserve at least 10 per cent of their programming budget or transmission time for European works created by the independent production sector. These measures were promoted by France, supported by Spain, Italy and Greece (Krebber 2002: 99). However, these countries were disappointed by compromises made during the enactment of TWF and tried to strengthen the measures when the directive first came up for revision in the period 1995–97. In particular, both articles had been weakened in order to soften the objections of 'liberal' member states, notably the U.K., Germany and the Netherlands. To be precise, the articles included the words, 'where practicable' and, furthermore, the quotas were only regarded as 'politically binding' rather than judiciable before the ECJ (Krebber 2002: 109 and 117).

Consequently, during its EU presidency in the first half of 1995, France exerted pressure on the Commission to make the broadcasting quotas binding, arguing that the integrity of European culture was at stake. However, stricter protectionism was opposed by key members of the European Parliament and the Council of Ministers. While some Mediterranean member states supported the French line, northern European member states led by the U.K. and Germany were strongly opposed (*European Voice* 1(3), 5 October 1995). In November 1995, the Council voted in favour of a political agreement to leave the rules as they stood, merely agreeing to set up a committee to ensure their proper implementation (*European Voice* 1(10), 23 November 1995). The European Parliament's culture committee immediately sought to reverse this decision, arguing that the Council had pre-empted Parliament, expressing its opinion under the co-decision rules recently introduced by the Maastricht Treaty. The committee argued, too, in favour of extending the scope of the quotas to new online services like video-on-demand (*European Voice* 2(2), 11 January 1996). In a June 1996 meeting, the Council stood its ground, opposing any change to the quota rules and their extension to new online services (*European Voice* 2(24), 13 July 1996). Notwithstanding its recently acquired co-decision right in this field, the Parliament's position was far weaker than that of the Council of Ministers. If revisions of the TWF Directive were to go to formal conciliation, and no agreement was reached, the existing terms of the Directive would simply continue to apply. This, clearly, would suit the Council more than the Parliament, which had in fact submitted no fewer than 200 amendments[4] (*European Voice* 2(30), 25 July 1996). The Parliament abandoned its demand for mandatory quotas when a vote in

November 1996 failed to gain the support of an absolute majority of all 626 MEPs[5] (*European Voice* 2(42), 14 November 1996). The quotas issue resurfaced in the debates surrounding the second revision of TWF that commenced in 2002 when the Culture and Audiovisual Affairs Council called for a review of the directive. This was supported by the EP. The Commission duly conducted two rounds of consultation (2003–2004, 2004–2005) and tabled a set of proposals (2006). The main purpose of the revision was to revise TWF to cater for new technological developments (online services, mobile communications, etc) which were introducing TV like activity through 'non linear'- in other words, non-scheduled, *on-demand* rather than scheduled, *broadcasting* – services. Controversy centred on the question as to whether the Directive should go beyond single market objectives and extend the cultural, social and public interest objectives to the new audiovisual services. Needless to say, France seized the opportunity to seek the extension of the quotas to on-demand services. Predictably, the result was another compromise. The Directive, enacted in 2007, merely called for providers of on-demand services to promote the production of, and access to, European works (Michalis 2007: 219–29).[6]

Another case of transfer of the French cultural policy model to the EU level resulted from a 'package-deal' arising from the negotiations over the TWF Directive (Krebber 2002: 62), namely, the introduction of a very modestly funded support programme for European film and TV co-productions, called 'MEDIA' (*Mesures pour encourager le dévelopement de l'industrie audiovisuelle*). While TWF was a purely regulatory policy, this distributive programme involved subsidizing a range of activities, from training through to language transfer and distribution. The first phase was launched by the Commission (DG X) in 1988, financed from the Commission's own budget. In December 1990, the Council of Ministers adopted 'MEDIA 1995' as a fully fledged five-year programme with its own EU budgetary appropriation of ECU 200 million. However, this only amounted to one-tenth of Commission spending on IT research and was less than what the French alone spent on subsidies for film and TV production. The U.K. and Germany in particular were reluctant to allow any higher expenditure (Humphreys 1996: 279–81). In 1995 European culture ministers agreed in the Council to increase funding to ECU 310 million for the period 1996–2000 under what was now called 'MEDIA 2'. The increase in the EU's budgetary provision for MEDIA was interpreted by some as compensation to the French for failure to tighten up the TWF protectionist quota regime. The French, however, had called for twice this sum (*European Voice* 1(14), 21 December 1995). Moreover, a French-inspired proposal from the Commission to establish a special mixed private/public loan guarantee fund for European film-makers was blocked altogether.

As a budget issue, the EU's contribution to such a fund required unanimity among the member states. An allocation of ECU 90 million from the EU budget for the guarantee fund was opposed by finance ministers from the U.K., Germany and the Netherlands (*European Voice* 2(24), 13 July 1996). A reduction of the proposed EU contribution to ECU 60 million failed to persuade the three northern European countries, now supported by Austria and Sweden (*European Voice* 3(25), 26 June 1997). The film guarantee scheme foundered against this opposition. Nonetheless, subsequently the member states agreed to allocate 'MEDIA plus' for the period 2001–2006 €453.6 million for distributing and promoting European audio-visual works, with a further €59.4 million for implementing a training programme for professionals in the European audio-visual industry.[7] Upon EU enlargement in 2004, the Commission proposed doubling the MEDIA budget. The current, fourth MEDIA 2007 programme (2007–2013) was actually allocated a budget of €755 million.[8]

International Trade and Cultural Diversity

The French also mobilized the EU to defend these measures against the United States under the leitmotiv '*l'exception culturelle*', in international trade negotiations. The Treaty of Rome had given the EU exclusive external competence over the common commercial policy for international trade in goods. Accordingly, where trade in goods was concerned, member states were unable to pursue unilateral policies, the European Commission represented the EU in negotiations and, where their approval was required, member states voted according to qualified majority voting (QMV).

However, the issue of competence for trade in services was less clear and led to tensions between the Commission and the member states during the the Uruguay Round of the GATT. The Council disputed the Commission's right to conclude agreements relating to services.[9] The Commission requested an opinion from the ECJ, which specified in its 1994 Opinion (ECJ 1994) that the Community and its member states shared competence to conclude the new General Agreement on Trade in Services (GATS). Accordingly, the Commission could still represent the Community in negotiations but the member states had to be constantly informed and negotiating positions and any decisions would have to be agreed unanimously. The GATS 1993 was actually signed by both the Commission and the member states in Marrakesh in April 1994 (Young 2002: 41). This need for a common position among the member states enabled France to enlist the EU in defence of the Europeans' right to apply protectionist programme quotas and to subsidize audio-visual production through national and EU TV audio-visual support funds. To date, the French 'protectionist' position with regard to the right of European countries to implement audio-visual quotas and subsidies has been the official EU position.[10]

However, there have been pressures to modify this stance. By no means all member states are culturally protectionist. There are complaints from certain European as well as U.S. media companies with transnational operations about European cultural protectionism. The Commission is internally divided on the issue. There has always existed the danger that further audio-visual liberalization might end up being part of a package deal on trade. The long-term prospects for a continuation of *l'exception culturelle* appeared to weaken when the European Convention on a treaty to establish a constitution for Europe proposed to move towards an exclusive competence for the EU for all external trade matters and to decide any issues by QMV, a position that was advocated by External Trade Commissioner Pascal Lamy (*European Voice* 9, 2003). However, on the insistence of the French government, an article was inserted into the draft constitution (European Convention 2003: 217, para. 4) which – by requiring Council unanimity for the negotiation and conclusion of external agreements in the field of cultural and audio-visual services – would effectively retain the member state veto. This draft was submitted to the European Council in Rome on 18 July 2003. The draft treaty was subsequently subjected to a tremendous amount of detailed elaboration in the Intergovernmental Conference, but the article survived in the final adopted version (Title 5, Chapter III, Article III-315). Despite the collapse of the Treaty process following the French and Danish referendums, the EU has continued to provide – if not an uncontested *exception culturelle* enshrined in international trade law – at least some measure of protection against cultural policy deregulation. In the DoHa Round of GATS negotiations, the EU has declined to make any liberalisation commitments in the audiovisual field. While the Lisbon Treaty, signed by EU leaders in December 2007, proposed to remove areas of mixed competence and provide the EU with exclusive competence for all aspects of trade, significantly it does still require member state unanimity for the negotiation and conclusion of trade agreements in the field of culture and audiovisual services where such agreements 'risk prejudicing the Union's linguistic and cultural diversity'.[11]

Competition Policy

EU competition law, particularly since the enactment of TWF, has very significantly expanded the EU's scope for media regulation. Indeed, Levy (1999: 81) has observed that 'the operation of European Community competition policy has already had more of an impact on Europe's broadcasting industry than any of the European regulation specifically targeted at the sector'. In Levy's view, 'EU competition policy will continue to be the dominant mode of European-level intervention in the digital TV market for some time to come.' This is because, under EU competition law, the European Commission has direct authority, without needing the approval of the European Council or the European Parliament, to make decisions that are subject only to review by the ECJ. Following the 1989 TWF Directive, the number of European media mergers and joint ventures increased dramatically and the European Commission Competition Authority's involvement in media decisions increased commensurately (Harcourt 2005; Levy 1999; Pauwels 1998). Harcourt (2005: 41) reports that between 1989 and 1999 the Commission made over fifty formal decisions, including a relatively high number of negative merger decisions: 8 as compared with 11 negative decisions of a total of 1,104 merger decisions in all sectors. The Commission also made its influence felt through a number of significant informal decisions, such as when it suggested that the British satellite broadcasting company BSkyB should be excluded from British Digital Broadcasting (BDB) when the U.K. regulator, the ITC, was issuing digital terrestrial broadcasting franchises in 1997 (Harcourt 2005: 41).

European competition decisions have impacted on the audio-visual sector in a number of distinct ways. Important decisions have been made about the acquisition and sale of rights to key kinds of programming, such as sports programmes – DG Competition's concern here being to ensure fair access to such content. Some of the Commission's earliest decisions went against the then-dominant positions of public service broadcasters in the rights marketplace, leading Collins (1994: 155–56) to suggest that DG IV appeared to be embarked on an 'implacable pursuit of the public service broadcasters'. However, more recent decisions have gone against commercial broadcasters. The Commission has intervened on a number of occasions to enhance competition in the programme supply market (e.g. in the case of the distribution of U.K. Premier League football rights). However, how far competition law can protect media pluralism more generally is questionable. As Gibbons (2004: 65) notes, there has been no real attempt to address the 'most critical bottleneck for the purposes of promoting media pluralism', which is the 'bundling of a programming package' by market-dominant commercial operators (see below).

The question of the future scope of the public service remit in the digital age soon became the most hotly contested competition policy issue bearing on public service broadcasting. In recent years, the European Commision (DG competition) has received a considerable number of complaints from the private sector about alleged distortion of the media market resulting from allegedly unfair benefits enjoyed by public service broadcasters. These were most notably seen to be their deployment of public funding to enter new media markets that could be left to the private sector (e.g. 24-hour news services, children's channels) and also – in many cases – their drawing supplementary funding from advertising, which involved them competing in the same market as commercial broadcasters. Commercial broadcasters, and their political supporters, argue that, in the multichannel era, public service broadcasters should be confined to areas of clear market failure, restricting themselves to providing what the market fails to deliver.

Contradictory signals have come from within the Commission about the future of public service broadcasting. On the one hand, there have from time to time been noises seemingly questioning the public service broadcasters' traditional comprehensive remit (i.e., to provide sport, films and other entertainment, as well as programmes that commercial broadcasters are less disposed to offer) and their possibilities for expansion into certain new media 'markets', notably online provision. A number of commentators and policy protagonists have expressed concern about the deregulatory potential that EU competition policy holds for traditionally comprehensive 'European-style' public service broadcasting (Harrison and Woods 2001: 498–99; Meier 2003: 337–38; Wheeler 2004: 350). On the other hand, as Ward (2002: 97–110) makes clear, most of the specific rulings that the Commission Competition authorities have made thus far regarding the development of new media services (notably niche TV channels, such as 24-hour news services and children's channels) by the public service broadcasters have been in their favour. On the initiative of the European Parliament, and strongly supported by the member states, the EU's commitment to protect a broad 'European-style' concept of public service broadcasting has been enshrined in treaty law in the form of a protocol on this subject, appended to the 1997 Treaty of Amsterdam. The Protocol states:

> The provisions of the Treaty establishing the European Community shall be without prejudice to the competence of the Member States to provide for the funding of public service broadcasting insofar as such funding is granted to broadcasting organisations for the fulfilment of the public service remit as conferred, defined and organised by each Member State, and insofar as such funding does not affect trading conditions and competition in the Community to an extent which would be contrary to the common interest, while the realisation of that public service shall be taken into account.[12]

The Treaty of Amsterdam also explicitly recognized the importance of public services by introducing a new provision in its Article 16 which emphasizes the importance of public services generally and the ability of member states to provide these services as they see fit, subject to competition provisions (Harrison and Woods 2001).[13]

In November 2001 the Commission released a Communication on the application of state aid rules to public service broadcasting (Commission of the European Communities [CEC] 2001). It cited the Protocol of the Amsterdam Treaty, confirming that the definition of the public service remit is a matter for the member states. The Communication states that state support for public service broadcasters does constitute state aid in the terms of the EC Treaty and therefore 'will have to be assessed on a case by case basis' (CEC 2001: Para. 17). But it makes clear that – so long as the remit is clearly defined by the member state – the Commission has to confine itself to evaluating the proportionality of that aid. The Commission Communication stresses the need for transparency. In the first place, there should be a 'clear and precise definition of the public service remit'. Second, the Communication guidelines make clear that in order to allow the Commission to carry out its 'proportionality test' for funding, a separation of accounts between public service activities and non-public service activities must be maintained to 'provide the Commission with a tool for examining alleged cross-subsidisation and for defending justified compensation for general economic interest tasks'. While the Commission thus accepts the competence of the member states to define public service broadcasting and also to determine how it is funded, it is evidently crucially important that in future the member states spell out clearly the remit of public service broadcasting that they deem to be socially, culturally and democratically appropriate. Equally, it is important that they have adequate monitoring and control mechanisms in place to ensure the fulfilment of the public service remit. If member states do not meet these demands, then they render their public broadcasting services vulnerable to an adverse ruling on competition grounds.

While in nearly all cases so far, the Commission has found in favour of the public service broadcasters, it has also bared its teeth on occasion. In 2004, the Commission compelled the Danish public service broadcaster TV2 to pay back 'excess compensation for public service tasks', thereby showing how seriously it viewed 'proportionality'. Moreover, complaints against public service broadcasters in Germany and the Netherlands have raised the issue of the scope and financing of their online activities. While the Commission does not question that such activities can be included in the public service remit, it is plainly concerned about their scope and financing (Michalis 2007: 234–36).

Other EU competition decisions have concerned digital alliances between commercial players. Thus, in 1994 and again in 1998, DG IV blocked bids to produce a digital pay-TV alliance by the leading German companies, Bertelsmann, the Kirch group and Deutsche Telekom AG. These commercial interests wanted to establish a digital joint venture to deliver pay-television and other interactive services such as video-on-demand through a proprietorial conditional access system (CAS). However, the Commission vetoed the alliance on the grounds that it would pose a threat to an open market in Germany for pay-TV and other future digital communication services.

The Commission justified its decision on the grounds that the alliance would create a dominant position in three markets. First, it would leverage the Kirch group's already dominant position over German television programme rights and libraries into the pay-TV market. Second, it would create monopoly control over the provision of conditional access and subscriber management systems for pay-TV and other new digital services. Third, the alliance would consolidate Deutsche Telekom AG's (then) dominance of the German cable market (Humphreys 1996: 285–86). Generally, though, as Ward (2002: 91) has suggested, the 'regulatory ground [established by the European Commission's approach to mergers and joint ventures] was favourable to companies looking to strengthen the audiovisual market by building up company portfolios and expanding the size of production by exploiting cross-border strategies within the common market zone', the aim being to promote 'European champions', like the RTL group (Bertelsmann), Telefonica and Vivendi. The few cases incurring negative decisions fell foul of the Commission's policy 'to promote pan-European market mergers rather than individual market concentrations' (Ward 2002: 94).

EU Media Ownership Regulation

However, the EU has plainly provided little 'positive integration' in the audio-visual field. The classic market-correcting measure to accompany TWF would be media-specific rules to ensure media pluralism and diversity, such as harmonized rules restricting media concentration. EU competition rulings – for instance against the aforementioned attempts by three of Germany's largest communications companies to produce a digital alliance – might have the effect of protecting a minimum of media pluralism. However, they are plainly no substitute for more elaborate media-specific rules to protect pluralism and a diversity of media output.

The TWF Directive said little about the problem of media concentration, despite the fact that market liberalization was bound – indeed, intended – to lead to the expansion of Europe's largest media concerns. The arrival of new media and, in particular, the digital convergence of the information and communications industries (see below) was also driving a marked trend towards media concentration as large, generally internationally-ambitious, private media corporations sought to exploit new economies of scale and scope. Much of the investment in the new media came from large corporations like News Corporation (Rupert Murdoch), Bertelsmann, Vivendi, Liberty and AOL Time Warner. The potential dominance of the new digital media landscape by a few powerful international media corporations greatly concerned European media unions and journalists' associations, as well as the European Parliament's culture committee. No matter how competitive the market was deemed to be in purely economic terms, media concentration raised questions of the potential abuse of editorial power by media owners and controllers, the narrowing of the range of viewpoints represented in the media, and at the very least a diminution of the diversity of media content. The Commission was at first inclined to view media pluralism rules as a matter for the member states. However, it was compelled to give attention to the issue by a succession of European Parliament resolutions calling for EU action. Even then, initially the Commission's main concern appeared to be that the patchwork of diverse national regulations on media ownership would impede the development of the internal market (Humphreys 1996: 286–93), although over time it came to take the media pluralism issues more seriously (Harcourt 2005).

A Commission draft directive was finally produced in 1996. This would have restricted any further acquisition by a private broadcasting company that owned channels capturing more than 30 per cent of a country's TV or radio audience and similarly restricted the expansion of any cross-media company (press, radio, TV) with a combined audience share of 10 per cent (it did not apply to public service broadcasters). However, the draft directive was shelved before it could become the subject of any negotiation in the Council of Ministers and with the European Parliament (Humphreys 2000a: 86–89; for much more detail, see Harcourt 2000, 2005). Divergent positions on media pluralism within the Commission had characterized, and impaired to an extent, policy formulation. Undoubtedly, however, the EC's 'non-policymaking' on the thorny issue of 'pluralism' was ultimately to be explained by the fact that it was unable to override both the determined resistance of influential member states (notably Germany) and powerful vested interests in the media field (like the European Publishers Council and large media corporations).

This failure of DG XV (Internal Market) to progress harmonization of media-specific anti-concentration rules designed to safeguard 'pluralism' contrasted with the Commission's relatively active application of general EU competition policy to the media field by DG IV (DG Competition). In itself, this is highly illustrative of the EU's liberal bias towards negative integration. It exemplifies the difficulty that the Commission encounters in pursuing more interventionist cultural and social policies (positive integration) that confront powerful vested economic interests and challenge member states' claims of primary competence for media policy (see Humphreys 2004: 112).

As a result of the EU's failure to achieve any harmonized baseline rules for media concentration, nothing has prevented a deregulatory 'race to the bottom'. Such a development was suggested by the marked deregulation of anti-concentration rules in both the U.K. and Germany in 1996, the next stage of which seemed to be heralded by even more dramatic deregulation by the U.K.'s Communications Act 2003.[14] In both countries, governments seemed to have accepted the media owners' argument that deregulation was needed for the international competitiveness of their national media industries. The prospects for restraining any such deregulatory race appear to be highly unpromising. As Gillian Doyle (2002: 94) has observed:

> At the level of each [European] state, arguments in favour of a more liberal ownership regime are often expressed in terms of the need to match the competitiveness of European media rivals. Similarly, at the European level, greater flexibility is argued for on the basis that the European audiovisual industry encounters great external competition from the American and Japanese industries.

Broadcasting/Telecommunications Convergence

By the latter half of the 1990s, the EU agenda concerning broadcasting-specific regulation, including the way media pluralism might be protected against media concentration, had been overtaken by a policy debate about the appropriate aims and methods of regulation in view of the 'convergence' of broadcasting, telecoms and IT (Humphreys 1999b). By now, technological innovation – notably digitalization – was breaking down the boundaries between these hitherto largely discrete sectors. Digitalization means that media can be carried via diverse communication channels, including the internet. Increasing numbers of homes in Europe are connected to high-bandwidth networks through which they can receive multimedia, on-demand and interactive 'new media' services as well as simple telephony and television. Digital 'convergence' of electronic media, telecoms and computing, traditionally sectors with widely varying degrees of sector-specific regulation, produces pressures for more flexible, 'technology-neutral' regulation. Some now argued that the collapse of traditional boundaries between the telecoms, IT and broadcasting industries meant that that regulation would have to converge, leading to a single 'horizontal' regulatory model for the entire 'converged' communications sector. Others, however, argued that content regulation, traditionally associated with broadcasting, should be kept distinct from carriage regulation to safeguard non-economic public-interest goals.

The European Commission broached the theme of the regulatory policy implications of 'convergence' in a Green Paper published in December 1997 (CEC 1997). The European Commission's Green Paper tried to appear open-minded about the future direction of regulation. It recognized that opinions and interests were divergent, indeed polarized, on the issue. Within the Commission there were different viewpoints, notably between DG X (cultural policy, broadcasting) and DG XIII (industrial policy, telecommunications and IT). Accordingly, the Green Paper presented three options. Essentially, these were:

1. To 'build on current structures' – that is, to adapt and refine the existing separate 'vertical' (i.e., sector-specific) regulatory approach.
2. To 'develop a separate regulatory model for new activities, to co-exist with telecommunications and broadcasting regulation' – that is, to move pragmatically towards a new 'horizontal' approach whilst leaving scope for 'vertical' regulation of distinctive services.
3. To 'progressively introduce a new regulatory model to cover the whole range of existing and new services' – that is, a radical regulatory overhaul involving a single 'horizontal' approach, in recognition of the dramatic extent of convergence.

DG XIII (Information Society) appeared to favour the third option (Levy 1999: 132). Plainly, its main concern was to break down existing national regulatory boundaries between the broadcasting, telecoms and IT sectors in order to promote investment in and the full exploitation of the new technologies, with a view to their potential major contribution to European economic competitiveness and job creation. However, DGX (Culture) was more concerned about the implications for broadcasting. During the consultation initiated by the Green Paper, strong support for the continued sector-specific regulation of broadcasting was expressed by many respondents. Notably, these were public service broadcasters and member-state governments, who emphasized that broadcasting would continue to have a unique relevance for the expression and formation of opinion, and therefore a 'fundamental role … for ensuring democratic pluralism, diversity and the sharing of culture' (CEC 1998: 4). Content regulation was excluded from the new 'horizontal' regulatory model for communications infrastructure and services, outlined by the Commission in 2000 and adopted by the Council of Ministers in a series of directives during 2002 (for details, see Ward 2002: 111–24).[15]

The 2002 regulatory package extended the scope of the EU's pro-competitive '1998 regulatory package' for telecommunications to all electronic communication networks and services. It was intentionally deregulatory in that it abolished the burdensome old telecoms licensing system, replacing it with a much lighter-touch style of authorization regime for all networks and services providing electronic communications carriage, including those (e.g. terrestrial, satellite, cable, etc.) providing broadcasting content. It also aimed progressively to roll back the member states' regulation of communications infrastructure and related services as their individual electronic communications markets (e.g. fixed line, cable, mobile, etc.) became competitive. However, because of the member states' special sensitiveness about the media, the framework accepted that broadcasting content would continue to be regulated 'vertically' according to member states' preferred socio-cultural models. To be precise, recital 5 of the Framework Directive stipulated that:

> This framework does not … cover the content of services delivered over electronic communications networks using electronic communications services, such as broadcasting content, financial services and certain information society services, and is therefore without prejudice to measures taken at Community and national level in respect of such services, in compliance with Community law, in order to promote cultural and linguistic diversity and to ensure the defence of media pluralism.

Recital 6 specified further that: 'Audiovisual policy and content regulation are undertaken in pursuit of general interest objectives, such as freedom of expression, media pluralism, impartiality, cultural and linguistic diversity, social inclusion, consumer protection and the protection of minors.'

Accordingly, the member states could retain licence requirements for content providers (i.e., 'broadcasters'). The regulatory requirements they placed on their national broadcasters could be much higher than the EU's minimum requirements specified in TWF (whose purpose was to render EU markets open to all broadcasters that met the TWF requirements). Moreover, in order to protect the network access of public service broadcasting (content), the Universal Services Directive, a key part of the new EU regulatory package, allowed member states to impose 'reasonable "must carry" obligations' for public service channel transmissions (services that meet 'general interest' objectives), on providers of electronic communication networks used for the distribution of radio or television broadcasts (Article 31).

In sum, communications carriage has been subject to further EU deregulation, but audio-visual content has clearly been spared the 'telecoms-style' deregulation that might have occurred. Under the convergence regulatory framework, strictly regulated public service broadcasting was safe from any hypothetical EU-inspired and convergence-justified deregulation. Equally, though, in the internationalized audio-visual environment, with its scope for regulatory arbitrage, international commercial media companies continue to enjoy extensive freedom from regulation. In this respect, Ward (2002: 131) contends that the failure to produce EU-level rules for audio-visual content (positive integration) left

> a fissure between national regulation and European regulation that technically allows companies to bypass stringent regulatory demands ... In remaining national in scope, the regulators are in danger of being left behind by current trends ... Big companies require big regulators ... At the moment we are in a position where, as the commercial sector becomes more internationalised, these channels increasingly enjoy minimal regulation.

Regulating Access to Digital Broadcasting

The limits of the EU's regulatory capacity in the audio-visual sector is further exemplified by the issue of regulating access to the new digital networks, the regulation of so-called conditional access systems (CAS), the 'digital gateway' systems which, through desktop boxes, scramble and unscramble TV signals and, together with subscriber management systems, allow only those consumers who have paid for a service to access it. According to a detailed study by David Levy (1999: 63–79), the European Commission, bruised by the disappointments surrounding its interventionist High Definition Television policy, abdicated from the responsibility to regulate for either common standards or access terms for digital TV networks and instead chose to defer to the decisions of an industry grouping – the Digital Video Broadcasting (DVB) project. This group reached agreement only over a common European digital transmission standard, but provided no common standard for conditional access systems. This allowed the market players to develop their own proprietory systems and resulted in the emergence of a fragmented European digital TV market, characterized by incompatible conditional access systems in different national or linguistic areas (e.g. BSkyB in the U.K. and Ireland). This fragmentation of the European digital TV market clearly went against the grain of the EU's principal audio-visual policy – namely, the creation of a single European market in order to promote a stronger European audio-visual industry (Humphreys 1996: 256–96).

Digital access also raised competition and media pluralism issues. Control of the set-top box presented the opportunity to discriminate through price or access terms against potential competitors in the field of pay-TV and new information society services. As John Birt, then Director-General of the BBC, famously declared in his 1996 MacTaggart Lecture: 'The battle for control of and a share of the enormous economic value passing through that gateway, will be one of the great business battles shaping the next century… [N]o group should be able to abuse control of that set-top box to inhibit competition' (*Guardian*, 24 August 1996, p. 27, cited in Humphreys and Lang 1998: 21). Warning against 'digital dictators', the *Guardian* newspaper even editorialized that the digital gateway 'should be enshrined in law as a common carrier owned and operated by users without prejudice' (*Guardian*, 29 October 1996, p. 16, in Humphreys and Lang 1998: 22).

Under pressure from the European Parliament, some statutory access provisions were actually included in the EU's 1995 Advanced Television Standards Directive. Its Article 4 specified that CAS providers should be required to supply third-party access (i.e., including to their rivals) to their conditional access services on 'fair, reasonable and non-discriminatory' terms. The directive also obliged national regulatory authorities to ensure that CAS operators kept separate financial accounts, published unbundled tariffs, and that they should not prohibit a manufacturer from including a common interface allowing connection with other access systems. However, as Levy has commented, the latter stipulation was a far cry from mandating the inclusion of a common interface. Manufacturers were most unlikely to include a common interface against the wishes of their customers. Moreover, the directive was 'so vague as to leave national officials unclear as to what provisions meant, and as to which needed to be written into national law. The result was that national implementation varied hugely' (Levy 1999: 73). This regulatory deficit on the part of the EU has hardly been remedied by the adoption of its new regulatory framework for the 'converging' electronic communications sector (see previous section). The Access Directive of the new framework largely reproduces the relatively weak provisions from the Advanced Television Standards Directive (Humphreys and Simpson 2005: 135–36).

Above all, however, as Tom Gibbons (2004) has argued, 'the most critical bottleneck for the purposes of promoting media pluralism is the bundling of the programming package. It is this activity, analogous to the editorial decision, which determines what content reaches the audience.' Purely concerned about the relationships between providers of networks, associated facilities and services in wholesale markets (in the case of CAS, the relationship between the controller of the digital gateway and other programme service providers), the EU Access Directive has nothing to say about the relationship between the controller of the digital gateway and the subscriber/viewer. Furthermore, as Gibbons notes, the Access Directive

> is precisely concerned with problems arising from the dependency on proprietary desk-top boxes … It cannot exert any effect on the contractual bundling arrangements made by the programme packagers, because they are not obliged to offer access to such bundles on fair, reasonable and non-discriminatory terms. That kind of access is presumed to be capable of being regulated by competition law, without such an ex ante condition being applied.

Gibbons illustrates the very limited purchase of the Access Directive for enhancing media pluralism by reference to the U.K. case, where

> most [though not all] broadcasters on BSkyB's digital satellite platform reach the viewers by being included in a BSkyB pay-TV package, so they do not need conditional access services. Similarly, broadcasters on cable systems also reach their viewers via the packaging arrangements made by the cable operators; they do not need any conditional access services. (Gibbons 2004: 64)

Conclusion

Given the fast-moving nature of developments in this field, any conclusions must be tentative. More research remains to be done.[16] Nonetheless, this chapter has explained how the EU has – and is likely to continue to have – a mixed degree of regulatory competence in the audio-visual field. The EU's influence is greatest in issues concerning the European internal market and competition issues with a Community dimension. Here the EU has direct responsibility. With regard to the internal market, there is some evidence to suggest that the impact of the EU has been to amplify other downward pressures (e.g. from technological developments) on national regulations and to stimulate a measure of regulatory arbitrage by satellite television services seeking out the most favourable regulatory locations. With regard to competition policy, there is certainly the potential for a negative impact on public service broadcasting. However, to date, the Commission would appear to have proceeded rather cautiously in view of the strong member state sensitivities on this subject. This caution contrasts with the Commission's activism against those private sector mergers and alliances deemed to threaten the development of a single market populated by strong pan-European champion companies. Nonetheless, the relationship between the Commission and public service broadcasters is heavily fraught with tension. In Richard Collins's (2002: 10) words, the 'structural conflict between the competition principles of the European treaty and the status and practice of PSB is both inescapable and likely to become more salient'. How this tension will be resolved is open to a considerable uncertainty, despite the Commission's production of guidelines in 2001. The Commission wields considerable discretionary power in making its competition judgements. The pressure from the private sector is bound only to mount with digital convergence. Moreover, the Commission's 2001 guidelines are currently the subject of consultation, with a view to adapting them to take account of the public service broadcasters' online media activities.

This chapter suggests that the Commission has been both a 'purposeful opportunist', seeking to expand its influence and, if possible, its competence in the audio-visual field, and a 'policy entrepreneur', grappling with the complexities of international market and technical change. However, there would nonetheless appear to be distinct limits to EU positive integration in the audio-visual sector because of the power of private media lobbies interested in a weakly regulated European market (see Doyle 2002; Harcourt 2005), and above all because of the politically sensitive nature of the sector and the member states' desire to retain primary responsibility for it (see Levy 1999). The relative weakness of the Commission in promoting positive integration, in the absence of a strong member state consensus on the need or desirability, is illustrated by the manifest failure so far to achieve harmonized media-specific anti-concentration rules designed to safeguard media pluralism, despite the fact that it remains a much vaunted concern.

Equally, it is manifest in the failure to produce detailed EU rules on conditional access regulation that would go further than just regulating access to the technology, but also require the controllers of digital gateways to safeguard and promote media pluralism. The contrast with the application of general EU competition policy to the media field by DG Competition is suggestive of a liberal EU bias towards negative integration. This highlights the difficulty that the Commission encounters in promoting more interventionist cultural and social policies (positive integration) that challenge powerful vested economic interests when there is a lack of member state support. The member states have been adamant that the sensitive field of media policy is primarily their field of competence; indeed, since the Maastricht Treaty (1992) established a vague EU cultural policy role, the audiovisual sector has been an area where the EU can take only 'supporting, coordinating or complementary action'. This leaves negative integration, the removal of regulatory barriers to the internal market, as the EU's main achievement to date.

However, the story has not been completely 'deregulatory'. EU negative integration in the shape of TWF has been accompanied by one noteworthy measure of 're-regulation', notably the EU-wide adoption of French-style culturally protectionist quotas, though, as we have seen, the French and their supporters in the European Parliament have so far failed in their attempts to have these quotas strengthened. Also, the deregulatory pill of TWF was sweetened a little (for the French) by a (very) modest measure of budgetary support for European audio-visual production. So far, on French insistence, the EU has served as an effective shield for these policies against U.S. pressure in international trade negotiations. Above all, it is noteworthy that the Commission's competition policy interventions over the launch by public broadcasters of new digital services, including online ones, have – so far – been supportive of a comprehensive understanding of public service broadcasting. In sum, whether or not the EU's impact has been deregulatory or re-regulatory is a question deserving of further empirically oriented academic research. All of the issues discussed herein remain open, in particular the tension between competition policy and public service broadcasting, the long-term external trade-related issues, and not least the long-term impact of the digital convergence between media, telecoms and IT.

Notes

1. The impact of the EU's policies on cultural diversity and public service broadcasting is part of a current ESRC-funded project ('Globalisation, Regulatory Competition and Audiovisual Regulation in 5 Countries') conducted by Professor P. Humphreys (School of Social Sciences, University of Manchester), Professor T. Gibbons (School of Law, University of Manchester) and Dr A. Harcourt (Department of Politics, University of Exeter). ESRC Ref. No. RES-000-23-0966. Duration: 1 February 2005 – 31 January 2008. The author acknowledges the input of his colleagues into the research design and would like to thank them for their helpful observations and corrections to this paper.

2. The federal government and national commercial media interests favoured the creation of a single European market, but not the *Länder*, which feared the impact of Europeanization on their cultural policy competence.

3. The 1974 Sacchi and the 1980 Debauve rulings.

4. These included two particularly controversial provisions – respectively requiring the insertion of V-chips in TV sets to strengthen parental control of children's viewing and protecting the rights to show certain 'listed' major national cultural and sports events from exclusive deals with pay-TV providers. These proposals led to a round of conciliation talks between the Parliament and the Council of Ministers. In the end, the Parliament dropped its support for the V-chip, about which both the Commission and the Council were highly sceptical, and concentrated its energy on the listed events issue, where there was much more scope for agreement. Indeed, an agreement with the Council was reached on the basis that these be national lists defined by the member states rather than drawn up at EU level, as MEPs had wanted.

5. Despite producing majority support.

6. The revised directive is called the 'Audiovisual Media Services' Directive. Directive 2007/65/EC of the European Parliament and of the Council of 11 December amending Council Directive 89/552/EEC ['TWF'].

7. For details, see: www.europa.eu.int/comm/avpolicy/media/index_en.html.

8. See: http://ec.europa.eu/information_society/media/overview/index_en.htm

9. And also to trade-related aspects of intellectual property rights (TRIPS).

10. Similarly, the French were able to mobilize EU-wide support, or at least acquiescence, from the more economically liberal member states, for audio-visual services to be exempted from international trade liberalizing agreements over telecommunications and foreign direct investment (Young 2002).

11. The treaty is accessible at: http://europa.eu/lisbon_treaty/full_text/index_en.htm.

12. Treaty of Amsterdam, 1997: 87.

13. The relevant section of Article 16 (former Article 7d) of the Treaty states that: '... given the place occupied by services of general economic interest in the shared values of the Union as well as their role in promoting social and territorial cohesion, the Community and the Member States, each within their respective powers and within the scope of application of this Treaty, shall take care that such services operate on the basis of principles and conditions which enable them to fulfil their missions.'

14. Prior to this, both of these countries had among the strictest anti-concentration rules in Europe. Evidence of a 'race to[wards] the bottom' was a key finding of the ESRC research project 'Regulating for Media Pluralism' (Grant no.: L12625109) conducted by the author and colleagues at the University of Manchester between 1996 and 1999, under the auspices of the ESRC's Media Economics and Media Culture Research Programme. For detail, see *inter alia*: Gibbons 1998a and 1998b; Humphreys and Lang 1998; and Humphreys 1998, 1999b, 2000a, 2000b and 2003. Also, see the study by Gillian Doyle (2002).

15. *Directive 2002/21/EC on a Common Regulatory Framework for Electronic Communications Networks and Services* (Framework Directive), OJ 2002 L108/33; *Directive 2002/19/EC on Access to, and Interconnection of, Electronic Communications Networks and Associated Facilities* (Access Directive), *OJ 2002* L108/7; *Directive 2002/20/EC on the Authorisation of Electronic Communications Networks and Services* (Authorisation Directive), OJ 2002 L108/21; *Directive 2002/22/EC on Universal Services and Users' Rights relating to Electronic Communications Networks and Services* (Universal Services Directive), OJ. 2002 L108/51.

16. As currently by the ESRC project described in note 1.

Bibliography

Cerny, P. 1997. 'Paradoxes of the Competition State: The Dynamics of Political Globalization', *Government and Opposition* 32(2): 251–74.

Collins, R. 1994. *Broadcasting and Audiovisual Policy in the European Single Market.* London: John Libbey.

———. 2002. 'The Future of Public Service Broadcasting in the United Kingdom', conference on *The Future of Public Broadcasting in a Changing Media Society, Institute of Mass Communication and Media Research, University of Zurich, 27–29 September.*

Commission of the European Communities. 1992. 'Pluralism and Media Concentration in the Internal Market', *Official Journal of the European Communities,* COM(92) 480.

———. 1997. *Green Paper on the Regulatory Implications of the Convergence of the Telecommunications, Audiovisual and Information Technology Sectors.* Brussels: COM, December.

———. 1998. *Working Document of the Commission: Summary of the Results of the Public Consultation on the Green Paper on the Convergence of the Telecommunications, Media and Information Technology Sectors: Areas for Further Reflection.* Brussels: COM, July.

———. 2001. *Communication from the Commission on the Application of State Aid Rules to Public Service Broadcasting, Official Journal of the European Communities,* 2001/C 320/04.

Council of the European Communities. 1989. 'Directive on the Coordination of Certain Provisions Laid Down by Law, Regulation or Administrative Action in Member States Concerning the Pursuit of Television Broadcasting Activities', 89/552/EEC, *Official Journal of the European Communities,* L 298/23, 17/10/89.

Cram, L. 1997. *Policy-making in the European Union: Conceptual Lenses and the Integration Process*. London: Routledge.

Doyle, G. 2002. *Media Ownership*. London: Sage.

European Convention. 2003. *Draft Treaty Establishing a Constitution for Europe*. Brussels: Convention Secretariat, CONV 850/03.

Gibbons, T. 1998a. *Regulating the Media*. London: Sweet and Maxwell.

———. 1998b. 'Aspiring to Pluralism: The Constraints of Public Broadcasting Values on the De-regulation of British Media Ownership', *Cardozo Arts and Entertainment Law Journal* 16(2–3): 475–500.

———. 2004. 'Control over Technical Bottlenecks – A Case for Media Ownership Law?', in S. Nikoltchev (ed.), *Regulating Access to Digital Television: Technical Bottlenecks, Vertically Integrated Markets and New Forms of Media Concentration*, IRIS Special. Strasbourg: European Audiovisual Observatory, pp. 59–67.

Goodhart, D. 1998. 'Social Dumping within the EU', in D. Hine and H. Kassim (eds), *Beyond the Market: The EU and National Social Policy*. London and New York: Routledge.

Harcourt, A.J. 2000. 'European Institutions and the Media Industry: European Regulatory Policies between Pressure and Pluralism', Ph.D. dissertation. Manchester University.

———. 2002. 'Regulatory Competition in the EU: A Case Study in National Media Regulation', *International Regulatory Competition and Cooperation, Robert Schuman Center, European University Institute, Fiesole/Florence, Italy, 21 November*.

———. 2005. *The European Union and the Regulation of Media Markets*. Manchester: Manchester University Press.

Harrison, J. and Woods, L.M. 2001. 'Defining European Public Service Broadcasting', *European Journal of Communication* 16 (4): 477–504.

Humphreys, P. 1996. *Mass Media and Media Policy in Western Europe*. Manchester: Manchester University Press.

———. 1998. 'The Goal of Pluralism and the Ownership Rules for Private Broadcasting in Germany: Re-regulation or De-regulation?', *Cardozo Arts and Entertainment Law Journal* 16(2–3): 527–55.

———. 1999a. 'Germany's 'Dual' Broadcasting System: Recipe for Pluralism in the Age of Multi-channel Broadcasting?, *New German Critique* 78: 23–52.

———. 1999b. 'Regulating for Pluralism in the Era of Digital Convergence'. *ECPR Joint Research Sessions, Mannheim, 26–31 March*. Workshop 24: 'Regulating Communications in the Multimedia Age'.

———. 2000a. 'Regulation for Media Ownership: Issues in Ownership and Competition', in J. Andrew, M. Crook, D. Holmes and E. Kolinsky (eds), *Why Europe? Problems of Culture and Identity*, vol. 2. Houndmills: Macmillan, pp. 71–93.

———. 2000b. 'New Labour Policies for the Media and Arts', in D. Coates and P. Lawler (eds), *New Labour in Power*. Manchester: Manchester University Press, pp. 221–39.

———. 2003a. 'Regulatory Policy and National Content', in M. Raboy (ed.), *L'Avenir de la réglementation de la radiodiffusion*. Québec: Centre d'études sur les médias, Université Laval, pp. 177–207.

———. 2003b. 'EU Policy on State Aid to Public Service Broadcasters', *SMIT-CEAS-Telenor Conference on the ICT and Media Sectors within the EU Policy Framework, Brussels, 7–8 April.*

———. 2004. 'Globalization, Regulatory Competition, and EU Policy Transfer in the Telecoms and Broadcasting Sectors', in D. Levi-Faur and E. Vigoda-Gadot (eds), *International Public Policy and Management: Policy Learning beyond Regional, Cultural, and Political Boundaries.* New York: Marcel Dekker, pp. 91–120.

Humphreys, P. and Lang, M. 1998. 'Regulating for Media Pluralism and the Pitfalls of Standortpolitik: The Re-regulation of German Broadcasting Ownership Rules', *German Politics* 7(2): 176–201.

Humphreys, P. and Simpson, S. 2005. *Globalisation, Convergence and European Telecommunications Regulation.* Cheltenham, UK, and Northampton, MA, USA: Edward Elgar.

Krebber, D. 2002. *Europeanisation of Regulatory Television Policy: The Decision-making Process of the Television Without Frontiers Directives from 1989 and 1997.* Baden-Baden: Nomos.

Levy, D. 1999. *Europe's Digital Revolution: Broadcasting Regulation, the EU and the Nation State.* London and New York: Routledge.

Majone, G. 1996. *Regulating Europe.* London: Routledge.

McKenzie, R.B. and Lee, D.R. 1991. *Quicksilver Capital: How the Rapid Movement of Wealth Has Changed the World.* New York: Free Press.

Meier, H.E. 2003. 'Beyond Convergence: Understanding Programming Strategies of Public Broadcasters in Competitive Environments', *European Journal of Communication* 18 (3): 337–65.

Michalis, M. 2007. *Governing European Communications.* Lanham, Maryland, USA: Lexington Books.

Pauwels, C. 1998. 'Integrating Economies, Integrating Policies: The Importance of Antitrust and Competition Policies within the Global Audiovisual Order', *Communications and Strategies* 30: 103–32.

Radaelli, C. 2000. 'Policy Transfer in the European Union: Institutional Isomorphism as a Source of Legitimacy', *Governance* 13(1): 25–43.

Scharpf, F.W. 1997. 'Introduction: The Problem-solving Capacity of Multi-level Governance', *Journal of European Public Policy* 4(4): 520–38.

———. 1999. *Governing in Europe: Effective and Democratic?* Oxford: Oxford University Press.

Schmidt, V.A. 1999. 'Convergent Pressures, Divergent Responses: France, Great Britain, and Germany between Globalisation and Europeanisation', in D.A. Smith, D.J. Solinger and S.C. Topik (eds), *States and Sovereignty in the Global Economy.* London and New York: Routledge, pp. 172–92.

Sun, J.-M. and Pelkmans, J. 1995. 'Regulatory Competition and the Single Market', *Journal of Common Market Studies* 33(1): 67–89.

Treaty of Amsterdam. 1997.

Vogel, D. 1995. *Trading Up: Consumer and Environmental Regulation in a Global Economy.* Cambridge, MA: Harvard University Press.

Vogel, S. 1996. *Freer Markets, More Rules: Regulatory Reform in Advanced Industrial Countries.* Ithaca, NY: Cornell University Press.

Ward, D. 2002. *The European Union Democratic Deficit and the Public Sphere: An Evaluation of EU Media Policy.* Amsterdam: IOS Press.

Wheeler, M. 2004. 'Supranational Regulation: Television and the European Union', *European Journal of Communication* 19 (3): 349–69.

Woolcock, S. 1994. *The Single European Market: Centralisation or Competition Among National Rules?* London: Royal Institute of International Affairs.

Young, A. 2002. *Extending European Cooperation: The European Union and the 'New' International Trade Agenda.* Manchester: Manchester University Press.

Chapter 9

EU Information Policies: A Case Study in the Environmental Sector

Max Craglia and Alessandro Annoni

Introduction

The creation of a European public sphere is a very topical issue at the current stage of development of the European Union. It has gained a particular momentum since the rejection of the Constitutional Treaty in the public referenda held in France and the Netherlands in 2005, but the emerging gap between the European institutions and the citizens of Europe had already been recognised in the early 1990s at the time of the Maastricht Treaty, and has been well documented since by successive public opinion polls organised by the Commission through its Eurobarometer surveys. The purpose of this chapter is to provide evidence of the initiatives put in place to develop such a European public sphere from the particular angle of information policies in general, and environmental information policies in particular. The political and contested nature of information policies is highlighted as a contribution to the debates about democracy and governance in the Union.

The chapter is organized as follows: after this introduction, it summarizes the current state of public opinion in Europe as measured by the latest Eurobarometer surveys. This sets the context for a review of recent initiatives at the European level aimed at closing the gap between the Union and its citizens, increasing participation, and strengthening the democratic process. The chapter then focuses on policies at the European level aimed at increasing access to public sector information in general and environmental information more specifically, before finally providing a case study of participative and bottom-up policy development in the environmental sector, highlighting the opportunities but also the challenges inherent in such an approach.

What Europeans Think of the European Union

Between February and March 2006, almost 25,000 Europeans in 25 countries were interviewed by the TNS Opinion and Social Network in a special Eurobarometer survey on the Future of Europe (TNS 2006a). This study complemented the regular survey of European public opinion, the latest of which was undertaken in March-May 2008 (TNS 2008a). The key findings of these two surveys are as follows.

In 2006, the vast majority of Europeans were happy with their family life (90 per cent) and current occupation (84 per cent), as well as being happy to live in their own country (90 per cent). The economy was a key area of concern, with over a third of respondents having difficulties 'making ends meet', and there was a significant degree of pessimism, particularly in the older EU 15, about the direction followed by their country (43 per cent) (CEC 2006a). Unemployment, crime, and the overall economic outlook were the three most widespread sources of concern, being mentioned by 49 per cent, 24 per cent, and 23 per cent of Europeans respectively (CEC 2006b). By 2008, concerns over employment have reduced (27 per cent) but for the first time inflation and rising prices have become very important issues (26 per cent) (TNS, 2008a)

With respect to attitudes towards the European Union, just over half of respondents are positive about membership of the Union, and another quarter see it as neither good nor bad, while only 14 per cent oppose membership. As shown in Figure 9.1, these trends have been relatively stable for the last ten years, although in the last year there has been a significant drop in support of the EU (-6 per cent), almost compensated by an increase in the neutral stance (+4 per cent).

With respect to specific policy areas, Table 9.1 shows that fighting terrorism, protecting the environment, and defence and foreign affairs are three areas for which decision making is required at European level, and the EU plays a positive role. Immigration and fighting crime are also areas for European decision making but here the degree of satisfaction is less pronounced, particularly in relation to immigration. To note also that more than 60 per cent of Europeans have a neutral or negative view

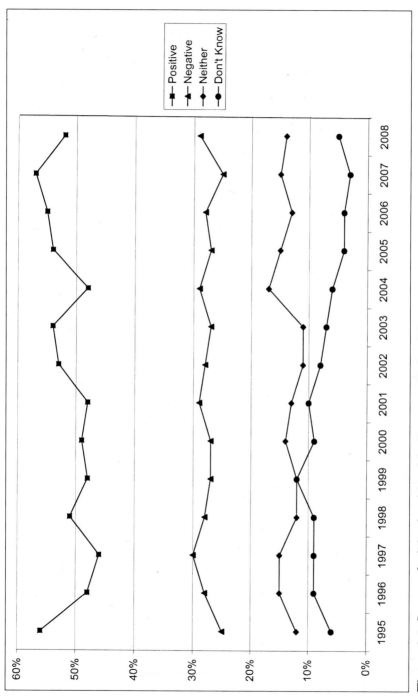

Figure 9.1: Support for Membership of the European Union (%).

Source: Derived from TNS 2008a

of the role of the EU in fighting inflation, which is one of the main areas of concerns across Europe at the present time.

Table 9.1: Support for European decision-making and perceived role of the EU.

In the following areas, decisions should be made...	Jointly within the EU	In the following areas, the EU role is... Positive	Negative	Neutral
Fighting terrorism	81%	57%	11%	22%
Protecting the environment	73%	52%	14%	24%
Defence and foreign affairs	67%	48%	12%	27%
Immigration	63%	29%	28%	31%
Fighting Crime	61%	41%	13%	36%
Transport	49%	29%	13%	45%
Fighting inflation	49%	21%	36%	31%
The economy	48%	39%	20%	29%
Fighting unemployment	40%	25%	24%	40%
Heath and social welfare	34%	22%	19%	47%
Education	32%	26%	16%	45%
Taxation	30%	16%	27%	43%
Pensions	26%	15%	21%	50%

Source: Derived from TNS 2008b.

With respect to democracy and participation in European affairs, the 2006 special survey indicates that interest in European affairs is still lukewarm, with 52 per cent not interested in European affairs, compared to 36 per cent who are not interested in domestic affairs (TNS 2006a).

Whilst voting is still perceived as the main method by far of participating in European affairs, the low turnout at European elections may be explained by the finding that in 2006 only 36 per cent of respondents believed that their voice was heard in Europe, while over 50 per cent believed that it was not (TNS 2006b). By 2008, the gap had widened further to 30 per cent and 61 per cent respectively, reflecting also the increased concerns over the economic outlook (TNS, 2008b). Overall, therefore, there is a real challenge in closing the gap between citizens and institutions at the European level – that is, improving the governance of Europe. The next section explores some of the elements of the debate and initiatives under way.

Improving the Governance of Europe

The debate on reforming the governance of Europe started in the late 1990s and was put as one of the four strategic objectives of the Commission in 2000. This came out of the recognition that leaders throughout Europe were facing a real paradox. On the one hand, their citizens wanted them to find solutions to pressing societal problems and, at the same time, they were becoming increasingly disenchanted with politics. Whilst this problem was widespread throughout Europe, it was all the more acute at the European level, with people losing confidence in a poorly understood and complex mechanism for delivering policies. A White Paper on European governance was put forward by the Commission in 2001 (CEC 2001) and open to an eight-month long public consultation, ending in March 2002. The White Paper argued that good governance is based on five key principles: openness, participation, accountability, effectiveness, and policy coherence. On this basis, it made proposals along four main strands:

1. Improving public involvement in shaping and implementing European policy, including increased access to relevant information.
2. Improving the quality, effectiveness and simplicity of regulatory acts, including greater use of social, economic, and environmental impact analysis.
3. Contributing more effectively to global governance by improving dialogue with stakeholders in third countries, taking more account of the global impact of its policies, and speaking with a single voice in international negotiations.

4. Refocusing European policies and institutions by identifying and communicating more clearly the long-term objectives, and making decision-making in the Union simpler, faster and easier to understand by the public, so as to make all the institutions more accountable.

The public consultation drew a relatively small number of responses (260), with some geographical areas not contributing at all. The four principles underpinning good governance were supported although additional principles such as democratic legitimacy and subsidiarity were also proposed. With respect to the Commission's proposals, most comments focused on increased public participation and the involvement of civic society, while the other strands drew fewer comments, possibly because they were perceived as being too managerial and driven by institutional self-interest (CEC 2003a). In this respect, an acknowledged limitation of the White Paper was the decision 'to bring forward only those proposals that could be applied within the existing institutional framework, in other words under the treaties as they stand' (CEC 2003: 5), as proposals for a new framework were becoming part of the mandate of the Intergovernmental Conference on the Constitutional Treaty to report in 2004.

An important lesson learnt from the consultation process on the White Paper is how difficult it is to engage stakeholders in a European debate, given the complexity of multilevel governance in Europe across public, private, and non-governmental sectors, and the extent to which 'European' issues are also interwoven with national and local political issues. Such complexity was demonstrated even more clearly with the debate on the Constitutional Treaty and its rejection in the referenda held in the Netherlands and France in 2005. Although the reasons for rejecting the proposed Treaty are complex, it has been suggested that some people perceived the Treaty as not doing enough to protect social rights in the face of globalization, whilst others used the opportunity to express discontent with their government rather than give an opinion on the contents of the Treaty itself (CEC 2006a; Wallström 2006). Certainly, the length of the Treaty itself, at 448 articles plus annexes, would not have helped an informed debate.

Following these rejections, and the lack of agreement among national governments on the way forward, it has become clear that developing an effective two-way communication between Europe and its citizens has to be a policy in its own right, with dedicated resources and long-term commitment. This is not just a task for the European institutions but primarily for the Member States, whose Heads of Government agreed in June 2005 to enter a period of reflection 'to enable a broad debate to take place in each of our countries, involving citizens, civil society, social partners, national parliaments and political parties' (CEC 2005a: 2). For its part, the Commission has supported these activities through the following actions:

1. Launch of an action plan to improve communicating in Europe by the Commission (CEC 2005a).
2. Development of a long-term set of actions to support democracy, dialogue, and debate. These include: support for national debates on the future of Europe in key policy areas such as social and economic development; listening to stakeholders' expectations in a range of different fora and through different media, including the new web portal 'your voice in Europe', (http://ec.europa.eu/yourvoice/index_en.htm); promoting European citizenship through dedicated funding for citizens' projects; promoting participation in decision-making, and turnout at European elections (CEC 2005b).
3. Increasing the openness of European institutions through greater access to documents, visits, and the launch of a transparency initiative to make the work of European institutions open to public scrutiny and their work more accountable (CEC 2006a).
4. Implementing impact assessment on all major initiatives launched by the Commission (CEC 2002a) and developing a common methodology for evaluating the administrative cost imposed by legislation (CEC 2005c).
5. Opening a public consultation on a European Communication Policy, the main purpose of which is to engage stakeholders throughout the Union on ways forward to close the recognised gap between European citizens and their institutions (CEC 2006b).

The latter makes an interesting case about the need to develop a European public sphere, as well as making Europe more relevant to the national and local public spheres. It argues that:

> In today's Europe, citizens exercise their political rights mainly at national and local level. Political rights linked to the European dimension have been introduced, such as the right to participate in the elections of the European Parliament. However, people learn about politics and political issues largely through their national education systems and via their national, regional and local media. They consider the manifestos of political parties dealing with

national, regional and local issues, and they discuss these issues mostly in their own communities. In short, the 'public sphere' within which political life takes place in Europe is largely a national sphere. To the extent that European issues appear on the agenda at all, they are seen by most citizens from a national perspective. The media remain largely national, partly due to language barriers; there are few meeting places where Europeans from different member states can get to know each other and address issues of common interest. Yet many of the policy decisions that affect daily life for people in the EU are taken at European level. People feel remote from these decisions, the decision-making process and EU institutions. There is a sense of alienation from 'Brussels', which partly mirrors the disenchantment with politics in general. One reason for this is the inadequate development of a 'European public sphere' where the European debate can unfold. (CEC 2006b: 4–5)

To develop such a European public sphere, the White Paper proposes a set of measures including greater access to information in multilingual settings, closer partnership with national institutions, and fora to connect citizens across national boundaries, and to connect citizens to their EU institutions. The consultation on the White Paper is still open at the time of writing, and it will be interesting to see the extent and geographical variation of the responses. There is little doubt, however, that developing such a European public sphere is a long-term challenge, if nothing else because of multilingual and multicultural variations across the Union, but also because of the need to strike a balance between retaining the diversity and identity of the local, regional, and national levels whilst introducing and developing a European discourse.

Equally important is the need to understand and engage with the power relations that underpin the institutional relationships within Member States, and between Member States and the Union. Within Member States there are long-term tensions between national and local/regional levels in a number of countries such as Spain, Italy, and Belgium, as well as more recent initiatives and debates on devolution vs. centralisation in the United Kingdom, and the ten states that became members of the Union in 2005 (Alden 2001; Newman 2000; Peter 2000). In these national power relationships the Union is not a neutral player or is not perceived to be. In the ten new member states, it was the process of accession itself that required the creation of new administrative structures at the subnational level (NUTS2 and NUTS3) in order to be eligible for financial support from the structural funds. In this case, therefore, there is a direct link between the European dimension and the regional one.

In other cases, there is at least a perception among some analysts that the regional dimension of European policies and funding strengthens the hand of the regions within national/regional power relations, and thus undermines the national level. Eser and Konstadakopulos (2000) make this argument in relation to the debate on the European Spatial Development Perspective. Tewdwr-Jones et al. (2000), in their analysis of the impact of EU policies on British national and regional planning policy guidance, demonstrate on the one hand that the 'Eurosceptic' Thatcher government up to 1997, consistently chose to ignore the European origin of much of the legislation affecting British planning by making exclusive reference to the national legislation transposing the European one, whilst on the other hand local and regional authorities, particularly in Labour-controlled Scotland and Wales and large conurbations, were becoming much more aware of the funding available from Europe and saw this as an opportunity to bypass to some degree the national level.

The national governments' tactics to 'blame Brussels' for any initiative that is politically unpalatable whilst taking the credit, or at least hiding the origin for those that are viewed favourably by the electorate or markets – as shown in Tewdwr-Jones et al. (2000) – can therefore be read as part of a wider and dynamic power relation between centre and periphery, and local vs. European levels. In this context, the national media plays an important part in shaping public opinion and in contributing to the political process. Information, misinformation, and counter information thus become important tools not just of an abstract democratic process but also of a power tussle between multiple stakeholders. Selected examples of misinformation have been collected on a Commission website aimed at debunking some the myths reported by the media – http://ec.europa.eu/dgs/communication/facts/index_en.htm – and include, for instance:

Bombay Mix to be renamed	
The Press:	Nutty EU officials want to rename Bombay mix Mumbai mix – to make the snack politically correct. They say the Indian city of Bombay has been called Mumbai since 1995 so the old name could offend because it dates back to colonial rule. (The Sun, 18 July 2006, p27)
The Facts:	Any suggestion that the EU would get 'mixed-up' in renaming this or any other snack is completely ludicrous. You couldn't make it up, could you? Well, The Sun did.

Viagra	
The Press:	All male members of staff at the EU institutions can be partly reimbursed for the medical costs of six Viagra pills a month (Sondagsavisen, 25 August 2002).
The Facts:	Some 47,000 members of staff at the EU institutions are covered by sickness insurance, to which they contribute every month. Out of these 47,000, ten get their medical expenses for six Viagra pills a month partly reimbursed – and only because impotence is a direct consequence of a very serious disease, for example cancer.

These examples and the ones collected on the website are only a minority amongst the many accurate reports but make the point against the rationalist argument that 'more information leads to better decisions', particularly in the context where public policy fails to recognise the complex power relations at play. As Georgiadou (2006) argues, quoting van de Donk (1998):

> The real world of information processing in the domain of public policy making ... is characterised by several types of information (manipulated statistics, high quality research, gossip, editorial comments, evaluation reports, corridor analysis); information pathologies (faulty receptors, failures in communication, information overload, systematic biases); and information politics (manipulation, non-registration, withholding, biased presentation, adding other information, timing, leaking and so on). (van de Donk 1988: 391)

Therefore, ignoring interests and ideology in public policymaking, or regarding them as illegitimate or as irrational components of resistance to the truth and beauty of research is to misread the nature of democratic decision-making (Georgiadou, 2006).

If information is an important component of the political process, so the latter plays an important part in shaping information policy. The next section explores this dimension at the European level.

Information Policy in Europe

The development of the 'Information Society' in Europe found a legal basis in the 1993 Maastricht Treaty, which gave the European Union responsibility in matters of trans-European networks in the transport, energy, and telecommunications sectors. At a time of high structural unemployment, the European Commission saw the development of an information-based society as the key to creating new job opportunities in the medium term. This vision and the opportunity to exploit information technology to modernise government and provide better and cheaper services continued to receive high-level political support through the 1990s, with seed funding from the EC to leverage national funding and private-sector capital. Although more recently, access to information has become an important component of the democracy and governance debate (see previous Section), it is important to recognise that the initial impetus was economic competitiveness. Within the overall framework of policies aimed at creating a single market for people, goods, and services, the process followed for the information market has focused first on increasing physical access to the information infrastructure, then on its information content, and finally (still ongoing) on liberalising services.

EU initiatives to liberalise physical access have included the privatisation of national telecommunications monopolies where greater competition has increased consumer choice and level of service. The common standard for mobile telephony (GSM) promoted by the EU in 1994 has created a multibillion-euro market, giving Europe a competitive edge in this sector (Standage 2001). An important development is the establishment of a regulatory framework for electronic communications networks and services to ensure transparency and to avoid market distortions by players exploiting their dominant position. This regulatory regime, agreed in April 2002, includes a Framework Directive (CEC 2002b), and Directives on Authorisation (CEC 2002c), Access (CEC 2002d), and Universal Service (CEC 2002e), in addition to the one on Personal Data Processing and Privacy enacted in 1997 (CEC 1997) and revised in 2002 (CEC 2002f). Aside from the details of these directives, the recognition that this aspect of economic and social life cannot be left exclusively in the hands of the market, and requires a set of agreed rules, checks, and balances is of considerable importance.

Against this set of initiatives, more limited success has been achieved in increasing and regulating access to information or content. A set of guidelines put forward by the EC in 1989 (CEC 1989) to promote access to information, transparency, and a level playing field were largely ignored, partly because of a lack of enforceable legal authority, and partly because of the immaturity of the EU Public Sector Information (PSI) market at that stage.

It took another ten years before the debate was relaunched, with the publication in early 1999 of the *Green Paper on Public Sector Information: A Key Resource for Europe* (CEC 1998). This consultation paper played a major role in raising the debate across Europe on the opportunities created by the increased availability of PSI in digital format for its reuse beyond the purposes for which it was originally collected. The document recognised existing barriers to accessing PSI, including different legal frameworks and pricing regimes, and posed pertinent questions on the extent to which such frameworks ought to be harmonised across Europe.

The political battle, particularly between the European Parliament pushing for a more liberal approach, and the Council, representing the Member States, trying to reduce any potential impact of the proposed directive on government departments, was vigorous and ranged across the scope of the directive, the boundaries of what constitutes PSI, its documentation, and crucially, the permissible charging regimes. 'Access' to PSI was dropped at an early stage from the scope of the directive, leaving it to Member States to define what information should be accessible. Moreover, it was accepted that where charges are made they can include a return on investment. Having survived these major battles, and also excluded educational, research, cultural, and broadcasting establishments from its provision, the debate then focused on ensuring a level playing field, transparency, and non-discriminatory practices in the conditions for the reuse and exploitation of documents that are already generally accessible. Although the final text approved was clearly a step in the direction of greater access, reuse, and transparency, the political battle left its scars, as shown by the disappointed assessment of the Dutch rapporteur of the European Parliament, Win Van Welzen, who noted:

> This small majority in the European Parliament would rather see that the private sector, and in particular SMEs, keep on paying the public sector (i.e. via the return on investment on the re-use of public sector information) and that there is no transparency on the re-use. Also, this small majority seems to think that more bureaucracy is favourable in this matter: the text as adopted today still leaves room for public sector bodies to approve (or not) the re-use of public sector information, while we are talking here about information that is already generally accessible! Having to ask for approval for re-use for generally accessible information in many cases even means a step backwards (source: http://www.wimvanvelzen.nl/e_statement.php3?statementid=46).

While the Information Society initiatives reviewed above have largely been driven by the Directorate General of the EC in charge of promoting the information market, and are thus underpinned by an economic perspective, new pressures for increased public access to information have developed in the environmental arena. At the international level, the 1998 Aarhus Convention on Access to Information, Public Participation in Decision-Making and Access to Justice in Environmental Matters (UNECE 1998), which came into force in October 2001, is important because it links the right to access information with human rights, including the right to participate in decision-making processes and the right to seek redress. It therefore moves away from the economic arguments about access as a way to develop the market, to more fundamental issues about democracy and social justice. The implications of adopting the Aarhus Convention bring economic arguments back centre stage.

At the European level, the Aarhus Convention required a reappraisal of several areas of policy, including the revision of the 1990 Directive on Access to Environmental Information (CEC 1990) which was drafted in the mid 1980s, prior to the internet era. The revised 2003 directive (CEC 2003b) exemplifies how 'progressing' into the digital age may be perceived as a threat to the business model of some government departments and agencies. Hence, while the original 1990 directive made a presumption in favour of access to information at marginal or no cost, and the Aarhus Convention referred to 'reasonable cost', the new EU directive had a clause inserted in its preamble at the last stages of conciliation, clarifying that, for those public agencies that provide environmental information on a commercial basis, market price was to be considered a 'reasonable cost'. A similar political battle has taken place in the context of a new directive aimed at increasing access to environmental data to support public policy and informed public participation, which is discussed in the next section.

Inclusive and Participatory Policymaking: a Case Study

Directive 2007/2/EC of the Council and the European Parliament (CEC, 2007) establishes the legal framework for setting up and operating an Infrastructure for Spatial Information in Europe (INSPIRE) based on infrastructures for spatial information established and operated by the member states. The purpose of such infrastructure is, in the first instance, to support the formulation, implementation, monitoring, and evaluation of Community environmental policies, and to overcome major barriers still affecting the availability and accessibility of pertinent data (see also Annoni and Craglia, 2005). These barriers include:

1. Inconsistencies in spatial data collection: spatial data are often missing or incomplete or, alternately, the same data are collected twice by different organisations.
2. Lacking documentation: description of available spatial data is often incomplete.
3. Spatial data sets not compatible: spatial data sets often cannot be combined with other spatial data sets.
4. Incompatible geographic information initiatives: the infrastructures to find, access and use spatial data often function in isolation only.
5. Barriers to data sharing: cultural, institutional, financial and legal barriers prevent or delay the sharing of existing spatial data.

The key elements of the INSPIRE directive to overcome these barriers include:

1. Metadata to describe existing information resources so that they can be more easily found and accessed.
2. Harmonisation of key spatial data themes needed to support environmental policies in the Union.
3. Agreements on network services and technologies to allow discovery, viewing, download of information resources, and access to related services.
4. Policy agreements on sharing and access, including licensing and charging.
5. Coordination and monitoring mechanisms.
6. Implementation process and procedures.

From the outset of this initiative in 2001 it was recognised that, to overcome some of the barriers highlighted above, it would be necessary to develop a legislative framework requiring Member States to coordinate their activities and agree on a minimum set of common standards and processes. This in turn requires the wide support of the Member States to the objectives of INSPIRE. Therefore, a very collaborative process was put in place to formulate the INSPIRE proposal. This process in particular involved the establishment of an expert group with official representatives of all the Member States, and working groups with expertise in the fields of environmental policy and geographic information to formulate proposals and forge consensus. From this process, it was agreed that the key principles of INSPIRE should be:

1. That spatial data should be collected once and maintained at the level where this can be done most effectively.
2. That it must be possible to combine seamlessly spatial data from different sources across the EU and share it between many users and applications.
3. That it must be possible for spatial data collected at one level of government to be shared between all the different levels of government.
4. That spatial data needed for good governance should be available with conditions that do not restrict its extensive use.
5. That it should be easy to discover which spatial data is available, to evaluate its fitness for a purpose and to know which conditions apply for its use.

Following three years of intensive consultation among the Member States and their experts, a public consultation, and the assessment of the likely impacts of INSPIRE (see http://inspire.jrc.it), the European Commission adopted the INSPIRE proposal for a directive in July 2004 (CEC 2004).

The European Parliament expressed its favourable opinion on the Commission's proposal in June 2005, and introduced a number of amendments to clarify the proposed legislation. The Council adopted a common position in January 2006, introducing a number of limitations to the data sharing arrangements put forward by the Commission. The text analysis of the original proposal and of the one adopted by the Council undertaken by Corbin (2006) (see Table 9.2) clearly shows the change in emphasis between the two and demonstrates once more that information access policies are strongly embedded in a political process which touches upon the different ways in which public sector organisations in general, and data producing ones in particular, are funded in the member states.

The second reading of the Commission's proposal by Parliament took place in June 2006, rejecting many of the restrictions imposed by the Council with a majority of 5:1. Given the extent of disagreement, it was necessary to convene a Conciliation Committee with representatives of both Council and Parliament to find an acceptable compromise that was the basis of the Directive adopted in March 2007.

Table 9.2: Comparison between Council and Commission INSPIRE text.

10 words or phrases used by the Commission that are not used in the Council draft	10 words and phrases not used by the Commission but used by the Council
accessibility	apply charges
commercial activities	click-licences
common licensing	corresponding fees
competition	cost-benefit
Decision 1692/96/EC25 *	excessive costs
distortion	limit sharing
focuses	payment
harmonised specifications	precondition
requisite	reciprocal
rights of use	viability

Source: Corbin 2006.* *(European Transport Networks)*

In parallel to this decision making process, three different services of the European Commission – DG Environment, DG Joint Research Centre and DG Eurostat – started coordinating the drafting of the implementing rules envisaged by the directive[1]. Such implementing rules are needed for each of the key components of the infrastructure, namely: metadata, harmonisation of key data themes to achieve greater interoperability network services, data and service sharing, and monitoring and reporting. Given the political context of the Directive, their drafting requires not only a high level of technical competence but above all the participation and engagement of all the key stakeholders in geographic information in Europe. To organise this process, two mechanisms have been put in place: the first is to engage the organisations that already have a formal legal mandate for the coordination, production, or use of geographic and environmental information (the Legally Mandated Organisations or LMOs) at European national and subnational level. The second is to facilitate the self-organisation of stakeholders, including both data providers and users of spatial data, in Spatial Data Interest Communities (SDICs) by region, societal sector, and thematic issue. SDICs should naturally form strategic partnerships: public-public, public-private, and private-private, to align the demand for spatial data and services with the necessary investments.

The central role that the SDICs play in the development of implementing rules includes:

1. To identify and describe user requirements (to be understood as in line with environmental policy needs, as opposed to 'maximum' requirements beyond the scope of INSPIRE and beyond realistically available resources).
2. To provide expertise to INSPIRE drafting teams.
3. To participate in the review process of the draft implementing rules.
4. To develop, operate and evaluate an implementation pilot.
5. To develop initiatives for guidance, awareness raising, and training in relation to the INSPIRE implementation.

In addition, the Legally Mandated Organisations (LMOs) play a central role in reviewing and testing the draft implementing rules, and in assessing their potential impacts with respect to both costs and benefits.

An open call was launched on 11 March 2005 for the registration of interest by SDICs and LMOs, who were also asked to put forward experts and reference material to support the preparation of the implementing rules. The deadline for the registration of experts was 29 April 2005. By that date, the following had registered on the INSPIRE website:

1. 133 Spatial Data Interest Communities.
2. 82 Legally Mandated Organisations.
3. 180 Proposed Experts.
4. 90 Referenced Materials.
5. 91 Identified Projects.

The analysis of the LMOs shows that the majority are national in character and dominated by producers of reference data. SDICs, on the other hand, characterise themselves primarily as research organisations and coordinating bodies. It is important to note that each SDIC bundles together many organisations representing different viewpoints and interests.

An example of a SDIC organised by region is the GDI NRW – a non-profit initiative of the state of North-Rhine Westphalia. In the GDI NRW, representatives of economy, administration and science work together in a Public-Private Partnership as geoinformation providers, enablers, brokers and users. The GDI NRW has more than 100 members, including various state authorities in North-Rhine Westphalia (land surveying office, geological survey, ministry of the environment, etc.), about twenty local authorities, several research institutions and multiple business companies.

There are also interesting examples of SDICs organised around thematic issues, such as the European Soil Bureau Network (ESBN), the European Environment Information and Observation Network (EIONET), the European Meteorological Infrastructure (EMI), and several others.

The ESBN, created in 1996, is a network of national soil science institutions. Its main tasks are to collect, harmonise, organise and distribute soil information for Europe, for which there is increasing demand, to address a number of environmental problems and issues, including: leaching of agrochemicals, deposition of heavy metals, disposal of waste, degradation of soil structure, risk of erosion, immobilisation of radionuclides, supply of water at catchments level, assessing the suitability and sustainability for traditional and alternative crops, and estimation of soil stability.

The EIONET was established in 1990 and aims to provide timely and quality-assured data, information and expertise for assessing the state of the environment in Europe and the pressures acting upon it. The EIONET is a partnership network of the European Environment Agency (EEA), a number of European Topic Centres and a network of around 900 experts from 37 countries in over 300 national environment agencies and other bodies dealing with environmental information.

The European Meteorological Infrastructure (EMI) is an operational infrastructure established by the European National Meteorological Services to deliver information services to decisionmakers, customers and users throughout Europe. EMI is part of the World Meteorological Organisation telecommunication system for the European Region.

These few examples show not only the thematic breadth of the SDICs contributing to the definition of INSPIRE, but also the extent to which the development of this spatial infrastructure needs to build on other infrastructures already existing in the different communities of interest, making sure that it can interoperate effectively with their architectures, technologies, standards and protocols, and organisational frameworks.

Whereas the communities described above already exist, the INSPIRE open call also forced several organisations to create new groups of interest or to join existing ones. As a consequence, many user groups that were often not considered by data producers in strategic decisions are now invited to be part of the SDICs and have started to gain greater influence in the processes defining data priorities and needs.

The number of SDICs and LMOs has continued to increase since April 2005 as the awareness of the INSPIRE process increases and, as of April 2008, includes 235 SDICs and 136 LMOs, while the number of registered projects and reference material has almost doubled, passing the 300 mark.

Of significant interest is the high number of experts (180) proposed by the SDICs and the LMOs. Considering that the experts proposed are not paid by the European Commission, but are supported instead by the organisations and communities that have nominated them, these figures indicate the degree of the call's success, and the extent of support offered toward the implementation of INSPIRE.

From the large pool of experts available, some 70 individuals were selected on the basis of their experience and with a view to balance the perspectives of data producers, users, and solution providers from the private sector. On the basis of this selection, and the advice of the representatives of the member states, five drafting teams were established, one for each of the implementing rules: metadata, data specifications, network services, data and service sharing, and monitoring and reporting. They started operations in October 2005 and already demonstrate how European-wide legislation can be developed with stakeholder contributions.

Three aspects are particularity important in understanding the work and the challenges of the drafting teams: first, each expert represents a community of interest and therefore has the responsibility to bring to the table the expertise, expectations, and concerns of this community and; secondly, each drafting team has to reach out to all the thematic communities that are addressed by INSPIRE. This is no small undertaking as the proposed directive covers more than 30 different data themes, including reference data and environmental data themes which are the responsibility of multiple agencies at national, regional and local level across 25 countries. As a matter of comparison, it is worth considering that a similar initiative in the U.S. – the National Spatial Data Infrastructure – defined only seven framework themes: geodetic control, orthoimagery, elevation, transportation, hydrography, governmental units, and cadastral information; for each of which it is possible to identify a Federal agency taking the lead in data collection and management. This is not the case in Europe where there are no European-level institutions in charge of data collection.

The implication for the drafting teams is that they have a much more difficult task in collecting and summarising reference material, seeking common denominators and reference models, and developing recommendations which satisfy user requirements without imposing an undue burden on those organisations that have day-to-day responsibility for data collection and management across Europe. Seeking compromise between different requirements and perspectives is crucial to the work of each drafting team. Last but not least, it is important to note that the drafting teams have the ownership of their work. They make recommendations and submit them to review to all the registered SDICs and LMOs, and the representatives of the Member States. It is only after they have taken on board all the comments received that the European Commission takes ownership of the draft implementing rule, and submits it to public consultation for further review.

The complex articulation of this participatory approach is certainly innovative, not only in relation to the developments of spatial data infrastructures but more generally to the formulation of public policy at the European level. In this respect, it is a good case study of the new European governance model advocated by the initiatives reviewed in this chapter. Being participatory and inclusive, it can facilitate the political process in that the interested parties can openly discuss their concerns and find solutions that balance the general interest with particular concerns. It must also be recognised, however, that this is not always the case, and that some of the participants have multiple agendas and conflicting objectives operating in parallel to the formal process, including direct lobbying, and misinformed press reports suggesting, for example, that the proposed directive would bankrupt leading government agencies or undermine national security (see Rennie 2006). Information policies and politics are always intertwined and this is also part of the democratic process.

Conclusions

The EU is at an important stage of its development process, recognising the need to close the gap between its citizens and the European institutions, and finding a new common sense of purpose and direction. To support dialogue and democracy in the Union, a package of initiatives is being developed to increase access to information in both directions to and from the institutions, to engage citizens in participating more actively in the democratic process, to demonstrate the relevance of the policies and initiatives taken, including more inclusive and transparent policymaking. Whilst the goals and even the measures to achieve them can be shared and agreed, this chapter has sought to provide evidence of the complexity of the process taken to get there.

In the first place, the initiatives taken cannot come only from the Commission and other European institutions, but have to rely on the active involvement of the Member States and their internal mechanisms of stakeholder participation. Here lies an initial tension, because the national dimension of public spheres in Europe is both part of the problem and of the solution. Moreover, attempts to develop either a European public sphere and discourse, or engaging European institutions in the national and local debates, can be the subject of criticism by those who might interpret such initiatives as attempting to undermine and interfere with the national level, or to impose a hegemonic discourse smothering local identities (e.g. Richardson and Jensen 2004).

In this sensitive context, increasing access to information is perceived as a prerequisite for more informed public debate, increased participation and trust, greater accountability and so on. Transparency, accountability, and trust are without doubt crucial elements for improved governance in Europe, and are supported by information access. Nevertheless, this chapter has sought to provide evidence that increasing information access is not a mechanistic proposition where it is enough to 'open the tap' or set up yet another website, but a negotiated outcome of a complex political process in which national, local, and organisational agendas and self-interest are played out through formal and informal channels, as demonstrated most recently by the rejection of the revised Constitutional Treaty (the Lisbon Treaty) by Irish voters in June 2008.. What is needed is to develop a framework which is open, transparent, and participatory, and where these legitimate self-interests can find a voice. This is not easy to manage when there are so many stakeholders involved, and requires time, effort, and commitment. Nevertheless, such efforts are worthwhile if they lead to a more democratic and trusted governance in Europe built through visible practice and not just enunciated principles.

Notes

1. A directive is a piece of legislation that defines the general principles and objectives to be met, while leaving Member States to define their own way to

reach these objectives through national legislation. Implementing rules include instead those technical details which are mandated by the Commission to all Member States to ensure the coherent implementation of the directive. The implementing rules are formally adopted through the comitology procedure that has been recently amended (CEC 2006c). Under the new regulation, the Parliament and the Council are now put on equal footing for all comitology procedures related to co-decision acts. As a consequence, all measures must be ratified by all three institutions to come into force.

Bibliography

Alden, J. 2001. 'Devolution since Kilbrandon and Scenarios for the Future of Spatial Planning in the United Kingdom and the European Union'. *International Planning Studies*, 6(2), 117–132.

Annoni, A. and Craglia, M. 2005. Towards a directive establishing an infrastructure for spatial information in Europe (INSPIRE) in *Proceedings of GSDI-8 From Pharaohs to Geoinformatics - The Role of SDIs in an Information Society*, Cairo, April 16-25th,
http://gsdidocs.org/gsdiconf/GSDI-8/papers/ts_47/ts47_01_annoni_graglia.pdf

Commission of the European Communities. 1989. *Guidelines for improving the synergy between the public and private sectors in the information market*. Brussels: CEC. ftp://ftp.cordis.lu/pub/econtent/docs/1989_public_sector_guidelines_en.pdf (accessed 22/8/2006).

Commission of the European Communities. 1990. *Council Directive 90/313/EC of 7 June 1990 on the freedom of access to information on the environment*. Brussels: CEC. http://europa.eu.int/scadplus/leg/en/lvb/l28091.htm (accessed November 6, 2002).

Commission of the European Communities. 1997. *Directive 97/66/EC of the European Parliament and of the Council of 15 December 1997 concerning the processing of personal data and the protection of privacy in the telecommunications sector*. Brussels: CEC.

Commission of the European Communities. 1998. *Public sector information: a key resource for Europe*. COM(98) 585 Final. Brussels: CEC http://europa.eu.int/ISPO/docs/policy/docs/COM(98)585/ (accessed 22/8/2006).

Commission of the European Communities. 2001. *European Governance: a White Paper*. COM(2001)428 final. Brussels: CEC.

Commission of the European Communities. 2002(a). *Communication of the Commission on Impact Assessment*. COM(2002)276 final. Brussels: CEC.

Commission of the European Communities. 2002(b). *Directive 2002/19/EC of the European Parliament and of the Council of 7 March 2002 on access to, and interconnection of, electronic communications networks and associated facilities (Access Directive)*. Brussels: CEC.

Commission of the European Communities. 2002(c). *Directive 2002/20/EC of the European Parliament and of the Council of 7 March 2002 on the authorization of electronic communications networks and services (Authorisation Directive).* Brussels: CEC.

Commission of the European Communities. 2002(d). *Directive 2002/21/EC of the European Parliament and of the Council of 7 March 2002 on a common regulatory framework for electronic communications networks and services (Framework directive).* Brussels: CEC.

Commission of the European Communities. 2002(e). *Directive 2002/22/EC of the European Parliament and of the Council of 7 March 2002 on universal service and users' rights relating to electronic communications networks and services (Universal service directive).* Brussels: CEC.

Commission of the European Communities. 2002(f). *Directive 2002/58/EC of the European Parliament and of the Council of 12 July 2002 concerning the processing of personal data and the protection of privacy in the electronic communications sector (Directive on privacy and electronic communications).* Brussels: CEC.

Commission of the European Communities. 2003(a). *Report from the Commission on European Governance.* Luxembourg: Office for the Official Publications of the European Communities.

Commission of the European Communities. 2003(b). *Directive 2003/4/EC of the European Parliament and the Council of 28 January 2003 on public access to environmental information and repealing Council Directive 90/313/EEC.* Brussels: CEC.

Commission of the European Communities. 2003(c). *Directive 2003/98/EC of the European Parliament and of the Council of 17 November 2003 on the re-use of public sector information.* Brussels: CEC.

Commission of the European Communities. 2004. *Proposal for a directive of the European Parliament and of the Council establishing an infrastructure for spatial information in the Community (INSPIRE),* COM(2004)516 final. Brussels: CEC.

Commission of the European Communities. 2005(a). *Action plan to improve communicating Europe by the Commission.* Brussels: CEC, http://ec.europa.eu/dgs/communication/pdf/communication_com_en.pdf

Commission of the European Communities. 2005(b). *The Commission's contribution to the period of reflection and beyond: Plan-D for Democracy, Dialogue and Debate.* COM(2005)494 final. http://eur-lex.europa.eu/LexUriServ/site/en/com/2005/com2005_0494en01.pdf

Commission of the European Communities. 2005(c). *Communication from the Commission on an EU common methodology for assessing administrative costs imposed by legislation.* COM(2005)518 final. Brussels: CEC.

Commission of the European Communities. 2006(a). *The Period of Reflection and Plan D.* COM(2006)212 provisional. Brussels: CEC, http://ec.europa.eu/commission_barroso/president/pdf/com_2006_212_en.pdf

Commission of the European Communities. 2006(b). *White Paper on a European Communication Policy.* COM(2006)35 final. Brussels: CEC, http://ec.europa.eu/communication_white_paper/doc/white_paper_en.pdf

Commission of the European Communities. 2006(c). *Council Decision of 17 July 2006 amending Decision 1999/468/EC laying down the procedures for the exercise* of implementing powers conferred on the Commission (2006/512/EC). Brussels: CEC.

Corbin, C. 2006. INSPIRE *Word-Phrase Analysis v.1.* Document posted to the european-gi-policy@jrc.it list on 2nd March.

Commission of the European Communities. 2007. Directive2007/2/EC of the European Parliament and of the Council establishing an infrastructure for spatial information in the Community (INSPIRE) *Official Journal of the European Union*, L .108/1 to 14 25/4/2007, Luxembourg: Office for the Official Publications of the European Communities.

Eser T.W., and Konstadakopulos, D. 2000. Power Shifts in the European Union? The Case of Spatial Planning. *European Planning Studies*, 8(6), 783–798.

van de Donk, W. 1998. 'Beyond incrementalism?' in W. van de Donk and I. Snellen (eds.) *Public administration in an information age.* Amsterdam: Elsevier, 381–401.

Georgiadou, Y. 2006. SDI Ontology and Implications for Research in the Developing World. *International Journal of Spatial Data Infrastructures Research*, 1, 51–64.

Newman, P. 2000. Changing Patterns of Regional Governance in the EU. *Urban Studies*, 37(5–6), 895–908.

Peter, J. 2000. The Europeanisation of Sub-National Governance. *Urban Studies*, 37(5–6), 877–894.

Rennie, D. 2006. 'EU gaffe could expose Navy's chart secrets', *Daily Telegraph*, 17 June, http://www.telegraph.co.uk/news/main.jhtml?xml=/news/2006/06/17/wmaps17.xml

Richardson, T. and Jensen, O. 2000. Discourses of Mobility and Polycentric Development: a Contested View of European Spatial Planning, *European Planning Studies*, 8(4), 503–520.

Standage, T. 2001. The Internet, untethered. October 11. *Economist.* http://www.economist.com/surveys/displaystory.cfm?story_id=E1_RTTJPQ (accessed 22/8/2006).

Tewdwr-Jones, M., Bishop K., and Wilkinson, D. 2000. 'Euroscepticism', Political Agendas and Spatial Planning: British National and Regional Planning Policy in Uncertain Times', *European Planning Studies.* 8(5) 651–668.

TNS Opinion and Social, 2006a. *The Future of Europe.* Special Eurobarometer 251 wave 65/1. Luxembourg: Office for the Official Publications of the European Communities, http://europa.eu.int/comm/public_opinion/index_en.htm

TNS Opinion and Social, 2006b. Standard Eurobarometer 65. Luxembourg: Office for the Official Publications of the European Communities.

TNS Opinion and Social, 2008a. *Standard Eurobarometer 69: First Results.* Luxembourg: Office for the Official Publications of the European Communities.

TNS Opinion and Social, 2008b. *Standard Eurobarometer 68* Luxembourg: Office for the Official Publications of the European Communities.

UN Economic Commission for Europe. 1998. *Convention on Access to Information, Public Participation in Decision-Making and Access to Justice in Environmental Matters done at Aarhus, Denmark, on 25 June 1998.*
http://www.unece.org/env/pp/documents/cep43e.pdf (accessed 22/8/2006).

Wallström, M. 2006. *Europe: Which way forward?* Speech to Copenhagen University
   19   May,   http://europa.eu/rapid/pressReleasesAction.do?reference=SPEE
   CH/06/318&format=HTML&aged=0&language=EN&guiLanguage=en
   (accessed 10/8/2006).

Chapter 10

Defending Communicative Spaces: The Remits and Limits of the European Parliament*

Katharine Sarikakis

Introduction

With the internationalization of communications policy, the role of international and supranational institutions in the process of decision-making has attracted the attention of academic research but also of actors in civil society. Surprisingly, perhaps, the European Parliament, given its special position as a unique institution of representational politics at an international level, has not been given the same degree of attention. There is a profound lack of studies of the role, potential and dynamics of European Parliamentary politics in issues of communications policy, whether these are related to media, telecommunications or more broad cultural policies.

This chapter examines the role of the European Parliament (EP) in the historical development of media policies in the European Union (EU). A historical overview of the institution in media policies provides information about aspects of internal EU policymaking processes, and therefore helps us understand the workings of the polity. Most importantly, however, it provides an insight into a unique case of supranational representation, which gains significance in its potential for dialogue with international social movements and social change. As a first-ever experiment in supranational representation, it provides the only source of historical data that can reveal the conditions under which emancipatory politics can be pursued at a governance level in a globalized world. The importance of the institution is inherent in its representative role for European citizens, its position vis-à-vis unaccountable international elites, the de facto facilitation of a European, albeit elite, political public sphere and its definitional positive predisposition to 'public good' idea(l)s.

Based on the historical analysis of key media and communications policies in the EU, this discussion will seek to identify the role of the EP in determining the discourses surrounding the process of developing policy. In particular, this chapter discusses issues of cultural domination on the European cultural and communication policy agenda Here, the notion of cultural imperialism is used as a broad concept that addresses cultural imbalances, not as a linear construction of top-down or one-way domination, but rather as a net of complex social and economic relations. The chapter first sets the background against which the EP is called to fulfil its mandate. It then analyzes the ways in which the institution has perceived and addressed key communications issues. This analysis takes into account that both the current 'singularity' of supranational political representation and the phenomenon of cultural imperialism are firmly located within the processes of globalization.

Unique or First of Its Kind? The Driving Context of a Supranational Parliament

In order to understand the nature of the EP, it is important to analyze and understand its positioning within the broader structure of the EU. It is widely accepted by the majority of integration theorists that the predominant objective in the creation of the EU polity was economic, even though the political grounds for pursuing integration were also strong, such as the aim of restoring and maintaining peace in Europe. Meanwhile, and especially with the expansion of EU jurisdiction, the integration process has been accompanied by criticism of the democratic deficit of the polity, improvements in the role of the EP notwithstanding. Increasingly, not only economic but also social issues are dealt with at an international level. However, political representation at this level involves only some representation of states and not of citizens. Furthermore, projects of regional economic integration are operational in the cases of NAFTA, MERCOSUR and the African Union. Questions of democracy and accountability at these levels of decision-making have become central in the continuation and legitimization of these regimes. In March 2004 the inauguration of a Pan-African Parliament was followed by proposals for the creation of a MERCOSUR Parliament in September 2004. These developments further emphasize the pressing need for democratic representation within international economic regimes. They also seriously question a popular argument among students of the EU that the polity is a 'unique' political system, making the existence of the Parliament a 'uniquely' European phenomenon.

On the contrary, although the EP is currently the only supranational Parliament (with democratic representation), it is reasonable to argue that, as an institution, it is both an 'answer' to and a product of globalization (Sarikakis 2002, 2004). Political integration as a means of legitimation seems to follow efforts in market integration; this phenomenon leans closer to the analyses offered by scholars such as Peter Cocks and Jacque Mistral. Cocks (1980) argued that the process of European integration can be traced back as far as the Middle Ages, making the EU project neither unique nor 'contemporary'. Instead, as market integration has forced political and administrative cohabitations, so has the European polity come into existence through a history of gradual but consistent steps towards regionalized globalization. Moreover, Jacques Mistral (1982, 1986) of the Parisian Regulation School sees the world economy as being simultaneously an 'organic totality' of capitalist accumulation and a hierarchy of hegemonic nations, a tendency towards market integration coexisting with the fragmentation of systems of accumulation. This is because, in each nation, the process of accumulation is autonomous, deriving from the general laws of capitalism and from social relations and cultural conditions that are more particular. The state of the international regime of production, accumulation and circulation requires an appropriate regulatory milieu that provides trading actors with a degree of predictability in political and economic conditions, as well as with familiar and low-cost trade environments. It also requires new institutions.

Our discussion of the construction of the EU and the subsequent development of its governing bodies leans closer to Mistral's analysis, who argued that an international regime consists of three elements: 1. a regime of capitalist accumulation that serves as a model; 2. a configuration of economic spaces, and 3. complementary relations between these spaces (Mistral 1986, in Robles 1994). The third element is expressed in the role of non-state actors such as transnational companies in international regulation. Although not having the same function, such actors are granted the same status as state institutions at an international level. The EU is a transnational regime within an international regime of accumulation and regulation that is largely facilitated and driven by communications technologies in the early twenty-first century. Here, the role of hegemony is to be found not only in the role of the American empire, most associated with the international regime and the question of cultural imperialism, but also in the immaterial realm, that of ideas and values. Therefore, the ideals of liberal democracy and freedom of expression or those of the 'European way of life' become some of the elements negotiated for their rhetorical and material value. Communications policies have come to the forefront of not only economic but also social and cultural struggle owing to the very nature of the role of communication as an inherent element of humanity.

The Policies

The development of the European Parliament has been subject to the larger institutional questions surrounding the development of the EU. Consequently, its formal powers to influence and direct policy within the EU have changed with the degree and nature of European integration. Its role in media policies has also followed this path, being heavily dependent upon the position defined for it by the nation states in their agreements (Intergovernmental Conferences). As an institution, it has grown from a decorative consulting body to a legislator almost equal with the Council of Ministers, made up of the representatives of member states. Its own institutional and formal increase of power, the changing function of the EU more generally and the external international economic regime have played an important role in defining the key issues in communications, in both the media and the broader field of cultural industries. Therefore, the analysis of the European Parliament's activity takes as its basis these two factors and coincides, in terms of the Parliament's 'efficiency' in influencing policy with the milestones in media policy at an EU level. The centrality of the European Parliament's role in dealing with this philosophical aspect as well as the 'pragmatic' issues of change in the media industries is visible in the very policy itself. Three periods of European Parliamentary activity in the last twenty years of media and cultural policy can be distinguished, each signifying the transformation of the media and cultural climate in Europe, the character of public debate and the position of strong actors in particular industries.

Phase 1: Making Waves

The first period of Parliament's active role in media policies involves the introduction of the fundaments of media and cultural policy discourses to the EU 'domain'. It covers the period from the first parliamentary resolution in 1982 (European Parliament [EP] 1980a, 1980b, 1982) for policy at a European level to the establishment of the most important single policy for the single pan-European market in 1989 – the Television Without Frontiers Directive (TWF) (Peterson and Bomberg 1999: 204– 5). In this first period of EU involvement in media policy, Parliament gained some legislative powers but was still in a disadvantaged position compared to the Council of Ministers. Media and communications markets were expanding from largely national to regional and international territories with the application of particular technologies.

Soon, by the end of the 1980s, media deregulation had become the single most common action taken by nation states, an integral part of the wave of privatization of public spaces and services. As is well known, existing dominant media conglomerates benefited the most from the deregulated environment. This observation was addressed as a phenomenon of internationalization or commercialization of media by an alarmed Parliament in one of its 1985 reports. The European Parliament saw the exacerbation of informational flow imbalances within the EU space as a particularly unfavourable condition for European media and culture industries but also for European integration.[1]

Earlier, the European Parliament had asserted the significance of the role of the media in their twofold capacity of creating a European identity and disseminating information about the European Community, tasks that would presume a degree of non-commercial organizsation of communicative spaces (EP 1980a, 1980b, 1982, 1984b). The predominant issues represented in the resolutions adopted by the institution were cross-border themes of such as the protection of freedom of speech, the protection of human rights, and the preservation of cultural diversity in Europe, echoing the rhetoric of the beginnings of the European project, namely – peace, democracy and respect for human rights. The decisive point of departure from the discourse was the inclusion of cultural diversity as a factor in, and object of, supranational policymaking. This has been a persistent and constant pursuit in policymaking for over two decades. The European Parliament's core argument was the development of a political union, through the development of a common consciousness (EP 1985a: para. M).

In the early days of EU media policy history, the European Parliament commenced the advocacy of a socially responsible media model, a model that still continues to inspire the Parliament's positions today. The institution's limited authority, however, meant that the tactic – and necessity – of 'being a nuisance' was necessarily adopted as the means to pursue this ideal. It succeeded in defining the way in which cultural and media matters were to be addressed in the following years. In this 'discourse-setting' period, the European Parliament introduced eleven media-related reports and resolutions. This remarkable body of work was channelled into the drafting of the TWF Green Paper and the subsequent, albeit compromised, directive. Across these eleven resolutions, (prepared by the the Committee of Culture), often regarded as one of the 'less significant' or, 'soft' committees in the European Parliament[2]) some common themes emerged:

1. The concept of pan-European spaces of culture and media information as the drivers of political and cultural European integration.
2. The supranationalization of policy relating to the media and cultural sector (not provided for in the founding treaties of the EU), and hence the advocacy of a form of public interest-centred intervention and proactively integrationist politics in the European polity.
3. An emphasis on the political significance of cultural expression of European peoples in relation to the polity and on the preservation of spaces dedicated to the creation of national/local 'stories' free from cultural imperialistic industries; according to the European Parliament, 'the cultural diversity in Europe threatened to be overrun by international media commercialisation … the media question [was] "a power question"' (EP 1985b: 272).[3]
4. Advocacy for a culture of public service broadcasting not sidetracked by commercial activities and for the independence of journalists particularly in commercial media.

It is interesting to note that 'cultural cohesion' has never been explicitly referred to in the work of the European Parliament, whereas 'cultural diversity' has become one of its main concepts. Cultural cohesion is conventionally thought to constitute a vital element of societies, alongside common language or other common cultural values. Scholars and politicians have sometimes attempted to approach the EU in terms of a society in need of cultural cohesion, but this has not been a view that the European Parliament shared. Although its propositions for action in fostering a 'European consciousness', and therefore a form of cultural cohesion, underlie much of its conceptual work, the European Parliament has been careful not to suggest connotations of cultural homogenization, and therefore of dominance. Rather, the European Parliament has based its cultural and media policy initiatives on the ideas of diversity as part of a newly assumed European identity. In its response to the Commission's Green Paper and during subsequent readings of the TWF, the democratization of the Community through democratic and attuned media became one of the important aims of future policy. However, the 'Cultural', as opposed to the 'Economic', was already gaining some ground (Sarikakis 2004). The protection of cultural diversity, the creation of a new cultural identity and the reception of products as cultural rights (EP 1985a: para. 7), as well as the economic potential of cultural production, appeared to go hand in hand with the political and economic dimensions of the polity.

Phase Two: Expanding, Defending and Stabilizing – Lessons in Compromise

With the completion of the TWF Directive, another cycle of deliberations began. Some scholars point to the fact that some of the most important European Parliament proposals, such as the content quota and advertising restrictions, failed to become part of a more social agenda in the largely market-oriented TWF Directive (e.g. Collins 1996). However, European Parliamentarians feel that the drafting of a directive was itself a successful achievement, given the difficulties of setting the whole process into motion (the decision-making process lasted almost a decade) (Sarikakis 2004).

With the European Parliament now armed with a considerable policy document advocating economic integration in the field of the media, the second phase of activity began by focusing on a number of key issues. Media pluralism and ownership concentration, public service broadcasting and the strengthening of domestic production and talent were the main areas that the European Parliament now concentrated its efforts on. At the end of this period – from 1989 to 1997 – the institutional arrangement through the Amsterdam Treaty gave the European Parliament legislative powers almost equal to the Council of Ministers. Furthermore, two significant policy outcomes concluded this cycle: the Public Service Broadcasting Protocol to the Treaty of Amsterdam and the withdrawal of the draft Media Pluralism Directive.

By the end of the 1990s the media market had reached entropy, with major acquisitions taking place. The revision and amendment of the TWF Directive revived a number of issues as matters of public debate, such as the definition (and expansion) of European works, obligatory contribution of resources towards the production of independent works, and restrictions – albeit seriously compromised – to advertising space. Also important were renewed efforts to provide content quotas (though for a second time such attempts failed to produce definitive and binding policy) and the proactive protection of media content pluralism (rather than media ownership) without abandoning measures for the protection of national players as commercial or PSB providers. Further attempts to define content pluralism and control ownership patterns within the auspices of a new definitive policy provision (the Media Pluralism Directive) were unfruitful as private interests proved too strong to be overcome by a disunited front of anxious public service broadcasters (PSBs), and member states and diverse local/regional conditions (Sarikakis 2004). Parliament even decided to withdraw a proposal regarding the establishment of an independent broadcasting committee, under pressure from the advertising lobby, among others. Even more radical proposals (such as a policy to tackle pornography) were rejected by the Council.

Since the founding treaties did not allow for culture to be addressed by the policy mechanisms of the EU, any references to this issue were characterized as beyond the jurisdiction of the Community. The European Parliament's representations during the TWF debate addressed not simply the legalistic question of culture as part of Community jurisdiction, but also posed the 'institutional question' – the question of democratic representation. This brought the European Parliament into direct opposition with member states who would not happily embrace other forms of integration. European governments and EU jurisdiction were drawn into confronting the uneasy question regarding the direction of European integration. It continued pressing for reform of the constitutional law that would enable it to attain more legislative powers and expand its range of activities. The Treaty on the European Union, which came into force in 1993, signalled a breakthrough in European politics: Article 128 includes the audio-visual sector under the jurisdictions of the Community, whereby action between the member states 'shall be aimed at encouraging and supplementing their action [in such fields as] artistic and literary creation, including the audio-visual sector' and that the community 'shall take cultural aspects into account in its action' (op. cit. in SCADPlus 2001).

Twelve years after the first call of the European Parliament for legislation in the cultural section, the founding Treaty of the European Community now included cultural products in its jurisdiction, thereby creating the necessary legal base while also expanding the jurisdiction of the Community as a whole. The area of culture, as directly related to that of consciousness and identity and furthermore as a significant component of democracy, became the point where even the redefinition of the essence of the Community could start taking place.

Alongside the battle to introduce cultural issues as part of the EU's agenda, the European Parliament had to address two of the most crucial media-related concerns facing Europe – pluralism and public service broadcasting. Within the space of just two years (1990–1992) the European Parliament introduced over ten reports specifically about the problem of ownership concentration and pluralism, leading to a highly controversial draft directive. This was soon withdrawn due to lack of agreement. Many MEPs clearly did not believe that a directive on pluralism would ever be developed some stating, the main reason for the failure in policy was the vulnerability of national governments, such as those in the U.K. and Germany, to transnational media moguls (see Sarikakis 2004). A similar observation about the power of industrialists was made by the European Federation of Journalists in their report on media ownership concentration in Eastern Europe (2003). Despite integral disagreements (as some MEPs were in favour of some degree of ownership concentration), consensus in the European Parliament acknowledged that uncontrolled and unlimited merger activities endangered the independence and freedom of journalists and the right to information (EP 1992: 6).

As the Maastricht Treaty introduced 'Culture', and therefore the means for cultural expression, into the sphere of the EU's jurisdiction, the European Parliament further argued for the protection of public media space, this time public service broadcasting systems. The inability and unwillingness of nation states and industry to allow a positive policy on the problems of ownership concentration and media pluralism to find fertile ground and, the profound insult against the legitimacy of Public Service Broadcasters role in the market were two of the most significant battles the European Parliament had to fight. Its arguments for the protection of PSBs were based upon the ideas of cultural diversity and the protection of communicative, cultural spaces from commercialization. As earlier, at the beginning of its advocacy work, the European Parliament repeated its calls for the establishment of pan-European channels – also based on the ideals of public service.

As the European Parliament argued, the public service broadcasting system 'before being a technical, legal or economic one, addresses the needs and concerns of citizens and consumers, whose interests in, *inter alia*, civil rights, employment, cultural diversity or consumer protection, are not necessarily the same as those of merchants' (EP 1998b: para. 2). This came as a response to the guidelines drafted by the Commission at the request and pressure of commercial broadcasters. According to these, the PSBs would have to choose one of the funding models suggested by the Commission: to be solely funded by public funding; dual funding; or funded by public tenders. The consequences for the funding of public service broadcasting and control over content production would have been disastrous, as PSBs would have little control over their long-term development as institutions and as economic factors. The European Parliament not only successfully advocated for the protection of PSBs, it also played a central role in the drafting of the public service broadcasting protocol to the Amsterdam Treaty. The Commission was soon forced to withdraw its proposal. In 1997 the Amsterdam Treaty made a specific commitment to the role of public service broadcasting in Europe. The European Parliament's resolution called on broadcasters to enrich their multicultural content and encourage a feeling of solidarity among different cultures (EP 1998b: para. 37); to improve their accountability to the public (para. 29); to set up a list of guidelines and principles that govern the PSBs' activities (para. 34) and to promote equal opportunities policies for the inclusion of women and men in their workforce and content (para. 27). Furthermore, the Resolution introduced the principle of universal access in the Information Society (i.e., in para. AB).

The alliance formed by national broadcasters, sympathetic governments and Directorates-General, and professional organizations supported the European Parliament's work, which resulted in the public service broadcasting protocol. The dominant position in the debate surrounding cultural and communications policy had been occupied by questions of media competition and the economic potential of emerging technologies. The well-known struggle over the introduction of content quotas in the TWF,[4] but also the 'cultural exemption' achieved at the end of the WTO negotiation rounds, due to the insistence of the European Parliament and the strong position by certain countries, were responses clearly addressing a belief in the role of culture and expression in sustaining human communities and in creating new ways of understanding one's own lifeworld. However, the European Parliament also perceived crude commercialization as the threat posed mainly by (U.S.) domination of cultural products.

Phase 3: Coming Full Circle – Reviving the Ghosts

The current third phase is characterized by the commercialization of cultural industries and constant pressures on PSBs' existence in most European countries. The commercialization of content in the public sector indicates the shift of cultural production towards easily consumable and marketable artefacts. As expected, the main beneficiaries are media and communications technology conglomerates, which dominate the market through vertical and horizontal integration of services and production. Responding to the Commission's monitoring report on the TWF's effects in European countries, the European Parliament (2001) and the recent review of the TWF Directive (December 2003) call for further amendment to the directive to include issues of technological development, despite the Commission's reluctance. A new amendment would be of particular interest, as it would demonstrate continuity or changes in the debates led by the European Parliament.

More importantly, the European Parliament, having fought some of the most significant battles in media policy at international level, returns to address the problems of media pluralism and ownership concentration with a number of its own initiatives. The most important of these initiatives are found in the resolution voted by the Parliament on the Commission's fourth report on the TWF (EP 2003) and its resolution on breaches of freedom of expression in the EU (EP 2004). Both documents call upon the Commission anew to draft policy that addresses the problem of media concentration. The European Parliament stated that a 'complete overhaul' of the TWF Directive is needed to address the effects of communications technologies. The proposed way is the synthesis of a legislative framework that brings together the directives of TWF, e-commerce and copyright.

The European Parliament also repeated its call for a transnational broadcasting council, this time in the form of a working group made up of representatives of public and private broadcasters as well as national regulators. In this resolution, the role of pluralism in cultural diversity, freedom of information and democracy is once again emphasized. However, nowhere is it more strongly argued than in the resolution adopted on breaches of freedom of information (EP 2004). This controversial report and resolution originally referred to the Italian politician and media proprietor Silvio Berlusconi by name, although during the debate in the European Parliament references to named individuals had to be omitted. Regarding media ownership concentration, it stated: 'the Italian system presents an anomaly owing to a unique combination of economic, political and media power in the hands of one man – the current President of the Italian Council of Ministers.' Referring to a study by the European Institute of the Media, the European Parliament expressed concern about the state of media ownership in the EU and the lack of a policy framework to deal with the increasing concentration of ownership and even abuse of power. For the drafting of both reports, a number of European Parliamentary committees were involved alongside the Committee on Culture and Education; the Committee on Civil Liberties, Justice and Home Affairs was, for instance, especially involved in the report on breaches of freedom of expression. Such broad-based involvement shows the extent not only of the European Parliament's concern about such issues, but also the media's impact across the spheres of individual liberties, human rights and internal affairs.

Historically, the development of media and cultural policies in the EU has its roots in the political engagement of the European Parliament. The European Parliament has emphasized the significance of the role of the public service broadcasting system for European societies and the special role of media in constructing a European identity. Media and cultural industries are viewed not only as tools to preserve and expand existing cultural traditions and languages but also as active facilitators of new cultures and identities. The active rather than passive (consuming) function of media is also advocated in their role in political processes and in the project of cultural integration, through the potential of technologies to act as two-way vehicles for the exchange of information among European peoples. The protection of content, pluralism and the public service broadcasting system have constituted the central focus of an ongoing debate for over twenty years. During this third phase of activity, the work of the European Parliament – now in its sixth term and with a still larger number of people and countries to represent – has become even more relevant to the international character of the media and cultural issues. In the preparation and review phase leading to the adoption of the new Audiovisual Media Services Directive (European Parliament and Council 2007; this is replacing the Television Without Frontiers Directive), brave positions were put forward by the European Parliament. For example, the underlying approach to media and culture as one based on basic principles irrespectively of their technological aspects of delivery or consumption has been one cultivated by EP's long term involvement in the protection of culture and citizens. Initial proposals related to the controlling of sexist, racist and other harmful content to be expanded to digital platforms and internet content derived also from long standing efforts by EP to introduce proactive regulation in the communications industry. Again this new directive manifests the signs of compromise between parliamentary based attempts for socially proactive policy and resistance for any but the minimum of regulation by industrial actors (see Sarikakis 2007).

The Relevance of the European Parliament's Work and Its Blind Spot

In its work, the European Parliament deals with an increasing volume of economic and social affairs that transcend the boundaries of select committees and jurisdictions. Despite internal disagreements and tensions about the degree of 'protection' of media and cultural industries, there is a consensus that media issues are too important to be left to competition policy. A significant number of interventions have been made by the institution that aim to shape the discourse and agenda of EU media policy. This requires that the European Parliament is on a constant 'alert mode', not least because private interests in media markets are immense – the industrial lobby is well organized and has strong allies among certain, technocratic, parts of the Commission as well as national governments. This does not mean that MEPs do not share free-market ideas; however, even the neo-liberal fraction signs up to the need for the protection of communicative spaces.

The history of the European Parliament, therefore, has produced some of the most significant cornerstones of transnational policy not only at EU level but also international level. Examples are the special reference to PSBs in the Treaty of Amsterdam, which is in effect EU constitutional law, and the exemption of cultural products alongside basic services of water, health and education. Despite such victories, the European Parliament can never afford to rest on its laurels, as threats to all these realms of human existence and activity are very real, and not simply rhetorical. The European Parliament's overarching aim has been to defend the media against commercialization and cultural domination, both through the preservation of existing communicative spaces and the active creation of new ones. It has therefore advocated for the protection of existing public-based communicative spaces such as the PSBs and the cultural industry, not only in its ability to produce goods that can compete but, most importantly, in preserving and nurturing nodes of diverse cultural expression. Minority languages, museums and cultural cities, audio-visual and electronic media production are some of the 'spaces' where the creation of a polity and European identity can emerge. Democratic ideals alone are not strong enough arguments for the development of policy in an environment that prioritizes production and accumulation. Therefore the economic potential of these communicative spaces has had to be proven not only to technocratic Commissioners and neo-liberal states but also to the European Parliamentarians themselves.

In its effort to protect communicative spaces, whether in the form of PSBs, domestic cultural production or even freedom of expression, the European Parliament has favoured certain spaces while failing to turn its attention to others. As part of its advocacy for space for cultural expression, the idea of cultural domination has played an important role, not simply as a normative justification for policy proposals but also as a perceived real threat to Europeanness. Content quotas, state aid to domestic independent audio-visual producers, media pluralism and diversity of languages have been approached as tools in the protection against cultural domination, and in particular American cultural imperialism. It is true that the single European market has benefited the United States more than any other single nation, which is not surprising as the hegemonic position of political and economic players is maintained through the integration of markets.[5] However, cultural dominations within the EU remain the blind spot of the European Parliament. And history has shown that, unless issues of immediate economic profit are brought up by the European Parliament, they will remain invisible in elite politics.

Policies designed to boost European production such as the MEDIA (and MEDIA Plus) programmes have borne fruit, The increase in film production can be mostly observed in nations with strong cinematic traditions within their own territory. Thus, France and Germany are the strongest producers, followed by Denmark and the Netherlands.

Furthermore, Spain, Italy and France have strong links to Latin America with co-productions occupying fourteen of the twenty top places in the Latin American box office in 2001. Germany, Spain, Italy and Great Britain are certainly the main producers in the EU but also the main beneficiaries from admissions sales. Overall, France is the dominant EU 'exporter' with 12 per cent of total admissions for French films, followed by Great Britain (7.5 per cent) Germany (3.9 per cent) and Italy (2.1 per cent) (Focus 2002). All other EU countries together account for the remaining 5.9 per cent, while Hollywood still maintains its dominance.

Media ownership concentration is reaching extraordinary proportions, resulting in actual oligopoly in some cases. Out of the top-five most successful British publishers, three belong to German transnationals, one is U.S.-based and one is British (Hodder Headline). More specifically, both Transworld, the number-one U.K. publishing house which produced over six million copies in 1998, and Random House, the fourth largest in sales, belong to Bertelsmann AG, the German media company; HarperCollins, the second largest in sales, belongs to News Corporation, which is owned by the Murdoch media empire (Stokes 1999: 13). The situation in Central and Eastern Europe (CEE) has recently been recorded by a study on behalf of the European Federation of Journalists (EFJ) (2003). The complex and murky patterns of media ownership reveal that the usual suspects are the dominant buyers in national media. These are mainly Germany, Switzerland and Scandinavia and, in particular: the German Passauer Neue Presse, which owns newspapers in Germany, Austria and, now, in the Czech Republic, Poland and Slovakia; Westdeutsche Allgemeine Zeitung (WAZ), which owns newspapers in Germany, Austria, most CEE countries and occupies a dominant position in Bulgaria (EFJ 2003: 8); and Axel Springer Verlag (Germany), which is the largest publishing company in Europe and owns a majority of magazines in Poland, Hungary and Romania. The Scandinavian group Orkla is also expanding into CEE countries, including Ukraine. Increasingly, the U.S. media is also gaining control of a large portion of media in CEE countries, through U.S. programming, satellite and cable broadcasting and the acquisition of media companies. Here, again we find the major U.S.-based/U.S.-owned media companies such as AOL Time Warner and Viacom dominating the media sphere.

The architecture of the EU facilitates the integration of 'fragmented' market spaces into a common space of integrated markets, in terms of capital, labour mobility and sustainability. But legitimacy of the project is a prerequisite for internal stability and predictability, a feature that is also especially attractive to governments of states eager to be part of the EU, despite the opportunity costs their countries will face. Governments are subjected to pressures from stronger nations with stronger market forces and are more vulnerable to media commercial interests (Galperin 1999; Hoffmann-Riem 1996). Nentwich and Falkner (1997) argue that, where corporatist interests prevail, the European Parliament is much less powerful than national parliaments. 'Unity in diversity' has been addressed by the European Parliament as the concept that seeks to epitomize contemporary Europe and provide a vision for a future EU, while cultural imperialism has been perceived as one of the most powerful 'enemies' of this vision. However, the threat of cultural inperialism is recognized only when it is imposed by external actors. The internal pathologies are only addressed in terms of conventional understanding of media pluralism. Again, even within this context, the European Parliament has not been able to develop its own 'panopticon' across the often subtle, yet nonetheless significant practices of dominance, which is expressed at multiple levels and in complex ways. Besides media ownership, language and cultural practices also become objects of imbalanced relations. With the accession of CEE countries into the EU, 20 million people will be added to the 40 million people currently speaking minority languages. Although the (currently eleven) official languages of the EU are the official languages of the member states, this is not a synonym for 'preferred' languages. Initially French and increasingly English have become the preferred languages of the EU, particularly in communications with third parties. It is clear that even policies designed to revive and protect this aspect of cultural diversity are not particularly effective. Although regional development programmes and language-targeted initiatives have assisted the revival of languages, such as Gaelic, most of Europe's languages are spoken only within their national or regional territories. As some critics point out, the languages of incoming countries will be official on paper, but in reality will be treated as second class (Carlson 2003).

A number of internal independence claims and distinct minority communities within the member states of the EU (the cases of Northern Ireland, Basque Country, and Scotland, for example) pose questions about the degree of recognition of their respective cultures, including those of language, education and religion. Most of the linguistic and nationality minorities in Europe have currently no legal status or media or official public presence (Minority 2000.net). Even so, some minorities are better represented than others, the different power positions of internal minorities also indicating the limitations of cultural policy attempts to encourage linguistic diversity.

As Europe becomes more diverse in its ethnic composition, the inclusion and organic integration of the protection of 'immigrant' cultures should also be pursued. Currently, over 30 million people living in the EU have no citizenship. The issues surrounding their cultural heritage are closely interrelated with current ideological and political predispositions about the nature of citizenship. The dimensions of the latter are addressed in particularly limited contexts, involving rights and responsibilities, attachment to nationhood and significant dependency on linguistic competency. The social and cultural dimensions of citizenship, however, are rarely addressed in the EU context, although generally cultural policy could be categorized as citizenship policy. Some of its unspoken effects in the lived experience of certain historically discriminated or minoritized groups go so far as to become matters of survival.

The political change in CEE states has been accompanied by an eagerness of their governments to 'fit into' the Western world. The conditions for accession to the EU prescribe that incoming countries should first satisfy the acquis communitaire, which includes meeting the economic criteria. Such conditions are actively promoting the 'adjustment' of educational, administrative and even linguistic practices to the order of a particular conception of the EU – a conception largely manufactured by particular social groups (elites). An example of this dimension of impacting on the internal organization of CEE societies is the effect of processes of adaptation on the economic, social and cultural lives of citizens. For instance, policies to 'streamline' administrative and economic systems are taking away earned women's rights. Already, research shows the ways in which the introduction of neo-liberal policies in Central and Eastern Europe is undermining women's socio-economic status. Masculinist cultures rise together with higher unemployment for women and the withdrawal of welfare systems especially important for women, such as childcare, and systems encouraging women's participation in formal politics and political representation (Watson 2000). Gender-imposed unemployment is one such example (Watson 2000). These are effects caused by the transition to a different socio-economic system (liberal capitalism) accompanied by and adhering to a patriarchal ideological system.

Remits and Limits of Supranational Representation

Culture and media in European policy occupy the two ends of an ostensibly defiant relationship between motives: for the European Parliament, they become the watchdog of integration – for others and, in particular, the technocratic Directorates-General of the Commission, an economic asset (Delgado-Moreira 2000; Sarikakis 2004). The transformative potential of cultural policy is left to the jurisdiction of regions in the same way that policy is designed to bring common initiatives into different spaces without bridging them. Even programmes aimed at fostering European co-productions, especially in the audio-visual field, may not necessarily provide the conditions for genuine cultural expression. Culture as a commodity is therefore heavily influenced by market pressure and industry deregulation. The policy adopted for the protection of 'indigenous' cultural production aims to counterbalance Hollywood's predominance in Europe. For this reason, initially internally but later also internationally, co-productions in the audio-visual sector are supported through funds and training programmes. The European industry has benefited from these programmes, but at the same time the benefits cannot be enjoyed equally. Moreover, the increased need for cooperation, due to the difficulty in securing funding outside the Hollywood industry, has resulted in leading international co-productions having to 'assume global characteristics … that is, forms that are culturally indistinct and which eschew political content' (Baltruschat 2003: 166). The outcome, a homogenized product tailor-made for international markets, bears little difference to the familiar Hollywood recipe.

The initiatives taken to promote 'Europeanness' aim to construct public consciousness about a particular space and form of society in the making. However, these policies are not confident in their definition of 'European'. Sassatelli (2002), analysing the policy behind and organization of the 'European Capital of Culture', emphasizes that the 'European' focus remains blurred; it is a combination of references to distinct points in the cultural and geopolitical space of the EU rather than something clearly 'of Europe'. What this tell us about is not the lack of or need for the construction of – or even the undiscovered existence of – pure Europeanness; rather, it indicates the ways in which conflicting images of Europe have been articulated in its policy trajectory.

The European Parliament as the embodiment of the institutionalized version of citizens' representation in elite suprastructures is a 'lonely' experiment in the current map of international relations, despite the fact that, increasingly, demands for an active input from European Parliamentarians in these processes have become more visible (freedominfo.org 2004). The reasonable expectation of the institution is that it should be closer to European citizens than to governments and to a great extent this is the case, seeking to ensure that citizens' views are put forward. Still, the power of national dynamics and in particular those of capital and government are strong, manifested in the effects of governmental or industrialist pressure on a range of policies. It is also demonstrated in the way in which European integration has been approached, not as a cosmopolitan or intercultural collaborative project but rather as a fiscal exercise in market integration that requires the expansion to other fields and the creation of new institutions (Mistral 1991).

The European Parliament expresses concerns about the state of the media in a very similar way to national parliaments. A number of the issues addressed through parliamentary resolutions, such as proposals for an independent broadcasting committee, the threat to pluralism and the problem of media ownership concentration and foreign ownership and the perceived threat of cultural imperialism, are common concerns among industrialized nations. The report on Cultural Sovereignty commissioned by the House of Commons of Canada includes almost identical proposals to those made by the European Parliament (House of Commons 2003).

However, similarly, the position of the institution within a state-like formation that is constituted by processes of production and accumulation sets the limits of its 'radicalism'. As Mistral points out, 'regular capital formation cannot be ensured without the existence of solid institutional frameworks' (1986: 181) that make the transition from differentiations into stable principles of action for private agents and rules of cohesion for states. Putting aside the negotiations and network games that are inherent in any decision-making process, the European Parliament is an institution that largely fulfils the purpose of the EU as a supranational administration, which entails, like any other state in the industrialized world, the concurrent existence of structural constraints and 'paradoxes' of spaces of resistance. The success of these moments and spaces of resistance depends on the network of alliances, the make-up of the political fractions and the positioning of national governments. Also, its own preoccupation with 'external' threats, which has dominated so much of its rhetoric for the development of policy, is based on largely ignoring internal processes of media and cultural domination, which indicates that the ideas and pragmatics driving the advocating work of the institution do not pose an irreversible threat to the interests of 'domestic' capital.

If the criterion that would quantify the degree of legitimization of or resistance to cultural domination were the degree to which it has supported national cultural industries compared to 'foreign' ones, then the European Parliament can be said to have exercised considerable resistance. The institution has certainly provided valuable advocacy for national PSBs and domestic productions; it has mobilized training programmes and has achieved a very moderate but nevertheless secure funding system for European works; it has intervened in matters of content provision and continues to defend the political significance of the cultural sphere in the context of international agreements (e.g. WTO negotiations and the World Summit on the Information Society). It enables further resistance in the space created for the debates over citizenship issues, the role of citizens and not just consumers, cultural entities in Europe, expression and diversity.

However, the European Parliament's angst over the domination of American culture in the European space reveals a blind spot in as far as internal processes of domination are concerned. Its rather unsystematic engagement with policies that resist practices of internal cultural domination at the expense of internal minorities and non-market-driven creative and other public spheres has served to legitimize a status quo that supports 'European' expression in order for it to compete in a market arena. Furthermore, 'culture' is addressed mostly as an object of commercial value or as an antiquated, static site for visitors, but rarely as the realm where social relations are formed and maintained. Attempts to deal with the cultural dimensions of the EU still are often blurred and at the bottom of the polity's list of priorities. Nevertheless, the possibility of debating an alternative to media and cultural consumerism, albeit restricted, provides an oppositional discourse to market sovereignty that can be used by civil-society organizations as an entry point for the representation of matters of social justice. Elite structures are hardly the place for radical politics, so resistance is extended mainly to the ways and degrees that citizens have an input in policymaking. Despite the problems, resistance takes place with the legitimization of certain debates and in particular those that are in conflict with private interests. Resistance also takes place in processes of mediation between masses and unaccountable elites. The European Parliament is actively involved in global media policy and signals the possibility that supranational representational politics might be one of the ways forward in a globalized world. In that form, parliamentary representation could provide further links to the global networking grassroots that seek to address universally shared concerns. Dependency on their electorate and relative autonomy from nation states also means that successful lobbying on behalf of civil society makes the European Parliament more accessible than other EU structures and certainly more than international organizations.

Notes

*   This is an updated and revised version of the article published in the *International Communication Gazette*, 2005, 67(2).
1.   The European Parliament responded to the Green Paper as follows: '[We are] facing the danger that the Community might miss the opportunity to realize a common media policy and, instead, through the use of technical development allow the formation of irreversible international media structures of a commercial character, and monopolies or information systems of non-European origin' (translated from German by the author). See also Sarikakis 2004.
2.   For a discussion on the inner dynamics of the European Parliament, see Sarikakis 2004.
3.   'Medienfragen sind ... Machtfragen'.
4.   See Collins 1994; Sarikakis 2004.
5.   The United States has a 65.4 per cent share of cinema admissions in the EU, and the deficit in the audio-visual sector trade between the EU and States is growing (Focus 2002).

Bibliography

Baltruschat, D. 2003. 'International TV and Film Co-production: A Canadian Case Study', in S. Cottle (ed.), *Media Organisation and Production*. London: Sage.

Bobrow, D.B., Eulau, H., Landau, M., Jones, C.O. and Axelrod, R. 1977. 'The Place of Policy Analysis in Political Science: Five Perspectives', *American Journal of Political Science* 21(2): 415–33.

Carlson, C. 2003. 'Dying Words: EU Expansion to Affect Minority Languages'. Retrieved from http://www.rferl.org/nca/features/2003/08/15082003160020.asp.

Cocks, P. 1980 , 'Towards a Marxist Theory of European Integration' *International Organisation*, 34 (1) 4.

Delanty, G. 1998. 'Social Theory and Transformation: Is There a European Society?' *Sociological Research Online* 3(1). Retrieved from http://www.socresonline.org. uk/socresonline/3/1/1.html.

Delgado Moreira, J.M. 2000. 'Cohesion and Citizenship in EU Cultural Policy', *Journal of Common Market Studies* 38 (3): 449–70.

European Audiovisual Observatory. 2002. *Focus 2002 World Film Market Trends*. Strasburg: European Audiovisual Observatory.

European Federation of Journalists. 2003. *Eastern Empires. Foreign Ownership in Central and Eastern European Media: Ownership, Policy Issues and Strategies*. Brussels: European Federation of Journalists.

European Parliament. 1980a. *Report on the Information Policy of the European Community, of the Commission of the European Communities and of the European Parliament (the Schall Report)*. PE Doc 1–596/80.

———. 1980b. 'The Threat to Diversity of Opinion Posed by the Commercialisation of New Media'. Doc 1–422/80. Cited in European Parliament 1984a.

———. 1982. 'Resolution on Radio and Television Broadcasting in the European Community, in European Communities', *Official Journal of the European Communities*, OJ No C87/109–112, 05.04.1982.

———. 1984a. *Resolution on Broadcast Communication in the European Community (the Threat to Diversity of Opinion Posed by the Commercialisation of New Media)*, OJ NoC117/198–201 30.4.84.

———. 1984b. *Resolution on a Policy Commensurate with New Trends in European Television*, OJ No C17/201–205 30.4.84.

———. 1984c. *Resolution on Broadcast Communication in the European Community (the Threat to Diversity of Opinion Posed by the Commercialization of New Media)*, OJ No C 117/198–201, 30.04.19841985b.

———. 1985a. *Bericht im Namen des Ausschusses für Jugend, Kultur, Bildung, Information und Sport über eine Rahmenordnung für eine europäische Medienpolitik auf der Grundlage des Grünbuchs der Kommission über die Errichtung des gemeinsamen Marktes für den Rundfunk, insbesondere über Satellit und Kabel*, (KOM(84)300 endg.), PE 92 783/endg.

———. 1985b. *Europäische Medienpolitik in Verhandlungen des Europäischen Parlaments*, Nr.2-329/272 12.09.1985.

———. 2001. *Report on the Third Report of the Commission to the Council, the European Parliament and the Economic and Social Committee on the Application of Directive 89/552/EEC 'Television without Frontiers'*, A5-0286/2001 Final.

———. 2003. *Report on the Fourth Report of the Commission to the Council, the European Parliament and the Economic and Social Committee on the Application of Directive 89/552/EEC* A5-0251/2003.

———. 2004. *Resolution on the Risk of Breaches of Freedom of Expression and Information in the Union, particularly in Italy*, T5-0373/2004.

freedominfo.org. 2004. 'IFTI Watch Update', February 24. Retrieved from http:// freedominfo.org/ifti.htm.

European Parliament and Council 2007 Directive 2007/65/EC of the European Parliament and of the Council of 11 December 2007 amending Council Directive 89/552/EEC on the coordination of certain provisions laid down by law, regulation or administrative action in Member States concerning the pursuit of television broadcasting activities

Galperin, H. 1999. 'Cultural Industries Policy in Regional Trade Agreements: The Cases of NAFTA, the European Union and MERCOSUR', in *Media Culture and Society* 21: 627–48.

Hamelink, C. 1994. *The Politics of World Communication*. London: Sage.

Hoffmann-Riem, W. 1996. *Regulating Media: The Licensing and Supervision of Broadcasting in Six Countries*. New York: Guilford Press.

House of Commons, Standing Committee on Canadian Heritage. 2003. *Our Cultural Sovereignty: The Second Century of Canadian Broadcasting*. Retrieved from http://www.parl.gc.ca/InfoComDoc/37/2/HERI/Studies/Reports/herirp02/herirp02-e.pdf.

Landau, M. 1977. 'The Proper Domain of Policy Analysis', in D.B. Bobrow et al., 'The Place of Policy Analysis in Political Science: Five Perspectives', *American Journal of Political Science* 21(2): 415–33.

Lees, T., Ralph, S., and Langham Brown, J. (eds). 2000. *Is Regulation Still an Option in a Digital Universe?* Luton: University of Luton Press.

McChesney, B. 2001. 'Policing the Unthinkable', *openDemocracy*. Retrieved from http://www.opendemocracy.net.

Mistral, J. 1986. 'Régime international et trajectories nationals', in R. Boyer (ed.), *Capitalismes, fin de siècle*. Paris: Presses Universitaires de France, pp. 167–202.

O'Rourke, B. 2002. 'Eastern Europe: Language Group Turns Its Attention to Minority Languages'. Retrieved from http://www.rferl.org/nca/features/2002/11/27112002170014.asp.

Peterson, J. and Bomberg, E. 1999. *Decision-making in the European Union*. London: Macmillan.

Robins, K. 1991. 'Tradition and Translation: National Culture in its Global Context', in J. Corner and S. Harvey (eds), *Enterprise and Heritage: Crosscurrents of National Culture*. London: Routledge.

Robles, A.C. 1994. *French Theories of Regulation and Conceptions of the International Division of Labour*. London: Macmillan.

Sarikakis, K. 2002 'Supranational Governance and Paradigm Shift in Communications Policy-making: The Case of the European Parliament', in M. Raboy (ed.), *Global Media Policy in the New Millennium*. Luton: University of Luton Press.

———. 2004. *Powers in Media Policy: The Challenge of the European Parliament*. Bern: Peter Lang.

———. 2007. (guest editor) 'Media and Cultural Policy in the European Union' Special Issue of *European Studies: An Interdisciplinary Series in European Culture, History and Politics* 24.

Sassatelli, M. 2002. 'Imagined Europe: The Shaping of a European Cultural Identity through EU Cultural Policy', *European Journal of Social Theory* 5(4): 435–51.

Schiller, H. 1969. *Mass Communications and the American Empire*. New York: Augustus M. Kelly.

———. 1996. *Information Inequality: The Deepening Social Crisis in America*. New York: Routledge.

Screen Digest. 1998. 'Mergers and Acquisitions. Focus on Distribution Channels'. Retrieved from http://www.screendigest.com/yp_98-04(2).htm.

Stevenson, N. 1999. *The Transformation of the Media: Globalization, Morality and Ethics*. London and New York: Pearson.

TVinsite. 2002. 'Top 25 Media Companies'. Retrieved 17 October 2002 from http://www.tvinsite.com/brodcastingcable.

Veronis Suhler Merchant Bank. 2002. 'Communications Industry Report'. Retrieved from http://www.veronissuhler.com/articles/article_202.html.

Vincent, R.C., Nordenstreng, K. and Traber, M. 1999. *Towards Equity in Global Communication*. Cresskill, NJ: Hampton Press.

Walerstein, I. 1974. *The Modern World System*. New York: Academic Press.

Watson, P. 2000. 'Politics, Policy and Identity', *Journal of European Public Policy* 5(1).

Chapter 11

Supranational Regulation: The EU Competition Directorate and the European Audio-visual Marketplace

Mark Wheeler

Introduction

The European Union's (EU) regulation of European television and audio-visual services was developed within a number of vague provisions in Article 151 of the basic European Treaty (EU 1997b), which defined a role for the EU in the field of culture. Recently, the European Commission's competence for audio-visual services has grown as technological reforms enabled operators to develop at a pan-European level and there has been a positive harmonization between the revised versions of the Television Without Frontiers (TWF) Directive with the extension of supranational communications packages. In developing a regulatory approach to television and audio-visual services, the EU's response signalled a conflict between the economic priorities of industrial competitiveness on the one hand and the desire to maintain the principles of European cultural identity on the other: 'Broadcasting and the audiovisual has therefore been a notable site where one of the "grand narratives" of the Community has been played out, the battle between the interventionists and free marketers, between *"dirigistes"* and "ultra liberals"' (Collins 1994: 23).

Technological reform, cross-sectoral convergence, economic opportunity, and the globalization of communications services have brought new entrants, strategic alliances, acquisitions and corporate media marriages and mergers into the European television marketplace. Thus, within an expanding market, one of the constant themes underpinning the EU's policy responses, including the TWF Directive, has been liberalization of the rules governing Europe's television industries. This, the Commission felt, would improve European media companies' competitiveness against the challenges of foreign broadcasters, most especially from the United States, and allow the companies to establish a worldwide presence.

Simultaneously, the EU's audio-visual policies sought to preserve the social, cultural and political priorities that have been associated with the provision of pluralism through diverse and 'high-quality' television services in democratic societies. While the Commission has been concerned with content regulation, it has been legally required to utilize economic or structural forms of regulation to intervene over cultural matters. Consequently, the EU has been concerned with the issues surrounding media concentration, to ensure open and fair competition.

This chapter will comment on the contradictions within the EU's approach to television and audio-visual services by focusing on competition policy, which has grown in importance in the era of convergence and cross-media ownership. The European Commission's (EC) Competition Directorate has become a crucial actor in EU audio-visual policy due to the Commission's failure to establish a directive concerning media concentration in the 1990s. To rectify this omission, the Directorate filled the void by encouraging economic efficiency in climates favourable to innovation and technical progress. Therefore, with regard to the European audio-visual sector it has sought to apply rulings concerning: 1. Mergers or concentrations; 2. State aids and 3. Restrictive agreements, concerted practices and dominant positions.

Consequently, this review will consider how the Commission has applied the EC Treaty's competition rules to guarantee the unity and integrity of the converging communications markets. In particular, the Competition Directorate's liberal orientation has determined its view that new economic opportunities should enable a range of suppliers to provide services for viewers and consumers. Thus, it has sought to avoid further monopolization of audio-visual markets by preventing firms from sharing controls via protective controls. Therefore, it has been responsible for establishing rulings concerning the complex development of alliances and mergers between 'cross-platform' companies to stem concentration in the converging communications sector. Further, the Commission has been concerned with the distortion of media markets associated with public enterprises receiving state aids and subsidies. As the Directorate has criticized public service broadcasters (PSBs) for constraining national audio-visual markets, it has pursued state aid cases to determine whether PSBs have detrimentally affected commercial broadcasters' competitive rights for advertising revenues.

Concurrently, it has developed anti-trust provisions over the selling of televised sports rights, most especially regarding football. The Directorate has been concerned about the collective selling or purchasing of rights and the exclusivity granted in respect of those rights. When rights are sold on a collective basis by sports authorities to extract greater revenues, there is a reduction in the availability of rights in the broadcasting market. The Commission believes the restrictive effects of collective selling agreements undermine competition amongst broadcasters and consumer choice. This position has led to the Directorate investigating the sale of live Champions League matches with pan-European football bodies such as European Football Union (UEFA) and conflicting with the English Football Association's Premier League (FAPL).

Finally, it is the purpose of this review to consider whether the usage of competition policy has meant the Commission has been able (or not) to balance the increasingly conflicting imperatives of economic competitiveness with the core values of cultural identity. It considers whether competition regulations have created adequate consumer protections in the face of the growing media concentration, the erosion of PSBs and the monopolization of rights markets that have accompanied the convergence of the European communications sectors. Moreover, it discusses the extent to which the Competition Directorate, through pursuing economic efficiencies, has protected the democratic principles of information services with regard to being public goods in the light of the powerful confluence of technological, economic, political and ideological pressures demanding market freedoms.

The EU's Competing Motives: Market Efficiency Alongside Core Values

The EU has been concerned about the relative weakness of European television industries within the global marketplace, as European television companies are too small to compete internationally. In particular, the European television industry has become characterized by the growing disjunction between a small number of well-capitalized broadcasters who control electronic delivery systems against a larger number of undercapitalized organizations who will become smaller and more fragmented (Davis 1998: 80).

These difficulties have meant that European television markets stood at a considerable disadvantage against U.S. producers who were more efficient in the distribution of their product to large international audiences, as they could pursue greater economies of scale and substantive price advantages because of the size of their own domestic market. This led to an imbalance between the demands for programmes (which reflected the growth in channels and airtime to fill) against the limitations governing European production capacity. In turn, there has been a reliance on U.S. imports for fictional programming such as dramas and situation comedies due to their cheap cost compared to domestic production.

Thus, with the expansion of television and audio-visual services, which was associated with the diversification of revenue streams available to media companies (resulting in an exponential rise in the number of television hours to be filled), the EU believed that its role should be to facilitate unification of the fragmented national European television industries. This would create a more sustainable European television economy which could develop a programming infrastructure to compete with the influx of U.S. imports. In particular, Commission officials suggested that the European companies might compete on a global basis through the removal of national forms of protectionism and felt that, once market barriers had been lowered, the: 'European countries would satisfy their demand for programming from increases in European production ... rather than gravely increased dependence on US imports' (Humphreys 1996: 261).

To foment the rapid growth of the European television market, the EU's (de)regulatory principles of liberalization and harmonization have underpinned its approach to the audio-visual sector throughout a series of directives such as TWF, and policy approaches concerning media concentration and regulation of competition. These provisions, for a European-wide liberalization of broadcasting markets, were in accord with the EU's overarching goal of single market integration, which had been enshrined by the 1992 Maastricht Treaty (EU 1992).

Simultaneously, within this era of single market integration and commercial opportunity, the Commission sought to preserve and protect

what it perceived to be the traditional core values and strengths of the
European broadcasting economies. These included:

1. *Pluralism* – the most fundamental public objective in the media sector.
2. *Cultural diversity* – especially regarding the preservation of national
   identities.
3. *The enhancement of citizens' choice* – in which consumers will be able
   to enjoy a wide degree of access to the new opportunities provided by
   market innovation (Ungerer 2002: 4).

The Treaty on the European Union, which came into force on 1
November 1993, makes a specific reference to the audio-visual sector,
requiring the Community to take all cultural aspects into account in its
actions concerning audio-visual services (EU 1992b). In 1999 the Prodi
Commission defined its position concerning the regulation of content in
a Communication entitled *Principles and Guidelines for the Community's
Audio-visual Policy in the Digital Age*, which was endorsed by the
Council and the European Parliament (EU 1999d). The Communication
reaffirmed that regulation within the audio-visual sector must safeguard
public interest objectives including pluralism, cultural and linguistic
diversity, copyright protection, the right of reply, and the protection
of minors. Thus, the Commission commented that the extent of any
subsequent regulation should be determined by the failure of the market
to realize these objectives. Moreover, it was contended that regulation
must remain proportionate (i.e., the minimum necessary to achieve the
Commission's goals) (Reding 2000).

Further, the divisions between liberalizers and dirigistes were
complicated by the expansion of services that emerged due to the
digitalization and convergence of communication services (television,
telecommunications and information communications technologies).
The increase within digital television platforms has meant that EU
regulators have become concerned with the conditional access systems
which allow consumer access to services through set-top boxes and the
need to ensure there should be no bottlenecks over content in the supply
of communication services to users.

The Regulation of Media Concentration in a Converging Communications Market

These contradictions became evident when the Commission attempted to
develop procedures concerning the regulation of media concentration in

the converging internal communications market. To ensure an open media marketplace in Europe, thereby stemming the possible concentration brought about by the growth of vertically integrated conglomerates, the TWF Directive stated its aim was to make sure that competition must not, in any shape, be distorted. However, Article 5 (which established the 10-per cent quota for independent production) was the only explicit measure in TWF that dealt with media concentration from an economically liberal viewpoint (Humphreys 1996: 287).

Therefore, to rectify this omission, in the early 1990s, the EU declared that it would establish a directive concerning the concentration of media ownership through the harmonization of national rulings. However, as Levy comments: 'there was disagreement between the Community's institutions as to whether the primary purpose of Community action was the safeguarding of pluralism or the competition of a single European audiovisual market' (Levy 1999: 51). The lines of demarcation within this dispute were indicated by the differences in approach between the 1992 Green Paper on *Pluralism and Media Concentration in the Internal Market* (EU 1992a) and *Europe and the Global Information Society* written by the Bangemann High-Level Group in 1994 (EU 1995).

The former set out to assess the need for Community-level action concerning media ownership with regard to the disparities that existed amongst member states. It outlined a lengthy process in which there would be a facilitation of a network of like-minded operators who would be consulted with regard to questions on pluralism and media ownership (Iosifidis 1997: 91–104). Conversely, the 1994 paper described a situation across Europe in which national ownership regulations had impeded television and telecommunications companies from taking new opportunities in the internal market, with regard to information services (EU 1995). In turn, it speculated that such regulatory restrictions would undermine the competitive advantage of European television organizations against non-European competitors (Iosifidis 1997: 94).

Former Commissioner Mario Monti tried to reconcile these goals when he presented a draft directive in 1996 whose measures included a 30-per-cent upper limit on 'monomedia' ownership for radio and television broadcasters in their own territories and a 'multimedia threshold' of 10 per cent for ownership of combined media (television, radio and newspapers) (Levy 1999: 50–52). These proposals floundered as the member states disputed the appropriate level of diversity within ownership for the different-sized markets (local, regional or national).

While the Commission favoured an overall measure of a 30-per-cent
market share within a specific region for a television or radio station,
some Community members (notably Germany and the U.K.) argued
that market share should be measured in accordance with the media
companies' national marketplaces, irrespective of where the service was
transmitted. Following on from this, a more flexible draft proposed a
30-per-cent share that could be varied in respect to each set of national
circumstances.

However, the Commission was unable to secure a compromise
between the European Parliament and the member states over the
degree of flexibility governing ownership thresholds at local, regional
or national levels (Papathanassopoulos 2002: 112–13). In the event, the
draft directive was abandoned in 1998 when the EU decided to establish
a set of rulings on ownership, plurality and diversity through a number of
policy documents and research reports. Invariably, the recommendations
and rulings within these policy documents were limited. This was
because the basic Treaty provisions, in accordance with the principles of
subsidiarity, stated that ownership rules should fall within the regulatory
supervision of the member states. Moreover, due to the political sensitivity
of any rulings concerning media ownership, the EU found it difficult to
establish a consensus amongst member states favouring Community-
level intervention regarding media ownership. This was also reflected
in the lukewarm response from the media industries themselves when
presented with the possibility of a set of harmonized European-wide
rulings governing cross-media ownership.

Therefore, the political controversy that arose concerning these rulings
showed the fundamental dichotomy in the EU's approach between
the desire for plurality in media provision and the need to establish a
competitive European television sector. These differences were also
played out within the Commission itself, notably between the main EU
Directorates (DGs). DGX (Education and Culture) continued to seek to
preserve the concepts of plurality, while DGXIII (Information Society,
at the time headed by Commissioner Martin Bangemann) pursued
policies which were designed to expand information services through
market liberalization, on account of the new market conditions that had
emerged under convergence. However, the inconclusive results of the
EU's legislative proposals concerning media concentration in the mid to
late 1990s suggest it will be difficult to ever achieve consensus amongst
the constituent stakeholders including the Commission's Directorates,

the Parliament, the member states and the media companies themselves. This has led to a number of commentators predicting that the EU will continue to be 'powerless to regulate (on) the issue of concentration, apart from scrutinising (media) mergers and acquisitions' (Papathanassopoulos 2002: 115). They suggest that the most effective mechanism for the EU to regulate media concentration will ironically continue to be that most apparently liberalizing of single-market principles – competition policy.

The Competition Directorate

The remit of the Competition Directorate is neo-liberal in economics and commercial in application. It guarantees the unity of the internal market so that companies can compete on a level playing field in all member states. Thus, the Directorate seeks to avoid the monopolization of markets by preventing firms from sharing markets via protective agreements that would enable them to insulate themselves from competition, maximize their profits and impede development. Competition rulings are designed to stem any perceived market failing and the Directorate intervenes to correct anti-competitive practices by making rulings concerning:

1. *Mergers (concentrations)*: a merger or 'concentration' is where a firm acquires exclusive control of another firm or of a firm it controlled jointly with another firm, or where several firms take control of a firm or create a new one. The Commission can examine mergers before they occur to decide whether they are compatible with the internal market.

2. *State aids*: any aid granted by a member state or through state resources that distorts or threatens to distort competitive trade between member states by favouring certain undertakings or the production of certain goods is deemed to be incompatible with the common market. However, exemptions exist, as state aids which have a social character and promote culture are compatible with the internal market.

3. *Public enterprises and liberalization of the market*: with regard to public enterprises to which member states have granted special or exclusive rights, member states are prohibited from enacting or maintaining measures that are contrary to the rules of competition. There are some derogations which stipulate that enterprises entrusted with the operation of services of general economic interests are subject to the competition rules, in so far as the application of such rules does not obstruct the performance, in law or in fact, of the particular tasks assigned to them.

4. *Restrictive agreements and concerted practices*: a restrictive agreement is an agreement between two or more firms that requires one or more of the parties to the agreement to adopt a specific type of conduct. A concerted practice is a step below a restrictive agreement. It involves coordination among firms which falls short of an agreement proper.

5. *The abuse of a dominant position*: a dominant position is a situation of economic power held by a firm that allows it to hinder effective competition in the relevant market. It puts the firm in a position to exert considerable influence on the conditions in which competition can develop and be able to act without having to take that competition into account.

Further, with regard to mergers, the 1989 regulation EEC No.4064 provided the Competition Directorate with the legislative framework through which to interpret concentration. It was designed to ensure that the aims of Article 3 of the Treaty were realized to include the non-distortion of the common market and that concentration did not undermine dynamic competition. Moreover, the regulation enabled the Directorate to set a timetable so it could pre-empt mergers before they occurred, rather than afterwards.

Competition Policy in the Audio-visual Sector

In applying these measures to the audio-visual sector, the Competition Directorate has become an active player in intervening in the European television markets. To preserve competition within the audio-visual sector, the Directorate has pursued the EC Treaty's competition rulings to make decisions with regard to: mergers, state aid, public enterprises and the liberalization of the market, restrictive agreements and concerted practices, and the abuse of dominant positions (Wheeler 2001: 3).

However, as it has expanded its jurisdiction, the Directorate's neo-liberal approach to Europe's audio-visual sector has led to questions concerning its ability to protect public services, enhance pluralism and promote a European public sphere. Most especially, competition policy has ignored the 'cultural' diversity of content as it cannot recognize citizens' rights and concepts of identity. This is because the Directorate does not conceive communications as being any more than a private exchange of goods between suppliers and customers. To illustrate these values, it will be necessary to reflect on the Directorate's rules concerning:

1. Mergers to stem cross-media and communication concentration.
2. The definition of state aid with regard to public service broadcasters.
3. The sale of sports rights to broadcasters (Wheeler 2001: 4).

Mergers

The Competition Directorate's most conspicuous interventions within the audio-visual sector have arisen when it has been called upon to assess new competitive ventures including alliances and mergers, under its merger control rules (Humphreys 1996: 212). The restructuring of media markets in Europe led to the creation of large media conglomerates of 'European dimension' whose size (assets of €5 billion or over worldwide) triggered EC merger control (Ungerer 2002: 8). Similarly, competition regulations have been invoked when defensive alliances have occurred in which two or more companies with strong positions in their domestic markets combine to strengthen their positions within the convergent markets (Van Miert 1999: 117).

The Directorate has sought to employ its merger regulations so that it can investigate any proposed cross-communications alliance or merger before its goes ahead rather than having to consider it retrospectively. In interpreting these complex rules, it has realized that rapid technological change may increase forms of market concentration, rather than reduce them. Thus, the competition 'watchdogs' have become concerned with the danger that the conditional access systems enabling platform operators to broadcast, or consumers to subscribe to encrypted services, may be held in the hands of an individual 'gatekeeper' and consumer choice will be undermined (Van Miert 1997). Therefore, according to former Competition Commissioner Mario Monti: 'A strong, effective competition policy is fundamental to the success of many sectors in Europe, and none more so than the audiovisual sector. A nuanced approach is required, given the complexity and importance of the sector. But that it is nuanced does not mean that it is laissez-faire' (Monti 2002).

The Competition Directorate has conducted several investigations at national, pan-European and international level to provide rulings concerning the merging or formation of alliances between media, telecommunications and multimedia corporations. At a national level, it intervened in the German pay-television market between 1994 and 1998 to prohibit the two leading German commercial television owners, Bertelsmann and the Kirch group, attempting to develop a joint venture with the German telecommunications monopoly Deutsche Telekom (DT), to be called Media Services Gesellschaft (MSG). The companies intended that the MSG conglomerate should deliver pay-television channels and interactive services such as video-on-demand through conditional access and decoder systems. In both cases, the Directorate found against MSG due to concerns of market dominance in programme rights, the supply of programming in pay-television channels and anti-competitive controls over the distribution of set-top boxes Levy (1999: 88–89).

At a pan-European level, the Directorate supported the authorization of the French Télévision par Satellite; Bertelsmann/RTL; Canal Plus's acquisition of Nethold and several joint ventures including Canal Plus/Lagardere/Liberty Media; Kirch/BSkyB; and RTL/Canal Plus (Monti 2002). At an international level, with regard to the mergers between AOL and Time Warner and Vivendi and Universal, the Directorate moved actively to establish specific rulings which allowed the mergers to go ahead within the remit of competition.

In November 2002 the Commission began a detailed investigation into the acquisition of Italian pay-television satellite channel Telepiù by Rupert Murdoch's News Corporation from Vivendi-Universal. With a share of more than two-thirds of the Italian pay-television market, Telepiù was the dominant player and News Corporation intended to merge the station with its own pay-television operation Stream to strengthen its position in the subscription-based marketplace. During this investigation the Directorate considered the impact of the merger on Italian broadcasting to determine whether News Corporation's entrance favoured new competitors or affected a monopoly (EU 2002b). On 2 April 2003 it cleared the acquisition by allowing News Corporation to own the merged company, enabling it to attain a near total monopoly of the Italian pay-television market.

The Directorate's officials argued the merger benefited consumers because Stream was a weak business which would have been shut down if the deal had been blocked. In making their decision, they took into account the inherent difficulties of the Italian pay-television sector, which remained financially unstable as programming costs, stemming from the expensive acquisition of premium film or sports content, had exceeded revenues. Moreover, the penetration of subscription services was hampered by the presence of twelve free-to-air Italian television channels provided by the state-owned RAI, Berlusconi's Mediaset commercial stations and a plethora of local broadcasters. Thus, former Competition Commissioner Monti concurred with News Corporation's 'failing company defence':

[in which] a transaction can be regarded as a rescue merger if the competitive market structure would deteriorate in a similar fashion even if the merger did not take place (i.e. because the undertaking would exit the market). [While] the Commission … considered [that] … the very strict legal requirements for the 'failing firm defence'… were not met in the [cases] of [Telepiú and Stream] … [it took into] … account … the chronic financial difficulties faced by both companies, of the specific features of the Italian market and of the disruption that the possible closure of Stream would cause to Italian pay-television subscribers. (EU 2003a)

Subsequently, the Directorate argued that its main responsibilities referred to the imposition of controls over the merged satellite monopoly, thereby ensuring that the market remained open. In particular, it was conscious that News Corporation would achieve a dominant position if it remained the sole 'gatekeeper' for the customers and rival operators' conditional access rights to the Italian satellite platform. Consequently, the Commission required News Corporation to cooperate with other satellite operators through simulcrypt arrangements across its platform, thereby ensuring the same set-top box could read different signals encrypted from different technologies. Moreover, it required News Corporation to enter into competitive selling and buying arrangements for film and sports rights. Further, Telepiù had to divest its remaining interests in the terrestrial analogue and digital markets (EU 2003a).

In reviewing merger cases, the ideologies and principles of economic liberalism have underpinned the Directorate's rulings. This usage of competition policy has proved myopic, as the European audio-visual industries have not been considered in terms of cross-media ownership but only with regard to the provision of the competitive marketing of services for consumer need. Therefore, the oligopolistic tendencies of media giants to control and stream cultural content has been ignored, to the detriment of the European citizenry.

State Aid with Regard to National Public Service Broadcasters

The Commission has sought to prevent the implementation of anti-competitive agreements and the abuse of dominant market positions by public monopoly operators or service providers. On 15 November 2001 the Directorate published its *Communication from the Commission on the Application of State Aid Rules to Public Service Broadcasting* in which it clarified the EU approach on the application of state aid rules to PSBs (EU 2001). These were that:

1. Member states are free to define the extent of the public service and the way it is financed and organized, according to their preferences, history and needs.
2. The Commission called for transparency on these aspects to assess the proportionality of state funding and to control possible abusive practices.
3. Member states will be asked whenever such transparency is lacking, to establish a precise definition of the public service remit, to formally entrust it to one or more operators through an official act and to have an appropriate authority monitor its fulfilment.
4. The Commission will only intervene in cases where there is a distortion of competition arising from the aid which cannot be justified with the need to perform the public service as defined by the member state and to provide for its funding (Wheeler 2001: 6).

Therefore, while member states are regarded as competent for the definition and choice of funding public service broadcasting, the Commission retains a duty to check for abusive practices and any absence of overcompensation on a case-by-case basis. This is in accordance with the 1997 Amsterdam Protocol (EU 1997a) which provided that member states could provide for the funding of public service broadcasting via the appropriate levels of public subsidies so that market distortion should not occur, and established that the Commission's consensus view would taken against the introduction of any state aid guidelines in relation to PSBs. In particular, the state aid mechanism has come into effect when the private broadcasters claim their public rivals have enjoyed a competitive advantage in receiving both public subsidies and advertising revenues. The commercial organizations maintain this has meant PSBs have a greater capacity to invest in programming and services, and argue that public financing must be more transparent and proportional to the public service remit.

In this respect, in February 1999, the Commission opened formal state aid procedures regarding PSBs within Italy, France and Spain (who receive revenues from both state subsidy and advertising) and found their collection of advertising revenues did not unfairly distort the national markets. The launch of new digital services by PSBs has also led to complaints by private rivals. In 1998 the Directorate ruled in favour of two German thematic channels, Kinderkanal and Phoenix, run by the ARD and ZDF public operations (Aid no.: NN70/98. EU 1999b) and supported Portuguese public broadcaster Radio Televisao Portuguesa (RTP) when it was challenged by the private company Sociedade Independente de Communicacao (Davis 1998: 94). Further, on 29 September 1999, the European Commission rejected a complaint from BSkyB that licence funding of the supply of BBC News 24 to cable television viewers was an abuse of European laws on state aids (EU 1999a).

On 3 February 2004 the Directorate launched a state aid probe into the Netherlands' eight PSBs and their umbrella organization, the Netherlands Broadcasting Corporation (NOS), to consider whether the Dutch state had provided them with excess funds of €110 million since 1992. This investigation acted in accordance with the Commission's preliminary conclusion that the Dutch PSBs received subsidies and ad-hoc payments over and above the funds necessary to finance their output. Most especially, they had received additional monies for the provision of commercial services which were deemed to be outside of the purview of their public service remits. Additionally, the Directorate investigated possible forms of 'cross-subsidization' in which the PSBs' activities in advertising markets and their acquisition of sports transmission rights distorted normal types of market behaviour (EU 2004a).

In May 2004, after a formal investigation, the Commission ordered TV2/Danmark, the Danish public broadcaster, to return the excess compensation of €84.4 million plus interest it had received from the Danish government during 1995–2002. The Directorate calculated the Danish state's financing of the PSB had contravened its rulings which stated that state aids might only be received if the financing was proportionate to the public service's net cost. In determining TV2's net cost, the Commission took into account the advertising revenues it had generated from the public service programmes and concluded that TV2 had received too much money in subsidies.

Moreover, the findings revealed that the Danish state, as owner of TV2, had unfairly distorted the national television market by reinvesting annual amounts of excess compensation into TV2. In such a manner, TV2 benefited from state measures including interest-free and instalment-based loans, guarantees for operating loans, a corporate tax exemption and ad-hoc capital transfers, and had received access to a nationally available transmission frequency on favourable terms.

These anti-competitive advantages were enhanced when excess forms of compensation: 'Unduly [favoured] the public broadcaster compared to [those] competitors that [did] not receive any State funding. In these circumstances, excess compensation can allow the beneficiary to depress prices in commercial markets to levels not attainable to those competitors that do not receive state aid' (EU 2004b).

Thus, in pursuing state aids, the Directorate-General for Competition has been hostile to PSBs. While, in the majority of cases concerning state aids, it has found in favour of PSBs as there was no clear evidence of market distortion despite the claims of commercial operators, the Dutch and Danish examples demonstrate a growing conviction within the EU's governing circles to stem public subsidies by pursuing more market-driven interpretations of anti-competitiveness. Despite the Directorate's attempts to introduce draft guidelines in the application of state aids, the majority view in the Commission remained that complaints against PSBs should be considered on a case-by-case basis. And its response to PSBs demonstrates that 'the internal market is hostile to public service broadcasting ... [as, when] seen from the vantage point of ... neo-classical economic theory[,] ... public service broadcasting is aberrant and offensive (Collins 1999: 162). As Levy has commented, state aids remain 'the area where there is perhaps the greatest potential for conflict between the policies adopted by national governments and the way in which [the Competition Directorate] might interpret the competition provisions of the EC treaties' (Levy 1999: 97).

The Sale of Sports Rights to Broadcasters

The Competition Directorate has stated that there should be no unjustified restrictions for competition in the sale of rights by sports bodies to broadcasting companies. There are, however, two particular issues related to the marketing of broadcasting rights of sports events: the collective selling and purchasing of broadcasting rights and the exclusivity granted in respect of those rights.

There are significant complexities for broadcasters, sports bodies and competition regulators when a group of football clubs sell rights to matches to the media collectively to extract more revenue. When rights are sold on a collective basis, there is a consequent reduction of the availability of rights in the broadcasting market. The restrictive effects of collective selling agreements undermine the levels of competition amongst broadcasters and consumer choice. In effect, they amount to price fixing, restrict the availability of rights for sports events and strengthen the market position of the dominant broadcasters.

On a pan-European scale, the Directorate investigated the UEFA's collective selling of Champions League rights to determine whether this contravened the competition criteria. It announced, on 3 June 2002, that UEFA's collective sale had distorted competition between broadcasters, encouraged media concentration and barred access to key content for the development of internet- and mobile telephony-based sport services. This, the Directorate felt, had contravened the interests of both fans and consumers alike. Therefore, it supported UEFA's new rules, which were designed to bring the Champions League's media rights within the reach of internet content providers, as well as a greater number of television and radio companies. This meant that, rather than UEFA selling the rights as a bundle to only one broadcaster per nation, it will sell several packages of rights for shorter periods of time. Moreover, the football clubs themselves will be able to exploit some of these rights by directly targeting their fan base (EU 2002c).

On 19 January 2005 the Commission announced that it had made legally binding the German Football League's (Ligaverband) commitments to liberalize the joint sale of media rights of the Bundesliga 1 and 2. Previously, the Competition Directorate had been concerned that the Ligaverband's exclusive selling of commercial broadcasting rights had violated the EC Treaty's ban on cartels and restrictive practices. However, in agreeing to a 'commitment decision' with the league, it was satisfied that the centralized forms of marketing would be dismantled, as the Ligaverband undertook to offer unbundled rights packages for a duration of no longer than three seasons. Therefore, rights would be regularly offered to a large number of operators to offset any form of media concentration. Moreover, the Commission believed that, through such competitiveness between traditional and new media players, football fans could view games via a range of service providers including broadcasters, internet suppliers and mobile phone networks (EU 2005a). According to the Competition Commissioner Neelie Kroes, 'Fans benefit from new products and greater choice. Leagues and clubs benefit from increased coverage of their games. Readily available premium content such as top football boosts innovation and growth in the media and information technology sectors. Moreover, open markets and access to content are essential safeguards against media concentration' (EU 2005a).

However, Kroes' vision proved more problematic in the British pay-television market. In December 2002 the Directorate announced that it would consider whether English Football Association Premier League's (FAPL) joint selling of matches to British and Irish television companies should continue on an exclusive basis. In practice, this meant only 25 per cent or 138 of the Premier League matches were broadcast live, and one major media group BSkyB (controlled by Murdoch's News Corporation) could afford the acquisition and exploitation of such a bundle of rights. This, the Commission commented in a statement of objections to the FAPL, led to high prices and unfairly blocked other competitors from acquiring key content.

In response, the FAPL submitted its formal reply to the objections on 18 March 2003, denying that the arrangements restricted competition. Subsequently, the Commission and the FAPL reached a provisional agreement in December 2003 in which the league promised to ensure that a 'meaningful' number of live games would go to a second broadcaster. However, as uncertainty remained over what constituted a 'meaningful' package of live games and, when BSkyB agreed a £1.024 billion deal to screen a record 138 matches in 2003, the Competition Directorate issued the FAPL with a Notice concerning the joint selling of media rights on an exclusive basis on 30 April 2004:

> The arrangements restrict competition in the upstream markets for the acquisition of media rights of football. These markets are closely linked with downstream markets on which those rights are used to provide services to consumers. The most commercially important of these markets are the television markets, where, for example free-TV broadcasters compete for advertisers and pay-TV broadcasters compete for subscribers: the restrictions therefore affect the downstream markets as well ... This is because the joint and exclusive sale of large packages of media rights created barriers to entry, various restrictions on the output of the FAPL limited the development of products and markets, and ... [the] restrictions ... [lead] to further media concentration. (EU 2004c)

Therefore, the Brussels officials made clear their objections to the continuation of BSkyB's thirteen-year monopolistic control over the live rights of English Premier League matches. They felt that the FAPL had been obstructionist by refusing to act on the agreements it had made with the Directorate in 2003. Throughout the summer of 2005 Commissioner Kroes demanded that the FAPL should sell only 50 per cent of its live match rights to one broadcaster and the rest of the games would be put out for competitive tender. She also wanted to extend the number of live matches shown from the present number of 138.

Conversely, the Premier League feared the Commission's intervention would jeopardize the £340 million per annum it had secured for its clubs from BSkyB in 2001. Further, it contended that, by extending the number of live games on offer, there would be an over-saturation of matches leading to a decline in the worth of the rights. Therefore, the FAPL Chief Executive, Richard Scudamore, stated that the league preferred to continue dividing the same number of live matches into four packages covering 30 to 40 live games which would be put out to competitive tender. It maintained that if a single broadcaster won all the packages they would be required to drop one set of games, which could go to the second highest bidder or be retendered. Following this logic, the FAPL argued that 'second-tier' pay-TV operators such as Setanta might circumvent entry barriers by winning the fourth package. Moreover, the FAPL's officers hoped that, as BSkyB would have to compete with other broadcasters to win the rights, they could come close to securing the £1.1 billion in revenues they had achieved in the 2001 deal despite negotiating in a declining rights market.

These differences in opinion led the Commission and the FAPL into direct conflict with one another when the discussions to finalize the selling of live rights collapsed in August 2005. Subsequently, in September 2005, Kroes threatened the league with a legal 'statement of objections', claiming it had operated in an anti-competitive manner and requiring it to pay 10 per cent of its revenues in fines. In the event, the Commission, at the behest of the U.K. government, withdrew its objection. Instead, on 25 October 2005, Kroes agreed to consider Scudamore's revised proposals, including concessions concerning BSkyB's exclusive access to live match rights through a 'meaningful' tendering of packages (Deans 2005).

Subsequently, on 17 November 2005, the Commission and the FAPL agreed to end BSkyB's monopoly of live Premiership match rights in the forthcoming 2007 tender. They announced that 138 matches would be divided into six 'balanced' packages of 23 games to be tendered so that no single broadcaster could purchase all six, nor pay a premium to win two or more bundles. This, the Directorate claimed, would encourage greater competition by allowing BSkyB's subscription rivals NTL and Irish broadcaster Setanta, along with free-to-air channels including the BBC, ITV and Channel Five, to mount serious bids for the rights bundles. Further, it was contended the FAPL could seek bids from new entrants including British Telecom, France Télécom and AOL to make the competitive tender 'platform' neutral (Gibson 2005).

Subsequently, it was announced on 5 May 2006 that BSkyB had paid the FAPL £1.31 billion under the revised rules to win four out of the six packages and the rights to cover 92 live matches per season. The other two packages were won by Setanta who, surprisingly, secured 46 live matches at a cost of £392 million. Yet, despite this success for the Irish broadcaster, the devil lay in the detail as BSkyB has maintained control of the lucrative, coveted fixtures such as Arsenal v Manchester United, and the Setanta packages includes more of the so-called 'runt' bundles made up from less popular games (Day 2006).

Thus, despite Kroes arguments that fans will benefit from a wider range of services, it is unclear whether the market logic of competition can encourage a greater dissemination of coverage, or if there is evidence of consumer demand for such a package of rights covering football matches. Indeed, as subscribers will now be required to pay both BSkyB and Setanta to receive all games, for which the broadcasters paid inflated prices for rights under the new rules, the exponential costs will be increased for consumers rather than matches becoming available to end-users at a more competitive rate. Further, as there has been a concurrent decline in 'listed' sports events and growth of the rights market, a sizable section of the population will continue to be excluded from access to live coverage, as witnessed by the English Cricket Board's decision to sell its package of rights to BSkyB from 2006. Therefore, despite the breakdown in relations between the Directorate and FAPL over the collective sale of the FA Premier League's live rights, the principles of competition have not offset the decline in public coverage of national sporting events that has occurred throughout the last decade.

Conclusion

In establishing its policy instruments for the European television marketplace, the EU has facilitated a regulatory framework which would enhance opportunities for expansion within the single market. Most especially, the EU identified the fundamental problem within the European television markets as being one of fragmentation, which it believes has stymied the growth of European television companies when they have tried to compete within the global market. Thus, in attempting to foment the rapid growth of the European television market, the EU has employed the principles of liberalization and harmonization. Simultaneously, the Commission sought to intervene in the Community's broadcasting markets to redress what it has understood as being the undesirable outcomes of an unfettered marketplace. The collision of these imperatives has created an inherent tension in the EU policy process between dirigistes and liberalizers.

Within the Commission's attempts to create a Media Concentration Directive, this dichotomy was at its most evident. For instance, the EU declared that it would establish a directive concerning media concentration through the harmonization of national rulings. However, due to the political sensitivity of rulings concerning media ownership, the EU found it impossible to establish a consensus amongst the responsible Directorates-General, the European Parliament and member states for the directive. In the event, despite calls from the European Parliament to readdress the directive on media concentration, the European Commission preferred to leave the decisions concerning concentration to the auspices of its Competition Directorate.

As a consequence, the EU Competition Directorate has become an active player in intervening over the European television market as the centralizing tendencies of media conglomeration have grown. The Directorate has conducted several notifications across national, pan-European and international markets concerning the merging or formation of joint alliances between media, telecommunications and multimedia corporations. In the case of News Corporation's monopoly of Italian pay-television, it was convinced by those claims maintaining that media concentration was a necessary evil because it allowed for the development of a limited number of subscription services rather than none at all.

The Directorate has become active regarding the issuing of state aids procedures concerning the distortion of markets by PSBs through their receipt of public subsidies. Most recently, in the Netherlands and Denmark it has intervened to require the investigation of and repayment of monies received by PSBs that have detrimentally affected opportunities for commercial competitors. Moreover, with the growth of the sports rights markets, the Commission has been involved in the complex regulation of joint selling of live football games by European and national associations. This has led to controversies, not least with regard to the English FAPL, as the anti-competitive dominance of rights markets by monopoly suppliers has been seen by the Directorate to enhance media concentration.

Thus, for some, competition policy in its approach to media concentration has been understood as providing the appropriate mechanism through which the EU can meet the conflicting imperatives of competitive gain with the demands of plurality and diversity. However, as Jonathan Hardy has commented: 'In assessing market power through economic considerations, competition law is unable to grasp more complex operations of cultural or symbolic power which the regulation of media (and now multi-media) pluralism has traditionally sought to address' (Hardy 2001: 15).

As the converging communication markets take on different characteristics, the democratic flow of information to the public has become a chief concern. To this end, it would appear that competition policy provides only a qualified degree of protection for information markets conceived of as a public good. This is an issue of vital concern, since communication must be considered as having a significant social worth as well as being understood as an economic commodity. In effect, the EU's neo-liberal competition policies may enhance market opportunities, but they fail to recognize the cultural complexities of an audio-visual and communications public sphere in which a diverse range of voices are required to encourage representation and aid participation for European citizens. These concerns return attention back to the dichotomy between the Commission's interventionists and liberalizers, and suggest that in regard to supranational competition policy it has been the latter who have won the day, despite significant qualifications, in establishing EU rulings governing the television and the audio-visual sectors.

Bibliography

Day, J. 2006. 'BBC Keeps Premiership Highlights', *The Guardian*, 8 June. Retrieved 15 June 2006 from http://media.guardian.co.uk/sport/story/0,,1793268,00. html.

Chapman, P. 2000. 'Monti Grabs Lead Role in the EU Media Show', *European Voice*, 6–12 July.

Collins, R. 1994. *Broadcasting and Audio-visual Policy in the European Single Market*. London: John Libbey.

―――. 1999. 'European Union Media and Communication Policies', in J. Stokes and A. Reading (eds), *The Media in Britain: Current Debates and Developments*. Houndmills: Palgrave.

Conlan, T. 2005. 'Football Rights War Goes into Extra time', *The Guardian* 17 November. Retrieved 18 November 2005 from http://media.guardian.co.uk/broadcast/comment/0,7493,1644925,00.html.

Davis, W. 1998. *The European Television Industry in the 21st Century*, Financial Times Specialist Report: Media and Telecoms. London: FT Business.

Deans, J. 2005. 'Hopes Rise in TV Soccer Talks', *The Guardian*, 18 October. Retrieved 7 November 2005 from http://media.guardian.co.uk/broadcast/story/html.

European Union. 1989. *Council Directive 89/552/EEC of 3 October 1989 on the Coordination of Certain Provisions Laid down by Law, Regulation or Administrative Action in Member States concerning the Pursuit of Television Broadcasting Activities.* Brussels: European Council.

————. 1992a. *Pluralism and Media Concentration in the Internal Market: An Assessment of the Need for Community Action.* COM(92)480 final. Brussels: European Commission.

————. 1992b. *Treaty on European Union* (92/C 191/01), signed at Maastrict, 7 February 1992. Brussels: European Union.

————. 1994. *Communication to Parliament and Council: Follow-up Consultation Process Relating to the Green Paper on 'Pluralism and Media Concentration in the Internal Market: An Assessment of the Need for Community Action'*, COM(94)353 final. Brussels: European Commission, 5 October.

————. 1995 *Europe and the Global Information Society: Recommendations to the EC* (The Bangeman Report), Brussels: European Commission, 25 May.

————. 1997a. *Protocol on the System of Public Broadcasting in the Member States*, Protocols to the Treaty of Amsterdam amending the Treaty on European Union, signed at Amsterdam, 2 October 1997.

————. 1997b. *Treaty of Amsterdam Amending Treaty on European Union Establishing the European Communities and Certain Related Acts*, signed at Amsterdam, 2 October 1997.

————. 1999a. *Commission Decision on State Aid Financing of a 24 Hour News Channel out of a Licence Fee by the BBC.* SG(99) D/10201. Brussels: European Commission.

————. 1999b. *Commission Decision on State Aid Financing of Kinderkanal and Phoenix Specialist Channels.* Brussels: European Commission.

————. 1999c. *Communication to the European Parliament, the Council, the Economic and Social Committee and the Committee to the Regions: The Convergence of Telecommunications, Media and Information Technology Sectors, and the Implications for Regulation: Results of the Public Consultation on the Green Paper (COM(97)623).* Brussels: European Commission.

————. 1999d *Principles and Guidelines for the Community's Audiovisual Policy in the Digital Age (COM 657)*, Brussels: European Commission, 14 December.

————. 2001. *Communication from the Commission on the Application of State Aid Rules to Public Service Broadcasters.* Brussels: European Commission, 15 November.

————. 2002a. *Commission Open Proceedings into the Joint Selling of Media Rights to the English Premier League*, media release. Brussels: European Commission, 20 December.

————. 2002b. *Commission Opens In-depth Probe into the Acquisition of Telepiù by Newscorp*, media release. Brussels: European Commission, 29 November.

————. 2002c. *Commission Welcomes UEFA's New Policy for Selling the Media Rights to the Champions League*, media release. Brussels: European Commission, 3 June.

————. 2002d. *European Parliament Calls for a Resolution on Media Concentration*, media release. Brussels: European Parliament, 20 November.

————. 2003a. *Commission Clears Merger of Stream with Telepiù Subject to Conditions*, media release. Brussels: European Commission, 2 April.

————. 2003b. *Commission Reaches Provisional Agreement with FA Premier League and BSkyB over Football Rights*, media release. Brussels: European Commission, 16 December.

————. 2004a. *Commission Launches Aid Probe into Dutch Public Service Broadcasters*, media release. Brussels: European Commission, 3 February.

————. 2004b. *Commission Order Danish Public Broadcaster TV2 to Pay Back Excess Compensation for Public Service Tasks*, media release. Brussels: European Commission, 19 May.

————. 2004c. 'Notice published pursuant to Article 19(3) of Council Regulation No. 17 concerning case COMP/C.2/38.173 and 38.453 – joint selling of the media rights of the FA Premier League on an exclusive basis (2004/C 115/02)', *Official Journal of the European Union*, 20 April. Brussels: European Commission.

————. 2005a. *Competition: German Football League Commitments to Liberalise Joint Selling of Bundesliga Media Rights Made Legally Binding by Commission Decisions*, media release. Brussels: European Commission, 19 January.

————. 2005b. *EU Competition Policy in the Media Sector (compiled 2005)*. Brussels: European Commission. Retrieved 7 November 2005 from http://europa. eu.int/comm/competition/publications/studies/ecompilation_2005.pdf.

Gibson, O. 2005. 'Sky to Lose Their Premier League Monopoly: New TV Agreement Opens Bidding for Six Packages. Games Open to Terrestrial and Broadband Providers', *The Guardian*, 18 November. Retrieved 18 November 2005 from http://football.guardian.co.uk/televisionandradio/story/0,13818,1645323,00.html.

Harcourt, A. and Radaelli, C.M. 1997. 'Limits to Technocratic Regulation and the European Union: The Case of Media Ownership Regulation', *The 47th Political Studies Association Conference, University of Ulster*.

Hardy, J. 2001. 'Border Crossings; Convergence, Cross-media Promotion and Commercial Speech in UK Communications Policy', *The 51st Political Studies Association Conference, University of Manchester, 10–12 April 2001*.

Humphreys, P.J. 1996. *Mass Media and Media Policy in Western Europe*. Manchester: Manchester University Press.

Iosifidis, P. 1997. 'Pluralism and Media Concentration Policy in the European Union', *The Public* 4(1): 85–104.

Jones, T. 2000. 'New Economy' Mega Media Marriage Prompts Age-old Competition Worries', *European Voice*, 19–25 October.

Levy, D.A.L. 1999. *Europe's Digital Revolution: Broadcasting Regulation, the EU and the Nation State*. London: Routledge.

Monti, M. 2002. *Does EC Competition Policy Help or Hinder the European Audiovisual Industry?* London: British Screen Advisory Council (BSAC), 26 November.

Papathanassopoulos, S. 2002. *European Television in the Digital Age.* Oxford: Polity.

Radaelli, C.M. 1999. *Technocracy and the European Union.* London: Longman.

Reding, V. [member of the European Commission responsible for Education and Culture]. 2000., *Community Audiovisual Policy in the 21st Century: Content Without Frontiers?* London: British Screen Advisory Council (BSAC), 30 November. Retrieved 7 November 2005 from http://www.europa.eu.int/comm/index_en.htm10.

Ungerer, H. 2002. 'Media in Europe: Media and EU Competition Law', *Conference on Media in Poland by the Poland Confederation of Private Employers, Warsaw.* Brussels: European Commission. 13 February.

Van Miert, K. 1997. 'A European View on Opening up Networked Industries to Competition: The Telecommunications Example', *The VIIIth International Antitrust Conference, Berlin, 27 October.*

———. 1999. 'Competition Rules OK', in A. Leer (ed.), *Masters of the Wired World: Cyberspace Speaks Out.* London: Financial Times/Pitman.

Wheeler, M. 2001. *EU Competition Issues in the Telecommunications and Audiovisual Industries.* London: British Screen Advisory Council (BSAC), November.

Chapter 12

The Process of Neo-liberalization and the Transformation of the Turkish Media Sector in the Context of the New Media Architecture

Gülseren Adaklı

Introduction

In the 1950s, when Turkey started intensively integrating with the capitalist world, the industrialization of the Turkish press also gained pace, as it both expanded in size and advanced technologically. In the 1980s, however, the press lost its relative autonomy vis-à-vis the state and 'capital' very quickly and the traditional patterns of ownership and control in the sector transformed drastically, as will be further discussed.[1]

The economic stabilization measures enforced on 24 January 1980, a milestone in Turkish economic and political history, appeared prominently throughout the process of transformation from press to media (Kaya 1999).[2] The 12 September 1980 coup d'état brought about a restructuring of the economy and the polity, and undermined citizens' ability to live as equal and free individuals in Turkish society. Following the 1980 coup d'état, collective political activity, unionization and freedom of assembly were all eroded.

It would be fair to argue that the press championed a specific role and function in the implementation of the programme and in creating social consent, as it is further explained below. However, the approach adopted in this paper does not endorse the dominant instrumentalist paradigm, which would consider the media as an agent independent from the apparatuses of the state and capital that directly inculcate the dominant discourse on neo-liberalism to the masses; rather, it argues that the media increasingly became an essential component of the new social model which began to operate in the 1980s. In this era, when democratic debate was dismantled by means of a specifically Turkish formulation of coercion/consent, big-capital groups joined the broadcasting game as dominant players and undermined the status of public service broadcasting. Turkey ratified the European Convention on Transfrontier Television in 1993, which aimed to ease the tension between public service broadcasting and increasing commercialization, integral to the neo-liberalization process. Turkish media policy was formulated through an adaptation of the convention's terms to Turkey's circumstances (see Pekman 2001) and negotiations between capital and the government. By avoiding any public debate, this process resulted in regulation that favours capital.

Turkey's process of harmonization with the European Union (EU) has gained in momentum in recent years and produced new topics for discussion for the media industry and for media policy. The EU agenda on freedom of expression and minority rights has created a social divide that has infused daily life through the dichotomies of Turkish v Kurdish, secular v Islamist, and the military v the government. In the meanwhile, the dominant Turkish media have served the deepening of this divide by putting on different masks, such as 'militarist', 'pro-EU', or 'moderate Islamist'.

In order to comprehend the current political conditions in which the media are undertaking an active role in daily politics in Turkey, it is a necessity to locate the implications of the neo-liberalization process in the last two decades or so in the media field.

In this respect, the first objective of this study is the analysis of the media embodied in the multidimensional capitalist enterprises. Such media are able to determine the demand curve in the market – thanks to the dominant role of commercial advertising – and contribute to the transformation of the patterns of collective consciousness. The second objective of the paper is to assess the structures of ownership and control in the Turkish press, which were subjected to drastic changes in the wake of the economic, political and cultural transformations that have been occurring globally since the 1980s under the rubric of neo-liberalization and 'new media architecture'.[3] This will lead to a discussion of some issues raised by the change in the patterns of ownership and control in the media.

In this context, this chapter will first set out the general consequences of neo-liberal economic policies on the traditional media, especially on the press. It will then attempt to depict the characteristic features of the Turkish press that emerged in the 1980s. I will use the terms 'artisan-like' and 'factory-like' to compare the old and new production forms respectively, with the reservation that the usage of these terms is open to further discussion. In the final part of the chapter, I will elaborate on how this Turkish media structure relates to the ways in which the EU accession is debated in the Turkish public sphere.[4]

Neo-liberalism and the Media Industries

The 1980s was a period in which the media emerged as an industry and became one of the driving forces of many countries' economies around the world, including the United States, the U.K. and Turkey. Even though the voluminous literature that has emerged under the rubric of 'globalization' offers different approaches to analysing this new period,[5] these different perspectives all assign a peculiar importance to the media, both as an extending industrial field and with respect to the new functions it acquired (see, e.g., Artz 2003; Moran 1998: 1–6).

In the new media architecture, commercial gain outweighs public service, and private enterprise has come to dominate the cultural field. As has been argued, the intervention of the communication industries in the cultural field takes two forms: 1. by expansion into productive sectors such as newspapers, magazines, broadcasting, film, music and theme parks, and 2. by means of advertising and sponsorship (Schiller 1989: 4). In a similar vein, Garnham explains the social role and function of the mass communication media under two headings. First, the mass communication media have a 'direct' economic role as the creators of surplus value through the production and exchange of commodities. Second, these media assume an 'indirect' role in the creation of surplus value in other sectors through advertising (Garnham 1979: 235 and 1990).[6] In this respect, the media industry, which has been affected by the new commodification forms, has assumed an all-embracing identity, through which neo-liberal economic policies have manifested themselves very explicitly.

In general terms, in this new era the convergence between the traditional media sectors (i.e., press, broadcasting and film) and the information and telecommunications sectors, together with the content producers, have created a very decisive impetus as the internal markets of the advanced capitalist countries have reached their limits. Once those countries exhausted their domestic markets, they pursued new strategic partnerships in external markets (see Albarran 1998) and consequently started expanding into Latin American and Asian markets, where the labour costs were considerably lower.

In the new architecture, the press guided the market as the prominent actor. The experience of the British press sector, which turned into an arena of struggle in the 1980s, particularly reflects all the characteristics of the neo-liberal Thatcher era. In this period, the conglomerates that now replaced the traditional press groups:

1. benefitted from the economies of scale by equipping the press enterprises that used to operate as relatively small businesses with extensive technology, resulting in a rapid expansion of operations;
2. downgraded the organizational and union powers of the press workers by splitting them along the lines of editorial and printing/technology operations; and
3. changed the special structures of these enterprises by replacing them with huge complex business centers, in which different media units operated together, sharing the same labour forces, technological infrastructure, organizational management, and so on.[7]

Gillian Doyle summarizes the emergence of this process in Britain in the mid 1980s as follows:

> The physical production and printing of newspapers is one area where costs have reduced dramatically since the early 1980s. Up until then, each page had to be typeset manually and newspapers were dependent on a highly skilled and (in the U.K.) heavily unionised workforce to keep their printing presses running. The arrival of new computer technology that allowed newspaper pages to be made up electronically suddenly meant that large numbers of typesetters were no longer required to carry out this task. In the U.K., the introduction of new technology was fiercely resisted by powerful print unions, until the country's largest newspaper publisher, News International, finally managed to introduce it at new production sites for its four national titles at Wapping in 1985. (Doyle 2002: 123)[8]

One of the outcomes of the convergence of different information and communication sectors and the formation of a new world market dominated by mostly U.S.-based multinational corporations (MNCs)[9] was the emergence of monopolization. For instance, while the number of big corporations in the U.S. was fifty at the beginning of the 1980s, this number decreased to a one-digit number in the 2000s. 'For the first time in U.S. history, the country's most widespread news, commentary, and daily entertainment are controlled by six firms that are among the world's largest corporations, two of them foreign' (Bagdikian 2000: viii).[10] Ben H. Bagdikian, who examined the monopolies over a twenty-year period, defines the sector that merged with the new communication media, such as the internet, as an 'international cartel' (2000: viii). During the period in question, the traditional media were introduced to the new communication technologies like the internet by amalgamating into giant holding companies. To summarize, we can see that media industries in advanced capitalist countries went through two fundamental shifts in the new period: 1. the introduction of new corporate strategies such as what in populist discourse is termed 'synergy' (e.g. with different companies operating under the same roof); and 2. an overwhelming emphasis on production for foreign markets, following on the exhaustion of local markets due to profit squeeze.

The initial consequence of these shifts at the political level was deregulation, which meant the elimination of public service broadcasting, the submission of the field of communication to market conditions and principles, and the corresponding forms of consciousness that were formed accordingly.[11] It was in this context that the ideological structure defined as 'new conservatism' or the 'new right' was disseminated. A new kind of individualism and the dismantling of the social state and social and economic rights became two main elements of this ideological structure. The patterns of consciousness created by this new ideological structure were functional in dismantling a whole set of public enterprises through privatization policies, which resulted in enormous infrastructural investments in sectors such as telecommunication and energy. In the new ideological climate, Turkish media did not only integrate with different industrial and trade sectors, but also became an ideological defender of these neo-liberal policies.

The process by which public broadcasting monopolies have been eliminated since the 1970s, especially in the countries of Western Europe, and of the propagation of private radio and television broadcasting, is called deregulation. Giant communication companies, which have strived to rid themselves of every kind of government constraint, have been the most ardent supporters of arguments that favour the elimination of all limits and obstacles to their so-called freedom, thanks to technological changes. According to those arguments, the state was an obstacle to development and democratization and was considered to be an almost counter-revolutionary force against the technological revolution that would ensure equal access to information for every individual. It was the duty of governments, therefore, to promote and facilitate the free operation of the market.

In fact, rather than eliminating state intervention, neo-liberal economic policies attributed a new function to the state. What has changed since the 1970s is merely the form of this intervention. In the capitalist system, state and market are intertwined with each other, and the inability of the market to regulate itself makes state regulation unavoidable (cf. Amin 2000: 9–10). The discourse of the free market and deregulation is a myth that has provided ideological support to the capitalist class, which in turn has relied upon state intervention.[12]

Until the 1980s, traditional media – especially the press and the broadcasting sector –generally provided services at the national level. Deregulation and the development of new communication technologies provided a new market dynamic that, alongside the neo-liberal policies promoting the IMF and the World Bank, all made the control of the media industry by the multinational corporations possible.[13] The media industry market is controlled by diverse strategic plans. The integration/concentration of the big media firms takes many different forms (see Gershon 2000: 13, 37–40), but they can broadly be characterized as three main types: 'horizontal', 'vertical' and 'cross'.[14] These integration strategies created the possibility of compensating for the decline of one sector with the concomitant rise of another. For instance, today the production of a film may have a triggering effect on the production of diverse mediums such as the soundtrack albums, books, video games, DVDs, television series, and so on.

On the other hand, besides this horizontal, vertical and cross[15] integration, in underdeveloped and/or dependent capitalist countries such as Turkey, there is another characteristic form of integration. This form of integration, which involves investments in other industries besides the media sectors, can be referred to as 'super-cross' integration. This occurs when capital groups that have accumulated their capital in other industries invest in the media with various motives – for example, to gain a powerful channel through which to advertise and promote their assets, to lobby for the group's short- and long-term interests against the government, or to promote a positive image in the public eye. The story of the transformation of the Turkish media, which will be told in the next part of this chapter, is typical of this form of integration.

Another aspect of neo-liberal policies facilitated by the search for new markets was the production of products not only for national but also for international markets.[16] New communication technologies created the key input to overcome the crisis, which had occurred with the decreasing of the rate of profit in the 1970s.[17] Giant corporations, which permanently faced the threat of profit squeeze, started getting involved in mergers and acquisitions in international markets rather than in the national markets. Data for some mergers between 1986 and 2001 in the media sector provide a general idea of the nature of the transformation (Table 12.1).

Table 12.1: New Company Formations in the Media (1986–2001)

Year	Events facts	Outcomes (new functions)
1986	News Corporation bought Fox Television Network	Broadcasting-distribution
1989	Time Warner bought Brothers	Development in content
1994	Viacom bought Paramount Pictures	Contentand extension of distribution
1994	Viacom bought Blockbuster Video	Renting video and retail distribution
1995	Paramount (Viacom) set up UPN television network	Broadcasting-distribution
1995	Disney acquired ABC/Capital Cities	Broadcasting-distribution
1995	Time Warner set up WB television network	Broadcasting-distribution
1996	Time Warner bought Turner Broadcasting	Cable content and network distribution
2000	Viacom bought CBS television	Broadcasting-distribution
2000	Vivendi acquired Universal	Content diversification
2001	America Online merged with Time Warner	Internet distribution

Source: Deak 2003

The number of major representatives of the global media industry, in which mergers and acquisitions continue apace and important examples

Table 12.2: Global Media Giants according to Revenue (2006)

Group / Source country	Total Revenues (billion)	Number of Employees	Famous Trademarks
TIME WARNER USA	$42.089[19]	84,900	CNN, Warner Bros, Turner Entertainment, Turner Broadcasting System, Hanna Barbera, Castle Rock, Time, Fortune, New Line Cinema, CompuServe, Atlanta Braves
WALT DISNEY USA	$31.9[20]	129,000	ABC, Miramax, Touchstone, Buena Vista, Disneyland, Disney Toys, Disney Publishing, Hyperion Books, ESPN Radio
NEWS CORPORATION AUSTRALIA	$23.859[21]	38,000	20th Century Fox, Fox TV, Direct TV, Star TV, BSkyB, HarperCollins, National Geographic Channel, News International, bTV, MySpace, National Rugby League
VIACOM INC. USA	$17.321[22]	38,350[23]	BET, Famous Music, MTV Network (MTV, VH1, Nickelodeon, Nick at Nite, Comedy Central, CMT: Country Music Television, Spike TV, TV Land), Paramount Pictures, Paramount Home Entertainment, Famous Music, DreamWorks
CBS CORPORATION USA			CBS Corporation, CBS Television, UPN, CBS Television Stations, Paramount Television, King World, Showtime, CBS Radio, CBS Outdoor, Simon & Schuster, Paramount Parks, CBS Digital Media, CSTV Networks, Inc., CBS Consumer Products
VIVENDI UNIVERSAL FRANCE	21.428[24]	37,906	Universal Music Group (92%), Vivendi Universal Games (99%), Canal+ Group (100%), SFR (55.8%), Maroc Telecom (51%), NBC Universal (20% pay)[25]
BERTELSMANN GERMANY	17	75,000	RTL Group, Gruner & Jahr, BMG (Bertelsmann Music Group), Random House, Direct Group, arvato

Source: Adakli 2006: 355

of which can be observed in the table, is very few. To put it another way, the global media market is dominated by a small group of giant corporations. In Table 12.2 there is a classification and ranking of the companies according to income level in 2006.[18] Film studios, television networks and 80–85 per cent of the global music market in the United States are under the control of those corporations (McChesney 2001). Furthermore, satellite broadcasting at the world scale, book and magazine publications, cable television broadcasting and the conventional publishing market in Europe are also under the control of those corporations.

The development pattern of broadcasting in the former Eastern Bloc countries has not been significantly different. All countries in the region privatized their press sectors in the 1990s. A combination of public and private entrepreneurship became dominant in radio and television broadcasting. In Asian and Latin American countries, investment in media has considerably increased and the media has largely been under the control of U.S.-centred corporations.

I will examine the transformation of the Turkish media sector in the following section. In order to do so, I will first highlight the basic traits of how the Turkish press, which first became an industry in the 1950s, evolved into a different structure in the 1980s. I will then illustrate how big media empires emerged within the process of marketization in the sector, in relation to their interest in the privatized public enterprises and with particular reference to their struggle for market dominance.

The Neo-liberalization Process in Turkey and the Transition from Press to Media

The Turkish press sector integrated with different media and industry branches in the 1980s, leading to drastic shifts in ownership and control. The current situation of the Turkish media sector reflects an inter-capital competition in which a small number of media groups are involved in a permanent struggle for domination. None of these groups have succeeded in obtaining a position of absolute superiority or permanence.[26]

Since the 1980s, in parallel to the new strategic paths taken by Turkish capitalism, the press sector has undergone a phase of structural transformation through integration with different media such as radio, television and the internet, as well as with non-press sectors. One of the prominent consequences of this transformation is that small-scale firms have either exited the press sector or have merged with the big capitalist conglomerates. Hence, there has been a considerable alteration of the patterns of control. Although the industrialization of the Turkish media started in the 1950s, it remained structured around what I have termed an 'artisan-like' editorial process until the 1980s when it began to become more 'factory-like'.

Traditional journalistic values were deeply challenged by senior executives who committed themselves to big capital and its emphasis on the maximization of profit. The contest took place in the field of employment policy and the discourses of both news and editorial. The dominant media groups took advantage of the economies of scale provided by high-capacity printing machines as they launched a plethora of new publications, deepening their strategy of product differentiation by targetting different newspapers and magazines at different audiences. Against this backdrop, low-level employees became alienated from their labour. The first union in the press sector was established in 1952, and its power was strengthened by the liberal climate of the times in the wake of the coup d'état of 27 May 1960. The owners and executives of the Dogan Group, however, led the way in eliminating the union, creating an unorganized media labour and thus eroding independent journalistic values in the early 1990s (see Özsever 2004; Adakli 2006). Not only did the traditional functions of the press almost totally disappear, but the press also lost its relative autonomy from the state and capital. Today a few media groups operating in horizontal, vertical, cross and super-cross integration (see above) share the whole market and media output is produced in accordance with the interests of those companies with which the sector is affiliated.

One of the consequences of the market-oriented strategy geared to economic modernization was that the Turkish economy became much more information-based. This, in turn, transformed the whole media structure and led to the concentration of ownership and the emergence of a media output that is based more than ever before on sensational news (Kaya 1994).

It was with the measures of 24 January 1980 – one of the most important structural adjustment programmes that have ever taken place in Turkey – that international financial institutions such as the IMF and World Bank were brought into the equation. These measures resulted in the withdrawal of the state from traditional areas of intervention, especially from the market, and correspondingly led to the privatization of the service sectors, such as telecommunications (Adakli 2003).[27] Among the buyers of the valuable public enterprises offered for sale during privatization, one can find emergent holdings such as the Uzan Group, which later dropped out from the market and was charged with accusations of financial corruption. Yet, the policy and practice of privatization have come to be highly criticized in the twenty-first century because its main purpose was dismantling the public sector. One remarkable case reveals how media companies were involved in tenders for the state enterprises.

A 51-per-cent share of the state petroleum enterprise Petrol Office (POAS) – the biggest petroleum distributor in Turkey – was sold in 2002 to the IS Bank and Dogan Holding consortium for a price of $1,260 million. Of this cost of sale, $500 million was paid immediately in cash while the rest was paid with credit withdrawn from state banks with future POAS revenues as the repayment guarantee. The government later breached the state's own privatization law by selling the remaining shares to the same consortium. It is striking to see that POAS, which was one of the ten companies consecutively paying the highest institutional tax in Turkey until its privatization, did not pay any tax at all after being privatized (Petrol-İş, 2005).[28]

The replacement of the 'real accumulation' strategy with 'financial accumulation' can perhaps be regarded as the most essential new aspect of neo-liberal policies that facilitated the emergence of a very peculiar relationship between the media and banking sectors. Tülay Arin discusses the impact of the financial liberalization[29] implemented in different forms and degrees in many countries as a result of the crisis that occurred in the late 1970s from the perspective of the theory of bifurcation and regulation:

> The pattern of financial accumulation that took place within and through the banking sector created serious systemic risks and resulted in a bifurcation of financial accumulation and real accumulation ... The banking sector, especially the commercial banking sector, has moved away from its basic function of providing credit to the real sector and especially to industry. The ratio of their credits to their deposits was a little more than 50 per cent. Bank credits were around 40 per cent of their total assets. Instead of credit extension, banks were buying government bonds and treasury bills. In 1997, banks were holding almost 85 per cent of government securities. However, ... government borrowing has not been used for real capital accumulation. Therefore, financial development was proceeding with a weaker relation to the real sector of the economy. (Arin 1999)

It was within this context that financial investments in Turkey, especially bank ownership, became an easy means to enrichment, thanks to the underwriting of risks by the state. The banking sector has met the credit requirements of different business groups, including the ones operating in the media sector, and contributed to their consolidation. The financial institutions, especially the banks, whilst becoming a main pillar of the new system, integrated with another emergent sector – the media. Cavit Ça(ar, the owner of Nergis Holdings, Kamuran Çörtük, the owner of Bayindir Holdings, and Korkmaz Yi(t, who was famous for selling luxury homes, are only the best-known names associated with companies that emerged in the 1990s in the tourism, construction and textile sectors who then went on to acquire banks that later deteriorated financially (Adakli 2004: 37). Cavit Ça(ar and Kamuran Çörtük are close friends of Süleyman Demirel, a former Turkish Prime Minister and President, and they were both under Demirel's supervision and protection for some time. Korkmaz Yi(t, on the other hand, has been involved in a series of corruption scandals, which led to the dissolution of the Turkey's 57th government. Korkmaz Yi(t's attempt to collaborate with the mafia in order to win a bid for the sale of a bank and, more importantly, the revelation of these relations to the public, was one of the biggest political scandals in the history of the Turkish Republic (Adakli 2001a).[30]

Recently, the transfer of Imar Bank, owned by the Uzan Group, and the transfer of Iktisat Bank, owned by Erol Aksoy, who launched the first pay-TV in Turkey – Cine 5, to Tasarruf Mevduati Sigorta Fonu (TMSF – Saving Deposit Insurance Fund), made TMSF and hence the government (controlled by the AKP – Justice and Development Party) the biggest media 'owner' in the country. The same bizarre situation also exists for many other media institutions whose shares are owned by the banks transferred to TMSF. TMSF went on to auction these media in September 2005 for sale to private buyers.[31]

Table 12.3 is made up of data collected from the information on banks and financial institutions affiliated with the media. It provides a schematic account of the integration of finance and media sectors.

Policies of the New Right and Media in Turkey

In Turkey, the architect of the 'New Right Project', the counterpart of Reaganism in the United States and Thatcherism in Britain, is Turgut Özal. Özal was the Deputy Prime Minister during the military government. He served as Prime Minister between 1983 and 1989 and as President from 1989 to 1993 (see Tünay 1993). In the 1980s the

Table 12.3: Banks and Other Finance Groups Related to the Media
Sector (2004)

Name	Group	Related media
Adabank[3]2	UZAN	Star TV, Star (Newspaper), Telsim
Asya Finans	FETHULLAH GÜLEN	Zaman, STV, Burç FM
Bank Express	KORKMAZ YIÇT	Milliyet, Yeni Yüzyil, Ates, Kanal6, KanalE, Genç TV
Bank Kapital	CEYLAN	CTV
Bayindirbank	BAYINDIR	BRT
Disbank	DOĞAN	Hürriyet, Kanal D, CNNTürk, Radyo D, DBR
Etibank	SABAH	Sabah, ATV, Aktüel
Garanti Bankasi	DOĞUÇ	NTV
Interbank[3]3	NERGIS	Olay TV
Ihlas Finans	IHLAS	TGRT, Türkiye
Iktisat Bankasi	AVRUPA VE AMERIKA H.	Cine 5
Imar Bankasi	UZAN	Star TV, Star Gazetesi, Telsim
Körfezbank[3]4	DOĞUÇ	NTV
MNG Bank[3]5	MNG	TV 8
Osmanli Bankasi	DOĞUS	NTV
Pamukbank	ÇUKUROVA	Aksam, Show TV, Turkcell, Digiturk
Türkbank	KORKMAZ YIÇT	Milliyet, Yeni Yüzyil, Ates, Kanal 6, Kanal E, Genç TV
Yapi ve Kredi Bankasi	ÇUKUROVA	Aksam, Show TV, Turkcell, Digiturk

relationship between the press and Özal, who won the majority of the votes (45.1 per cent) in the general elections of November 1983, was strained.[36] This tension was especially exacerbated by the increase in the price of paper, the basic tool of the journalistic sector. The highest price increase and the elimination of subsidies for paper dates back to 25 January 1980 and was one of the most contentious issues between Özal and the newspaper owners, as it played an important role in the deterioration of the financial structure of the press in the 1980s. Between 24 January 1980 and 1988 paper increased in price by 7,890 per cent.

During the three years following the coup d'état of 12 September 1980 and during the ANAP governments of 1983–1991,[37] the press had to face not only economic pressures, such as the increase in the price of paper mentioned above, but also restrictions to its traditional public functions. Policies aimed at restricting the freedom of the press prevailed not only during the military government, but also during the Özal period, which also brought the rhetoric of the New Right onto the agenda. In fact, Özal, with his image of a technocrat more concerned with numbers than ideology (Ahmad 2000: 197), implied that he was more concerned with the economic sphere than the political. A concern with the latter would necessitate tackling the problem of giving back democratic rights, but Özal preferred to remain indifferent to the issue of political freedoms. Özal's slogan was 'first the economy then the democracy' (Ahmad 2000: 193). In this respect, Özal appeared to have implicitly agreed demarcated spheres of influence with the army after the 12 September coup d'état. He believed that regulation of the economy and the military would consequently guarantee 'law and order', and that the restoration of law and order required the severe disciplining of the press.

Özal's commitment to the IMF programmes contributed significantly to the formation of a press that was in harmony with the new economic policies implemented in Turkey, but Özal himself remained in a constant struggle with the press until the 1990s. The fact that Özal and his so-called 'princes' – a circle of young bureaucrats and politicians – were in very close relations with the bosses and managers of the private sector created a different dynamic in the Turkish political culture.[38] The most significant consequence of this shift in the political culture was the increasing importance of taking part in cliques in order to benefit from state subsidies or acquire privatized companies, and this eventually hindered public supervision and control over the system.

Thus, in the 1990s, the press began to respect and advocate much of what it had criticized in the 1980s.[39] During the Özal period, many newspaper owners, managers and columnists played a pivotal role in publicizing his projects, and helped him to achieve an iconic status.[40]

Elimination of the State Monopoly in Broadcasting and the Introduction of Private Broadcasting

In the 1980s the press sector and other capital groups in broadcasting made many significant initiatives. The first initiative observed by the present study was launched by Abidin Cevher Özden, known as the 'Banker Kastelli', who was one of the best-known, if not the strongest, representatives of capitalists during this period.[41] During his rise as a businessman, Özden paid billions of Turkish liras to the the state broadcasting monopoly, TRT (Turkish Radio and Television Corporation), for advertising and signalled that he would enter the broadcasting sector by setting up the first private television channel – the second channel after the public channel broadcasted by the TRT.

Özden's private broadcasting initiatives and the aspirations of thousands of people who have been attached to his dreams turned out to be a complete failure in the early 1980s and 'Banker Kastelli' fled overseas in mid 1982. 'Banker Kastelli' had promoted an easy way of earning more money from the sums of personal funds by offering very high interest rates, and had appealed to the working classes, who could never have made such returns by simply saving their wages.[42] After Özden, other companies from the press were also involved in establishing private broadcasting stations. The owner of *Dünya* newspaper, Nezih Demirkent, made a formal application to the RTYK (Higher Council of Radio and Television) on 23 September 1985,[43] and Erol Simavi and Aydin Doğan applied for a licence in 1987 to launch a private broadcasting company.[44] Although both applications were rejected, the big capital groups in the press sector revealed their intentions to operate in private broadcasting in the future.[45]

On 23 September 1983 the military government proposed a draft law to the Advisory Assembly entitled 'Law on Turkish Radio and Television' (no. 2954), which came into force on 11 November 1983. The law established the RTYK which was to determine whether the

TRT's 'principles were congruent with national politics'. As with all vital public sectors, there was indeed a need for a regulatory authority on broadcasting. The RTYK prepared a report to open up the debate on private broadcasting. To pave the way for private broadcasting in Turkey, the report suggested an amendment to Article 133 of the Constitution, which sustained the state monopoly in broadcasting.[46] Article 133 was amended in June 1993, three years after the launch of private broadcasting operated on a de facto basis in Turkey.

Another legal development was the alteration of the function of the supreme council responsible for the regulation of radio and TV broadcasting. The 'Law on the Establishment and Broadcasts of Radio and Television' (no. 3984) came into force with its publication in the *Official Gazette* No. 21911 on 20 April 1994 and consequently the RTÜK (Radio and Television Supreme Council) took RTYK's place (RTÜK remains the main regulatory body for private broadcasting to this day). Apart from the supervision and auditing role already ascribed to RTYK, RTÜK was assigned with the additional role of frequency planning. Its essential mission was declared to be the achievement of frequency allocation and the regulation of ownership structure.[47]

Another development concerning the marketization of broadcasting was that the PTT (Post, Telephone, Telegram), which operated as a public monopoly in communication and did not have a direct role in broadcasting, became a new actor in this latter field. The Main Plan for Communication 1983–1993, prepared under the military regime in 1982, stipulated a mandatory introduction of digital technology, which implied an important change in the broadcasting infrastructure. This plan illustrated the military government's clear objective of ascribing the PTT a new function with respect to mass communication. Within the framework of the plan, which would later be implemented by the ANAP governments, the launch of cable TV by the PTT and the transfer of the TRT transmitters to the PTT have helped transform this institution into a service unit providing broadcasting infrastructure to the private sector. The PTT launched the first pilot for cable TV on 23 December 1988, which covered only a limited area (the Cankaya quarter of Ankara). The RTYK questioned the legality of this trial, given the fact that the PTT had violated the monopoly rights of the TRT as guaranteed by the Constitution, but failed to prevent the PTT from takings its plans further (Kejanlioglu 2004: 297).

Law no. 3517 of 12 January 1989 transferred the radio and television transmitters owned by the TRT, together with 1,354 personnel, to the PTT.[48] This transfer from the public monopoly to the PTT[49] was seen as an important step in facilitating the entry of private-sector actors into the broadcasting sector.[50] From that date onwards, companies seeking to set up private broadcasting stations benefitted from the opportunities and facilities created by PTT, such as the increase in the number of channels, live broadcasting, and so on.

Private broadcasting started with the trial broadcasts of Star 1 in March 1990 by the company Magic Box-MBI Movie and Advertisement AS, affiliated with Rumeli Holdings, owned by the Uzan family. The involvement of Ahmet Özal, the son of President Turgut Özal, in this initiative was revealed nine months after the launch of trial broadcasts.[51]

In a speech of January 1989, President Özal laid a milestone for private broadcasting: 'Tomorrow someone could say if private broadcasting is forbidden in Turkey, then I will set it up abroad and beam the broadcasts in Turkish via satellite to Turkey.' Three months after this statement, the Uzan Group, together with Ahmet Ozal, launched the first Turkish private channel from Germany.

The process of private broadcasting, which started with Star 1, accelerated with the entry of the big capital groups into the press sector. Almost all the organizations that have a market share in today's TV landscape started broadcasting before 1994. The second private channel, Teleon, was initiated by the Uzan Group on 27 January 1992. Show TV followed Teleon on 1 March 1992. Show TV, which transmitted a broadcasting signal from its central office in Paris by renting a channel for 5 million dollars from the French satellite Eutelsat 2-F2, launched the trial broadcast on 7 February 1992 and signed up many celebrity journalists and entertainers. The major partners of Show TV, whose capital was announced as 36 billion dollars, were Erol Aksoy (50 per cent), who moved from the banking to the media sector and the *Hürriyet* (20 per cent) and *Sabah* groups (20 per cent).[52] The minor partners were the producers Grundig, Profilo, Ahmet Ertegün, and AKS TV Advertisement and Movie Industry and Commerce, all of which were affiliated to Show TV (Capli and Dündar 1995; Yengin 1994: 144; Adaklı 2001a).

After Show TV, two other new channels entered the broadcasting sector in 1992. One of these was HBB, where the major partner was Has Holdings, which started broadcasting on 9 October 1992. The other was

Channel 6, set up by Ahmet Özal (after leaving the Uzan Group), which began broadcasting on 4 October 1992.[53] Erol Aksoy added a pay-TV channel, Cine 5, to Show TV in 1993 and on 22 April 1993 the Ihlas Group started broadcasting as the TGRT. Channel D was run by the Dogan and Dogus Holdings; ATV, where Dinc Bilgin was the major partner, and the STV, set up by the daily *Zaman*, also entered the market (Yengin 1994; Adakli 2001a).

The structure of ownership and control, dominated by five big-capital groups (Dogan, Bilgin, Aksoy, Ihlas and Uzan) that became private monopolies, radically changed with the ambitious entry of the newcomers, namely, Dogus (Sahenk Family), Cukurova (Karamehmet Family) and Park (owned by Turgay Ciner). Table 12.4 is a compilation of the recent information on the big actors of the oligopolistic media industry, with the best-known brand names and segments.

Turkish Media and the Move towards EU Membership

Turkey's EU adventure, beginning with the Ankara Treaty on 12 September 1963, has become one of the main problems of the painful transformation[60] of Turkish society in the last decade. Turkey, while being pushed into the arena of neo-liberal competition on the one hand, is trying to cope with a social backlash that can be defined as the 'nationalism of globalization'[61] on the other. Within this process, the Turkish media, while championing EU accession, have helped to trigger social unease and unrest by highlighting issues such as the tensions between Kurds and Turks and secularists and Islamists, particularly in its news coverage.

In general, Turkish media capital assumes that accession to the EU, which is, in fact, the representation of global capitalism on a regional scale, will bring a significant market advantage. The EU candidacy process has been an important political issue throughout the 1990s, when a series of coalition governments ruled the country. It gained major momentum when the Islamist AKP came into power and increased the legislative drive towards integration.[62] This legislative harmonization with the EU includes several provisions concerning the media. One strongly debated issue was the legislation of an amendment allowing broadcasts in the 'mother-tongue languages'. Article 4 of the 'Law on the Establishment and Broadcasts of Radio and Televisions' (no. 3984), which regulates broadcasting guidelines, was amended by Law no.

Table 12.4: Major Cross-Media Groups in Turkey (2005)

	Dogan (Owner: Aydin Dogan)	Merkez (Owner: Turgay Ciner)	Çukurova (Owner: Mehmet Emin Karamehmet)
National terrestrial television[54]	Kanal D, CNN-Türk,[55] Star[56]	ATV	Show TV
Cable/Satellite[57]	Dream, FunTV, Galaxy	Kanal1	SkyTurk, DigiTurk digital package[58]
Radio[59]	Hür FM, Radyo CNN-Türk, Radyo D	Radio City	Alem FM
Newspaper	Hürriyet, Milliyet, Posta, Radikal, Referans, Gözcü, Turkish Daily News, Fanatik	Sabah, Yeni Asir, Takvim, Pasfotomaç, Cumhuriyet (Partial)	Aksam, Günes, Tercüman
Publishing	Online publishing, magazine publishing, book publishing, print distribution, music publishing, music and books retail, printing	Online publishing, magazine publishing, book publishing, print distribution, printing	Online publishing, magazine publishing, book publishing, printing
Other media	Production, DHA News Agency, media marketing	Production, Merkez News Agency, media marketing	Eksen facility provider, media marketing
ICT	ISP, telecoms, cable operator		GSM operator Turkcell, telecoms, ISP, cable operator
Non-media	Energy, automotive, health, trade, manufacturing	Energy, construction, hospitality	Trade, automotive, steel, manufacturing, hospitality, maritime and air freight

Source: rearranged and reformulated by the author from Capli and Tuncel 2005

4756 to allow broadcasts in the different languages and dialects used by Turkish citizens (see Capli and Tuncel 2005: 245). Although the most important topics regarding the transformation of the Turkish media industry in the context of EU harmonization are related to pluralism and diversity, which are directly related to the ownership structure, these issues have almost never come up in public debate. The lack of an open democratic debate has meant that the decision-making on such issues has occurred through private and mutually self-interested deals between the government and the dominant media groups – a process that can be clearly observed in the case of digital switchover, which was never discussed publicly but presented as a top-down policy.[63]

Big-capital groups, which campaign for Turkey's accession to the EU no matter 'what it costs', and the military, which in general backs EU membership but keeps away from a clear position, use the media against some nationalistic and left-wing groups that oppose the idea of EU membership on the basis that it will eradicate national sovereignty. The emphasis in the debate on the EU in the dominant media is generally that the EU would bring more freedom and wealth. The imposition and rules on economic issues that will come with EU integration have, by contrast, not been widely deliberated.

One can argue that Europe has a lot to learn from the Turkish experience of rapid liberalization of the media. Turkey's political and economic dependency on the Anglo-American world since the Second World War has turned into a neo-liberal type of dependency after the economic measures of 24 January and the subsequent coup d'état in 1980. Turkey has moved away from the social welfare state and import substitution model of the 1960s and 1970s faster than most European countries, and it is therefore now faced with the social cost of this rapid transition.

Conclusion

To sum up, the media sector has displayed a tendency to expand and consolidate in the 1980s and 1990s, when neo-liberal policies were implemented on a global scale and the media thus became an important space for big-capital groups. As the constitutive component of the new media architecture, the Turkish press sector more than ever requires business-minded editorial cadres. Those managers participate in direct decision-making processes concerning both media output and allocation of resources. This change is an inevitable requirement of the new architecture.

As a close follower of global media capital, Turkish media capital attempts to reinforce the managerial positions of the media holdings, which are mostly family companies, enhancing standardization and professionalization and, if possible, achieving an integration with foreign markets. Yet, there exist serious obstacles and limits to the achievement of those objectives for a peculiar capitalist formation such as Turkey.

In the last analysis, Turkish media capital, engaged in ambitions parallel to those of European capitalists, can 'contribute' to the EU public sphere around common capitalist interests. In Turkey, these interests will be realized on issues such as ownership, pluralism, diversity, digitalization, and so on, which arise from the internal disputes within the EU (see Chapter 8 by Peter Humphreys). As it is not possible to ignore the historical difference between European and Turkish capitalism, the issue of whether the EU's media regulation will create a new public sphere in Turkey depends on the formation of a new capitalist model or the possibility of a different emancipatory project.

The transformation of the Turkish media industry as outlined above may provide an insight into the development of the assumed or proposed EU public sphere, especially with regard to the problems that may arise in the integration of dependent capitalist countries. In a social formation where social opposition is suppressed by force frequently; where economic freedoms cannot be extended to political freedoms; where the historically rooted problems such as the Cyprus and Kurdish issues is used to surpass the frequent economic and political crises, rapidly accompanied by violence and jingoism; where the income gap is growing and where the right to organize cannot be more than an aphorism, it is extremely difficult to realize the universal norms of 'public service broadcasting', 'pluralism' and 'diversity'.

Though the Turkish example is not independent of the EU example, these norms are not easy for the EU to fulfil either. The problem is that the contradictions embedded in liberal philosophy cannot be resolved.[64] If Europe's advanced capitalist countries want to create a real pluralist and democratic public sphere, they must begin by to putting the brakes on the neo-liberal economic policies that they employ in the field of broadcasting, as in every other field of social life.

It is always possible to argue more and provide more empirical information about the relationship between neo-liberalization processes and the structural transformation of the Turkish media industry in relation to the EU, due to the constantly changing and dynamic nature of the sector itself. However, the scope of this paper was limited to outlining the basic framework and 'headlines' of the process. Undoubtedly, there is need for further and deeper research that focuses on the political and ideological consequences of neo-liberalization and the transformation of the media industry through comparative and cross-country analysis.

Notes

1. From the outset, I should emphasize that the argument on the 'relative autonomy of the Turkish press' is closely related to its relative weakness in the process of industrialization. Otherwise, in contemporary capitalism, it would not be possible for a press that is more or less institutionalized to be 'independent' from the state and capital. In this chapter, it is presumed that the existence of a press that has not reached the masses as much as it has today and has succeeded in preserving a certain power of opposition in the given set of social relations of the 1960s and 1970s supports the thesis of relative autonomy. In contrast, the press's steps towards industrialization in the 1980s have eliminated this independence with respect to infrastructural investments, working conditions, regulations and legislation in the media as well as in its content.

2. The expression of the 'transition from press to media' is first described by Professor Dr Rasit Kaya in an article which has also been cited here (1999). This transformation entails the fact that the press, which existed exclusively as a dominant communication apparatus until the 1980s, later became a component of the media holdings that expanded in size by the gradual integration of different businesses. This refers to a transition from a world of journalism where there was room only for relatively small enterprises, to a web of media whose activities are diversified – from book publication to television broadcasting – and which has, in different ways, close cooperation with the political regime.

3. I use the 'new media architecture' as a concept related to the new role attributed to the media in the process of neo-liberalization. The concept implies that, in a context shaped by a new coalition between state and capital, the dominant media turns out to be a component of the big capital groups and is organized in the form of holdings. The important aspects of this transformation are the fact that the market of communication is more discriminatory for entry to small business groups and more favourable to big business and the infringing upon and/or elimination of workers' rights, including rights to unionize in the media sector and the use of sensational news and misinformation in the content of the media. Despite the increasing number and diversity of market outputs such as radio and TV programmes, newspapers, magazines, books, music albums, the value and quality of those products with regards to the content are low in the sense that they are very similar to each other. The actors of the new media architecture, who paved a solid ground both ideologically and economically to

the strategies of redistribution at the global scale, have created a very suitable social environment for the flourishing of the depoliticization strategies brought about by the 12 September regime in Turkey.

4. I am indebted to Assoc. Prof. Dr D. Beybin Kejanlioglu, who has carefully read the draft and made invaluable criticisms and provided insights, as well as to my friend Demet S. Dinler, who provided meticulous assistance with regards to the language of the paper. In addition, I am grateful to my colleagues Hakan Tuncel, Burcu Sumer and Beycan Mura for their cordial help and for their amendments to this article.

5. Globalization is defined by critics and opponents as a process in which 'the peculiar characteristics of each country are ignored, the export oriented sectors rather than the ones which would meet the needs of the country benefit, national markets are opened to foreign products and investors almost without any conditions, where the polarisation between the Communist East and Capitalist West – which was balancing each other in the post second world war period – ceded its place to one between the rich North and the poor South' (Fis, Talay and Oncu 2003). For a summary of the critical approaches in the political economy literature on globalization, see Cohn (2000, esp. pp. 10–12).

6. In this study I was guided essentially by some of the works where a critical political economy approach to the field of communication/media is either explained or used. Some of those works are Garnham 1990; Murdock and Golding 1973, 1979, 1983, 1991, 1997; Murdock 1977, 1980, 1982; Boyd-Barrett and Newbold 1995; and Mosco 1996. Within those works the perspectives of Nicholas Garnham have been the most influential in the formation of my own approach. In his collection of articles under the title of *Capitalism and Communication*, Garnham suggests important arguments for a historical materialist analysis of the field itself. By referring directly to the works of Marx, he suggests macro frameworks for the processes of communications – a quite complicated subject. Golding and Murdock, on the other hand, have elaborated invaluable arguments on both theoretical and practical issues within the field. These two British scholars have been close observers and analysts of the field at the global scale, including the English media and communication industry.

7. Whilst Thatcher in the U.K. and Reagan in the United States were seen as the political actors of the neo-liberal policies that gained pace in the 1980s, in Turkey the then Prime Minister (1983–89) Turgut Özal, who was later also the President of the country between 1989 and 1993, was regarded as their successor on a local scale (see Tünay 1993). Clearly, all of these neo-liberal actors/architects also had great influence on the emergence of the new media architecture. The summary of the British case that is cited here also took place simultaneously in Turkey. The aspects underpinning this transformation will be considered further in this chapter.

8. For a clear evaluation of the company strategies followed by the English press in the neo-liberal period, see Doyle (2002: 119–40). Among these strategies one can cite promotional giveaways, price reductions and supplements, accompanied by a tendency to create 'dumbed-down tabloids'. It is possible to observe this in

The Times owned by Rupert Murdoch, as its sales figures regularly increased after 1993.

9. 'By 1998, there were about 19,000 MNCs, which accounted for 25 to 30 per cent of the gross domestic product of all market economies and 80 per cent of the trade in managerial and technology skills' (Cohn 2000: 11).

10. The companies indicated by Bagdikian (2000: x) are General Electric which acquired NBC in 1985, AOL-Time Warner, News Corporation, Viacom and Bertelsmann, which I will elaborate on in the following section.

11. For a good explanation of the consequences of neo-liberal policies with regards to the cultural industries, see Hesmondhalgh (2002).

12. See, for instance, Mosco (1990), who writes about the mythification of deregulation in the telecommunications sector.

13. One of those corporations, Time Warner and Disney, recorded non-U.S.-based revenues of 15 per cent in 1990, a percentage that increased to 30 per cent by 1997. Moreover, advertising, which was considered to be one of the most important components of the sector, has become one of the mostly rapidly industrialized ones. While in 1981 four big companies controlled 6 per cent of the world market, this figure reached 40 per cent in 2002 (von Nordenflycht 2003).

14. In 'horizontal integration', companies acquire additional units at the same production level (e.g., an attempt to acquire different publishing houses in the book publishing sector). 'Vertical integration' occurs, by contrast, where a company extends its production to other levels in the production chain (e.g., where a newspaper company takes control of different activities like the production of paper, printing, distribution and advertising). 'Cross-integration' refers to the concomitant ownership of different media (see Doyle 2002: 17–38).

15. Doyle (2002: 23) uses the term 'diagonal' for a similar integration type.

16. For example, ITV's export income was £20 million (2.8 per cent of its total income) in 1982, and reached £47 million (5 per cent of its total income) after only two years. Between 1984 and 1985, 70 per cent of the total income (£35 million) of the BBC, which sold programmes to more than a hundred countries, came from exports. In the sale of films and TV programmes, the United States is dominant. In 1981 the ratio of American films to the total foreign films broadcasted on British television was 94 per cent. This ratio is 80 per cent in France and 54 per cent in West Germany (Thompson 1996: 195–205).

17. According to Freeman and Soete (2003: 78–81), the 1970s preceded the period of the rise of the Fifth Kondratieff Wave, which is characterized by information and communication technologies.

18. Various lists and updates can be accessed at the companies' websites. For a schematic and overall picture of those lists, see the following websites: http://www.freepress.net/ content/ownership, http://www.cjr.org/tools/owners, www.adage.com, http://www.publicintegrity.org, http://www.pbs.org/wgbh/pages/frontline/shows/cool/giants/, http://en.wikipedia.org.

19. These are the 2004 figures. Revenues for the previous year are $39.563 billion. See http://ir.timewarner.com/downloads/3Q05presentation.pdf.
20. http://corporate.disney.go.com/investors/quarterly_earnings/2005_q4.pdf.
21. 30 June 2005.
22. Viacom figures for first three quarters of 2005 prior to the split. Total revenues for the same period of the previous year are $15,952 billion. This amounts to a growth of 9 per cent between 2004 and 2005. See *Viacom Reports Third Quarter 2005 Results*, available from http://www.cbscorporation.com/media/pdf/qr3q05.pdf.
23. The number of employees is unclear due to the split. These sources quote a number of 38,350: http://en.wikipedia.org/wiki/Viacom, http://www.hoovers.com/cbs-corp/--ID__12435--/free-co-factsheet.xhtml.
24. Total revenues of 2003 were €25.482 billion.
25. http://www.vivendiuniversal.com/vu/en/files/20050428_key_figures_2004.pdf.
26. This situation should not give the misleading idea that there are conditions of 'perfect competition' in the Turkish media sector, as argued by eminent academics in Turkey, as this is never supported by scientific evidence in academic publications. As a general tendency, monopolization can be observed in every capitalist formation in a so-called golden age that follows the short period of 'complete competition'. Though this tendency exists in the media sector as well, the real given situation refers to, technically speaking, an oligopolistic market.
27. Since this study focuses on the 'media industry', other, closely related fields of communication such as telecoms have not been dealt with. Yet in order to understand neo-liberal policies, it is important to consider the communications sector as a whole. The telecoms sector in Turkey, with all its infrastructure investments, has been one of the key sectors in the privatization programme launched by the government. After long debate on its privatization and a fairly long bidding process, Turk Telekom was sold as a block to a consortium led by Oger of Lebanon. The sale of 55 per cent of Turkish Telekom's shares started with the announcement of the tender on 25 November 2004, and the institution was sold to Oger Telecoms Joint Company OGG, which gave the highest price of $6,550 million (www.oib.gov.tr).
28. On 2 September 2005, Dogan Group bought all POAS shares belonging to Is Bank for $616 million, increasing its percentage share to 88.36 per cent, and thus took over complete control of the company. On the other hand, the consolidated profit of the group for the first nine months of 2005 was mainly due to POAS, apart from the immediate cash (€985 million/$1,28 billion) coming from the sale of Disbank (which belonged to Dogan Group) to Fortis (a company owned by a Dutch and Belgium consortium (*Milliyet*, 26 November 2005).
29. One of the most important consequences of the collapse of the Bretton Woods system, which was established in the post-war period and based on the control of capital flows and foreign exchanges, is the liberalization of financial structures and transition to floating exchange rates. Theodore H. Cohn points to two main problems created by the liberalization of capital controls: 'The removal of capital controls, combined with technological advances in such areas as

telecommunications, contributed to a massive growth in speculative capital flows, which had far-reaching effects on the world's financial markets. In the face of these changes, two problems developed with the floating exchange rate regime: volatility and misalignment of exchange rates. *Volatility* refers to short-term instability in the exchange rate, and *misalignment* refers to the long-term departure of an exchange rate from its competitive level' (Cohn 2000: 152).

30. As will be described later in this chapter, the intertwining of political power relations and the transformation of the media sector, as well as the degradation of the norms of journalism, posed serious concerns in public opinion. Even though the relationship between political power and the press was no different in the past, the current situation goes beyond it so that the scandals become weapons used by the media in case there is a need for altering the balance of forces between different capital groups. Not all aspects of the case of Korkmaz Yiğit were presented to the public, despite the declarations of the parties involved, including Yiğit himself, on several occasions.

31. After this chapter was written, new developments occurred relating to the broadcasting organizations that are affiliated with the group. For instance, the broadcasting of Star TV has been stopped by RTÜK because of its debt from advertisement shares, and this has led to tension between TMSF, which seeks common ground with Uzan Group and RTÜK, and the government (*Sabah*, 14 September 2004). On the other hand, there was speculation almost every day in the press about the sale of Star TV and the *Star* newspaper. One rumour was that Roman Abramovich, the Russian petroleum mogul and owner of the English football team Chelsea, would buy them (www.medyatava.net, 20 October 2004). One year later, on 21 September 2005, TMSF auctioned seven radio and two television stations and one newspaper within the Star Media Group. The radio Super FM was sold to CanWest, which is one of the biggest media corporations in Canada, for $33.1 million on 22 September 2005. Because of the article in the RTÜK Law that limits foreign shares in a media company to 25 per cent, CanWest participated in the bid along with CGS Television and Radio Broadcasting Trade Company, together with the Global Investment Company. The owner of Global Investment, Mehmet Kutman, is a relative of one of the former Prime Ministers, Mesut Yilmaz. On 26 September 2005, Star TV, which was the flagship of the Star Media Group, was sold to Dogan Media Group, considered to be the biggest media corporation in Turkey. One of the Dogan Group companies, Isil Television Broadcasting Trade Company, offered the highest bid of $306.5 million (twice as much as the asking price of $155 million), and the sale was approved by the Turkish Competition Authority (*Referans*, 26 October 2005). In fact, the interest of foreign capital in the bids is striking. Domestic capital groups such as Cukurova and Ciner groups have also been very interested in the bids. Yet, TMSF has not approved the sale of Kral TV (a thematic channel) to Cukurova Group, which had offered $45 million (*Zaman*, 4 October 2005). Cine 5, a pay-TV channel formerly owned by Erol Aksoy, is still waiting for auctioning by TMSF.

32. Major shareholders of Adabank were Kemal Uzan, Aysegul Uzan, Hakan Uzan, Cem Cengiz Uzan and Yavuz Uzan.

33. The major shareholders of Interbank were Cavit Caglar's Nergis Holdings and Credit Industrial.
34. The major shareholders of Körfezbank were Sheikh Mohamad Bin Hamad Al Thani, Kemal Ali Saleh, Mohamad Hamad Al-Mana, Al-Ahli Bank Of Quatar, Garanti Holding, Dogus, Ayhan Sahenk, Filiz Sahenk, Ferit Sahenk, Aymak Makine, Antur Turizm, Ana Yatirim, Dogus Holding and Datmar Turizm.
35. The major shareholders of MNG Bank were Mehmet Nazif Gunal, Gunal Insaat, Mapa Insaat, MNG Holdings and Hasan Tayyar Anica.
36. Özal's image in the press was negative during the 1980s. The most characteristic feature of Özal was his political style. According to a study of the articles from the Turkish dailies *Hürriyet*, *Sabah*, *Milliyet* and *Cumhuriyet*, out of the 4,493 statements on Özal, 1,440 (32.05 per cent) related to his style (Uzun 1993: 47–48). A massive 67.9 per cent of the statements included a negative judgement (Uzun 1993: 48–49).
37. The 45th government = the first Turgut Özal government (13 December 1983 – 21 December 1987); the 46th government = the second Turgut Özal government (21 December 1987 – 9 November 1989); the 47th government = the Yildirim Akbulut government (9 November 1989 – 23 June 1991); the 48th government = the first Mesut Yilmaz government (23 June 1991 – 20 November 1991).
38. 'These were the "bright young men" who brought with them ideas and schemes from Reagan's America on how to make quick and easy money, and a familiarity with computer and space age gadgetry. This was a universal phenomenon and India's Rajiv Gandhi had also brought a similar type into his government in 1984' (Ahmad 1993: 193).
39. For a study underlining the face-to-face relations between government officials and top business managers as an aspect of the post-1980 transformation in Turkey, see Kaya 1994.
40. Iconization is one of the typical features of the new period. The image of the capitalist as the exploiter class in the pre-1980 period, when there was a strong working-class opposition, ceded its place to a positive boss profile appreciated for creating employment. Sakip Sabanci is one of the typical examples of those icons (see Adakli 2001b).
41. Özden became famous in the 1960s by selling and buying savings bonds and *Hürriyet* bonds in the second-hand market. Özden's business was ruined when the government decided to charge taxes for this type of bond. In the mid 1970s Özden returned to the banking market with three intermediary companies called Banker Kastelli, Bimtas, and Mentas, and acquired a 'saviour' image in some sections of society, thanks to his advertising campaigns (see Yildirim 1998; Kafaoglu 1981, 1982).
42. The so-called 'Banker Disaster' was the subject of a film by director Zeki Ökten in 1982 that won the best film award at the Antalya Film Festival. The name of the film, *Rush on Interest* (*Faize Hucum*), evokes Chaplin's *Gold Rush*. The story tells of a retired worker who invests all his savings with a banker because of the high interest rates he offers, unleashing a family drama after the banker goes bankrupt.

43. In a 1987 interview Nezih Demirkent commented on the rejection of his application: 'They do not want to say "no", but in order to say "yes" some conditions should change' (*Nokta*, 27 September 1987).

44. In 1987 the Hürriyet, Veb Ofset and Ulusal groups founded a company called Super Channel in order to lease broadcasting time from the TRT and thus commence private broadcasting. For more on Super Channel, see Topuz et al. (1989: 73) and Kejanlioglu (1998: 189). That same year Fora AS (owner: Refik Erduran), Ulus Elektronik AS (owner: Nezih Demirkent), Milliyet group (owner: Aydin Dogan) and Sabah group (owner: Dinc Bilgin) made attempts at private broadcasting (*Nokta*, 27 September 1987).

45. Extensive information and analysis on the privatization of broadcasting in Turkey can be found in Capli 1990 and Kejanlioglu 1998.

46. The Sixth Five-year Development Plan aspires to 'establish private TV stations'.

47. Despite this assignment, RTÜK has not yet accomplished the frequency allocation because of Turkey's peculiar political conditions.

48. Another sign of the curbing of TRT's monopoly in TV broadcasting is the contracting out of programme production. While previously the programmes were either made by TRT producers themselves within the corporation or imported, TRT began outsourcing production to independent production companies. Between 1985 and 1991, 101 companies produced 206 programmes to be broadcast on TRT (Celenk 1998: 79–80). In that period, many producers and technical staff left TRT and began working in these independent production houses or set up their own companies. Celenk argues that the relation between the TRT and the production companies was very functional in establishing the necessary ground for the transition to private broadcasting (1998: 80).

49. Law no. 3517 was nullified with the decision of the Constitutional Court (18 May 1990, No.: 1990/8), yet the debate on the issue and the legal procedures long remained unresolved. Finally, in 1997, it was decided that the transmitters should be returned to the TRT. The rights of the personnel transferred from the TRT to the PTT have been violated and their salaries decreased by 50 per cent (Kejanlioglu 2004: 300).

50. A statement by Günes Taner, an MP from the Motherland Party (ANAP), at the parliamentary session on 1 July 1999, clearly exposed the government's intentions in 1989. On the return of the transmitters to TRT, he commented: 'Look at what happened in 1989. This initiative was to facilitate the establishment of private television and radio stations in the context of a monopoly. Then SHP appealed to the Constitutional Court ... Today there is no SHP. Also then there was PTT; today there is no PTT. At that time there was Article 133 of the Constitution; today there is no such an article – it has been amended' (*TBMM Tutanak Dergisi*, 1 July 1999, 28th Session).

51. In fact, by the time Star 1 began broadcasting, an earlier attempt at private TV broadcasting had been undertaken by the Ulusal TV group, owned by Erol Simavi (*Hürriyet* newspaper), Haldun Simavi (the former owner of *Gunaydin* newspaper) and Turker Inanoglu (Ulusal Video). Ulusal dealt with video distribution, satellite set-up, studio rentals and programme production for TRT

as well as owning a very wide library of Turkish films, thus their copyrights, thanks to Inanoglu. Apart from Ulusal, Ihlas Holdings produced some series for a future TGRT, *Sabah* newspaper was involved in technical infrastructure investment and Karacan continued its programme production for TRT.

52. In December 1991, Ulusal Radio and Television (URT), in which Hürriyet and Türker Inanog[breve on g]lu were partners, and Sabah Television Production AS (SATEL), which owned three national TV channels and two radio stations where Sabah group partnered with Image TV (established in 1986), merged to form Birlesik Iletisim Radyo ve Televizyon Yapim AS.

53. Early in 1990, because of a disagreement between Cem Uzan and Ahmet Ozal, the channel was renamed Interstar. The conflict arose when Ozal claimed his rights over Star 1. For the details of the legal dispute between Ahmet Ozal and Uzan Group, see Yengin (1994: 136).

54. All national terrestrial channels are also available on cable and satellite.

55. CNN-Turk is a news channel available nationwide. CNN-Turk is a joint venture with Time Warner, USA.

56. Star TV, a company of the Uzan Group whose ownership was transferred to TMSF with the acquisition of the Imar Bankasi, was bought by the Dogan Group for a price of $306.5 million in the 25 September 2005 bid.

57. All national cable channels are available on satellite as well.

58. Digiturk is 66 per cent owned by Fintur, from the Netherlands. Fintur, on the other hand, is 58.55 per cent owned by TeliaSonera and 41.45 per cent owned by Turkcell, another Cukurova company. However, TeliaSonera owns 37.09 per cent of Turkcell itself.

59. Local radio assets of the groups are not listed.

60. The negative effects of this transformation are visible, especially in Turkish agriculture. It is evident that the EU membership process is undermining Turkish agriculture. 'In terms of employment, the agriculture sector represented about 33 per cent of the whole labour force in 2003 (including forestry, hunting and fisheries), equivalent to some 7 million workers, as compared to 35 per cent in 2001 and 34 per cent in 2002. The number of agricultural holdings decreased by 25 per cent over the last ten years; from 4 million in 1991 to 3 million in 2001' (Elveren and Kar 2006). Despite its importance, both in economy and in social life, this issue is ignored by the mainstream Turkish media to a great extent.

61. Mary Kaldor (2004: 162) uses the term 'new nationalism' for this phenomenon: 'What I call the "new nationalism" is both shaped by, and shapes, the various phenomena we bunch together under the rubric of globalisation. I would argue that the "new nationalism" is regressive, and, in so far as it persists, will contribute to a wild, anarchic form of globalisation, characterised by violence and inequality.'

62. Turkey's candidacy for full membership of the EU was accepted at the Helsinki Summit on 10–11 December 1999. The National Programme accepted on 19 March 2001 followed the Accession Partnership Document of 4 December 2000. Turkey's constitution was amended by Law no. 4709 on 3 October 2001 to extend the sphere of fundamental rights and freedoms.

63. The government foresees that the digital switchover will be completed by 2009, although no actual road map has been laid out.
64. See Carchedi and Carchedi (1999) for a critical evaluation of the EU as a capitalist and imperialist integration.

Bibliography

Adakli, G. 2001a. 'Yayincilik Alaninda Mülkiyet ve Kontrol', in D.B. Kejanlioglu, S. Celenk and G. Adakli (eds), *Medya Politikalari*. Ankara: Ğnge, pp. 145–204.

———. 2001b. 'Popüler Ikon Olarak Sermayedar: Sakip Sabanci', *Praksis* 4: 242–66.

———. 2004. 'Türk sermayesinin ugursuz evliligi: Bankalar ve Medya', *Ekonom* 25 (August), pp. 37–8.

———. 2006. *Türkiye'de Medya Endüstrisi: Neoliberalizm Caginda Mülkiyet ve Kontrol Iliskileri*. Ankara: Ütopya.

Ahmad, F. 1993. *The Making of Modern Turkey*. London: Routledge.

Albarran, A.B. 1998. 'Media Economics: Research Paradigms, Issues, and Contribution to Mass Communication Theory', *Mass Communication & Society* 3(4): 117–29.

Amin, S. 2000. *Degisim Halindeki Dünya Sistemi*. trans. F. Baskaya. Ankara: Türkiye ve Orta-Doğı Forumu Vakfi.

Arin, T. 1994. 'Altyapi Hizmetlerinde Teknolojik Degisme, Ozel Sermaye ve Metalasma Biçimleri', *Dünü ve Bugünüyle Toplum ve Ekonomi* 6 (May): 5–67.

Artz, L. 2003. 'Globalization, Media Hegemony, and Social Class', in L. Artz and Y.R. Kamalipour (eds), *The Globalization of Corporate Media Hegemony*. New York: SUNY, pp. 3–32.

Bagdikian, B.H. 2000. *Media Monopoly*. Boston, MA: Beacon.

Boyd-Barrett, O. 1995. 'The Political Economy Approach', in O. Boyd-Barrett and C. Newbold (eds), *Approaches to Media: A Reader*. London: Arnold, pp. 186–92.

Capli, B. 1990. 'Televizyon Sistemlerinde Yeni Düzenlemeler: Bati Avrupa'da Kamu Tekellerinin Kaldirilmasi ve Türk Televizyon Sisteminde Dönüsüm Arayislari', Ph.D. dissertation. Istanbul: Istanbul University, Social Sciences Institute.

Capli, B. and Dündar, C. 1995. '80'lerden 2000'lere Televizyon', *Cumhuriyet Dönemi Türkiye Ansiklopedisi-Yüzyil Biterken* 15: 1376–86.

Capli, B. and Tuncel, H. 2005. 'Türkiye', in *Avrupa'da Televizyon: Düzenleme, Politikalar ve Bagimsizlik*. OSI/EU Monitoring and Advocacy Program, pp. 193–259.

Carchedi, B. and Carchedi, G. 1999. 'Contradiction of European Integration', *Capital & Class* 67: 119–53.

Celenk, S. 1998. 'Türkiye'de Televizyon Program Endüstrisi: Bagimsiz Prodüksiyon Ğrketleri Üzerine Bir Inceleme', MA thesis. Ankara University, Social Sciences Institute, Radio Television Cinema.

Cohn, T.H. 2000. *Global Political Economy: Theory and Practice*. New York: Addison Wesley Longman.

Deak, E.J. 2003. 'Technological Change, Convergence and the Strategic Struggle for Dominance in the Entertainment Industry', National Business and Economics Society 2003 Conference, Renaissance Conference Center, St. Thomas, U.S.V.I., March 5–8.

Doyle, G. 2002. Understanding Media Economics. London: Sage.

Elveren, A.Y. and Kar, M. 2005. 'Turkey's Economic Integration into the EU: Challenges and Opportunities', Working Paper No. 2005–10. Salt Lake City, UT: University of Utah, Department of Economics. Retrieved 27 May 2006 from http://www.econ.utah.edu/activities/papers/2005_10.pdf.

Fis, A.M, Talay, M.B. and Oncu, A. 2003. 'Türkiye Politik Ekonomisinde Etkin Devlet Tartismasi', VII. ERC/ODTU Uluslararasi Ekonomi Kongresi, Ankara, 6–9 September.

Freeman, C. and Soete, L. 2003. Yenilik Iktisadi, trans. E. Turkcan. Ankara: TUBITAK.

Garnham, N. 1979. 'Contribution to a Political Economy of Mass Communication', Media, Culture and Society 1: 123–46.

———. 1990. Capitalism and Communication: Global Culture and the Economics of Information. London: Sage.

Gershon, R.A. 2000. 'The Transnational Media Corporation: Environmental Scanning and Strategy Formulation', The Journal of Media Economics 13(2): 81–101.

Golding, P. and Murdock, G. 1973. 'For a Political Economy of Mass Communications', in R. Miliband and J. Saville (eds), The Socialist Register. London: Merlin, pp. 207–23.

———. 1979. 'Capitalism, Communication and Class Relations', in J. Curran et al. (eds), Mass Communication and Society. London and Worcester, MA: Edward Arnold, pp. 12–43.

———. 1983. 'Privatizing Pleasure', Marxism Today (October): 32–36.

———. 1991. 'Culture, Communications and Political Economy', in J. Curran et al (eds), Mass Media and Society. London: Edward Arnold, pp. 15–32.

———. 1997. 'Kültür, Iletisim ve Ekonomi Politik', trans. D.B. Kejanlioglu, in S. Irvan (ed.), Medya Kültür Siyaset. Ankara: Ark.

Hesmondhalgh, D. 2002. The Cultural Industries. London: Sage.

Kafaoglu, A.B. 1981. 24 Ocak Uygulamalari ve Bazi Gerçekler. Istanbul: Kardesler Basimevi.

———. 1982. Bankerler Olayi. Istanbul: Yaylacik Matbaasi.

Kaldor, M. 2004. 'Nationalism and Globalisation', Nations and Nationalism 10(1/2): 161–77.

Kaya, R. 1994. 'A Fait Accompli: Transformation of Media Structures in Turkey', METU Studies in Development 21(3): 383–404.

———. 1999. 'Türkiye'de 1980 Sonrasi Medyanin Gelisimi ve Ideoloji Gereksinimi', Türk-İş '99 Yilligi. Ankara: Türk-İş Yayinlari, pp. 633–60.

Kejanlioglu, D.B. 1998. Türkiye'de Yayincilik Politikasi: Ekonomik ve Siyasal Boyutlariyla Türkiye'de Radyo Televizyon Yayinciligi, Ph.D. dissertation. Ankara: Ankara University Social Sciences Institute, Radio Television Cinema.

———. 2004. Türkiye'de Medyanin Dönüsümü. Ankara: Imge.

McChesney, R.W. 2001. 'Global Media, Neoliberalism, and Imperialism', *Monthly Review* 52(10): 1–19
Moran, A. 1998. *Copycat TV. Globalisation, Program Formats and Cultural Identity.* Luton: University of Luton Press.
Mosco, V. 1990. 'The Mythology of Telecommunications Deregulation', *Journal of Communication* 40(1): 36–49.
————. 1996. *The Political Economy of Communication.* London: Sage.
Murdock, G. 1977. *Patterns of Ownership; Questions of Control.* London: Open University Press.
————. 1980. 'Class, Power, and the Press: Problems of Conceptualization and Evidence', in H. Christian (ed.), *The Sociology of Journalism and the Press.* Keele: University of Keele, pp. 37–70.
————. 1982. 'Large Corporations and the Control of the Communications Industries', in M. Gurevitch et al. (eds), *Culture, Society and the Media.* London and New York: Routledge, 114–147.
Nordenflycht, A. von. 2003. 'The Rise of the Global Advertising Holding Companies: Scale & Scope or Financial Intermediation?'. Retrieved 24 July 2004 from http://web.mit.edu/vonetc/www/ AdConsolidation.pdf.
Özsever, A. 2004. *Tekelci Medyada Örgütsüz Gazeteci.* Ankara: İmge.
Pekman, C. 2001. 'Çokuluslu reklamcilik, uluslararasi düzenlemeler ve ulusal uygulamalar: kurallari kim ister?' in D.B. Kejanlioglu, S. Celenk, and G. Adakli (eds), *Medya Politikalari.* Ankara: İmge, pp. 205–42.
Petrol-İş. 2008. Özelleştirme ve Türkiye, http://www.petrol-is.org.tr/Web_Arastirma/Ozellestirme/Turkiye/OZELLESTIRME_VE_TURKIYE.htm (Access date: 18 October)
Sabah. 2004. 'Devlette Star savasi: RTÜK ile TMSF arasinda "Star Wars" yasaniyor. RTÜK'ün borçlari nedeniyle Star televizyonunu kapatma kararina TMSF isyan etti', 14 September.
Schiller, H.I. 1989. *Culture Inc.: The Corporate Takeover of Public Expression.* New York: Oxford University Press.
Thompson, J.B. 1990. *Ideology and Modern Culture. Critical Social Theory in the Era of Mass Communication.* Stanford University Press.
Topuz, H. et al. 1989. *Basinda Tekellesmeler.* Istanbul: Mozaik.
Tünay, M. 1993. 'The Turkish New Right's Attempt at Hegemony', in A. Eralp, M. Tünay and B. Yesilada (eds), *The Political and Socioeconomic Transformation of Turkey.* London: Praeger, pp. 11–30.
Uzun, R. 1993. *Siyasal Iletisim Sürecinde Lider Imaji. Basinda Turgut Ozal*, MA dissertation. Ankara: Gazi University Social Sciences Institute.
Yengin, H. 1994. *Ekranin Büyüsü: Batida Degisen Televizyon Yayinciliginin Boyutlari ve Türkiye'de Ozel Televizyonlar.* Istanbul: Der.
Yildirim, A. 1998. 'Bankerler Krizi ve Kastelli', in *Bilanço 98: 75 Yilda Para'nin Serüveni.* Istanbul: Tarih Vakfi, pp. 218–21.

Notes on Contributors

Gülseren Adakli has been a member of staff at Ankara University, Faculty of Communication since 1995. Currently she teaches various undergraduate and postgraduate courses, including 'Communication and Media Policies', 'History of Communication' and 'Political Economy of Media' at the same faculty. Before joining the teaching team, she worked as a media professional in the public and private sector. She received her Ph.D. in 2003 with her dissertation entitled 'Turk Medya Sektorunde Mulkiyet ve Kontrol Iliskileri (1980–2003)' (Turkish Media Industry: Ownership and Control in the Age of Neo-liberalism) (Turkiye'de Medya Endustrisi: Neoliberalizm Caginda Mulkiyet ve Kontrol Iliskileri, Utopya, 2006). She was one of the editors of *Praksis*, a Marxist quarterly in social sciences. She has also co-edited *Medya Politikalari: Turkiye'de Televizyon Yayinciliginin Dinamikleri* (Media Policies: The Dynamics of Television Broadcasting in Turkey) (Ankara: Imge, 2001). Currently she is working on a post-doctoral research project that is a comparative analysis of the British and Turkish media professionals ('New Employment Structure and Job Security Issues in the Media Industry in the Context of Neo-liberal Politics') at the University of Westminster. Email: gulseren.adaleli@gmail.com

Dr Alessandro Annoni is a geophysicist with more than twenty years' experience working in various environmental fields (forestry, agriculture, hydrology, landscape, nature protection and conservation), dealing with spatial planning, spatial analysis, environmental modelling, geoinformation and related technologies (GIS), remote sensing, image processing, system design and software development. Since 1997 he has been working in the European Commission's Joint Research Centre (JRC) in Ispra, Italy. He is currently the Head of the Spatial Data Infrastructures Unit, which includes a highly competent and motivated technical team of about thirty scientists working on Spatial Data Infrastructures, the largest group in Europe in this field. In 2001 he was appointed the Technical Coordinator of the INSPIRE (Infrastructure for Spatial Information in Europe) initiative. Alessandro participated in several European projects related to spatial information and is a member of the Board of the International Society for Digital Earth.

Alessandro is an author, co-author and editor of more than a hundred publications related to GIS and remote sensing. Email: Alessandro.annoni@ jrc.it

Dr Cristiano Bee is a researcher at the Jean Monnet European Centre of the University of Trento, Italy, where he is involved in a project titled 'Becoming European: Actors, Networks and Processes in the Construction of European Identity' He is also member of the University of Trento's team involved in the networks of excellence GARNET (Global Governance, Regionalization and Regulation: The Role of the EU) and CINEFOGO (Civil Society and New Forms of Governance in Europe) financed by the VI Framework Programme of the European Commission. He recently concluded his Ph.D. in Political Sociology at the Department of Political Science of the University of Florence, with a thesis on the development of the EU's Information and Communication Policy with a focus on a qualitative analysis of European Commission official documents and in-depth interviews with representatives of networks and relays dealing with European communication. Email:cristiano.bec@soc.unitn.it

Dr Valeria Bello has recently obtained her Ph.D. in Sociology at the University of Florence's Department of Political Science. Her Ph.D. thesis – 'The Construction of Identity and the EU Network Governance' – concerns the role of civil society in the identity construction process. She currently works as a researcher at the Jean Monnet European Centre of the University of Trento. She is a member of the University of Trento's unit of the national scientific research project 'Becoming European: Actors, Networks and Processes in the Construction of European Identity', in which she is studying the role of the EU's self-image. Email: valeria.bello@soc-unitn.it

Dr Max Craglia is the research coordinator of the Unit of the Joint Research Centre (JRC) of the European Commission, which has responsibility for the technical development of the Infrastructure for Spatial Information in Europe (http://inspire.jrc.it). He is also the editor of the *International Journal of Spatial Data Infrastructures Research* (http://ijsdir.jrc.it). Prior to joining the JRC in 2005, Max was a Senior Lecturer at the University of Sheffield teaching GIS for urban planners, and researching areas of spatial data infrastructure deployment and use, as well as data policy. Whilst at Sheffield, Max coordinated several European projects related to geographic information, and was Director of the Centre for Geographic Information and Spatial Analysis (SCGISA). Selected recent publications include: M.

Blakemore and M. Craglia (2006), 'Access to Public Sector Information in Europe: Policy, Rights, and Obligations', *The Information Society* 22(1): 13–24; M. Craglia and M. Blakemore (2004), 'Access Models for Public Sector Information: The Spatial Data Context', in G. Aichholzer and H. Burkert H. (eds), *Public Sector Information in the Digital Age*. Cheltenam: Edward Elgar, pp. 187–216; M. Craglia, L. Leontidou et al. (2004), 'Towards the Development of Quality of Life Indicators in the "Digital" City', *Environment and Planning B* 31(1): 51–64; M. Craglia and I. Masser (2003), 'Access to Geographic Information: A European Perspective', *Journal of the Urban and Regional Information Systems Association (URISA)* 15(APA I): 51–59. Email: massimo.cragtia@jrc.it

Jackie Harrison is Professor of Public Communication in the Department of Journalism Studies at the University of Sheffield and Chair of the Centre for Freedom of the Media (CFOM). She has published several papers relating to European audio-visual law and policy and has co-authored *European Broadcasting Law and Policy* with Lorna Woods from Essex University, published as part of the Cambridge University Press series Studies in European Law and Policy in 2007. Her three principle research interests are the study of news; European communication, information and audiovisual policy and regulation; and public service broadcasting and communication. In 2000 she published *Terrestrial TV News in Britain: The Culture of Production* (Manchester University Press) and in 2006 *News* (Routledge). In 1998 she published with Barrie Gunter *Violence on Television in Britain: An Analysis of Amount, Nature, Location and Origin of Violence in Programmes* (Routledge) and in 2003 with Lawrence Erlbaum *Violence on Television: Distribution, Form, Context and Themes* (Routledge). She has undertaken funded research projects for the television industry and regulatory bodies and has held membership of several professional associations: the Royal Institute of International Affairs, Association of British Editors, Society of Editors, the World Press Freedom Group and the Royal Television Society. Email: j.harrison@sheffield.ac.uk

Professor Peter Humphreys has taught comparative European politics at the University of Manchester, U.K., since 1986. He has published extensively on comparative media and tele communications policy. His past work includes two co-edited collections and a co-edited book (all with Kenneth Dyson) – namely, *The Politics of the Communications Revolution in Western Europe* (Frank Cass, 1986), *The Political Economy of Communications: International and European*

Dimensions (Routledge, 1990) and *Broadcasting and New Media Policies in Western Europe* (Routledge, 1988) – and two sole-authored books – *Media and Media Policy in Germany* (Berg, 1994) and *Mass Media and Media Policy in Western Europe* (Manchester University Press, 1996). In 2002 he edited a special issue on *Telecommunications Regulation in Europe* of the journal *Convergence* (Summer 2002, Vol. 8, No. 2). His most recently published book (co-authored with Seamus Simpson) is *Globalisation, Convergence and European Telecommunications Regulation* (Edward Elgar). In 2003 Peter Humphreys completed a three-year ESRC-funded collaborative research project looking at policy transfer in three liberalized utility sectors within the EU, and was responsible for the research on the telecommunications sector. Prior to that he conducted a three-year project (1996–1999) under the ESRC's Media Economics and Media Culture research programme, examining policy developments in the U.K., Germany and at the EU level concerning laws and regulation designed to limit media concentration and promote pluralism in broadcasting. Currently he is engaged on another three-year ESRC-funded project exploring audio-visual regulation in Canada, France, Germany, U.K. and the United States with regard to public service broadcasting and the promotion of pluralism and cultural diversity. Email: peter.humphreys@manchester.ac.uk

Nicholas W. Jankowski is Associate Professor, Department of Communication, Radboud University Nijmegen, and Visiting Fellow at the Virtual Knowledge Studio for the Humanities and Social Sciences, Amsterdam, The Netherlands. He has served as Visiting Fellow at Oxford Internet Institute, Oxford University, and as Visiting Professor at universities in Leuven and Ljubljana. Jankowski has been involved in the investigation of community media and small-scale communication initiatives since the mid-1970s. His publications include: with O. Prehn and J. Stappers, *The People's Voice: Local Radio and Television in Europe* (Libbey, 1992); with L. Hanssen, *The Contours of Multimedia* (University of Luton Press, 1996); *Community Media in the Information Age* (Hampton Press, 2002); and, with K.B. Jensen, *A Handbook of Qualitative Methodologies for Mass Communication Research* (Routledge, 1991). He recently co-edited, with R. Kluver, K. Foot, and S. Schneider, an international study of the Web and elections: *The Internet and National Elections: A Comparative Study of Web Campaigning* (Taylor & Francis, 2007). In 2007 he also edited a themed issue of the *Journal of Computer-Mediated Communication* on e-science (Vol. 12, No. 2). Jankowski is initiator and co-editor of the journal *New Media & Society*. He is a founding board member of the European Institute of Communication and Culture (*Euricom*) and editorial board member of the journal *Javnost–The Public*. Email: nickjan@xs4all.nl

Dr Erkki Karvonen is Professor of Information and Communication Studies at the University of Oulu, Finland. He was originally educated in journalism studies, but later he made himself conversant with public relations and organizational communication studies. He has published articles and two books – *Imagologia: Imagon teorioiden esittelyä, analyysiä, kritiikkiä* (Imagology. Presentation of Public Image Theories: An Analysis and Critique), Acta Universitatis Tamperensis 544 (Tampere yliopisto, 1997) and *Elämää mielikuvayhteiskunnassa. Imago ja maine menestystekijöinä myöhäismodernissa maailmassa* (Living in the Image Society: Successful Public Image and Reputation Building in the Late-modern Era) (Gaudeamus, 1999) – on questions of public image, political image, political communication, media management and corporate reputation management. He has also been interested in media ethics and journalism criticism. Recently he has been working on the themes of the celebritization of politics and the uneasy relationship between journalists and politicians. Professor Karvonen's earlier academic activity includes participation in the research project 'Information Society in Finland' (1996–2000), run by the Academy of Finland. Email: erkki.karvonen@oulu.fi

Dr Katharine Sarikakis is Director of the Centre for International Communications Research and Senior Lecturer in Communications Policy at the Institute of Communications Studies, University of Leeds. Her subject expertise includes international communications and media policy. Her work focuses on the ways in which political economic dimensions of communications have an impact on the nature and objects of communications policies, nationally and globally. An important strand of this research is the study of the development of supranational representational politics and its role in European communications policies and governance. Furthermore, she is interested in the ways in which communications policy is expressed in lived experience with particular reference to the 'organic' exercise of citizenship and social justice. She is the co-editor of the *International Journal of Media and Cultural Politics*. Recent publications include: *Feminist Interventions in International Communication* (ed with L. Shade, Rowman + Littlefield 2008); *Media Policy and Globalization* (with P. Chakrararty, Edinburgh University Press, 2006); *Powers in Media Policy: The Challenge of the European Parliament* (Peter Lang, 2004); *British Media in a Global*

Era (Arnold, 2004). She has edited the *European Studies* 2007 special issue 'Media and Cultural Policy in the European Union; and, with D.K. Thussu, *Ideologies of the Internet* (Hampton Press, 2006). She has served as an elected Vice-President of the International Association of Mass Communications Researchers and Secretary General of ECCR (currently ECREA). Email: k.sarikakis@leeds.ac.uk

Nick Stevenson is a Reader in the School of Sociology and Social Policy, Nottingham University. In 1991 he became a lecturer in the Department of Sociological Studies at Sheffield University where he remained until joining Nottingham University in 2001. In 1995 Nick published *Understanding Media Cultures: Social Theory and Mass Communication* (Sage). This volume has since been translated into Spanish and Chinese, and appeared in a second edition in 2002. In 1996 Nick and his colleagues Peter Jackson and Kate Brooks won an ESRC grant to study the production, content and reception of men's lifestyle magazines. The results of this study were published as *Making Sense of Men's Life Style Magazines* (Polity Press, 2001). He has also published the research volume *The Transformation of the Media: Globalisation, Morality and Ethics* (Longman, 1999) and the edited collection *Culture and Citizenship* (Sage, 2002). More recently, he has been working on the themes of culture, citizenship and cosmopolitanism. A number of papers are available on these themes, and in 2003 Open University Press published *Cultural Citizenship: Cosmopolitan Questions*. Currently he is researching cultural citizenship and education. Email: nick. stevenson@nottingham.ac.uk

Damian Tambini is a Senior Lecturer at the London School of Economics and an Associate Fellow at the Institute for Public Policy Research (IPPR), at the Oxford Internet Institute, and at Oxford University Said Business School. He is also a Fellow of the Royal Society of Arts and serves on the Advisory Groups of the Oxford Media Convention, the Creative Archive License Group, and Polis. From June 2002 to August 2006 he was Head of the Programme in Comparative Media Law and Policy at Oxford University. Before that he was at Nuffield College, Oxford (Postdoctoral Fellow, 1998); Humboldt University, Berlin (Lecturer, 1997); and the European University Institute, Florence, Italy (Ph.D., 1996). His research interests include media and telecommunications policy and democratic communication. He co-edited *Cyberdemocracy* (Routledge, 1998) and *Citizenship, Markets, and the State* (Oxford University Press, 2000). Other recent publications include: *Nationalism In Italian Politics* (Routledge,

2001), *Collective Identities in Action: Theories of Ethnic Conflict* (Ashgate, 2002) and *Privacy and the Media* (IPPR, 2003). He is the co-editor of *New News: Impartial Broadcasting in the Digital Age* (IPPR, 2002) and *Codifying Cyberspace: Self-regulation of Converging Media* (UCL Press, 1996). Email: d.tambini@ise.ac.uk

Renée van Os is a Ph.D. candidate at the Radboud University Nijmegen, Department of Communication, The Netherlands. She completed her MA in 2002. Her Ph.D. project focuses on the potential of the internet for enhancing the European democratic process and contributing to a European public sphere. Van Os is author or co-author of journal articles and book chapters, and has contributed to conference proceedings in which she has investigated aspects of the concept of European public sphere in an online environment. A recent article of the French EP election has been published in *Information Polity: An international journal of government and democracy in the Information Age*. Email: r.vanos@maw.ru.nl.

Bridgette Wessels is a Lecturer in Sociology. Her writing and research focuses on the production and use of various forms of new media and iDTV, innovation and change, information society, new media in policy, public services/public sphere and everyday life. She has conducted European research in the areas of the innovation of telematics in national public spheres across the EU and in the dynamics of inclusion and exclusion in Europe. She took the role of expert for the EU Information Society Technologies (IST) programme in the 5th Framework, and for the Office for Science and Technology project on Cyber-trust and Crime Prevention and in a Royal Society project on 'Public Perceptions of Cyber-trust' (2003/04). Her publications include: *Information and Joining Up Services: The Case of an Information Guide for Parents of Disabled Children* (Policy Press 2002) with Bagnall, *Inside the Digital Revolution: Policing and Changing Communication with the Public* (Ashgate 2007) and *Understanding the Internet: a Socio-cultural Perspective* (Palgrave, 2009). She has also published articles in *New Media and Society*, *The Information Society*, and *Journal of Computer Meditated Communication*. Email: b.wessels@sheffield.ac.uk

Professor Fred Wester has taught qualitative methodology at the Faculty of Social Sciences at Radboud University, Nijmegen, The Netherlands, since 1973. In 2003 he became Professor in Communication Science. He has published extensively on qualitative methodology and content analysis methods. His doctoral thesis discussed Glaser and Strauss's Grounded

Theory methodology. He is the author of *Strategieën voor kwalitatief onderzoek* (Strategies for Qualitative Research) (1987; 3rd edn 1995) and, together with Vincent Peters, of *Kwalitatieve analyse: Theorie en praktijk* (Qualitative Analysis: Theory and Practice) (Muiderberg, 2004). He is (co)editor of collections on symbolic interaction research (1985), on interpretive research (1988), on the interview (*The Deliberate Dialogue*, 1996), on research types in communication science (1995), on applied forms of qualitative research (2000), on reporting of qualitative research (2003) and on content analysis (2006). His research concentrates on interpretive studies of media content and media reception. Since 2002 he has been the chairman of Kwalon, a platform and journal for discussions on qualitative research in the Netherlands and Belgium. Email: f.wester@maw.kun.nl

Dr Mark Wheeler is a Reader in Politics, Department of Law, Governance and International Relations, London Metropolitan University. He joined the department in 1991 on completion of his graduate studies. His research interests include the political economy of the global mass media, the political and social implications of the internet, policy reforms to media systems within the U.K. and EU, and the political relations between Hollywood and Washington. He regularly presents conference papers on media politics and has contributed several articles for journals including *Democratisation, Convergence, The European Journal of Communication, The Harvard International Journal of Press/Politics* and *The Canadian Journal of Communications.* He has published *Politics and the Mass Media* (Blackwell, 1997) and *Hollywood: Politics and Society* (British Film Institute, 2006), and is joint author with Petros Iosifidis and Jeanette Steemers of *European Television Industries* (British Film Institute, 2005). He is also a research officer for the British Screen Advisory Council (BSAC). Email: m.wheeler@londonmet.ac.uk

Index